THE CULT OF KINGSHIP IN
ANGLO-SAXON ENGLAND

*The transition from
paganism to Christianity*

The Cult of Kingship
in Anglo-Saxon England

THE TRANSITION FROM
PAGANISM TO CHRISTIANITY

WILLIAM A. CHANEY
Lawrence University

UNIVERSITY OF CALIFORNIA PRESS
Berkeley and Los Angeles · 1970

239614

University of California Press
Berkeley and Los Angeles, California

Standard Book Number: 520-01401-4

Library of Congress Catalog Card Number: 72-79041

Printed in Great Britain

Contents

To
My Mother

Preface

History as record, like history as event, has its own origins and development. The following work began years ago in studies of ruler-cult written in the historical seminars of that *erhabener Geist* and great master of medieval kingship, the late Ernst H. Kantorowicz. I record here my unending debt to his teaching and to his friendship. For much of the actual research and writing of this book, as well as the necessary ancillary studies in the many related fields, I am indebted to the time and freedom which I enjoyed as Junior Fellow of the Society of Fellows of Harvard University, and the final re-casting of this study was done during a leave of absence from Lawrence University. Among the many to whom I owe so much, I should like to express special gratitude for help and encouragement to the late Professor Paul B. Schaeffer (Berkeley), the late Professor Arthur Darby Nock (Harvard), the late Professor Crane Brinton (Harvard), Sir Maurice Bowra (Oxford), President Douglas Knight (former President of Lawrence and of Duke University), and former President Curtis W. Tarr (Lawrence). My thanks are due and gladly given to the many courtesies of the librarians of Harvard University, the Bodleian at Oxford, Cambridge University, the University of Exeter, the University of California (Berkeley), the University of Wisconsin, and Lawrence University.

I acknowledge with gratitude permission given by the editors of the following journals to use those parts of the work which have appeared previously: the *Harvard Theological Review* (copyright by the President and Fellows of Harvard College), the *Journal of British Studies*, the *American Journal of Legal History*, *Church History*, the *Journal of Church and State*, and *PMLA* (reprinted by permission of the Modern Language Association of America). All writers blessed with efficient and constantly cheerful secretaries will understand my debt to Mrs. Ruth Lesselyong. My love and gratitude to the lady to whom this book is dedicated cannot be sufficiently expressed.

Introduction

In Anglo-Saxon as in Christian history, many roads lead to Rome. This has been correctly and at times over-emphasized in matter, ranging from Augustine to Whitby, from numismatics to laws from banners to Bede. Indeed the Roman road has been so broad and so well marked with recorded *miliaria* that we may have missed the growth-ridden Germanic by-paths which were actually trod by the tribes in England. But surely the impact of culture on cult is as important in history as the reverse, and the terms in which the newly converted Anglo-Saxons interpreted the Christian religion were shaped by the tribal culture, impregnated, as it was, by the heathenism of the old religion. Gregory the Great's famous letter to the Abbot Mellitus,[1] advising that pagan temples in England be used for the worship of the Christian God, that the people *ad loca quae consuevit, familiarius concurrat,* and that the sacrificial animals of heathenism be now devoted to Christian festivals, agrees with the *responsa* of the same pope to Augustine concerning the choosing of local customs best suited to the conditions of the converted.[2] Thus many features of the Conversion period which have been interpreted *post eventum* as Christian were undoubtedly seen with other—and familiar—overtones by the Woden-sprung rulers and their people.

Although no Anglo-Saxon work gives us full information on pre-Christian religion in England, almost no poem from before

[1] Ven. Bede, *Historia Ecclesiastica,* I, 30; J. E. King, ed., *Baedae Opera Historica* (Loeb Classical Library, no. 246; London and Cambridge, Mass., 1954), I, p. 162. This edition has been used throughout the following chapters.

[2] *Hist. Eccl.,* I, 27; King, ed., I, p. 120. On the genuineness of the *responsa,* cf. Wilhelm Levison, *England and the Continent in the Eighth Century* (Oxford, 1946), p. 17, n. 1. M. Deanesly and P. Grosjean, 'The Canterbury Edition of the Answers of Pope Gregory I to St. Augustine,' *The Journal of Ecclesiastical History,* X (1959), pp. 1–49, have recently examined the arguments against the authenticity and have concluded that, within limited distinctions not touching the *responsa* cited here, 'the *libellus* may be held to be Gregorian'.

the Norman Conquest, no matter how Christian its theme, does not reflect it,[3] and the evidence for pagan survivals and their integration into the new faith goes beyond even the literary sources. The rites of pre-Saxon gods in England, such as Helith at Cerne Abbas and Gourmaillon at Wandlebury, survived the coming of both the Anglo-Saxons and Christianity,[4] and the Germanic precursors of the Christian God seem to have been no less vigorous. Also vigorous was the integration of that English heathenism into the total structure of Anglo-Saxon society, its life and world-view. When the conversion to Christianity occurred among the *folc* of the island realms, the binding force of religion was no more lessened than the tribal *mores* were immediately changed. In history a people does not shed its skin overnight, and when it is the societal flesh and bones that are affected, the transition must be even more gradual. The new religion of the English must for some years have been interpreted largely in terms already familiar to a cult-centred culture; fundamental elements of the latter continued, it will be seen, under Christian guise throughout Anglo-Saxon history. We shall examine this continuity from paganism to Christianity as it relates to kingship and the religious, sacral nature which permeated that institution among the English under both the old and the new cults.

In northern heathenism the primary leader of the tribal religion was the ruler.[5] The king's god was the people's god, and the king as *heilerfüllt* stood between his tribe and its gods, sacrificing for victory and plenty, 'making' the year. Tied into temporal and cosmic history by divine descent, he represented and indeed *was*

[3] Cf., e.g., Friedrich Brincker, *Germanische Altertümer in dem angelsächsischen Gedichte 'Judith'* (Hamburg, 1898), p. 5, where this point is insisted upon, and *passim.*

[4] Walter of Coventry, *Memoriale, sub anno* 1045 (R.S., I), p. 60: 'In quo pago olim colebatur deus Helith.' T. C. Lethbridge, *Gogmagog: The Buried Gods* (London, 1957), esp. pp. 23, 81–82, 159 (in which the imaginative author tells of a May 1st night spent looking in vain for still-surviving rites at the head of the fertile Cerne Giant); cf. also T. C. Lethbridge, 'The Anglo-Saxon Settlement in Eastern England: A Reassessment', *Dark Age Britain: Studies presented to E. T. Leeds* (D. B. Harden, ed.; London, 1956), p. 119.

[5] This is developed below, especially in chapters 2–3.

the 'luck' of his people. Thus it was the king's relationships with the gods which 'saved' his folk as much as did the gods themselves; this royal function, when translated into Christian eschatology, was to be part of medieval rulership throughout the following centuries. The ruler's role is also the major factor in the Germanic conversion; inasmuch as English kings were converted without violent incident, by so much is tribal conversion without great external drama; when politico-cultural opposition is greater, as often occurred in Scandinavia, as under Olaf Tryggvason and Olaf the Holy, by so much is religious opposition greater.[6] The new Christian God consequently—'the Almighty, the Lord of great kings', as the Anglo-Saxon *Christ* calls Him[7]—was seen in these terms of the god of the king, and the latter continued his sacral relationship between the realms of the divine and the mortal.

The following study is devoted to an exposition of the nature and elements of this sacral kingship among the Anglo-Saxons. It is not a history of the *regna* and even less of the growth of political unity in England. These have been treated frequently, and although they still present problems, they are not, for the most part, our problems. Nor is this a formal, chronological history of the relationship of Church and State before the Norman Conquest, although an analysis of the religious aspects of kingship will necessarily raise questions similar to those of such a study. Instead, I shall attempt to investigate the often nebulous but nonetheless vital sources which illuminate the way in which the folk saw their king, as a sacral figure which held their tribal world together and related it to the cosmic forces in which that world was enmeshed. The ruler was himself a centre of the societal cult, and it is this cult of kingship in Anglo-Saxon England that is our subject.[8]

[6] Helmut de Boor, 'Germanische und Christliche Religiosität', *Mitteilungen der Schlesischen Gesellschaft für Volkskunde*, XXXIII (1933), pp. 26–51.

[7] *Christ*, ll. 941–942.

[8] In its larger aspect, beyond the confines of England, it was the subject of the Eighth International Congress For The History of Religions, held in Rome in April 1955. Papers of the Congress on this theme have been published in *The Sacral Kingship: Contributions to the Central Theme of the VIIIth International Congress for the History of Religions (Rome, April 1955)* (Leiden, 1959).

It is often maintained that sources for English paganism are almost non-existent. This is indeed true of written accounts of its beliefs and practices, for the triumphant Church for the most part obliterated knowledge of the older religion, except when references to it were necessary for its suppression. Christianization of heathen references in literary works was apparently common. Nonetheless, these sources are far richer than is generally realized, when the contributions of archaeology, literary studies, comparative religions, folklore, place-name investigations, numismatics, and other fields are combined. Germanic heathenism has left many traces to accompany the sixty sites of its worship which can now be located in England.[9] A problem in the interpretation of the English evidence, however, is the degree to which Scandinavian material can be used to fill the gaps. The extreme caution which paralysed much early investigation has now, happily, given way to a more balanced use of the available information. It is not simply a matter of looking for the coin where the light is better rather than in the darkness in which it was lost. The Scandinavian tribes, prior to the migration, had been near neighbours of the Angles and Saxons, and heathenism continued among them, with comparatively little southern, Roman influence, for several centuries longer than in the new island home of the English.[10] It would, of course, be foolish to assume that the two branches of the old religion were not different in important ways or that these differences had not multiplied during the generations since the migrations. Nonetheless, the constant discovery of analogies in ideas, cult objects, and societal emphases between the two areas can no more be ignored than the fact that previous problems of Anglo-Saxon investigations are often illuminated or even solved when examined in the light of comparable Scandinavian sources. Such comparisons have their dangers, but these loom less large

[9] P. H. Reaney, *The Origin of English Place-Names* (London, 1960), p. 117.

[10] The emphasis must be, of course, on 'comparatively'. For the contacts between Scandinavia and the rest of Europe, cf. Peter Hunter Blair, *An Introduction to Anglo-Saxon England* (Cambridge, 1956), pp. 55–58. However, the extensive trade cannot be taken as evidence for the importation of Christian elements into northern paganism.

than those inherent in ignoring the increasingly significant body of comparative studies which modern scholarship has made possible. Indeed, the success of such comparisons in bringing understanding of at least the context of problems may itself be a test of Anglo-Saxon paganism's similarities to the religion of early Scandinavia, that 'womb of nations', as Jordanes calls it. One must proceed with caution, but the Sutton Hoo finds, for example, have revealed hitherto unsuspected connections between at least the East Anglian royal house and the Uppland district of Sweden.[11] The 'Romanist' interpretation of Anglo-Saxon England has held sway in so many areas that its Germanic past has too often been seen through Mediterranean eyes. I claim that the varied data, some full and direct, others scanty and only suggestive, bearing on England during its transition from paganism to Christianity all fit into a coherent, understandable picture when seen against the Germanic background; when this Teutonic past is ignored, insoluble problems appear. Certainly, at least, the case for Anglo-Saxon continuity with the Germanic North deserves to be presented in full.

To become an Anglo-Saxon, pagan or Christian, is impossible, but we divorce too much, I think, Anglo-Saxon Christianity from the culture, shaped by paganism, which formed and even warped it. Our view of both politics and religion is consequently influenced. I do not think, for example, as we shall see, that one can understand King Oswald, 'the most holy and very victorious king of Northumberland', as Bede calls him, without considering the relation of the cross which he erected at Rowley Water and northern pillar cult, the hand and knee as sacral objects, Germanic tree cult and its connections with Heimdall and Christ, pillars of light above Anglo-Saxon royal saints, royal protection against pestilence, division of the king's body after the battle of *Maserfelth* with dismemberment of kings to protect their realm, the hanging of sacrifices to Woden, King Oswald as a Bavarian and Tyrolean

[11] F. P. Magoun, Jr., 'Beowulf and King Hygelac in the Netherlands', *English Studies*, XXXV (1954), pp. 203–204; for an extensive bibliography of Swedish–East Anglian connections, cf. Prof. Magoun's review of D. Whitelock's *The Beginnings of English Society*, in *Speculum*, XXVIII (1953), p. 220.

lord of the weather, and the raven of Woden and Oswald as a sacral bird. If only some of these make sense, a dimension is given to the wars of Northumbria and Mercia. And if, to move from example to thesis, culture and cult are related, a dimension is added in the past-enmeshed Conversion story in the transition from paganism to Christianity in Anglo-Saxon England. In that transition the cult of kingship will be seen to have played a strategic role.

CHAPTER I

The Woden-sprung kings: Germanic sacral kingship and divine descent

Cyning sceal rice healdan begins an Anglo-Saxon gnomic poem,[1] and Anglo-Saxon history as well opens with kings holding the rule. Neither history nor tribal tradition records a form of government other than kingship for any of the states established in England by the Germanic invaders. Attempts of nineteenth century constitutional historians to hear the ancestral spirit of parliamentary democracy are vain for the migration period. There is no good evidence for a national *witan* separate from the royal court, for the existence of the hundred as a governing unit prior to the tenth century, for legislative authority of the shire, or indeed for the concept of local self-government.[2] Kingship is the Anglo-Saxon political institution *par excellence* and gives cohesion to the realms established by the invading tribes. In each kingdom the royal race—the *stirps regia*—which sprang from its founder provided the source from which the individual rulers were chosen,[3] and beyond the earthly founder was the god who was the divine ancestor of almost every Anglo-Saxon royal house, Woden. The antiquity of the monarchic institution is reflected in the developed terminology for kingship, as in the

---

[1] *Maxims* II, l. 1a, in Elliott Van Kirk Dobbie, ed., *The Anglo-Saxon Minor Poems* (Anglo-Saxon Poetic Records, Vol. VI; New York, 1942), p. 55. Although the poem reached its present form probably in the late ninth or early tenth century, it may well contain pre-Christian matter; *Ibid.*, p. lxvii.

[2] All of these myth-shattering conclusions drawn by H. M. Chadwick, *The Origin of the English Nation* (Cambridge, 1924), pp. 144–146, still stand.

[3] Chadwick, *Origin*, p. 147, n. 1, points out that the three exceptions, other than foreign conquerors—Aelle of Northumbria, Harold II, and probably Ceolwulf II—did not found permanent dynasties, but rather 'in each of these cases the kingdom practically came to an end with the usurper.'

B

twenty-six synonyms for 'king' used by the *Beowulf* poet alone,[4] and time itself was recorded according to the regnal years of these Woden-sprung monarchs.[5] Their accessions and deaths are recorded in such histories as have survived, which are filled above all with the deeds of kings.

In spite of the paucity of sources, even in later traditions, for the age of migrations and the Anglo-Saxon settlement in the island, it is clear that the institution of kingship was a survival from pre-conquest Germanic custom and did not arise as rule peculiar to the insular development. Tacitus records it for the Teutonic tribes of the *Germania*, in which descent-chosen kings are found sharing power with war-chiefs. *Reges ex nobilitate, duces ex virtute sumunt*, he asserts.[6] The 'king or chief' (*rex vel princeps*) speaks first in the tribal assembly, but here he rules more 'by right of advising' (*auctoritate suadendi*) than by any absolute right of command.[7] Fines are paid in part to the king or state,[8] and the king or chief participates in the priestly office of interpreting the most sacred auguries, the neighing of the white horses.[9] Thus, far from an autocrat, the Teutonic king of the *Germania* exercises power which is honorific and priestly but neither unlimited nor arbitrary;[10] kingship, however, is a firm part of this generalized portrait of Germanic society, and the Tacitean distinction between *reges* and *principes* seems to rest not so much on a fixed division between the two titles as on multiple rulership, with more than one prince, drawn from the *stirps regia*, ruling over a

[4] C. M. Bowra, *Heroic Poetry* (London, 1952), p. 244.

[5] Wilhelm Levison, *England and the Continent in the Eighth Century* (Oxford, 1946), p. 84, which also discusses the introduction of the Dionysian era. Dating by regnal years was, of course, common Germanic practice. For the use of indictions in England, an imitation of Rome adopted only by Kent among the English kingdoms, cf. Charles W. Jones, ed., *Bedae Opera de Temporibus* (Cambridge, Mass., 1943), pp. 382–383.

[6] Tacitus, *Germania*, c. 7; Maurice Hutton, ed., *Tacitus. Germania* (Loeb Classical Library; London, 1946), p. 274.

[7] *Germania*, c. 11 (p. 280).

[8] *Germania*, c. 12 (p. 280).

[9] *Germania*, c. 10 (p. 278).

[10] *Nec regibus infinita aut libera potestas: Germania*, c. 7 (p. 274).

single tribe.[11] Kingly government is general to early Germanic society, though two or more kings are sometimes found sharing rule over a single tribe. Even later, in Anglo-Saxon England, there are examples of multiple-rulership. Horsa and, after Horsa's death, Hengest's son Aesc shared the rule over Kent with Hengest, as Cerdic and his son Cynric were joint-kings over the West Saxons. Sigehere and Sebbe were later co-rulers in East Anglia, and five West Saxon kings were slain in a single battle by Edwin of Northumbria.[12]

What scanty information we have of specific tribes from classical authors supports the fact of the institution of royalty, especially with reference to the northern and eastern tribes. Tacitus claims a stronger royal power for the eastern Goths, Rugii, Lemovii, and Suiones,[13] and H. M. Chadwick, who has sifted the available evidence, demonstrates that the Marcomanni, Quadi, Hermunduri, Semnones, and probably the Langobardi were also ruled by kings.[14] For the Western Germanic regions, except for eastern tribes who have migrated, such as the Burgundians and Suebic groups, Chadwick has found only six references to pre-fourth century kings. The fact that only *duces* and *principes*, the former as war-chiefs and the latter as magistrates, occur elsewhere supports the reasonable hypothesis that the general picture of the *Germania*, with its distinction between *reges* and *duces*, is based more on the western tribes on the borders of Empire, and hence better known to Roman authors, than on the eastern peoples with their more monarchic government. More important for us, however, as evidence for the continuity of Anglo-Saxon kingship with its earlier existence on the Continent, is its early prevalence among the tribes neighbouring the region of the pre-migration Angli, ancestors of the English.[15] The Suebic peoples to the

[11] Chadwick, *Origin*, p. 291. See below, n. 52. On dual chieftainship in the North, perhaps derived from twin gods, cf. E. O. G. Turville-Petre, *Myth and Religion of the North* (New York, 1964), pp. 218–220.

[12] These examples are cited by C. Brooke, *The Saxon and Norman Kings* (London, 1963), p. 92.

[13] *Germania*, cc. 43–44 (pp. 324–326).

[14] Chadwick, *Origin*, pp. 288–292.

[15] On the probability for Angel, north of the lower Elbe, as the home of the

south of Angel and the Cherusci, the most easterly tribe of the West Germans, were under the sway of kings, and to the north 'in Scandinavian history and tradition,' as Chadwick rightly asserts, 'kingship is universal.'[16] In the first century A.D., then, the period in which Tacitus writes, it is most probable that the Angli, of whose government in this early age we have no direct information, also shared this institution.

Kingship is a characteristic of the ancestors of the Anglo-Saxon tribes in the later age of migrations as well. Only the House of Mercia, which was descended from the late fourth and early fifth century kings of Angel, near Schleswig, has been established definitely as linking Anglo-Saxon kings with royal ancestors of the pre-conquest Continent. However, Chadwick's seminal studies have overthrown the earlier theory that kings may have arisen in England only after the migration by demonstrating not only that the Angles and Jutes were ruled by kings from times immemorial but that the Saxons and Angles of Britain were probably of common stock and not two distinct tribal groups. Thus the lack of kings among the Continental Saxons, who in historical times were ruled by non-monarchic *satrapae*, a term Bede may have used even to indicate their king-like rulership,[17] is not at all fatal to the extension of English kingship back through the ancestral Continental tribes and the invasions to the dawn of the Christian era.[18] The history of the Anglo-Saxons is, then,

---

Angles, cf. Chadwick, *Origin*, pp. 97–110; Sir Frank Stenton, *Anglo-Saxon England* (2nd ed.; Oxford, 1947), pp. 12–13. On the relationship of Anglo-Saxon royalty to the Danish island of Sjaelland, cf. Chadwick, *Origin*, pp. 272–273.

[16] Kings Italicus and Chariomerus of the Cherusci (Tacitus, *Annales*, XI, c. 16; Dio Cassius, LXVII, c. 5) are among the six known references to kings among the West Germanic tribes; Chadwick, *Origin*, p. 289, and for Scandinavian tradition, pp. 289, 291.

[17] Richard Schröder, 'Der Allsächsische Volksade lund die Grundherrliche Theorie,' *Zeitschrift der Savigny–Stiftung für Rechtsgeschichte, Germanistische Abteilung*, XXIV (1903), pp. 352–355; the emphasis in *satrapa* is not merely on nobility or distinction, for which Bede had other terms, but on rulership.

[18] On the probable identity of Angles and Saxons, cf. Chadwick, *Origin*, ch. 4, 'The Saxons, Angles and Jutes in Britain', pp. 51–84; on kings in Angel

enmeshed with kingship and, as we shall see, with the sacral and religio-political nature with which that ancient office was endowed among the Germanic tribes. Consequently, a general picture of the role of kingship in the pagan Germanic north will be useful, before examining in detail its survival, even under the impact of the new and triumphant religion of the Cross, in the island realms of the Anglo-Saxons. The bases of this kingship are not a subject of inquiry by Roman authors, such as Tacitus, who have given us so much information on other aspects of it; runic and other northern sources are richer in the light they shed on the fundamental premises and beliefs underlying Germanic rulership. An introductory survey of this background will serve our purposes here, with a detailed examination of the Anglo-Saxon evidence and its northern parallels awaiting a closer study of the separate problems.

The most fundamental concept in Germanic kingship is the indissolubility of its religious and political functions.[19] The king

---

and Jutland (if the Jutes are related to that region), pp. 111–136; on the lack of kings among the Old Saxons but their existence among the neighbouring Frisians, pp. 96, 153. Cf. Stenton, *Anglo-Saxon England*, pp. 36–37. For the decline in significance in England by the early eighth century of original tribal differences, the possible effect of a sense of kinship on the acceptance of a single Church, and the recognition by the English that they and the Continental Saxons were 'of one blood and one bone' (in the words of Boniface), cf. Dorothy Whitelock, ed., *English Historical Documents c. 500–1042* (English Historical Documents, vol. I; London, 1955), p. 8.

[19] The best introductions to Germanic sacral kingship are Otto Höfler, *Germanisches Sakralkönigtum* (Tübingen, 1952), I, which, however, must be used with caution; O. Höfler, 'Der Sakralcharacter des Germanischen Königtums', *The Sacral Kingship. Contributions to the Central Theme of the VIIIth International Congress for the History of Religions (Rome, April 1955)* (Leiden, 1959), pp. 664–701; Jan de Vries, 'Das Königtum bei den Germanen', *Saeculum*, VII (1956), pp. 289–309; Hans Naumann, 'Die Magische Seite des Altgermanischen Königtums und Ihr Fortwirken in Christlicher Zeit', *Wirtschaft und Kultur: Festschrift zum 70. Geburtstag von Alfons Dopsch* (Baden bei Wien, 1938), pp. 1–12; Turville-Petre, *Myth and Religion of the North*, pp. 190–195; Helmut de Boor, 'Germanische und Christliche Religiosität', *Mitteilungen der Schlesischen Gesellschaft für Volkskunde*, XXXIII (1933), pp. 26–51; H. M. Chadwick, *Origin*, pp. 295–303.

is above all the intermediary between his people and the gods, the charismatic embodiment of the 'luck' of the folk. The relation of the divine and the tribal is primarily one of action, of 'doing', and to assure the favourable actions of the gods toward the tribe the king 'does' his office as mediator between them, sacrificing for victory, for good crops and for peace, 'making' the year. It is not that he is simply a priest; he is the leader of the folk and the guarantor of their *heil* who acts so that the gods may bless them. Thus, later distinctions between priestly and political functions are caught up into a union, a personal embodiment of the link with the divine on which the tribe's well-being depends. In a world in which the kingdoms of men depend upon the realm of the divine, the earthly king moves in the vital strand which binds them together. In a very real sense, then, the god is first of all the god of the king, whose role it is to assume this burden of favourable relationship with the deity, and only secondarily the god of the tribe, whose 'luck' is mediated by that of the ruler. When the king's 'luck' or charismatic power is maintained, the favour of the god rests with the tribe; when he has lost his 'luck' and is impotent to secure the divine blessings, his people are justified, even obliged, to do the only thing possible, to replace him with another who can make the office once more effective.

Germanic history and saga are filled with this underlying current of the king's sacral 'luck'. 'It is hard to fight against the king's luck' and 'much avails the king's luck' maintain ancient proverbs, and frequent examples occur of the radiation of this royal 'luck' out to his folk: 'And yet I know surely, we shall not bring this matter about, if your royal luck does not help us in it'; 'since they had excellent forces and the good royal luck was with them, they all came safely from it'; 'I gladly add my king's luck to your own and to the safety of all of you.'[20] Similarly, in Snorri Sturluson's account of the Battle of Stamford Bridge, King Harold of England interprets the fall of King Harold Sigurdson

[20] Vilhelm Grönbech, *The Culture of the Teutons* (London, 1931), I, ch. 4, 'Luck', pp. 127–154; ch. 5, 'Luck is the Life of the Clan', pp. 155–174; vol. III, pp. 14–17, excursus on 'Anglo-Saxon *Speð*, Luck'. For the specific quotations above, cf. I, p. 133, and H. Naumann, 'Die Magische Seite', p. 1.

from his horse as a flight of the royal 'luck'; 'Do you know the stout man who fell from his horse, with the blue kirtle and the beautiful helmet?' the English king asked. 'That is the king himself,' they answered. 'A great man,' said King Harold, 'and of stately appearance is he, but I think his luck has left him.'[21] The defeat of the Norwegian king and his people, of course, ensued.

— A king's riches are a sign of his 'luck'; for example, the Anglo-Saxon terms *eadig* and *saelig* are used to mean both 'lucky' and 'rich', and wealth is taken as a token of that quality on which the gods shower their blessings.[22] Further, at the root of the Anglo-Saxon *wyn* as a kenning for the ruler is this concept of the 'luck' upon which his followers depend, a meaning which remains basic for the continuation of the appellation into Christian times and ecclesiastical usage.[23]

Jan de Vries has argued that the priestly, 'luck'-centred role of kingship was originally distinct and is reflected in the Tacitean differentiation between the *rex* chosen by his birth and the *dux* or war-chief chosen by his *virtus*. These two aspects of kingship, he contends, are in their turn rooted in the different functions of the gods Tiwaz (Tyr) and Woden.[24] The priestly functions we have been considering reflect the sacral aspect of the ruler, centred in Tiwaz, god of order and law, and displayed in Tacitus' conjunction of *sacerdos ac rex*. The *dux*, on the other hand, is the function

[21] Samuel Laing, transl., *Heimskringla* (Everyman's Library; London, 1930), p. 229. This same concept of royal 'luck' may perhaps be behind William Rufus' exclamation, 'Kings never drown', when he set out into a gale in the English Channel, on his way to suppress a revolt in Normandy; Grönbech, *Culture of the Teutons*, I, p. 132.

[22] Ernst Leisi, 'Gold und Manneswert im "Beowulf",' *Anglia*, LXXI (1953), pp. 259–260, with references on p. 260, n. 1. Beowulf is *sigoreadig secg*, 'a warrior blessed with luck, *mana*' (ll. 1311, 2352).

[23] Hertha Marquardt, *Die Altenglische Kenningar* (*Schriften der Königsberger Gelehrten Gesellschaft, Geisteswissenschaftliche Klasse*, 14 Jahr., 3 Heft; Halle, 1938), pp. 257–258, places the kenning in the tradition that *der Gefolgsherr ist für die Seinen der Inbegriff des Glücks . . . Die altenglischen Elegien zeigen deutlich, wie für den Gefolgsmann kein Glück denkbar ist ohne seinen Fürsten.* Its ecclesiastical and Christian use as a kenning for the Deity is attributed to the customary influence of royal kennings on divine kennings and not *vice versa*.

[24] De Vries, 'Königtum', pp. 296–297.

of kingship centred in Woden, god of the creative element, and expressed in the regal role of war-leader. During the early Germanic migrations, de Vries holds, the necessary dominance of the latter role, and consequently of Woden, brought Tiwaz into eclipse, as the *dux*, by establishing a dynastic kingdom, became a *rex* and merged the two functions in a charismatic, Woden-centred kingship.[25]

However close to historical reality this ingenious hypothesis may be, it must lie indeed in the realm of prehistorical conjecture; nonetheless, when the light of history and tradition falls on Germanic kingship of the age of migrations, the king is leader of the war-hosts but also the charismatic mediator with the divine, the sacral holder of the tribal 'luck'.[26] Thus Germanic and Scandinavian history of the early Middle Ages knows no strong priesthood set apart from the secular rulers. The temples were private possessions, pagan parallels of the medieval *Eigenkirche*, and the head of the household was the temple's priest.[27] The Germanic king himself offered sacrifices.[28] Whether or not the *sacerdotes* of Tacitus are in reality only the *principes* in their magical and priestly role,[29] by the time of the early migrations the chief of the *principes*—the king—has become the tribal high-priest, the 'warden of the holy temple', as northern poetry calls him.[30] Sacrificing for good crops and for victory in battle, he assured plenty among his people, but when the gods deserted him and his 'luck' no longer flowed from him, he could be deposed or even killed in time of tribal disaster. So Ammianus Marcellinus

[25] De Vries, 'Königtum', pp. 290, 296–297, 298–300.

[26] Among the Old Saxons of the Continent, who had no king, the war-leader was chosen by lot from among the many *satrapes*; Bede, *Hist. Eccl.*, V, 10; J. E. King, ed., *Baedae Historia Ecclesiastica Gentis Anglorum* (Loeb Classical Library; London, 1930), II, p. 242.

[27] See below, pp. 63–65, 73–77.

[28] Turville-Petre, *Myth and Religion of the North*, pp. 260–261.

[29] Naumann, 'Die Magische Seite', p. 7.

[30] Gudbrand Vigfusson and F. York Powell, eds., *Corpus Poeticum Boreale* (Oxford, 1883), II, p. 478. For references to him as the 'pontiff of temple worship', cf. p. 479. This convenient, often-cited collection of northern poetry will be referred to below as *C.P.B.*

records that Burgundian kings under whom crops or victory failed were deposed,[31] and when bad harvests continued in Sweden under the Ynglingar King Domaldi, in spite of rich sacrifices by the ruler, he was killed.[32] His descendant, King Olaf Tretelgia of Sweden, failed to make *blot*, neglecting the rites necessary for good crops, so that the latter failed; the Swedes, who 'used always to reckon good or bad crops for or against their kings', burned the king in his house as an offering to Oðin.[33] Thus when the king maintained a proper relation with the gods, his realm was bathed in fullness, but when his 'luck' left him, it was a sign that the gods themselves had deserted him; hence Odoacer, although an Arian Christian, when he was struck down by Theodoric the Ostrogoth in Ravenna, uttered his dying cry of despair at this withdrawal of the king's deity—'Where is God?'[34]

The early Germanic king is, consequently, not a god and not all-powerful, but he is filled with a charismatic power on which his tribe depends for its well-being. This is the king's *mana*, 'a force utterly distinct from mere physical power or strength, the possession of which assures success, good fortune, and the like to its possessor.'[35] This power permeates not the king alone but the entire 'royal race', the whole kin from among whom the folk elect him, and its source is probably to be sought in the descent of this *stirps regia* from a god. The Woden-sprung monarchs of

[31] Ammianus Marcellinus, XXVIII, c. 5, §14; John C. Rolfe, ed., *Ammianus Marcellinus* (Loeb Classical Library; London, 1939), III, p. 168.

[32] *Ynglingasaga*, c. 15 (18); E. Wessen, ed., *Snorri Sturluson. Ynglingasaga* (*Nordisk Filologi*, Series A, no. 6; Copenhagen, 1952), p. 18.

[33] . . . *ok gáfu hann Oðni ok bletu honum til árs sér* (and gave him to Othin as a sacrifice for goods crops): *Ynglingasaga*, c. 43 (47) (*Heimskringla*, I, 75–76); E. Wessen, ed., pp. 45–46. On the meaning of *blot* in this passage as reference not so much to worship of the gods as magical ceremonies for assuring the fertility of the earth, cf. Chadwick, *Origin*, pp. 237, 302.

[34] Recorded only in Johannes Antiochenus (214a); Naumann, 'Die Magische Seite', p. 2.

[35] J. de Vries, *Altgermanische Religionsgeschichte* (*Grundriss der Germanischen Philologie*, Vol. XII : 2; Berlin and Leipzig, 1937), II, pp. 32–43, with bibliography. The definition above of *mana* (O.N. *mattr*, *megin*), p. 32, is quoted from F. P. Magoun, Jr.

the Anglo-Saxons, like the god-descended royal houses of the Continent, contain within the clan the special virtue, the *mana* from on high, but hereditary as this power was, the office of kingship which embodied it might be filled by any member of the 'divine race'. 'It was the virtue of their blood,' as Fritz Kern writes, 'that lifted the sons of Woden, the Astings, the Amals, and so on, out of the ranks of the folk, though without bestowing upon any individual prince a right to the throne independent of the popular will. The family's possession of the throne was as inviolable as the right of any individual prince to succeed to it was insecure.'[36]

In this light, the tribal election of the sacral ruler was not so much a 'democratic' institution, as nineteenth-century constitutional historians, obsessed with the antecedents of parliamentary government, loved to portray it; rather it was the right to assure itself the possession of the *mana*-filled, god-sprung king, selected from the royal race for his obvious 'luck'. The election was thus the tribal right to choose the one who was the 'incarnation of the mystical powers of the whole community of the folk'[37] and

[36] Fritz Kern, *Kingship and Law in the Middle Ages* (S. B. Chrimes, transl.; Oxford, 1939), p. 14. Kern interprets the charismatic power as a magical *mana*, as do Naumann, Tellenbach, Chadwick, *et al.*; de Vries rejects the notion of magical *mana* embodied in the king's person and interprets the royal sacral power not as a magic, personal *Heil* but as a religious concept based on descent from the ancestral god: *Das Heil des Königs ist . . . mit dem Geschlechte verbunden, aus dem er entsprossen ist . . . und findet seine Quelle in dem Urahn. Die Überlieferung zeigt nachdrücklich: der Urahn ist ein Gott* (p. 295). I see no essential difference here, except in de Vries' dislike of the term 'magic'; flowing as it does from the divine ancestor, with whom the priestly king is the tribe's mediator, as well as with the other gods, the power is nonetheless a special, even magical, charisma embodied in the person of the ruler and constitutes, in Naumann's phrase, *die magische Seite* of kingship. Chadwick distinguishes 'between the migration period and the preceding age—so far at least as the more northern nations are concerned—by the statement that in the former the king was the descendant of a god, while in the latter he was a god himself'; *Origin*, p. 303. In the period with which I am concerned, the influence of divine descent is more apparent.

[37] De Vries, 'Königtum', p. 298. O. Höfler, 'Sakralcharacter', pp. 692–695, presents evidence that *thing*-kingship can be reconciled with sacral kingship, since the *thing* (assembly) itself is sacral. Thus the king, chosen by the *thing*, can be both sacral and *primus inter pares*.

whose divinely inspired word gives the *auctoritas suadendi* by which he rules that assembled folk.[38] This tribal selection of the ruler dominates Anglo-Saxon elevations into kingship from our earliest sources for it down to its close when 'all the people chose Edward (the Confessor) as king'.[39] At the same time, as we shall see, all of the royal houses of the Anglo-Saxons for whom genealogies remain claimed divine descent, as choice was in effect limited to the god-sprung family to which the 'luck'-giving *mana* was apparently confined. Even in Christian times, the importance of this descent-based authority was recognized, as Alcuin testifies: 'Scarcely any of the ancient royal kindred remains, and by as much as their origin is uncertain, by so much is their power less.'[40] This, in Christian kingship, has its origin in the pagan Germanic sacral monarch who, with his lineage placing him in the line of Woden, made *blot* for his folk to maintain the blessings of the gods. The Woden-sprung rulers thus represent not only their folk but the gods between whom and their people they mediate.[41]

[38] Tacitus, *Germania*, c. 11; see above, p. 8 and n. 7.

[39] Anglo-Saxon Chronicle, *sub anno* 1042; J. Earle and C. Plummer, eds., *Two of the Saxon Chronicles Parallel* (Oxford, 1892), I, p. 162 (MSS. C, D). This edition will be used for the Chronicle through this work.

[40] *Et vix aliquis modo, quod sine lacrimis non dicam, ex antiqua regum prosapia invenitur, et tanto incertioris sunt originis, quanto minoris sunt fortitudinis:* letter of Alcuin to the nobles and people of Kent, A.D. 797; *Mon. Ger. Hist., Epistolae*, IV, Ep. 129, p. 192. J. E. A. Jolliffe, *The Constitutional History of Medieval England* (2nd ed.; London, 1947), p. 44, errs in giving the source as one of Alcuin's letters to Archbishop Eanbald.

[41] Otto Höfler, *Germanisches Sakralkönigtum*, I, pp. xi–xii, on some of the problems and manifestations of this divine 'representation'. All of these elements mentioned above, as well as materials cited later, necessitate rejection or severe qualification for Anglo-Saxon England of the theories in P. Grierson, 'Election and Inheritance in Germanic Kingship', *Cambridge Historical Journal*, VII (1941), pp. 1–22. In contrast to the theory of royal race and election, he contends that election and inheritance occur but not together and that no proof exists of an inherent divine right to the kingship in a god-sprung line. He limits his examination to the Goths and Lombards—East Germanic peoples—only, however. The importance of descent in Anglo-Saxon kingship, the god-sprung lineage of all known royal lines, the appearance of *electio* (even if simply acclamation or assent), and other evidence cited must lead us to place the Anglo-Saxons in a different tradition.

The role of divine descent as the connecting link between the two and as the possible basis of sacral kingship in Anglo-Saxon England demands further analysis.

In a kin-centred society such as that of the Anglo-Saxons and other Germanic peoples, common descent bound the social group together and provided the basis of unity.[42] As in modern society an individual tends to be identified by his occupation, in Germanic society he identified himself by his lineage and by the lord whom he followed. 'We are sprung of a strain of the Geatish people, Hygelac's hearth-companions,' Beowulf answers, when challenged to say who he is; 'my father was famous among the folk, a noble chieftain, Ecgtheow his name!'[43] Or again, 'I will make known my lineage to all,' the young Aelfwine declares in the *Battle of Maldon*, when he rallies the hosts, 'that I was of a mighty race in Mercia.'[44] It is descent that helps to establish both claim to rank and a standard of conduct worthy of the nobly born. So Aelfwine recites his descent from Ealhhelm as proof of how he himself should act, so that 'thegns shall have no cause to reproach me among my people'. Descent called its bearer to heroism. At *Brunanburh* 'Edward's sons'—King Athelstan the Glorious and his brother, the aetheling Edmund—'clove the shield-wall, . . . for it was natural to men of their lineage to defend their land, their treasure, and their homes, in frequent battle against every enemy'.[45]

As with lords of men confidence and trust were established by a noble line, so Divinity itself could be thought of as appealing to the same source of authority. In the *Andreas*, for example, 'the

---

[42] On Germanic kinship system, cf. Chadwick, *Origin*, pp. 303–323; Elizabeth E. Bacon, *Obok: A Study of Social Structure in Eurasia* (New York, 1958), pp. 144–147; on kinship in Anglo-Saxon England, cf. Stenton, *Anglo-Saxon England*, pp. 312–314; Bertha S. Phillpotts, *Kindred and Clan in the Middle Ages and After: A Study in the Sociology of the Teutonic Races* (Cambridge, 1913), pp. 205–244.

[43] *Beowulf*, ll. 260–263.

[44] *Battle of Maldon*, ll. 216–217; M. Ashdown, ed., *English and Norse Documents Relating to the Reign of Ethelred the Unready* (Cambridge, 1930), p. 30.

[45] Anglo-Saxon Chronicle, *sub anno* 937, where the account is in alliterative verse in five of the seven MSS.; Earle and Plummer, eds., *op. cit.*, I, p. 106.

Lord of hosts, the Spirit of heavenly holiness, spoke . . . : "Now I shall bid a sign appear, . . . (to) tell in true speech what is my lineage—thereby men shall have faith in my race."[46] This heavenly reflection of the 'royal race' lends added weight to the concept of descent-given and God-given royal authority which, as Alcuin says, is weakened for kings 'by as much as their lineage is uncertain'. The Anglo-Saxons understood the authority of Christ because He was the Son of God, as their pagan forebears understood the authority of the king because he was sprung from a god.

The deification of humans is not unknown in the North. *'Colunt et deos ex hominibus factos,'* says Adam of Bremen concerning the Swedes and cites as evidence the worship given after death to King Eric.[47] But an explanation of royal divine descent by the deification of an individual human ancestor is both unnecessary and dependent on very little evidence indeed. The veneration of the dead king relates, as we shall see, to the *mana*-filled ruler whose blessings are still desired. In an age in which gods often walked the earth and mingled in the affairs of rulers, a deified human ancestor is no more needed for divine descent in the north than it is for the descent of Homeric chieftains from the gods. At any rate, the problem of origin is both chronologically and in concept antecedent to our investigation. The fact of belief in the divine descent of kings is independent of its origin and is firmly established, not only among the Anglo-Saxons. Scandinavian rulers trace their line from the god Yngwi, later assimilated to Frey, and are styled 'the scion, the offspring, the descendant of Yngwi or the God (Tyr), the branch of Woden's own race'.[48] Heimdal or Rig is the ancestor of all kings, according to the *Lay of Rig*,[49] and the assumption of royal divine origin is common in

[46] *Andreas*, ll. 727–734; G. P. Krapp, ed., *The Vercelli Book* (Anglo-Saxon Poetic Records, Vol. II; London, 1932), p. 23.

[47] Adam of Bremen, IV, c. 26, with reference to *Vita Ansgari*; Bernhard Schmeidler, ed., *Adam of Bremen, Gesta Hammaburgensis Ecclesiae Pontificum* (3rd ed.; Hanover and Leipzig, 1917), p. 259.

[48] *C.P.B.*, II, p. 478.

[49] *C.P.B.*, II, p. 478.

northern poetry. 'Let us sit and weigh the Races of Kings,' the goddess Freyja says in the *Hyndluljoð*, 'of all men that sprung from the gods';[50] in one of the oldest epics, the *Hamðismal*, 'the god-sprung king roared mightily, as a bear roars, out of his harness'.[51] If, as shall be seen, Anglo-Saxon monarchs also came of a divine race, they shared this in common with other Germanic ruling houses.

As has been observed, the entire royal kin and not merely the holder of the kingship was elevated into the divine race by this descent from deity. The royal dignity was transmitted to the family; 'the realm belongs to the royal race', as Liebermann says.[52] Any member of the royal house might therefore hope for the throne, a fact which helps to account for the numerous fratricidal wars and struggles for it which fill Anglo-Saxon history.[53] A parallel of this familial inheritance of the royal *mana* is seen in Procopius' account of the Herulian embassy to their northern home, probably near that of the Angles, to seek out a king. After slaying their own ruler, the Heruli who lived among the Romans sent a mission to their homeland of Thule to select a new king from the old *stirps regia*. 'They found many there of the royal blood' and chose one, Procopius writes, and, when the latter died on the return journey, the embassy returned yet again and selected another. Although the Heruli had in the meantime repented and had asked the Emperor Justinian to give them a ruler, when the latter went out to meet his rival in combat upon the embassy's return, his entire army deserted to the scion of the ancient royal house, even though Justinian's appointee was also

---

[50] *Sitja við skolom, / ok um iaofra aettir doéma: / gumna eirra es frá goðom kvómo:* C.P.B., I, p. 227.

[51] *Þa hraut ríkt inn regin-kungi / baldr í brynjo sem biaorn hryti: ibid.,* p. 58.

[52] Felix Liebermann, ed., *Die Gesetze der Angelsachsen* (Halle a. S., 1912), II, p. 553. Cf. F. Kern, *Kingship and Law*, p. 13: 'The whole dynasty, not merely the individual, was called to the throne. . . . All members of the ruling family are royal'. The distinction, consequently, between the *rex* and the Tacitean *princeps* is, as Kern points out (p. 13), 'one of degree rather than of kind'.

[53] For examples of wars by rival claimants and of consequent royal exiles, cf. D. Whitelock, ed., *Engl. Hist. Doc.,* pp. 26–27.

a Herulian.[54] Not only is there evidence here of the hold upon a folk of the tradition of the 'royal race' but also of the entire house as the potential source of kingly office. This relation of king and kin was founded upon common descent from an ancestor whose *mana* permeated the royal line. That ancestor was a god.

This charismatic quality bestowed by divine descent on the whole royal kin is probably to be detected behind the various Germanic titles used for the king. Jan de Vries, in his investigations of the philological and semantic origins of these terms, has concluded that the new Germanic word *kuningaz* and its variations came into use in place of the older Indo-Germanic *râj-rêx-rîks* variants precisely to emphasize the religious character of the 'divine race'. Furthermore, the kin-centred basis is seen in the Anglo-Saxon work *cyning* (king) itself, which, it has been suggested, meant originally 'son of the *cyn* or family', with special application to the royal house; that it was widely used among the Germanic tribes before the Anglo-Saxons came to Britain is reflected in the distribution of the Old German *cuning* and Old Norse *konungr*. The ruler's relation to kin and folk appears also in the Old English *aetheling* and its Germanic parallels, in the Gothic *kindins* ('leader of the commonly descended race or clan') and the Burgundian *hendinus* (probably 'leader of the *kind*'), in the Anglo-Saxon *ðeoden* and its parallels, terms of folk-kingship, in the Anglo-Saxon *leod* (meaning both 'prince' and 'folk'), in the Anglo-Saxon *ðengel* (O.N. *þengill*, perhaps 'foremost of the *thing* or assembled tribe'), and in other cult-centred and descent-centred appellations for the *mana*-possessing king.[55] Uncertain as the early meanings of most of these must be, the accumulated results point in one direction: sacral kingship was reflected in terms used for the ruler, whose kin-centred authority they also embody.

[54] Procopius, *History of the Wars*, VI (*Gothic War*, II), chs. 14 §42 and 15 §§27–36; H. B. Dewing, ed., *Procopius. The History of the Wars* (Loeb Classical Library; London, 1919), III, pp. 412, 420–424.

[55] De Vries, 'Königtum', pp. 298–305; cf. Chadwick, *Origin*, p. 296, in which the hereditary aspect of the Anglo-Saxon word *cyning* is discussed. For Anglo-Saxon terms for king, see below, pp. 47–48.

Furthermore, divine descent and possibly an original divinity of the king himself are seen not only in the general designations for the office but also in the names chosen by these god-sprung monarchs. In Sweden, for example, the necessity of fulfilling the ancient royal role extended to the choice of name. When a son was born to the Swedish king on St. James' Day and was consequently named James by the bishop, the folk were greatly displeased, because no king of the Swedes had ever been named this. As a result, he was forced to take the ancient royal name Oenund. If the king's 'luck' depended on his descent, it was dangerous to the kingdom for its ruler to be called by a name not saturated in that tradition. Prefixes to the royal names further suggest the *mana*-possessing nature of the dynasty. Thus Merovingian rulers were often named with *Child-* (= battle) and *Chramn-* (= raven, the sacral bird of Woden) prefixes, and the frequent occurrence of such names as Segimerus, Segimundus, and Segestes among the Cherusci indicates the victory-giving *mana* of their house.[56]

Similarly, the tradition of a sacral royal name appears as explicitly in Anglo-Saxon England. The prefix 'Os-', signifying '(heathen) god' or 'divine' occurs in the names of twelve Northumbrian kings. Margaret Murray finds comfort for her extreme theory of the Divine King in England in the fact that all but two of these died violent deaths and so are, to her, royal sacrificial victims.[57] We need not go this far, since in seventh and eighth century Northumbria it was difficult not to become a royal sacrificial victim; nonetheless, the names are not without significance for the penetration of the *heilerfüllt* king of paganism into Christian times.[58] The 'Os-' prefix has also been seen as a reminiscence of the Aesir, spirits of the North and a word applied in

---

[56] De Vries, 'Königtum', p. 295.

[57] Margaret Murray, *The Divine King in England* (London, 1954), pp. 45–46, 218. On methods of alliteration in Germanic royal genealogies, cf. G. T. Flom, 'Alliteration and Variation in Old Germanic Name-Giving', *Modern Language Notes*, XXXII (1917), pp. 7–17.

[58] In Scotland, the spurious laws of Kenneth MacAlpin parallel blaspheming God's name and the king's name and condemn the blasphemer of either to have his tongue cut out; A. W. Haddan and W. Stubbs, eds., *Councils and Ecclesiastical Documents Relating to Great Britain and Ireland* (Oxford, 1871), II : 1, p. 122.

Icelandic to all the gods. They appear only once in Anglo-Saxon, in a charm against rheumatism, in which they are combined with elves and hags.[59] But harking back to an age in which elves were larger, one may well conjecture that the syllable 'Os-' rang bells in a seventh century Northumbrian head that it does not in ours. ' "Os" is the beginning of every speech', declares the early Anglo-Saxon Rune Poem.[60] This god who is *ordfruma aelcre spraece* is probably Woden, the giver of poetry and runes[61] and the ancestor of the Anglian kings who incorporated the divine name into their own. The connection of Woden and 'os', 'god', must remain vague, but it is suggested by the association of both with the giving of speech and with the early Anglo-Saxon kings of Northumbria. It must be recalled, moreover, that the priest-kings of the *Germania* ruled in the assembly *auctoritate suadendi*;[62] if the source of their inspired word was the god from whom later Germanic kings traced their descent, Woden, so the god who gave magic words was 'the beginning of every speech', as in turn the sacral king's speech was the first in the assembly.

In selecting from this divinely descended race, the practical problem of choosing a king who was a worthy war-chief as well as a vessel of sacral 'luck' often led to a preference for an older collateral relative instead of a child of the deceased monarch. Indeed, as William Stubbs has pointed out, the history of Wessex

[59] G. Storms, *Anglo-Saxon Magic* (The Hague, 1948), pp. 50, 142–143, 147; the northern smith, a figure of magic, also makes his appearance in this charm: pp. 140–141, 146–147 (in which he is related to Weland the Smith). On 'Os-' = Aesir = Anses, cf. *C.P.B.*, II, p. 515.

[60] L. 10: ᚩ (*os*) *byþ ordfruma aelcre spraece*; Elliott van Kirk Dobbie, ed., *A.S. Minor Poems*, p. 28. On its probable date of eighth or early ninth century, cf. p. xlix, and on meaning and origin of *os*, p. 154.

[61] See below, p. 34. Cf. H. M. Chadwick, *The Cult of Othin* (London, 1899), pp. 29–30. In the prose text of *Salomon and Saturn* the giant *Mercurius*, the Woden of the *interpretatio Romana* (cf. Engl. 'Wednesday' and Fr. 'Mercredi') is credited with the invention of letters; J. M. Kemble, ed., *The Dialogue of Salomon and Saturnus* (Aelfric Society Publ., III; London, 1848), p. 192 (v. 58), and on the identification of Woden with Mercury, p. 197; Ernst Philippson, *Germanisches Heidentum bei den Angelsachsen* (*Kölner Anglistische Arbeiten*, Vol. IV; Leipzig, 1929), pp. 148–149.

[62] See above, p. 8 and n. 7.

from A.D. 685 to 839 gives not a single example of a son succeed-
ing his father directly,[63] and in later times an emergency almost
inevitably led to the selection of one old enough to cope with it.
Thus in the exigencies of the Viking invasions in the second half
of the ninth century, Aethelbald of Wessex was succeeded upon
his death in A.D. 860 by his brother Aethelberht, the latter, after
a reign of five years, by his brother Aethelred, and he in turn by
his brother Alfred the Great.[64] Similarly, when King Edmund
was killed in A.D. 946, he was succeeded by his brother Eadred,
even though he had a son, Eadwig.[65] The concept of hereditary
'luck' in the god-sprung house consequently combined with the
early tribal right of electing the best embodiment of the type of the
folk to place, in theory, the ablest of the blessed on the throne.[66]

This pagan notion of the sacral-able king was not only continued in Christian times but strengthened when it was translated
into ecclesiastical terms. The Church opposed the succession of
illegitimate children to the throne, and in this support of the
sanctity of marriage helped to elevate the sanctity of kingship,
though in terms of the new religion. When the Synod of A.D. 786
ruled that illegitimacy barred a candidate for king, it paralleled the
royal office with the priestly, into which only one born in wed-
lock could enter.[67] Thus kings and priests must have a descent, or
at least birth, proper to their office, a Christian translation which

[63] William Stubbs, *The Constitutional History of England* (5th ed.; Oxford,
1891), I, p. 152.

[64] Anglo-Saxon Chronicle *sub annis* 860–871; Earle and Plummer, eds., I,
pp. 66–73. When Alfred's son, Edward the Elder, succeeded to the throne, the
aetheling Aethelwold, the son of Alfred's older brother, King Aethelred, seized
two royal residences and finally deserted to the Danes; *ibid.*, pp. 92–93 (*sub
anno* 901[899]).

[65] *Sub annis* 946, 955; Earle and Plummer, eds., pp. 112, 113.

[66] This absence of primogeniture for one hundred and fifty years goes
farther than 'the fairly regular application of primogeniture, with the normal
proviso that minors could not succeed to the throne', asserted for Anglo-Saxon
England by P. Grierson, 'Election and Inheritance', p. 3. On possible methods
of succession, cf. Kern, *Kingship and Law*, p. 12, n. 3.

[67] Haddan and Stubbs, eds., *Councils and Ecclesiastical Documents*, III, p. 453.
Cf. E. Eichmann, 'Königs- und Bischofsweihe', *Sitzungsberichte der Bayerischen
Akademie der Wissenschaften*, Philol.-Philos. Klasse (1928), no. 6, p. 64.

would probably be seen by the folk so soon after the Conversion as paralleling the proper descent necessary for the pagan priest-king.

The final Christian addition to the theory of succession within the royal house is the notion that one born 'in the purple', after his father's accession to the throne, was more legally in line of succession than his older brothers. Common in Byzantium and used in Germany in support of Otto the Great's younger brother Henry in A.D. 936,[68] this argument is found in England in the disputed election of 975 after the death of King Edgar. An objection to Edward the Martyr, who is supported by the ecclesiastical party led by Dunstan, is that he was not born to a crowned king and his wife: *quia matrem ejus, licet legaliter nuptam, in regnum tamen non magis quam patrem ejus dum eum genuit sacratam fuisse sciebent.*[69] The sacred rite of making a king bestowed a special character on the monarch which set apart those sons born to the anointed from his earlier children. This is a different view from the earlier one of the special character bestowed by divine descent, even though an approach to the same problem, the elevated nature of kingship, and a similar solution in rooting that special character both in royal birth and in a divine source. As shall frequently be seen, the new religion translates the older, pagan, and Germanic view of kingship in its various aspects into Christian terms.

One final word must be said on the nature of kingship based on divine descent and yet within the royal kin, before examining that descent itself. The marriage of a king to his father's widow is found in England, as among the Warni and other Continental tribes. Although this custom is usually found in societies which give women a subordinate role and consequently regard the widow as chattel to be inherited by the son, yet in the early North Harald Hildetand in Denmark, Halfdan the Black in Agdir, and his son Harald in Sogn all came to their thrones through their

[68] Kern, *Kingship and Law*, p. 18, n. 10.

[69] Eadmer, *Vita Dunstani*, c. 35. E. A. Freeman, *The History of the Norman Conquest of England* (3rd ed., revised; Oxford, 1877), I, p. 639, points out that the same objection could be made to Edward's brother and rival Aethelred, who was also born before King Edgar's coronation at Bath, and that the objection was perhaps intended only to place the candidates on an equal basis.

mothers. Although among the fourth century Angli succession through the male line was the custom in the royal house, yet in the first century their principal deity was apparently a goddess; there is no proof that they were agnatic in these earlier centuries when the Anglian pantheon may have been dominated by a female deity.[70] It is clear that Bede knows of goddesses in English heathenism.[71] Furthermore, Chadwick has suggested that the worship of Frey in Sweden was a later development, replacing an original female cult of Freyja. This would account for the evidence he has adduced both that 'it was the queens and not the kings of the Swedes who were originally regarded as the representatives of the deity' and 'that the position of the Swedish kings as representatives of Frey was, like the god himself, a secondary development—that originally they were regarded as representatives of Freyia.'[72]

All of this must be kept in mind in assessing any signs of female descent in royal divine genealogy or in Anglo-Saxon claims to the throne. For example, the marriage of King Cnut to Emma, the widow of King Aethelred the Redeless, his predecessor, which has often puzzled historians, may well have been influenced by these ancient customs. As Freeman says, 'there is indeed something very strange about the whole thing',[73] but not only for the reasons he cites. The Encomiast in his history of Emma says nothing of her earlier marriage with the West Saxon monarch and even refers to her twice as a *virgo*—in spite of her three children by Aethelred; although this can be taken simply as 'woman', the context makes it clear that the Encomiast intended to deceive his readers. Emma's own apparent aversion to her first marriage is a possibility also.[74] Nonetheless, Cnut's marriage to a

---

[70] On these problems, cf. Chadwick, *Origin*, pp. 305–320.

[71] See below, p. 60.

[72] Chadwick, *Origin*, pp. 237–238; quotations from p. 238.

[73] Freeman, *Norman Conquest*, I, p. 735.

[74] Alistair Campbell, ed., *Encomium Emmae Reginae* (Camden Third Series, Vol. LXXII; London, 1949), pp. xliii, xlvi, 32 (Bk. II, c. 16); Freeman, *Norman Conquest*, I, pp. 736–737. The origin of the accounts of her dislike of Aethelred is William of Malmesbury, who is not explicitly supported by the Encomiast, who never mentions Emma's first marriage.

woman much older than himself and whom he had probably never seen was undoubtedly a matter of policy and makes complete sense only in light of the ancient Scandinavian and possibly pre-migration Germanic succession to the throne of him who married the old king's widow. As the northern ruler had once been the husband of Freyja,[75] the new king must possess the old queen who came to represent that deity. It is this principle rather than the acquisition of paternal chattel which royal marriages to the dead king's widow demonstrate. That Cnut's marriage was understood in this manner not only in his Danish realms but in England—rule over which he was strengthening by this act—as well is supported by sources suggesting that this kind of marriage was an ancient Anglo-Saxon custom also. Eadbald, son of the first Christian monarch in England, Aethelberht of Kent, married his stepmother when he came to the throne upon his father's death, an act which calls down upon him violent vituperation from Bede,[76] but which may have been ancestral custom to the still heathen Eadbald. Indeed, St. Augustine faced the problem of marriage with the stepmother in Anglo-Saxon society and included it among the *quaestiones* which he referred to Gregory the Great.[77]

Further, Judith, queen of the ninth century Aethelwulf of Wessex, was married to his son, King Aethelbald, when the old king was dead.[78] And among the Warni, a tribe closely connected with the Angles, King Radger married the widow of his father, Hermigisil, following the latter's deathbed advice to him to follow this custom of their ancestors.[79] A dim echo of a time when

[75] Chadwick, *Origin*, pp. 237–238.

[76] Bede, *Hist. Eccl.*, II, 5; King, ed., I, p. 228.

[77] Bede, *Hist. Eccl.*, I, 27; King, ed., I, pp. 122–124.

[78] Asser, *Life of King Alfred*, c. 17, asserts that this was 'contrary to God's prohibition and Christian dignity' but obviously errs in claiming it was 'also against the usage of all pagans'. On this and other marriages in context of marriage with the dead king's widow, cf. J. G. Frazer, *Lectures on the Early History of Kingship* (London, 1905), pp. 243–244.

[79] Frazer, *Lectures*, p. 244; on the relation of the Warni and Angli, cf. the detailed treatment in Chadwick, *Origin*, pp. 102–110. On matrilineal succession among the non-Teutonic Picts of northern Britain, cf. H. M. Chadwick, *Early*

maternal descent was deity-related may, finally, be detected in Simeon of Durham's citing of King Oswald's noble descent in his maternal as well as paternal line: *nec tantum paterna sed et materna quoque origine clarissimam duxit genealogiam.*[80] However, important as these evidences are for a former royal relationship with the gods through the female line, there is no doubt that the Anglo-Saxon kingdoms of historical times are agnatic; descent is above all through the male line, and divine descent in the royal house is also through paternal lineage.

The *stirps regia* as a race set apart by its task of mediating between the gods and man has, from many aspects, been seen to rest upon its charismatic quality derived from divine descent. Its ancestor was a god, and for the kings of Anglo-Saxon England that god was Woden. Hengest and Horsa, the legendary leaders of the Germanic invasion, were, according to Bede, the great-great-grandsons of Woden, *de cuius stirpe multarum provinciarum regium genus originem duxit;*[81] 'from that Woden,' a Northumbrian addition to the Anglo-Saxon Chronicle confirms, 'has descended all our royal family, and that of the Southumbrians also.'[82] The Anglo-Saxon royal genealogies are an immensely rich and equally complex source for early English traditions. However, their usefulness for our problem does not involve the textual and exegetical complications centring in the problem of how to distinguish the historical content of the genealogies from their fictitious 'divine'

Scotland (Cambridge, 1949), pp. 89–98; F. T. Wainwright, ed., *The Problem of the Picts* (Edinburgh, 1955), pp.25-28: J. Fraser, 'The Alleged Matriarchy of the Picts', *Medieval Studies in Memory of Gertrude Schoepperle Loomis* (New York, 1927), pp. 407–412 (whose author is not to be confused with Sir James Frazer, who has written on the same subject).

[80] Thomas Arnold, ed., *Symeonis Monachi Opera Omnia. Historia Ecclesiae Dunhelmensis* (Rolls Series, Vol. LXXV:1; London, 1882), p. 18 (Bk. I, c. 1). That his mother Acha was a sister of King Edwin is mentioned by Bede, III, 6, but without Simeon's 'genealogical' interpretation.

[81] Bede, *Hist. Eccl.*, I, 15; King, ed., I, p. 72.

[82] Ms. E *sub anno* 449, which gives the same generations of Hengest and Horsa in descent from the god as does Bede and is probably derived from the latter; Earle and Plummer, eds., I, p. 13.

elements.[83] Their lack of historicity is seen doubly, for example, in the fact that only three generations separate the fifth century humans Hengest and Horsa from the god Woden, who was worshipped at least as early as the first century A.D. Nonetheless, they are all clear on the divine origins of the English royal houses.

Eight genealogies survive. Of these, seven—those of Kent, Wessex, East Anglia, Mercia, Bernicia, Deira, and Lindsey—all record the descent of their kings from Woden. The kings of Essex trace their lineage from Seaxnet, a god known among the Saxons of the Continent, identified both as a son of Woden and as the god Tiw (Tyr);[84] only the Sussex royal genealogy is not known, but there is little reason to believe that it too was not Woden-sprung. The early English belief that their rulers were Woden-descended is not affected by the ancestors which several of these pedigrees give to Woden himself, since these additions date from a later age, when the kings received their *mana* from another God. As Kenneth Sisam has summarized in his magisterial analysis of the genealogies: 'Few will dissent from the general opinion that the ancestors of Woden were a fanciful development of Christian times. There is no evidence of an ancient tradition

[83] The best recent monograph on the genealogies is Kenneth Sisam, 'Anglo-Saxon Royal Genealogies', *Proceedings of the British Academy*, XXXIX (1953), pp. 287–346. Royal genealogies are printed in Erna Hackenberg, *Die Stammtafeln der Angelsächsischen Königreiche* (Berlin, 1918). For bibliography, cf. also Karl Hauck, 'Lebensnormen und Kultmythen in Germanischen Stammes- und Herrschergenealogien', *Saeculum*, VI (1955), pp. 189–190; E. A. Philippson, *Die Genealogie der Götter in Germanischer Religion, Mythologie, und Theologie* (Urbana, Ill., 1953), p. 88, n. 152. Source references are collected in Whitelock, ed., *Engl. Hist. Doc.*, p. 12, n. 11.

[84] Walther Schücking, *Der Regierungsantritt (Die Urzeit und die Zeit der Ost- und Westgermanischen Stammesreiche*, I; Leipzig, 1899), p. 176, consequently errs in claiming *alle Herrscher der angelsächsischen Reiche leiteten ihren Ursprung von Woden ab*, and *alle überlieferten Stammtafeln der Könige führen das Geschlecht auf Woden zurück*. E. A. Philippson, *Die Genealogie . . .*, p. 60, also goes too far when he states *alle acht Teilkönigreiche leiteten ihre Dynastien von Woden ab*. On Seaxnet, cf. p. 34, and the same author's *Germanisches Heidentum . . .*, pp. 117–119. These two valuable works of Philippson are cited hereafter as *Die Genealogie* and *Germ. Heid.* Turville-Petre, *Myth and Religion*, p. 100, suggests Seaxnet's association with Njörðr or Frey.

about them among the Germanic peoples of the Continent and Scandinavia. Bede gives no hint of pedigrees going beyond Woden. The list in the *Historia Brittonum* begins with him. Cerdic's pedigree (R^a) in the West Saxon Regnal Table, important because it is a text of Alfred's time earlier even in this part than the Parker MS., ends with Woden; and so do the Chronicle pedigrees, except Aethelwulf's under 855 and Ida's under 547.'[85]

Of the rulers of Kent, eight generations take their line from King Aethelberht, the first royal convert to Christianity among the Anglo-Saxons, to his divine ancestor, Woden. As we have noted, both Bede and the Anglo-Saxon Chronicle, probably derived from Bede, give Hengest and Horsa's descent from Woden, and Bede that of Aethelberht from Hengest.[86] The early king-list compiled by the British chronicler Nennius, probably in the late seventh century, also traces the descent of these invaders from Woden, and this is in agreement with Bede's account.[87]

More genealogical sources are available for the House of Wessex than for any other. Lineages to Woden are given in the Anglo-Saxon Chronicle for Cerdic, the founder of that kingdom, in the genealogical preface to Parker MS. A[88] and *sub annis* 552,[89] 597,[90] and 855, the latter being the famous lineage of King

[85] K. Sisam, 'Anglo-Saxon Royal Genealogies', p. 308; on the generations from Woden to the god Geat, cf. pp. 307–314. Gordon J. Copley, *The Conquest of Wessex in the Sixth Century* (London, 1954), ch. 13 ('The West Saxon King-lists: Adam to Elesa'), pp. 129–139; R. W. Chambers, *Beowulf: An Introduction to the Study of the Poem* (3rd ed.; Cambridge, 1959), pp. 198–201, on 'the stages above Woden'.

[86] Bede, *Hist. Eccl.*, I, 15, and II, 5; King, ed., I, pp. 70–72, 226. Earle and Plummer, eds., I, p. 13.

[87] A. W. Wade-Evans, ed., *Nennius's 'History of the Britons'* (London, 1938), pp. 53–54.

[88] Earle and Plummer, eds., 1, p. 2. Another copy, but independent of A, is B.M. Cotton Tiberius A iii, fol. 178, and probably was prefixed to the Chronicle MS. B. An independent ninth-century version, B.M. Addit. MS. 23211, is printed by H. Sweet, *The Oldest English Texts* (Early English Text Society, Original Series, no. 83; London, 1885, reprinted 1957), p. 179. Bruce Dickins, *The Genealogical Preface to the Anglo-Saxon Chronicle* (Occasional Papers, no. 2; Cambridge, 1952), *passim*. [89] Earle and Plummer, eds., I, p. 16 (Parker MS. A).

[90] Earle and Plummer, eds., I, p. 20 (Parker MS. A).

Aethelwulf.[91] The Chronicle pedigree of Ida *sub anno* 688 goes only to Cerdic, who is also claimed *sub anno* 786 as the ancestor of Brihtric of Wessex, but without any lineage to Woden appended.[92] The descent from Woden of the Wessex ruling family is also recorded by Asser in his *De Rebus Gestis Aelfredi*, derived from the Chronicle's ancestry of Alfred's father, Aethelwulf.[93]

For the East Anglian kings neither Bede nor the Anglo-Saxon Chronicle supplies genealogical information, but that royal house, which Sutton Hoo has demonstrated to have previously unsuspected, strong links with Sweden,[94] sprang from the god whom both Scandinavian and pagan English kings venerated. An early ninth century manuscript traces its descent from Woden,[95] and the even earlier genealogy of the *Historia Brittonum* of Nennius confirms this.[96]

More information exists for the Anglian kingdom of Mercia, whose *stirps regia* alone among the Anglo-Saxon royalty is firmly connected with ancestral kings known to have held sway on the Continent before the invasion. The great pagan warrior-king Penda is of the stem of Woden, although his predecessors on the throne are names only.[97] Perhaps in an attempt to blot out divine descent which lingered so long even after the Conversion, the genealogy of Penda has been erased from one of the Chronicle's principal manuscripts, Parker MS. A. Descent from Woden is also traced in the same source, however, for the ruler of Mercia during the age of its hegemony under Offa.[98] British Museum

[91] Earle and Plummer, eds., I, p. 66 (Parker MS. A). Cf. Chadwick, *Origin*, ch. II, 'King Aethelwulf's Mythical Ancestors', pp. 252–283.

[92] Earle and Plummer, eds., I, pp. 40, 52 (given as A.D. 784).

[93] W. H. Stevenson, ed., *Asser's Life of King Alfred* (Oxford, 1904), pp. 2, 157–160 (note). From his maternal genealogy (p. 4) it is clear that Alfred was Woden-sprung on both sides of his ancestry.

[94] See above, Introduction, n. 11.

[95] B.M. Cotton Vespasian B vi, written probably between A.D. 811 and 814; H. Sweet, ed., *Oldest English Texts*, p. 171. For date and provenance of ms., cf. p. 167.

[96] C. 59; A. W. Wade-Evans, ed., *Nennius's 'History'*, p. 77. For the probable seventh century date of its original form, cf. p. 25.

[97] Anglo-Saxon Chronicle, *sub anno* 626; Earle and Plummer, eds., I, p. 24.

[98] Earle and Plummer, eds., I, p. 50, *sub anno* 755 (757). Cf. B. Thorpe, ed.,

Cotton MS. Vespasian B vi, the source for the East Anglian line, gives independent confirmation of the divine origin of the Mercian house, as does Nennius.[99]

In Northumbria both the kings of Bernicia and of Deira are Woden-sprung, even though from different sons of the god. The Chronicle adduces the Bernician line *sub anno* 547 from King Ida to Baeldaeg, son of Woden, and the Deiran *sub anno* 560 from King Aelle to Waegdaeg, another son.[100] Although variations appear, Cotton Vespasian B vi and Nennius both confirm the divine descent, the former in the Deiran line from Aelle's son, Edwin, and in the Bernician line from Ecgfrith. Nennius also brings the lines from Woden down to these two kings.[101] Finally, the kings of Lindsey, whom no early writer mentions and whose existence is known only from the ninth century manuscript edited by Sweet, are also shown by it to have shared this common descent of the Anglo-Saxon royal houses from Woden.[102]

Thus a notion of common divine origin apparently linked all —or almost all—of the kingly families of the Anglo-Saxons.[103]

Florentii Wigorniensis Monachi Chronicon ex Chronicis (London, 1848), I, p. 251. The ancestry of Aethelbald of Mercia is traced in the Anglo-Saxon Chronicle *sub anno* 716 (717) to Pybba, 'whose ancestry is given above'; Earle and Plummer, eds., I, p. 42.

[99] H. Sweet, ed., *Oldest English Texts*, p. 170; Wade-Evans, ed., *Nennius's History* . . ., p. 78 (*Hist. Brit.*, c. 60). Cf. R. W. Chambers, *Beowulf*, pp. 195–198 ('The Mercian Genealogy'), in which the ninth century C.C.C.C. MS. 183 is also adduced as evidence.

[100] Earle and Plummer, eds., I, pp. 16, 18. The other Northumbrian genealogies *sub annis* 670, 685, 731, 738 do not give the complete descent. Baeldaeg has been identified by Aethelweard, Snorri, and some modern scholars with the god Balder; Turville-Petre, *Myth and Religion*, pp. 70, 121–122.

[101] H. Sweet, ed., *Oldest English Texts*, pp. 169–170; Wade-Evans, ed., *Nennius's History* . . ., pp. 76–77, 78–79.

[102] H. Sweet, ed., *Oldest English Texts*, pp. 170–171. Frank Stenton, 'Lindsey and its Kings', *Essays in History presented to Reginald Lane Poole* (H. W. C. Davis, ed.; Oxford, 1927), pp. 136–137.

[103] G. Copley, *Conquest of Wessex*, p. 130, parallels this with the 'community of hero-worship'—with Old English poetry, for example, celebrating the deeds of Danes, Swedes, Burgundians, Franks, and Frisians—which also may reflect 'a sense of common origin'.

Of the two remaining kingdoms, no royal genealogy survives for Sussex, but the argument from silence does not invalidate the great weight of evidence from the neighbouring realms. The only royal genealogy extant not to ascend to Woden is the ninth century line *de regibus orientalium seaxonum*,[104] which ends with Seaxnet or Seaxneat. This god is undoubtedly to be identified with the Continental Saxon deity, Saxnot, who appears with *Uuoden* and *Thunaer* in the seventh or eighth century Old Saxon renunciation formula.[105] 'The need of the Saxons', Seaxnet's name is in its second element an attribute of the Norse Oðin, but, although in his identification with Tyr and Balder, perhaps a son of Woden, this relationship is late in developing.[106]

It is, then, from Woden that most of the kings of the English traced their divine descent, a god-sprung lineage on which may well have rested originally their peculiar mediatorship with the divine. Woden—the *Wuotan* of Old High German and the *Othinn* (Othin, Odin) of Old Norse—in Scandinavia was the Lord of Valhöll and the special deity of war, poetry, and magic. The Woden cult may have had its origin in the Rhineland,[107] but the problem is by its nature insoluble. Many nineteenth-century scholars—Müllenhoff, Weinhold, and Mogk among them— maintained that his worship began originally among the Istvaeones and was spread by the Rhine-Franconians, but numerous traditions have brought the Wanderer to the North from the southeast of Europe, migrating undoubtedly with the tribes that worshipped him.[108] What concerns us here is only the nature of his divine role as it affects tribal kingship.

Although it is dangerous, of course, to equate the theological

---

[104] H. Sweet, ed., *Oldest English Texts*, p. 179.

[105] E. Philippson, *Germ. Heid.*, p. 117.

[106] Philippson, *Germ. Heid.*, pp. 117–118. His name does not survive in any place-name of the East Saxons, but for possible place-name incorporations of *Neat*, cf. p. 118. Woden's name survives in Essex in two lost field names, *Wodnesfeld* in Widdington and *Wedynsfeld* in Theydon; P. H. Reaney, *The Origin of English Place-Names* (London, 1960), p. 118.

[107] E. Philippson, *Die Genealogie*, pp. 14, 16.

[108] Karl Helm, *Wodan—Ausbreitung und Wanderung Seines Kultes* (Giessener Beiträge zur Deutschen Philologie, Vol. LXXXV; Giessen, 1946), *passim*.

attributes of the Anglo-Saxon Woden with those of his Scandinavian cognate, a comparison of select features may itself shed light, if similarities are found, on the closeness of English and Scandinavian paganism. The relationship of Woden-Othin to kingship is noteworthy in both cases. In the North, his importance is not only as the father-god, and of especial importance the *Stammvater*,[109] but as virtually a 'class' god of monarchs. The term 'father' is combined with his name in the *Völuspa* and *Grimnismal*; he appears as the *Alföðr* ('All father') in the latter and in *Skaldskaparmal*, and *Lokasenna* 45 terms all the gods 'sons of Othin'. 'Othin is called All-father, because he is the father of all the gods,' *Gylfaginning* 20 confirms, even though Norse theology does not interpret this in a physical sense. But it is not only of the gods that he is father; mankind, too, can claim him. 'He can be called All-father, because he is the father of all gods and men,' *Gylfaginning* 9 asserts.[110]

However, his primary role for the tribe is not as the father of mankind but as the god of kings and warriors. He is the deity above all associated with the chiefs of the tribe. 'Woden owns all the gentlefolk (*iarla*) that fall in fight, but Thor the thrall-kind,' says the *Harbarðsljoð*.[111] His peculiar association with the Anglo-Saxon royal houses would confirm this. The origin of Woden as god of kings and warriors is lost in the obscurities of pre-history, but de Vries' pregnant suggestion that the original polarity of the *rex*—the priestly, Tiwaz-centred aspect of kingship—and the *dux*

---

[109] For a good discussion of this deity, cf. Karl Helm, *Altgermanische Religionsgeschichte* (Heidelberg, 1953), II:1, pp. 251–268. On Woden as god of poetry, magic, and runes, cf. Turville-Petre, *Myth and Religion*, pp. 35–50; E. Philippson, *Germ. Heid.*, pp. 152–153. In the *Rigsthula*, e.g., he is featured not only as magician but as *Stammvater* and king (= Rigr = Rig = Othin). Cf. B. Pering, *Heimdall* (Lund, 1941), pp. 206–208. Axel Olrik's theory that the *Rigsthula* rests on Iro-Celtic sources (*ibid.*, pp. 40–42) has been attacked by A. Bugge (*ibid.*, p. 39, n. 1). On Woden or Othin as *Ahnherr*, cf. Turville-Petre, pp. 55–56; Philippson, *Germ. Heid.*, p. 152.

[110] On the above and other references in northern literature to Othin as father, cf. *C.P.B.*, II, pp. 461, 511. On the later Germanic *Herr der Geschlechte* as a mixture of Othin and the Christian God, cf. Axel Olrik, *Nordisches Geistesleben in Heidnischer und Frühchristlicher Zeit* (Heidelberg, 1908), p. 96.

[111] *C.P.B.*, I, p. 120.

—the martial, Othin-centred leadership—was conflated into the Othin-worshipping, sacral warrior-kings of the migration would help to account for that god's association with the two.[112] His command of the dark mysteries of runes and magic would also unite him to the sacrificial king. The god-sprung warrior-king who leads his hosts into battle makes a martial sacrifice to the deity, for the dead of the slaughter are dedicated to Woden.[113] His very name—*Woden id est furor*—shows his role as god of battles.[114] Half the slain belong to him, the *Grimnismal* informs us, and half to Freyja.[115]

Axel Olrik is thus correct when he asserts *Odin ist ein Gott für Häuptlinge, für die geistig Entwickelten*, but he goes too far when he concludes, *aber er vermag nicht, das Zutrauen der Menge zu gewinnen*.[116] As the sacral king led his people in sacrifices for the year, the peculiar royal association with Woden made the people dependent on that deity for their round of life. It is undoubtedly this which is responsible for the relationship which folklore has made between Woden and the harvest, as even in Christian times superstition made Wednesday, the day of Woden, still a lucky day for sowing and planting the crops, although it was otherwise generally an unlucky day.[117] However, beyond that, his widespread cult and his numerous holy places attest to a worship which must have had its popular aspects.

It is to England that we shall confine our attention, to search for evidence of the cult of this god from whom the Anglo-Saxon kings were descended. He rarely appears in Old English literature,

[112] De Vries, 'Königtum', pp. 296–297.

[113] H. M. Chadwick, *The Cult of Othin*, pp. 7–14.

[114] Adam of Bremen, IV, c. 26; B. Schmeidler, ed., p. 258. Cf. O. E. *wodendream* = madness, fury; Wilfrid Bonser, *The Medical Background of Anglo-Saxon England* (London, 1963), pp. 257–258.

[115] *Grimnismal*, ll. 51–52; C.P.B., I, p. 71. Cf. H. R. Ellis, *The Road to Hel* (Cambridge, 1943), pp. 66, 75.

[116] A. Olrik, *Nordisches Geistesleben*, p. 41.

[117] P. D. Chantepie de la Saussaye, *The Religion of the Teutons* (B. J. Bos, transl.; Boston, 1902), pp. 226–227. Its unlucky character probably derived from Christianity and may have been bestowed by the identification of Woden with the Devil.

which was written entirely in the Christian epoch,[118] but his cult can be well established in that country. Not only the royal genealogies attest to knowledge of him but evidences of his cult-locations are widespread in place-names in southern and central England.[119] The ancient earthwork of Wansdyke (*Wodnes dic* or 'Woden's dyke' in a charter of A.D. 903),[120] above the Vale of Pewsey in Wiltshire and Somerset, was probably a cult-centre of the god, running as it does between *Wodnes beorg* (in a charter of A.D. 825[121] and the Anglo-Saxon Chronicle *sub annis* 592 and 792

[118] See, however, J. S. Ryan, 'Othin in England: Evidence from the Poetry for a Cult of Woden in Anglo-Saxon England', *Folklore*, LXXXIV (1963), pp. 460–480.

[119] The following place-name evidence is based on Bruce Dickins, 'English Names and Old English Heathenism', *Essays and Studies*, XIX (1933), pp. 154–155; F. Stenton, *Anglo-Saxon England*, pp. 99–100; E. Philippson, *Germ. Heid.*, pp. 156–161. For Woden-cult in England, cf. E. O. G. Turville-Petre, *Myth and Religion*, pp. 70–72.

[120] Walter de G. Birch, *Cartularium Saxonicum* (London, 1887), II, no. 600. This work, in three volumes (1885–1893), is cited hereafter as Birch, with the number of the charter. Woden's Dyke was also known after the introduction of Christianity as the 'Devil's Ditch', and local tradition maintained that it was built by the Devil on a Wednesday—which is, of course, Woden's day; L. V. Grinsell, *The Ancient Burial Mounds of England* (2nd ed., London, 1953), pp. 72, 79. Sir Cyril and Lady Fox, 'Wansdyke Reconsidered', *Archaeological Journal*, CXV (1958), pp. 1–48, suggest that the east part of Wansdyke was probably built by Ceawlin of Wessex c. 584–592 and the west part at a later time, perhaps at the time of the peace between Penda of Mercia and Cynegils of Wessex in 628. A criticism of this by J. N. L. Myres, 'Wansdyke and the Origin of Wessex', *Essays in British History presented to Sir Keith Feiling* (H. R. Trevor-Roper, ed.; London, 1964), pp. 1–27, suggests alternatives, but both Fox and Myres agree that the earthwork is named for Woden, though for different reasons. Fox (pp. 40–41) holds that it may have been dedicated to the god, along with the surrounding region marked by place-names incorporating Woden's name, when Wansdyke was erected by the Saxons in a time of crisis; Myres, on the other hand, suggests that 'the name *Wodnesdic* is most naturally to be explained as a name given by pagan Anglo-Saxons to an impressive monument whose origin and purpose they did not know and could not guess, and which was therefore attributed by them to supernatural agency' (p. 17). For a map of the region showing Wansdyke, *Wodnes beorg*, and *Wodnes dene*, as well as *Wodnes geat* in his *dene*, see Fox, fig. 28, and Myres, p. 10.

[121] Birch 390.

[MS. E]), 'Woden's barrow', and *Wodnes dene*, 'Woden's valley'. In central Mercia the present place-names of Wednesbury (*Wadnesberie* of Domesday Book, 'Woden's fortress') and Wednesfield (*Wodensfeld* of Domesday Book, 'Woden's open country') attest to his worship, as do the village of Wensley (*Wodnesleie*, 'Woden's grove') in Derbyshire, the half-hundred of the same name or Wenslow (*Weneslai* in Domesday, but *Wodneslawe* in A.D. 1169) in Bedfordshire, and the hundred of *Wodenslawe* ('Woden's mound'), also in Bedfordshire, all in Anglian lands. Another *Wodnesfeld*, perhaps to be identified with Wanswell in Gloucestershire, is mentioned by Florence of Worcester *sub anno* 911. In the kingdom of the Jutes are found the present Kentish villages of Woodnesborough (*Wanesberga* in Domesday, but *Wodnesbeorge* in the early twelfth century Domesday of Christ Church) and Wormshill. These and others testify to the god's presence in the realms of the Anglo-Saxons. Further, under his alias of Grim he appears in *Grimes dic*, 'Grim's dyke', and in other locations in England.[122] Thus, as Sir Frank Stenton testifies, 'as memorials of popular heathenism these names give a useful indication of the general English attitude towards the god who was claimed as an ancestor by most English kings. They bring him out of the aristocratic mythology in which dynastic traditions wrapped him, down to his holy places in the country-side. They show that he was worshipped by common men belonging to each of the three principal races of which the English nation was composed.'[123] And the translation of more than one of them into Christian terms, as we shall see, testifies to the religious hold of these sacred sites of the old god.

It is not in genealogical and place-name sources alone, however,

---

[122] Grimr, 'the masked one', is also a Norse alias of Othin. Cf. the score of place-names incorporating this name in E. Philippson, *Germ. Heid.*, pp. 66–67. Cf. A. H. Smith, *English Place-Name Elements* (English Place-Names Society, Vol. XXV; Cambridge, 1956), p. 210. In A.D. 1272 Woden's Dyke was called *Grimesdich*; P. H. Reaney, *Origin of English Place-Names*, p. 119. The place-name evidence consequently makes the English identification of Woden by his name Grim highly probable, even though other proof is lacking.

[123] Stenton, *Anglo-Saxon England*, p. 100.

that witness is given to Anglo-Saxon knowledge of Woden. The middle day of the week, the Old English *Wodnes daeg*, is still named for him, of course.[124] He is also the only pagan Germanic god named in the Anglo-Saxon charms.[125] He is perhaps designated by the rune *Os* in the *Runic Poem*.[126] Furthermore, the human mask portrayed on Ango-Saxon coins, the *sceattas*, may possibly have been that of Woden, the masked god.[127] And finally, there is evidence that human sacrifice to Woden, known on the Continent,[128] was practised in England. One form of sacrifice to Othin in the North was, the evidence suggests, for the human offering himself to leap over a cliff to his death. So a family in the *Gautreks Saga* enter Valhöll,[129] and the missionary Hjalti testifies to this as a known mode of sacrifice.[130] The survival of this practice in England may perhaps be witnessed by Bede's reference to the voluntary leaping over precipices by groups of men, forty or fifty together, in time of famine among the South Saxons.[131] This

---

[124] Richard Jente, *Die Mythologische Ausdrücke im Altenglischen Wortschatz* (*Anglistische Forschungen*, Vol. LVI; Heidelberg, 1921), pp. 78–79.

[125] G. Storms, *Anglo-Saxon Magic*, p. 188. Cf. W. Chaney, 'Paganism to Christianity in Anglo-Saxon England', *Harvard Theological Review*, LIII (1960), pp. 202–203. His name survived into modern times in a charm against sickness recorded in Lincolnshire in the late nineteenth century: 'Father, Son, and Holy Ghost, / Nail the devil to this post— / With this mell I thrice do knock / One for God, and one for Wod, and one for Lok.' The latter reference is to the northern Loki. Philippson, *Germ. Heid.*, p. 153. This may, however, stem from a Viking source, in view of the Danish settlement in Lincolnshire.

[126] Turville-Petre, *Myth and Religion*, p. 71.

[127] E. Salin, *La Civilisation Merovingienne* (Paris, 1949), I, p. 288. Cf. the 'face-plate' of Irish kings, 'a gold plate the size of the face ... anciently given as compensation for insult to a king'; Whitley Stokes, ed., *The Martyrology of Oengus the Culdee* (Henry Branshaw Society, Vol. XXIX; London, 1905), p. lii; also Vernam Hull, 'Cert Ríg Caisil: The Right of the King of Cashel', *Medieval Studies*, XI (1949), p. 238.

[128] H. M. Chadwick, *The Cult of Othin*, pp. 3–14. See below, pp. 117–118.

[129] 'There is a cliff near our house called Gilling's cliff, and a steep thereon called the Family-steep; over it we throw ourselves if any misfortune falls upon us, and so we go to Woden'; *C.P.B.*, II, p. 354.

[130] H. R. Ellis, *Road to Hel*, p. 73. Cf. *C.P.B.*, I, pp. 410–411.

[131] Bede, *Hist. Eccl.*, IV, 13; King, ed., II, p. 74. On the day the South Saxons were baptized, however, rain fell and the crops were in time replenished.

lends added credence to a late source, Matthew Paris, who notes under the year 665 that 'pestilence prevailed so much in England that men, coming in crowds to the cliffs of the sea, hurled themselves into it, preferring to die by a swift death than to perish consumed by lengthy torment', although a forgotten custom may linger behind his explanation.[132]

Another form of sacrifice to Woden for which evidence may be found in England is the dedication to him of the war-dead. That the pagan sacrifice to him for the acquisition of victory and courage was known among the English is witnessed by the tenth century chronicler, Aethelweard, himself a Woden-sprung scion of the House of Wessex: *Hi* (Hengest and Horsa) *nepotes fuerunt Uuoddan regis barbarorum, quem post infanda dignitate ut deum honorantes, sacrificium obtulerunt pagani, victoriae causa sive virtutis.*[133] Direct evidence of such sacrifices, except in one case, does not exist. There are indirect indications, however, of the dedication of the dead of battle to Woden for victory. On the Continent, for example, Procopius records the human sacrifice of Goths by the Frankish King Theudebert in A.D. 539 as the 'first-fruits of the war. For these barbarians, though they have become Christians, preserve the greater part of their ancient religion'.[134] In England, the slaughter at Anderida in A.D. 491, when Aelle and his son Cissa captured this fortress-town and slew everyone within its walls— *ne wearð þaer forþen an Brit to lafe*—has overtones of a religious vow of dedication upon one of the first landings in Sussex.[135] As King Eirek the Victorious dedicated the army of his enemy Styrbiörn to Othin prior to battle c. A.D. 960–970,[136] so Aelle may have offered the god this human sacrifice before his onslaught against the British.

[132] Matthew Paris, *Chronica Majora* (H. R. Luard, ed., Rolls Series, Vol. LVII:1; London, 1872), p. 294.

[133] Aethelweard, *Chronicon*, I (no chapter), in J. Stevenson, ed., *The Church Historians of England* (London, 1854), II:2, p. 411; cf. Bk. II, c. 2, p. 416.

[134] Procopius, *The Gothic War*, II (VI of the *History*), c. 25; H. B. Dewing, ed., IV, p. 86 (transl., p. 87).

[135] Anglo-Saxon Chronicle, *sub anno* 491; Earle and Plummer, eds., I, pp. 14–15. This conclusion, which I had arrived at independently, is also suggested by Chadwick, *Cult of Othin*, p. 31, and E. Philippson, *Germ. Heid.*, p. 151.

[136] *Styrbiarnar þattr*, c. 2; Chadwick, *Cult of Othin*, p. 7.

D

Another dim reflection of dedication for destruction, but in this case without sacrifice, is perhaps to be seen in Bede's famous story of Coifi, the pagan priest of the Northumbrians, who deserted his old gods in favour of Christ.[137] Among the pagan Germanic followers of Woden a spear was cast over the hostile host to dedicate it to the god.[138] So when Coifi, of a priesthood which was traditionally without arms, took up a spear, the weapon of Woden, and hurled it into the temple he had served, it was perhaps not only an act of defiling the place of peace but also a ceremonial act devoting it to destruction. The Christian Bede tells us nothing of this pagan context of Coifi's deed, but the yet pagan tribe which witnessed it no doubt saw the casting of the spear and its significance in terms of the old religion.

Further, when King Aelle of Northumbria threw the famous Ragnar Lothbrok into a pit of adders, we may have another offering to the same deity.[139] H. R. Ellis is correct when she says that 'this sounds like some kind of sacrificial death, and if so, this would explain Ragnarr's firm conviction that he would be received by Othin, and would be in accordance with other passages dealing with human sacrifice'.[140] Although both the sources and the victim are Scandinavian, if any historical truth is at the centre of this well-known episode, it is still the action of a Christian Anglo-Saxon ruler that must be explained.

Finally, and with strong enough support to warrant it being styled direct evidence, is the death of King Oswald of Northumbria. As Vikar, Aun, and Olaf Tretelgia were northern royal sacrifices to Othin, so the dismemberment and the hanging of the English king by the pagan Penda of Mercia after his victory at *Maserfelth* was a sacrifice to Woden in the most common traditional mode of offering to that god. But this act of the Mercian

137 Bede, *Hist. Eccl.*, II, 13; King, ed., I, pp. 284–286.

138 *Flatey-bok*, II, 72, where Eirek, casting a spear against the hostile army, devotes it to Woden ('Woden owneth you all'); *C.P.B.*, I, p. 425, with other references. Turville-Petre, *Myth and Religion*, p. 47.

139 *Krakumal*, v. 27 (ll. 131–135); *Wolsunga* vellum no. 1824, v. 25 (ll. 97–100); both in *C.P.B.*, II, pp. 344–345, 350–351.

140 H. R. Ellis, *Road to Hel*, p. 74.

royal worshipper of his ancestral god is closely related to ritual king-slaying and must be left for later analysis.[141]

An actual epiphany of the god in England remains to be mentioned, even though it was in the Danelaw and to a Christian Dane that he manifested himself. Siward the Stout, Jarl of Northumbria, a renowned supporter of Cnut the Great, met on the rocky coast of his earldom an old man who prophesied Siward's future, gave him advice, and bestowed upon him a banner, called *Ravenlandeye*, which he took from his clothing. This banner was given by the Jarl to the city of York, which placed it in St. Mary's Church. It has been demonstrated that the old man with the magical gift of prophecy and the raven-banner of Woden was the god himself, even though the twelfth century Christian chronicler of Crowland who has given us the account did not know what underlay his tale.[142] And what more dramatic example could be hoped for of the Christianization of pagan remains than the translation of Woden's banner into a venerated possession of Old St. Mary's in York? As we shall see from many aspects, the vestiges of the old religion were taken into the Church, if not as literally as the *Ravenlandeye*. It is to the Christianization of royal divine descent that we turn now.

The pagan genealogies of the Woden-sprung kings were in time assimilated to Christianity. In the mythical lineage of King Aethelwulf of Wessex in the Anglo-Saxon Chronicle *sub anno* 855, Woden is sixteenth in descent from 'Sceaf, who is the son of Noah and was born in Noah's Ark'.[143] Appropriate as it is to have generated in the Ark one who in traditions recorded by Aethelweard and William of Malmesbury had drifted as a child in a boat to his future kingdom,[144] this 'arcane' transition makes the West

---

[141] See chapter III, pp. 116–119.

[142] O. Höfler, *Germanisches Sakralkönigtum*, pp. 237–238, n. 527. The source is the twelfth-century chronicle of Crowland by William Ramsey.

[143] Thus in MSS. B and C; the Parker Chronicle omits three generations and has Hrathra born in the Ark; cf. Sisam, 'A.S. Royal Genealogies', p. 315, on Bedwig as the ancestor in the Ark.

[144] Chadwick, *Origin*, pp. 256–267, in which the Scyld-Sceaf traditions are analysed, and pp. 272–276.

Saxon rulers collateral relatives, as Professor Magoun has pointed out, of our Lord.[145] This has its parallel in Wales in the court-pedigree of Hywel the Good, who traced his descent from 'Amalech, who was the son of Beli the Great and his mother Anna, whom they say to be the cousin of the Virgin Mary, the Mother of our Lord Jesus Christ';[146] since Anna is probably Ana or Anu, a variant of Danu, the Earth Mother, and Beli Mawr may well be the god Beli or Belenus,[147] our Lord would be the relative of the Mother of the gods, and the assimilation of a royal genealogy to the new religion would indeed be analogous to the Anglo-Saxon transition. The importance of divine descent for Anglo-Saxon kings is thus testified to not only by the persistence with which it was clung to even after their conversion but by its translation into terms of the new religion. Divine descent bound the monarch into temporal and cosmic history and served as a link between them. It was in part attributable to this descent that the Woden-sprung king stood between his tribe and the tribal god, whether pagan or Christian, as a royal priest.

---

[145] F. P. Magoun, Jr., 'King Aethelwulf's Biblical Ancestors', *Modern Language Review*, XLVI (1951), pp. 249–250. Luke iii, 36–38, is the suggested source for the Biblical names.

[146] A. W. Wade-Evans, ed., *Nennius's History* ..., p. 102; Rev. John Williams Ab Ithel, ed., *Annales Cambriae* (Rolls Series, Vol. XX; London, 1860), p. x, n. 1.

[147] Nora K. Chadwick, ed., *Studies in Early British History* (Cambridge, 1954), pp. 132, 196. On the possible identification of Beli with Bilwis, a pagan Germanic ruler of the underworld, and on Bilwis = Beli as the hypostasis of Woden, cf. A. H. Krappe, 'Bilwis', *Mitteilungen der Schlesischen Gesellschaft für Volkskunde*, XXXIV (1934), pp. 18, 26.

CHAPTER II

The royal priesthood

Although no single Anglo-Saxon work gives us full information on pre-Christian religion in England, varied sources nonetheless allow a picture, inadequate though it may be, to be pieced together. The concern here is ultimately only with the royal role in the heathen faith and then its translation into the new religion of Christianity. However, the continuity of theology is a crucial element in the transition from paganism to Christianity and shaped the continuing role of the monarch as a more than political figure.

In the first place, heathenism itself continued. Eadbald, son of the converted Aethelberht, led his people *ad priorem vomitum*,[1] and there is no evidence that paganism was outlawed in Kent until A.D. 640, when King Eorcenberht ordered the destruction of the idols. In the last surviving Kentish law code, dating from the very end of the century, it is still necessary for King Wihtred to forbid both free men and slaves from making offerings to devils.[2] In the realm of the East Saxons the people could not be recalled to faith in Christ even after King Saberht's pagan sons had been slain in battle, until Sigbert the Good's conversion almost half a century later.[3] In Wessex the earliest law code, that of King Ine, a contemporary of Wihtred of Kent, does not legislate against heathenism, but, as Professor Whitelock has recently reminded us,[4] this

[1] Bede, *Historia Ecclesiastica*, II, 5; J. E. King, ed., *Baedae Historia Ecclesiastica Gentis Anglorum* (Loeb Classical Library; London, 1930), I, 228.

[2] Wihtred, cc. 12–13; F. L. Attenborough, ed., *The Laws of the Earliest English Kings* (Cambridge, 1922), p. 26. For dating of code, cf. p. 3.

[3] *Hist. Eccl.*, II, 5, and III, 22.

[4] D. Whitelock, ed., *English Historical Documents c. 500–1042* (London, 1955), p. 331. In Alfred's use of Mosaic material in the introduction to his own code, he 'translated from the Bible that he who sacrificed to idols should die. He added to the prohibition to swear by heathen gods that nobody invoke them.

proves nothing about the latter's survival, since we have these laws only in Alfred's edition of them. The numerous references to heathen practices in Anglo-Saxon laws after the Viking invasions—under Alfred, Edward the Elder, Athelstan, Edmund, Aethelred the Redeless, and Cnut—stem largely from their revival in an age when, as Pope Formosus wrote to the bishops of the English in the 890s, 'the nefarious rites of the pagans have sprouted again in your parts'.[5]

One must hesitate, however, to attribute the resurgence of heathenism to the presence of large numbers of pagan Scandinavians alone. There is no certain evidence that even the largest Viking army in England in the ninth century contained more than two or three hundred men.[6] The revival is no doubt also due to the rich soil present among the Anglo-Saxons for the germination of pagan practices among the native stock. It is to be noted that in the abundance of Anglo-Saxon laws and canons directed against such customs after these invasions, what is to be found is legislation not so much against a specific worship of Woden, Thunor, and the other deities of the old religion as against the sort of superstitious practices which could accompany a formal acceptance and worship of Christ—incantations and auguries, the veneration

---

In the Decalogue, in accordance with the Roman Catholic practice, he left out the second commandment against the worship of images, only a century after the English and Frankish Churches had protested against the Greek Iconodules. But while the Church, in order to complete the number ten of the Decalogue, split the tenth commandment into two, Alfred appended the prohibition of metal idols from a later verse in Exodus, an insertion directed against the heathenism introduced by the Danish invaders.' F. Liebermann, 'King Alfred and the Mosaic Law', *Transactions of the Jewish Historical Society of England*, VI (1908–1910), pp. 25–26.

[5] N. E. S. A. Hamilton, ed., *Willelmi Malmesburiensis Monachi De Gestis Pontificum Anglorum* (Rolls Series, Ill.; London, 1870), p. 59 (Bk. I, c. 38).

[6] H. Sawyer, 'The Density of the Danish Settlement in England', *University of Birmingham Historical Journal*, VI (1957), p. 16. Use of Scandinavian methods and nomenclature of administration by the land-ruling aristocracy, he suggests, has led to an overestimation of Scandinavian influence in other areas, based on very little evidence. It is this very paucity of evidence, however, that makes the size of either Danish armies or Danish settlers in this period anything but conjectural.

of stones, trees, and wells, magic potions, ancient customs concerning the sun and moon, and witchcraft. Stimulated by the arrival of believing pagans from Scandinavia, there was undoubtedly a renewed outburst of such practices, but that they had ever died out among the English or that they reflect solely the customs of the newcomers from the North must be denied. The early Penitential of Theodore and the Penitential ascribed to Bede give evidence of the strength of a continuing paganism prior to the invasions, as does the legatine report to Pope Hadrian in A.D. 789.[7] Thus, along with the active paganism of the Viking settlers,[8] must be seen an encouraged revival of superstitions which had never died out. However much the merging of the two strands complicates the problem of survival,[9] the latter is well attested,

[7] For the latter, cf. Canon 19 of the legatine synods; A. W. Haddan and W. Stubbs, eds., *Councils and Ecclesiastical Documents Relating to Great Britain and Ireland* (Oxford, 1871) III, pp. 458–459. References to heathen practices are referred to especially in the Penitential of Theodore (A.D. 668–690, with later elements), the Penitential of Egbert, the so-called Confessional of Egbert, the so-called Canons of Edgar, the homilies of Wulfstan (especially No. 12, *De Falsis Deis*) and Aelfric (especially No. 17, 'On Auguries'), and Anglo-Saxon laws. References are collected in F. Grendon, 'The Anglo-Saxon Charms', *Journal of American Folklore*, XXII (1909), pp. 140–142. Cf. A. J. Robertson, *The Laws of the Kings of England from Edmund to Henry I* (Cambridge, 1925), p. 352; J. T. McNeill and H. M. Gamer, eds., *Medieval Handbooks of Penance* (Records of Civilization, XXIX; New York; 1938), pp. 198 (from Penitential of Theodore; cf. pp. 179–182 for date), 216 (from so-called Canons of Theodore), 228–229 (from so-called Penitential of Bede; cf. pp. 217–221 for discussion), 246 (from so-called Confessional of Egbert); Dorothy Bethurum, ed., *The Homilies of Wulfstan* (Oxford, 1957), pp. 39, 296, 309, 319–320, 331, 333–339; W. W. Skeat, ed., *Aelfric's Lives of the Saints* (Early English Text Society, LXXXII; London, 1885), pp. 368–376. Cf. W. Bonser, 'Survivals of Paganism in Anglo-Saxon England', *Transactions of the Birmingham Archaeological Society*, LVI (1932), pp. 37–70. On the so-called Canons of Theodore, cf. Wilhelm Levison, *Aus Rheinischer und Fränkischer Frühzeit* (Düsseldorf, 1948), pp. 295–303.

[8] Thus, Olaf Ball, a thegn of King Ragnald who held the land from Eden to the river Wear, swore 'by my mighty gods, Thor and Othin'. *History of St. Cuthbert*, c. 23; Whitelock, ed., *Engl. Hist. Doc.*, p. 262.

[9] E.g., in Wulfstan's *Sermo ad Anglos*, probably preached in A.D. 1014, in discussing the presence of 'wizards and sorceresses' in England, he uses the word 'valkyries' (*waelcyrge*) for the latter but apparently not in the customary

especially in the Anglo-Saxon charms. Whether incorporating the doctrine of elf-shot as a cause of disease or reflecting Woden as the hanging god, these manifestations of popular belief bear witness to the continuation of heathenism in Anglo-Saxon England.[10]

In the transition from paganism to Christianity, the new theology was translated into terms of northern life, and crucial to this was the royal nature of God. The concept of God or Christ as King of Heaven is, of course, common to many theological metaphors besides those of Germanic peoples. It was, however, peculiarly congenial to Anglo-Saxon, as to Scandinavian, thought. It is not simply that the imagery is frequently startling, with 'the Chief of princes, the Ruler of all peoples' giving *mund* to his *fyrd* from his high-seat in the wine-hall of Heaven.[11] The fundamental basis of Anglo-Saxon kennings for God is the concept of God as heavenly monarch.[12] The most frequent kenning for God is

---

Scandinavian sense of the term; Whitelock, *Engl. Hist. Doc.*, p. 859 and n. 1. Cf. Nora K. Chadwick, 'The Monsters and Beowulf', *The Anglo-Saxons: Studies in Some Aspects of their History and Culture presented to Bruce Dickins* (Peter Clemoes, ed.; London, 1959), pp. 175–177, on *waelcyrge* as pre-romantic, vengeful underworld spirits, with their presence traced in Anglo-Saxon England.

[10] On heathenism in the charms, cf. G. Storms, *Anglo-Saxon Magic* (The Hague, 1948), pp. 6–11; F. Grendon, 'Anglo-Saxon Charms', pp. 112, 114–115, 148. On elf-shot, cf. W. Bonser, *The Medical Background of Anglo-Saxon England* (London, 1963), pp. 158–162. On Woden and the Hanging God, see E. O. G. Turville-Petre, *Myth and Religion of the North* (New York, 1964), pp. 42–50.

[11] See, e.g., *Christ*, l. 514; *Christ and Satan*, ll. 93, 219, 309; *The Lord's Prayer II*, ll. 47–48. Cf. Jean I. Young, 'Glaed waes ic gliwum—Ungloomy Aspects of Anglo-Saxon Poetry', *The Early Cultures of North-West Europe. H. M. Chadwick Memorial Studies* (Sir Cyril Fox and Bruce Dickins, eds.; Cambridge, 1950), p. 276.

[12] The most thorough study of Anglo-Saxon kennings for the Deity is Hertha Marquardt, *Die Altenglischen Kenningar* (*Schriften der Königsberger Gelehrten Gesellschaft, Geisteswissenschaftliche Klasse*, 14 Jahr, Heft 3; Halle-Salle, 1938), pp. 267–291. Cf. also H. van der Merwe Scholtz, *The Kenning in Anglo-Saxon and Old Norse Poetry* (Utrecht and Nijmegen, 1927), pp. 92–98; on kennings for God as ruler, cf. Douglas C. Collins, 'Kenning in Anglo-Saxon Poetry', *Essays and Studies*, XII, n.s. (1959), pp. 10–16. K. Gutermann, *Herrschaftliche und Genossenschaftliche Termini (für Gott, Christus, den Teufel, und Ihre*

cyning,[13] and as the king is *aldor, brego, frea, fruma, hlaford, ord,* and *þeoden,* so is the Deity.[14] Besides these general terms of lordship, other principal categories of kennings for God also parallel those for the king. Thus one group concerns the office of rulership; like the monarch, the Deity is 'possessor' (e.g., *lifes agend, sigores agend*), 'wielder' and 'governor' (*wealdend*), and 'counsellor' (*theoda raeswa, raedend*).[15] Also God is the protector of his folk as *helm, hleo, hyrde,* and *weard.*[16] In a third major division of kennings, the kinglike Deity is gift-giver, the dispenser of divine rewards to his band of followers.[17]

The structure of all of these kennings, however, suggests, as Hertha Marquardt concludes in her study of them, not simply a translated application of royal terms to God but a 'divinization' of them in which the basic element of the kenning is that for a

---

Umgebung) in der Geistlichen Epik der Westgermanen (Diss. Kiel, 1910) was unavailable to me.

[13] Marquardt, *Die Altenglischen Kenningar,* pp. 270–271, lists approximately 180 references in Anglo-Saxon literature to God as *cyning.* The concept of 'king of Heaven', rarely to be found in Old Saxon and Old High German poetry, is common in Anglo-Saxon, in contrast to the idea of a heavenly lord of the *comitatus,* which is common to Germanic literature; *ibid.,* p. 269.

[14] Marquardt, *Die Altenglischen Kenningar,* pp. 271 (for God as *aldor*), 271–272 (*brego*), 272–273 (*frea,* approximately forty references), 273 (*fruma, hlaford, ord,* and *þeoden*). Approximately ninety references are found to Him as *dryhten* (p. 272), which is used for the earthly lord only in poetry and (more rarely) in law; *ibid.,* p. 250. For the application of the above terms to the king, *ibid.,* pp. 248–250; Scholtz, *Kenning,* pp. 89–92. For God as lord of a *comitatus*-like following of men and angels, cf. Marquardt, pp. 286–288.

[15] Marquardt, *Die Altenglischen Kenningar,* pp. 275–277; for similar kennings for king, pp. 251–252.

[16] Marquardt, *Die Altenglischen Kenningar,* pp. 277–279; for king, pp. 252–255. That the term *helm,* as discussed below in the consideration of it as a royal insigne, may have cult significance is supported by Marquardt's suggestion that the simple meaning of 'protector' is scarcely ample for such a kenning as *helm heofena* (*Beowulf,* l. 182); *ibid.,* p. 254.

[17] Marquardt, *Die Altenglischen Kenningar,* pp. 279–280; for king, pp. 255–256. There are, of course, groups of kennings for God as creator, judge, fate-giver, helper, saviour, joy, etc. (*ibid.,* pp. 280–284), but the concern here is with the dominant image of God as king. Kennings for God as father are, as in Old Norse, fairly rare; *ibid.,* pp. 267, 280.

chieftain of this world—*cyning, frea, helm, gifa*, etc.—but the combined variant is not the same but rather reflects the greater scope of divine power.[18] Thus, whereas the earthly monarch is, for example, *cyning, folcfrea, helm Scyldinga*, and *beaggifa*, God is *heofoncyning, engla frea* or *lifes frea, dryhtfolca helm*, and *sawla symbelgifa*.[19] This 'divinization' is quite concrete in its expression, as is true of kennings in general, so that the more abstract Latin *rex gloriae* and similar terms become materialized in terms of earthly rulership.[20]

The resulting image of God which dominates Anglo-Saxon writing is of a king but of one whose glory and authority outshine those of the earthly leader of the *folc*. Consequently an old religion which merged with king-cult would more readily blend with a new one which displayed its triumphant God as the sublime monarch, both the heavenly reflection and archtype of the worldly monarchs known to the Anglo-Saxons as the protectors of their people, the treasure-givers of the war-band, the lords and advisers of the tribe. So Christ is portrayed as 'the mighty Lord, the Prince of splendor, (who) summoned His thegns, the well-loved band, to Bethany',[21] and his apostle Andrew has thegns who, as in the Anglo-Saxon secular world, will not desert their leader lest they be despised for their action.[22] 'Defend the camp of God', Alcuin

[18] Marquardt, *Die Altenglischen Kenningar*, p. 267.

[19] Marquardt, *Die Altenglischen Kenningar*, pp. 249, 253, 256, 270, 272, 273, 277, 280.

[20] Marquardt, *Die Altenglischen Kenningar*, p. 267. However, as Marquardt states (p. 267), *im Gegensatz zu den altnordischen Kenningar, die mit Vorliebe auf den irdischkonkreten Himmel hinweisen, zeigt sich aber in den altenglischen Gotteskenningar von Anfang an ein starker Hang zur Ausmalung des Übersinnlichen. Der Himmel ist nicht die Bahn der Wolken und Gestirne, sondern die Wohnung oder 'Burg' der Engel und Seligen, wo Glanz und Herrlichkeit herrscht und ewiger* 'dream'. For the demolition of Rankin's theory of the Latin origin of Anglo-Saxon kennings for God, cf. pp. 289–291.

[21] *Christ*, ll. 456–458; G. P. Krapp and E. V. K. Dobbie, eds., *The Exeter Book* (Anglo-Saxon Poetic Records, III; London, 1936), p. 15. This extract is translated in C. W. Kennedy, *Early English Christian Poetry* (New York, 1952), p. 98.

[22] *Andreas*, ll. 401–414. G. P. Krapp, ed., *The Vercelli Book* (Anglo-Saxon Poetic Records, II; London, 1932), p. 14.

exhorts Bishop Higbald of Lindisfarne.[23] Thus if Gunnlaug Snakestongue could sing of King Aethelred II that 'all the host reverence the generous King of England like God Himself',[24] so in reverse God is seen as king; so an Anglo-Saxon abbot can write to a monarch that the latter has gained his sovereignty from the 'King of kings and Lord of lords'.[25] This image of the earthly king ruling under the heavenly one runs throughout the Old English period after the Conversion. It is found in the early privilege in which *Ic Wihtred eorplic cing, fram ðan heowenlice Cinge onbryd* grants a privilege to the ecclesiastical foundations of Kent[26] as, at the end of Anglo-Saxon rule, in the Confessor's charter to Christchurch, Canterbury, by the *cyng ond Englalandes wealdend under Christe þan heofenlican cyninge*.[27] Thus the old special relationship of king and gods in paganism continues in Christian terms. God is *aethelinga helm*,[28] and princes serve under their Lord's rule. 'Just as Augustus reigned over all the earth ere Christ came', says an Anglo-Saxon homilist, 'so now Christ has the aldordom of this and the next world'.[29]

[23] *Defendite castra Dei.* Letter of Alcuin to Bishop Higbald, A.D. 793; *Mon. Ger. Hist., Epistolae*, IV, Ep. 20, p. 57. Cf. Einar Sculason's mid-twelfth century *Drapa* on Olaf Tryggvason, in which the saint-king is described as 'now living in the Hall of Christ' and as a 'bright beam of God's hall'; Gudbrand Vigfusson and F. York Powell, eds., *Corpus Poeticum Boreale* (Oxford, 1883), II, pp. 285–286. This is referred to hereafter as *C.P.B.*

[24] *Herr sesk allr inn ǫrva Englandz sem Goð þengil:* refrain of Gunnlaug's *Praise on Aethelred* from the *Gunnlaugs-saga,* c. 9; *ibid.*, II, p. 111. The text is edited (with the verse in c. 7) in P. G. Foote, ed., *Gunnlaugs Saga Ormstungu* (Icelandic Texts, I; London, 1957), p. 15. Cf. the *Praise on Cnut* from the *Skioldunga* of Hallvard: 'Cnut defends his land as the Lord of all does the glorious hall of the mountains (Heaven)'; *C.P.B.*, II, p. 161.

[25] Abbot Ceolfrid to Naitan, King of the Picts, in Bede, *Hist. Eccl.*, V, 21; King, ed., II, p. 358.

[26] B. M. Cotton MS. Domitian A. viii; Haddan and Stubbs, eds., *Councils and Eccl. Doc.*, III, p. 244.

[27] A. J. Robertson, ed., *Anglo-Saxon Charters* (Cambridge, 1956), pp. 180, 427n.

[28] Cf., e.g., *Andreas*, l. 277; G. Krapp, ed., *Vercelli Book*, p. 10.

[29] Vercelli Homily V; John R. Sala, *Preaching in the Anglo-Saxon Church* (Chicago, 1934), p. 129. For an Irish parallel, cf. Whitley Stokes, ed., *The Martyrology of Oengus the Culdee* (Henry Bradshaw Society Publications,

The royal nature of God is, then, clear. Again it must be stressed that the concept of God as king is common in Christian theology and, needless to say, not a monopoly of the Anglo-Saxons. It was, however, congenial to their world-view and readily adopted as their dominant image of the Deity. The less the break that was necessary with both the political and theological background of the folk, the less hostile would be the latter toward the reception of Christianity.

Specific northern deities and the possible continuation of their cult are also related to sacral kingship. Thus, the name of the god Frea or Frey, whose cult apparently continued in England, was in origin probably a title, meaning 'lord', and used as an abbreviation of Yngvi-Frey.[30] His cult was peculiarly associated with the Swedish kings of Uppsala, but connotations of this deity may well have been present in the use of *frea* as a common kenning for an earthly lord and for the Anglo-Saxon king. The term is used seventeen times in *Beowulf* for 'lord'.[31] The *frea Myrginga* appears in *Widsith* (l. 96), *folcfrea* and *frea leoda* in *Genesis* (ll. 1852, 2098), and in the same poem (l. 1475) Noah is called *flotmonna frea*.[32] However, 'Frey', which has become identified with 'lord', is also used for '*the* Lord'. *Geseah ic tha frean mancynnes* (I saw there the 'Frey' of mankind), says the *Dream of the Rood*, and this title, so clearly associated with northern heathenism, is used elsewhere as well for the Christian Lord.[33] God is *heofona frea, rices frea, engla frea, lifes frea*, in image after image which to the northern ear

---

XXIX; London, 1905), p. 23 (from the Prologue): *in ri conic aïngliu, is coimmdiu cech thire* (the King that ruleth angels is lord of every land).

[30] H. M. Chadwick, *The Origin of the English Nation* (Cambridge, 1924), p. 237, and, on relation of Frey, Freyja, and Gefion, and the probable continuation of the cult in England, pp. 243–267. Nerthus = Niörðr; the latter, the father of Frey and Freyja, was worshipped by the Continental Angles. On Frey in England, cf. also R. Jente, *Die Mythologische Ausdrücke im Altenglischen Wortschatz* (*Anglistische Forschungen*, LVI; Heidelberg, 1921), pp. 89–94.

[31] Branston, *The Lost Gods of England* (London, 1957), p. 137.

[32] References in Marquardt, *Die Altenglischen Kenningar*, p. 249. Cf. p. 250 for *freawine folca* (*freowine folca*) in *Beowulf*, ll. 430, 2357, 2429.

[33] *Dream of the Rood*, l. 33; G. P. Krapp, ed., *The Vercelli Book*, p. 62. Branston, *Lost Gods of England*, p. 137.

could well have overtones of Yngvi-Frey and the heathen *frea* of peace and plenty.[34] Thus, although direct evidence for the worship of Frey in England is lacking, this use of *frea*, the boar cult associated with the deity, and Anglo-Saxon knowledge of Ing (in the Runic Poem) all support the hypothesis that he was known and firmly associated with earthly chieftains. Consequently, Christ and the Scandinavian Frey, god of plenty and of the king, may perhaps have blended in the new religion, even though the goddess Freyja and her maidens nowhere appear to have been 'converted' into the Virgin Mary and the three (or nine) Marys, as they were in the Scandinavian North.[35]

The *Dream of the Rood*, important sections of which are carved on the pre-Viking Age Ruthwell Cross (c. A.D. 700), also draws almost undoubtedly in its non-Biblical portrayal of the Crucifixion upon northern heathenism, the death of the god Balder; here 'the young hero' mounts 'the marvellous tree' and is wounded by darts: 'the warriors left me standing laced with blood', says the Rood, 'I was wounded unto death with darts'—certainly a strange exaggeration of the spear at the Crucifixion but as Balder was in the pagan myth, when the sport of throwing darts at him turned into the cosmic tragedy of the 'bleeding god'.[36] That this divine favourite of the gods themselves was hated by Loki, who merged with the Christian Devil, heightens the parallel of Balder and Christ.

[34] Marquardt, *Die Altenglischen Kenningar*, pp. 272–273, gives forty examples of the use of *frea* for the Christian God.

[35] B. Pering, *Heimdall* (Lund, 1941), p. 173. Cf. A. Ohlmarks, *Heimdalls Horn und Odins Auge* (Lund and Copenhagen, 1937), I, pp. 106 (on Freyja as the angel of the Last Trump), 218 (on the nine mothers of Heimdall as the three Marys). Cf. Christabel F. Fiske, 'Old English Modification of Teutonic Racial Conceptions', *Studies in Language and Literature in Celebration of the 70th Birthday of James Morgan Hart* (New York, 1910), p. 281, on use in Zeeland of both *Frejerock* and *Mariärock* for the constellation Orion's Belt.

[36] *Dream of the Rood*, ll. 61–62; G. P. Krapp, ed., *The Vercelli Book*, p. 63. Branston, *Lost Gods of England*, pp. 157–162. Like the blind Hödr, whom Loki directed to throw the dart of mistletoe, Longinus, who pierced the side of Christ with the lance, was blind, according to legend; cf. E. Philippson, *Die Genealogie der Götter in Germanischer Religion, Mythologie, und Theologie* (Urbana, Ill., 1953), p. 87, n. 141 (on 'ritual blindness'). On the similarities between Balder and Christ, cf. Turville-Petre, *Myth and Religion*, pp. 119–120.

The god is related to ruler-cult as well through the use of the Anglo-Saxon *baldor* (*bealdor*), whose basic meaning is 'more bold', for king or chieftain as a title of honour. Besides the *winia bealdor* of *Beowulf* (l. 2567), it is applied to rulers in *Guthlac* (l. 1358), *Genesis* (l. 2694), *Judith* (ll. 9, 49, 339), and *Elene* (l. 344).[37] Marquardt's emphasis on the application of *maegþa bealdor* to Juliana (l. 568) as referring primarily to her bold fight against the Devil is singularly appropriate in view of the presentation of the Christ-Balder of the *Dream*.[38] The word is, further, applied to Christ Himself in *Andreas*, where the Lord appears as *þeoda baldor*.[39] It has also been maintained that the famous whalebone Franks Casket (c. A.D. 700) portrays an Anglo-Saxon version of Balder's death, equating the runic 'Erdaeg' of the Casket with Balder (= morning star, O.E. *daeg* [*steorra*]) and the Baeldaeg of the Anglo-Saxon royal genealogies.[40] Thus although it has been questioned whether the Anglo-Saxons were acquainted with the god Balder and even that the deity's name has the meaning of 'lord',[41] Balder, Christ, and the king may indeed share parallelisms in Anglo-Saxon England and increase the suggestive identification of paganism with Christian theology and that ruler-cult which was a vital element in both.

A startlingly direct parallel between the Divine King and his

[37] References in Marquardt, *Die Altenglischen Kenningar*, p. 249. A Scandinavian parallel of Balder and a king is to be found in the *Flyting of Ivar and Woden*, in a prose paraphrase of the *Skioldunga Saga*: 'Which of the gods', asks King Ivar, 'may Halfdan the Sharp be likened to?' Horðr replies, 'He is Baldur among the gods, whom all the powers mourned for—very unlike thee'; *C.P.B.*, I, p. 124.

[38] Marquardt, *Die Altenglischen Kenningar*, p. 250.

[39] *Andreas*, l. 547; G. P. Krapp, ed., *The Vercelli Book*, p. 18. The four English place-names which seem to stem from the name of this deity probably derive from Scandinavian influence and from the Anglo-Saxon name Bealdhere; R. Jente, *Die Mythologische Ausdrücke*, p. 95.

[40] Karl Schneider, 'Zu den Inschriften und Bildern des Franks Casket und einer ae. Version von Balders Tod', *Festschrift für Walther Fischer* (H. Oppel, ed.; Heidelberg, 1959), pp. 8–17.

[41] Turville-Petre, *Myth and Religion*, pp. 117, 120–122; Balder may, however, be identified with Woden's son, Baldaeg, whom some Anglo-Saxon royal genealogies make an ancestor of English kings; *ibid.*, pp. 70, 121.

human counterpart is found in the ninth century Viking kingdom of York. There King Guthfrith, a former slave whose conversion and elevation to the throne are attributed to the appearance of St. Cuthbert in a vision, is identified with the Cnut—the baptismal name of Guthfrith—who is known from Northumbrian numismatics.[42] This Viking king, who died in A.D. 894, and his successor Siefred (Siegfred, Siegferth, or Sievert), who fought along with Hasting at Exeter in A.D. 892, both struck at York silver coins bearing the royal name—CNVT REX or SIEUERT REX, with variants—on the obverse and MIRABILIA FECIT on the reverse.[43] Although this phrase from the *Cantate*—*Cantate Dominum canticum novum, quia mirabilia fecit*—echoes the divine praise, the implication cannot be escaped that it is also the earthly monarch who 'has done marvellous things'. Especially is this true since there are also coins from one or both of these reigns with the obverse inscription MIRABILIA FECIT and on the reverse DOMINUS DEVS REX, with variants.[44] King Cnut and King Siefred are thus both brought into parallel with the Lord God King, both heavenly and earthly monarchs having done 'marvellous things'.

[42] Anonymous *History of St. Cuthbert*, c. 13; T. Arnold, ed., *Symeonis Monachi Opera Omnia* (Rolls Series, vol. LXXV:1; London, 1882), I, p. 203; transl. in part in Dorothy Whitelock, ed., *English Historical Documents c. 500–1042* (London, 1955), p. 261. Cnut was elected by being led at the ninth hour to the hill known as 'Oswiu's down', where a gold armlet was placed on his right arm. On 'sitting on a howe', see below, pp. 104–105. On the identification of Guthfrith-Cnut, cf. C. F. Keary, *A Catalogue of English Coins in the British Museum: Anglo-Saxon Series* (R. S. Poole, ed.; London, 1887), I, pp. lxvii, 202, and H. A. Grueber, *Handbook of the Coins of Great Britain and Ireland in the British Museum* (London, 1899), p. 17.

[43] Keary, *Catalogue*, pp. 209, 225, nos. 914–917, 1041–1042, and plate 24, no. 13, plate 27, nos. 1–2; Grueber, *Handbook*, p. 19, no. 105. On the Northumbrian Viking coinage, cf. also P. Grierson, *Sylloge of Coins in the British Isles. Fitzwilliam Museum, Cambridge. Part I. Ancient British and Anglo-Saxon Coins* (London, 1958), coins 472–519. For the division of the reverse legends into a cruciform pattern on the types discussed, a peculiarly English arrangement introduced by Alfred the Great, and for the royal name arranged at the ends of limbs of a cross, probably derived from the *denarii* of Charles the Bald, cf. Keary, *Catalogue*, p. 204.

[44] Keary, *Catalogue*, pp. 228–229, nos. 1065–1076, and plate 27, nos. 10–13; Grueber, *Handbook*, p. 19, no. 109.

The structure is completed with yet another series of silver coins from the kingdom of York in these reigns which have CNVT REX or SIEUERT REX as the obverse legend and DOMINVS DEVS REX or variants on the reverse.[45] That this parallel is not confined to the Scandinavian rulers of York is suggested by the continuance of this coin type in the chaotic period in Northumbria following Siefred's death, if a coin inscribed ALVVALDV (Alvaldus) and DNS. DS. REX is correctly attributed to Aethelwald the Aetheling, the son of King Aethelred I and cousin of Edward the Elder, who contested the throne of Wessex on Alfred the Great's death and who held the Northumbrian kingdom before his death in battle at Holme in A.D. 905.[46] Whether the concept behind the inscriptions was derived by the Northumbrian monarchs from Scandinavia or England cannot be determined, for although royal and divine parallels are found in both, there is in neither area an exact equivalent. However, no Scandinavian ruler minted his own coins in the North before Sweyn Forkbeard and Cnut the Great in Denmark, Earl Haakon Eiriksson and King Olaf the Holy in Norway, and Olaf Skautkonung in Sweden, all eleventh-century contemporaries. Pagan parallels of ruler and God are known, though, as we have seen, both in the Scandinavian home of the rulers of York and in the English realms over which they held sway.[47]

Finally, the continuity of theology is seen in another aspect

---

[45] Keary, *Catalogue*, pp. 209, 225–226, 228, nos. 918, 1043–1051, 1064, and plate 24, no. 14, plate 27, nos. 3–4; Grueber, *Handbook*, p. 19, no. 106.

[46] Keary, *Catalogue*, p. 230, no. 1078, and plate 28, no. 2; Grueber, *Handbook*, p. 19, no. 111. Garbled inscriptions, some bearing variations on the name of the mint-city of York (*Eboracum*)—e.g., EBR.AI.CE.C, ERRA.IC.EC—also are found on Northumbrian coins of this epoch with reverse inscriptions of MIRABILIA FECIT or DOMINUS DEUS REX. Cf. Keary, *Catalogue*, pp. 227–228, nos. 1052–1061, 1063, and plate 27, nos. 5–7, 9; Grueber, *Handbook*, p. 19, nos. 107–108.

[47] E.g., Gunnlaug Snakestongue's *Praise on Aethelred*: 'All the host reverence the generous King of England like God Himself'; see above, p. 49 and n. 24, for this and other parallels. Although Scandinavian in origin, Gunnlaug's *drapa's* reception at the English court proves such encomia were neither unknown nor unacceptable there.

which bears on rulership, in the Christianization of pagan *mana* into heavenly Grace. We have already noted the existence of *mana*—as *miht*, *maegen*, and *craeft*—in Germanic rulership in general and Anglo-Saxon kingship in particular.[48] Professor Magoun's investigation of *mana* in *Beowulf* has led him to the conclusion that 'though very likely not mathematically demonstrable, the probabilities are high that in certain passages *mana* lurks just behind a thin veil of so-called "Christian colouring".'[49] When 'the prince of the Geats firmly believed in his glorious *maegen*, favour of the Creator',[50] or when in his struggle with Grendel 'he remembered the might of *maegen*, generous gift which God had given him (*gimfaeste gife, ðe him God sealde*)',[51] the divinely bestowed power not only echoes the *mana* of paganism but translates it into Christian terms of God-granted Grace. A hero who is *eadig* and *sigoreadig*,[52] blessed with luck, Beowulf has been showered with free Grace by the Christian God. Magoun also sees evidence for the ancient *mana* of the king in the *Beowulf* poet's remark of King Heremod that 'God Almighty had advanced him in the joys of *maegen*, by deeds of might put him ahead of everybody'.[53] Thus the hero, in the case of Beowulf, and the king, in the case of Heremod, serve as literary parallels of the kings of more historical reality. Like both pagan and Christian rulers, they are the vessels through which the Christianized *mana* of the great man is poured by God. The folk is blessed in possessing a divinely strengthened protector who is himself 'blessed with victory-bringing luck' (*sigoreadig*), but it is this chieftain with whom God has a special relationship and on whom *mana* is bestowed. In both religions the king is the cosmic point through which is mediated divine help from above and sacrificial right relations with God

[48] See above, pp. 15–17. Francis P. Magoun, Jr., 'On Some Surv vals of Pagan Belief in Anglo-Saxon England', *Harvard Theological Review*, XL (1947), pp. 35–37.

[49] Magoun, 'On Some Survivals of Pagan Belief', p. 39. The following examples of *mana* as Christianized Grace in *Beowulf* are from pp. 39–42

[50] *Beowulf*, ll. 669–670.

[51] *Beowulf*, ll. 1270–1271.

[52] *Beowulf*, ll. 1225, 1310, 2352.

[53] *Beowulf*, ll. 1716–1718.

E

from below; he is the tribal vessel between Heaven and earth through which Grace is shed on the folk. Ancient as *mana* was to the Germanic peoples, its parallel with Christian Grace again facilitated the conversion of the Anglo-Saxons. Christian kingship like its pagan predecessor and the 'transition kingship' we have been examining saw an exaltation of the ruler in comparison with the ordinary Christian. Paganism gave way to a triumphant Christianity, but the king still remained a central and sacral figure. This is also evident in his role at the heathen festivals, at which he 'made the year', and the transition of that role into Christian terms.

Among the Anglo-Saxons as among other Germanic peoples, the religious calendar depended on the turns of the year's cycle. In Scandinavia, for example, there were three great festivals: the mid-Winter sacrifice for good crops (*til groðrar*);[54] the festival for victory (*til sigrs*), which was the great sacrifice to Woden to mark the war-year, at the beginning of Summer; and Winter's Day, the beginning of Winter and probably a New Year's festival for plenty and peace (*til ars ok friðar*).[55] It was Woden, the *Ynglingasaga* declares, that established all three festivals of sacrifice,[56] but it is with victory in battle that he is above all associated. As Woden was the deity primarily connected with the Summer offering for victory, so Frey was the northern god of plenty. Thus Adam of Bremen recounts that Swedish sacrificial offerings are made to Thor during plague and famine, to Woden in war-time, and to

[54] *Ynglingasaga*, c. 8; *C.P.B.*, I, p. 405. According to the St. Olaf's Saga (*Heimskringla*), c. 114, it was for 'peace and a good Winter'. H. M. Chadwick, *Origin*, p. 227.

[55] For these three festivals, cf. *Ynglingasaga*, c. 8: On Winter's Day there should be blood-sacrifice for a good year, and at Mid-Winter for a good crop, and the third sacrifice should be on Summer's Day for victory in battle; E. Wessen, ed., *Snorri Sturluson. Ynglingasaga* (*Nordisk Filologi*, Series A, no. 6; Copenhagen, 1952), p. 12; also Ari's *Life of Haakon the Good*, c. 16, in *C.P.B.*, I, p. 405. Chadwick, *Origin*, pp. 227–228, 248. On *blot* among the Germanic tribes, cf. Vilhelm Grönbech, *The Culture of the Teutons* (London, 1931), II, pp. 201–215; E. O. G. Turville-Petre, *Myth and Religion of the North*, pp. 251–262; Karl Helm, *Altgermanische Religionsgeschichte* (Heidelberg, 1953), II: I, pp. 208–213 (on seasons of festivals).

[56] *Ynglingasaga*, c. 8; E. Wessen, ed., pp. 11–12.

Frey for fertility at wedding nuptials.[57] The blessing of plenty-bringing fertility was traditionally associated with Frey, as we shall note later, as well as with his father Njörðr or Niord—probably the female Nerthus of Tacitus; also the one time northern literature specifically dates a sacrifice to Frey it occurred at the beginning of Winter.[58] Furthermore, in Ari's account of the feast accompanying a heathen sacrifice, the first toast was to Woden for victory and, again associating that god of kings with his royal worshippers, for 'the happy rule of the king' (rikiss konungi sinom). The second toast was then to Niord and Frey 'for good seasons and peace'.[59]

For Anglo-Saxon England, Bede gives some information, tantalizingly brief though it is, in his De Temporum Ratione. The Winter's Day sacrifice at the beginning of that season can be seen in the slaughter of cattle to the pagan gods in November. This month was the Old English blodmonath, the month of blot or sacrifice, Bede records, the mensis immolationum quod in eo pecora quae occisuri erant, diis suis voverent.[60] One of the great high festivals of heathenism was thus the November sacrifice, when the cattle which could not be maintained during the long Winter were sacrificed, probably in England as in the Scandinavian North for 'plenty and peace'—the blodmonath of England, the Thortrunk and offering til ars ok friðar of the North.

The first day of the first month of the old Germanic calendar

<hr />

[57] Adam of Bremen, Gesta Hammaburgensis Ecclesiae Pontificum, Bk. IV, c. 27.

[58] Offered at the 'Winter's nights' by Thorgrim Freysgoði ('priest of Frey'), who lived in the mid-tenth century, 'to greet the winter and to sacrifice to Frey'; it occurs in the Gisla Saga Surssonar, XV and XVIII. Chadwick, Origin, p. 228; Turville-Petre, Myth and Religion, pp. 166–167, dating the Winter nights in mid-October (p. 314) in Scandinavia, where the season's beginning may have been earlier than in England.

[59] C.P.B., I, pp. 404, 405. The sacrifice before Winter is also said to be to the Anse (Thor), p. 405.

[60] Ven. Bede, De Temporum Ratione, c. 15 (De Mensibus Anglorum); C. W. Jones, ed., Bedae Opera De Temporibus (Cambridge, Mass., 1943), p. 213. On the use of blotan, blot, and related words for 'sacrifice', cf. Richard Jente, Die Mythologische Ausdrücke im Altenglischen Wortschatz (Anglistische Forschungen, LVI; Heidelberg, 1921), pp. 38–41.

of sixty-day months and the date of one of the great pagan festivals was in early November and indeed perhaps on November 11th.[61] In Christian times this November feast perhaps accounts for the elevation in importance of the Feast of St. Martin (November 11th), for Anglo-Saxon law makes clear that a Christian translation took over for this festival many of the elements of its pagan counterpart.[62] The cult of this saint in England, accommodated to the pagan Germanic new year, was of Anglo-Saxon and not Celtic origin. The two earliest dedications to him, of the early church of St. Martin and of the porticus of the church of SS. Peter and Paul, both in Canterbury, date from the close of the sixth century, and the next earliest, that at Whithorn, probably not before the late seventh century.[63] The Anglo-Saxon cult of this Merovingian saint was probably stimulated by the accommodation to it of the early November *blodmonath* celebration. And the festive fires of paganism, overcoming the dread of Winter, still burn in England on Guy Fawkes Night, November 5th.[64]

The original Germanic division of the year into two parts— Winter and Summer, the only seasons for which there is Germanic etymological evidence and which Bede states specifically to have been the divisions of the Anglo-Saxon year[65]—was, Ernst

---

[61] Ernst A. Philippson, *Germanisches Heidentum bei den Angelsachsen* (*Kölner Anglistische Arbeiten*, IV; Leipzig, 1929), p. 205. There is a possibility, however, that November 7th marked the beginning of the Anglo-Saxon Winter; cf. Heinrich Henel, 'Altenglischer Mönchsaberglaube', *Englische Studien*, LXIX (1935), p. 347. Its accommodation to St. Martin's Day (see below), however, would be in line with Pope Gregory the Great's advice concerning the selection of a saint's day near in date to the replaced pagan festival. Bede, however, says the early Anglo-Saxons celebrated the New Year at Christmas but the pagan observance is uncertain.

[62] See below, chapter VII, 'The Economics of Ruler-Cult in Anglo-Saxon Law'.

[63] Nora Chadwick, ed., *Studies in Early British History* (Cambridge, 1954), pp. 181–182, 200. There is no evidence that St. Martin's, Canterbury, was so dedicated in Roman times.

[64] On this and Hallowe'en fires, cf. Christina Hole, 'Winter Bonfires', *Folklore*, LXXI (1960), pp. 217–223.

[65] *De Temporum Ratione*, c. 15: *Item principaliter annum totum in duo tempora, hiemis videlicet et aestatis, dispertiebant*; C. W. Jones, ed., p. 212.

Philippson has argued convincingly, augmented by the agricultural 'high' occasions of planting and harvest. The solemn procession of the fields with the plough has survived in the folklore-based Plough Monday rites of present-day England, on the Monday after Twelfth Day; the many Spring ceremonies of the field, probably originating in the ancient Nerthus festival, have been translated into the Christian festivals of Easter, Rogationtide, and Whitsunday, but rural folk-customs preserve their original fertility-connected significance.[66] There may in time have been a conflation of ceremonies originally divided between two feasts: one in late December and early January, the New Year's Day of the Anglo-Saxons, who celebrated the year's beginning, according to Bede, at Christmas, *ab octavo kalendarum ianuariarum die*, and which was translated into the Christmas–Epiphany festivities, and the second, later in the Spring. Both, however, were associated with the death of Winter and the hope for crops.[67] The first of these periods coincides with three days

[66] See below, pp. 101–102. Cf., e.g., G. E. Evans, *Ask the Fellows who Cut the Hay* (London, 1956), pp. 90–92, 214. H. M. Chadwick, *Origin*, ch. 10, 'The Cult of Nerthus', pp. 220–251, esp. pp. 245–249, who associates the Nerthus and Gefion cults with *blotmonath*; however, cf. E. Philippson, *Germ. Heid.*, p. 204.

[67] *De Temporum Ratione*, c. 15; C. W. Jones, ed., pp. 211–212. Philippson, *Germ. Heid.*, pp. 204–205. When I witnessed the *Sommertag* celebration in Heidelberg in March, 1960, it was still marked by the *Umzug*, with flower-crowned figures of straw and a folk-song, sung by the children, proclaiming the death of Winter. In Germany, the plough ceremonies were apparently in February, but their January occurrence in English Plough Monday rites suggests their relationship with an Anglo-Saxon mid-Winter or New Year's festival. February or *solmonath* was, however, also a month of sacrifice; see below. This New Year—which is Christmas Eve—Bede calls *modranect* ('the night of the mothers'?), *ob causam, ut suspicamur, ceremoniarum quas in ea pervigiles agebant* (*De Temp. Rat.*, c. 15). 'Hast thou done anything like what the pagans did, and still do, on the first of January, in (the guise of) a stag or a calf?', asks the *Corrector* (Bk. 19 of the *Decretum*) of Burchard of Worms, with reference to dressing as a sacral animal on the pagan New Year; John T. MacNeill and Helena M. Gamer, eds., *Medieval Handbooks of Penance* (Records of Civilization, no. 29; New York, 1938), p. 334. Cf. p. 335, on 'spinning, sewing, winding magic skeins' on the same day. The great nine-yearly festival at Leire was in *mense Ianuario, post hoc tempus quo nos theophaniam Domini celebramus*; Thietmar

—December 31st, January 1st and 2nd—regarded by the Anglo-Saxons as 'lucky' birthdays.[68] The Germanic Autumn festival of the harvest occurred in mid-September,[69] and the Fall procession of Frey for the plenty of the earth has been associated with this season. That this Autumn festival was known in pagan England is confirmed by Bede's appellation of *halegmonath* (holy month), the *mensis sacrorum*, to September.[70] Finally, an Anglo-Saxon Midsummer festival apparently celebrated the triumph of light and the sun and was translated in time into the Midsummer ceremonies on or near the Feast of St. John the Baptist.

In the Anglo-Saxon system of sixty-day months which Bede employs, Philippson conjectures that the six months of the year begin on November 11th, January 13th, March 17th, May 12th, July 12th, and September 17th. His analysis of the folklore and early literary evidence for Germanic pagan festivals places these in mid-November, mid-January, mid-March, mid-May or mid-July, and mid-September.[71] Thus, in spite of the tentative nature of the sources for English heathenism, there is above all evidence for paralleling these holy days or seasons. Bede's information and folklore survivals show parallels for virtually all of these. In summary, they occur in November, the month of *blot*; late December and early January, the rites of *modranect* and plough ceremonies; February or *solmonath*, *mensis placentarum quas in eo diis suis offerebant*;[72] in March, when offerings were made to the goddess Hred;[73] mid-Summer, a light and fertility feast; and

---

of Merseburg, *Chronicon*, Bk. I, c. 17 (9), in *Mon. Ger. Hist.*, *Scriptores Rerum Germanicarum*, n.s., IX, p. 24. For the connection of the New Year's celebration with the Germanic *Julfest*, cf. Philippson, *Germ. Heid.*, pp. 206–207. On the relation of the Anglo-Saxon *modranect* to the Scandinavian *disablot*, a Winternight feast, cf. Turville-Petre, *Myth and Religion*, pp. 224–227.

[68] Max Förster, 'Die Altenglischen Verzeichnisse von Glücks- und Unglückstagen', *Studies in English Philology. A Miscellany in honor of Frederick Klaeber* (Minneapolis, 1929), pp. 258 ff.

[69] On October 1st among the Continental Saxons; cf. Philippson, *Germ. Heid.*, p. 205.   [70] *De Temporum Ratione*, c. 15; C. W. Jones, ed., pp. 211, 212.

[71] Philippson, *Germ. Heid.*, p. 205.

[72] *De Temporum Ratione*, c. 15; C. W. Jones, ed., p. 212.

[73] *De Temporum Ratione*, c. 15; C. W. Jones, ed., p. 212.

September, the *halegmonath*. The relationship and common origin of Anglo-Saxon and Continental Germanic heathen festivals is, although perhaps expected, quite clear.

The question remains: what role did the king play in these high days of his folk? In the first place, the existence and role of any non-royal priesthood must be examined, to see if the sacral leadership was shared with other priestly participants. As we have seen, Tacitus records that the *sacerdos ciuitatis* acts with the king or *princeps* in interpreting the augury of the sacred horses before the meeting of the tribal assembly; in the latter itself it is the priest who silences the gathering before the king addresses it.[74] Further, the priests carry the sacred emblems of the tribe into battle, and punishments of the folk are permitted only to these *sacerdotes, velut deo imperante*.[75] However, in the age of the migrations a separate priesthood has diminished in importance in the Continental North. *Reges et populi, omnes et singuli* offer gifts at the solemn sacrifices at Uppsala, although a professional priesthood officiates there;[76] the priestly functions in Scandinavia are often performed by the pagan temporal nobility, who even own the temples as *Eigentümer*; a priesthood exists, but Old Norse literature bears witness to no high-priesthood, exclusive of kings, dominating the religion.[77] This is paralleled in Christian England, where the Domesday survey shows not only lay ownership of churches but treatment of the latter as entirely the possession of the families which founded them.[78]

In pagan England a pagan priesthood certainly existed. Bede's account of the conversion of Northumbria tells of a *pontifex sacrorum* who had long served the gods and who, rejecting the old faith, defiled the temple at Goodmanham. He asked King Edwin

[74] *Germania*, cc. 10, 11; see above, p.8 and n. 7.

[75] *Germania*, c. 7; Maurice Hutton, ed., *Tacitus. Germania* (Loeb Classical Library; London, 1946), p. 274.

[76] Adam of Bremen, *Gesta Hammaburgensis Ecclesiae Pontificum*, Bk. IV, c. 27.

[77] On the northern priesthood and the priestly role of rulers, cf. Turville-Petre, *Myth and Religion*, pp. 260-262.

[78] Heinrich Boehmer, 'Das Eigenkirchentum in England', *Texte und Forschungen zur Englischen Kulturgeschichte* (Halle, 1921), pp. 301-353; John Godfrey, *The Church in Anglo-Saxon England* (Cambridge, 1962), pp. 318-320.

for harness and a stallion—'for it was not permitted for a priest of the sacrifices either to bear arms or to ride a stallion'—and, riding to the temple, desecrated it by hurling his spear into it, calling upon the tribe to destroy it with fire.[79] Judging from the evidence, the pagan Anglo-Saxon priesthood was thus not allowed to carry weapons, and arms brought into the temple defiled it. The explanation of this, as Chadwick suggests,[80] probably is to be sought in the worship of Nerthus among the pre-invasion Angli. When the goddess in her cow-drawn shrine made her peregrination, *non bella ineunt, non arma sumunt; clausum omne ferrum.*[81] Thus, since the peace of the goddess banished weapons, the priests who attended this peace-goddess would be forbidden to carry arms. The forbidding of weapons or the riding of stallions to the Anglian priesthood may indeed derive from this, although it may also indicate an original order of priestesses, serving the deity of peace and plenty, forbidden emblems of war and martial life, and related to the priest *muliebri ornatu* whom Tacitus ascribes to the Nahanarvali.[82]

Another of the rare references to an Anglo-Saxon pagan priesthood occurs in Bede's comment on the *idolatris . . . pontificibus* whom the citizens of London preferred to serve instead of

[79] Bede, *Hist. Eccl.*, II, 13; King, ed., I, pp. 282–286. Cf. the Icelandic *Landnamabok*: a man 'had a good sword, and he carried it into the temple, wherefore Ingimund (the chief and priest) took the sword away from him'; *C.P.B.*, I, p. 407. In King Alfred's translation of Bede, Coifi is called *ealdorbisceop*, which, with *bisceop*, is the customary Anglo-Saxon word for a heathen priest, in the few references to that office in the vernacular. The authentic Germanic term, *blotere* (from *blotan*, the common Anglo-Saxon term for sacrificing of animals), is found in one Anglo-Saxon gloss but may have been the common word in pagan times. On these Old English terms, cf. R. Jente, *Mythologische Ausdrücke*, pp. 1–5, esp. pp. 1, 4. On Coifi casting his spear as an act of dedicating the temple to destruction, see above, p. 40.

[80] H. M. Chadwick, *Origin*, p. 302.

[81] *Germania*, c. 40; Hutton, ed., pp. 318–320.

[82] *Germania*, c. 43, in Hutton, p. 324. On the relation of Germanic king and *Seherin*, cf. Ortwin Henssler, *Formen des Asylrechts und Ihre Verbreitung bei den Germanen* (*Frankfurter Wissenschaftliche Beiträge, Rechts- und Wirtschaftswissenschaftliche Reihe*, VIII; Frankfurt-am-Main, 1954), pp. 109–110.

submitting to Bishop Mellitus.[83] A *princeps sacerdotum idolatriae* is, furthermore, seen in action in Eddius' *Vita Wilfridi*, standing on a high mound, cursing the Christians and attempting to bind them with magic spells. A companion of Wilfrid, however, slung a stone which had been blessed by the Christians of the bishop's band, and the *magus*, struck in the forehead, was slain.[84] It was this sort of magic spell which King Aethelberht of Kent wished to prevent by meeting the *magus* of the new religion, Augustine, in the open,[85] for, although the open air does not seem to have hindered the attempt by Wilfrid's heathen adversary, the incantation's power was apparently regarded as less dissipated in an enclosure.[86] But in all of this, there is little evidence of a priestly hierarchy and none for a 'national' shrine nor for a strong priesthood either rivalling or independent of the sacral king. The dominance of King Edwin at the seventh-century council which determined his kingdom's religious future and the advisory role of Coifi, on the contrary, suggest a priesthood subordinate to the monarch.

It is to the king as priest that we must look for the religious head of the folk. Among the Germanic tribes, to whom political and religious authority were not bifurcated, the king, who not only was the war-chief of his people but who embodied their 'luck', was their high-priest who dealt with the gods. As has been noted, the Tacitean conjunction of *sacerdos ac rex* had become by the age of the migrations the divinely descended priest-king who sacrificed for tribal well-being. In the North, not only is the king the 'warden of the holy temple', but Norwegian and Icelandic nobles own their own temples and perform the sacrifices as their

[83] Bede, *Hist. Eccl.*, II, 6; King, ed., I, p. 234.

[84] *Vita Wilfridi*, c. 13; B. Colgrave, ed., *The Life of Bishop Wilfrid by Eddius Stephanus* (Cambridge, 1927), p. 28.

[85] *Caverat enim ne in aliquam domum ad se introirent, vetere usus augurio, ne superventu suo, si quid maleficae artis habuissent, eum superando deciperent:* Bede, *Hist. Eccl.*, I, 25; King, ed., I, p. 110.

[86] The lofty hill, perhaps a burial mound, helped; cf. the witch's incantation against the Isle of Ely, made from a high place, during William the Conqueror's campaign against Hereward the Wake. B. Colgrave, ed., *Life of Bishop Wilfrid*, p. 160.

own *goði*.[87] The priestly functions of Germanic—and Anglo-Saxon—kings in sacrificing for plenty and peace and for victory in battle, as well as the accompanying ritual sacrifice of king-slaying, will be examined later. It may suffice here to recall that when the Swedish king, Olaf Tretelgia, failed to perform his priestly role, he was burned in his house by his subjects as an offering to Othin.[88] Certainly heathen Germanic kings, then, were priests. It is as a Christian continuity of this tradition, indeed, that we may see the Anglo-Saxon king speaking as a homilist, as he does in the laws, attending assemblies primarily lay, primarily clerical, and intermediate, and signing a charter at the head of the bishops and at the head of the princes.[89] So also the early English king himself spoke the words of the protective commination when a council granted land to the Church,[90] and it was Edward the Confessor who on Easter Sunday related the saga of Olaf Tryggvason to his court as an exemplary life.[91] 'In the king's righteousness', wrote Alcuin to King Aethelred of Northumbria in A.D. 793, 'is the prosperity of the whole folk, victory of the army, mildness of the seasons, abundance of the land, the blessing

[87] *C.P.B.*, II, pp. 477, 479. Cf. Philippus Oppenheim, *Der Heilige Ansgar und die Anfänge des Christentums in den Nordischen Ländern* (München, 1931), p. 87: 'Im Throndheimschen war jeder der älteren kleinen Könige und der späteren Häuptlinge zugleich Priester seines Geschlechts und seines Bezirks. Ähnlich war es auf Island, wo jeder Häuptling oder Gode in seinem Herrschaftsbezirk (Godord) seinen Tempel, seine Götter, und seinen Gottesdienst hatte'.

[88] See above, p. 15. On heathen kings as priests, cf. O. Henssler, *Formen des Asylrechts*, p. 103, n. 2.

[89] Walter de G. Birch, *Cartularium Saxonicum*, no. 201 B; this work, in three volumes (1885–1893), is cited here and below in the customary manner, as Birch, with the number of the charter. Cf. Felix Liebermann, *The National Assembly in the Anglo-Saxon Period* (Halle, 1913), p. 17.

[90] This is recorded of Wulfhere of Mercia at a council attended by Archbishop Deusdedit, A.D. 664; C. Mellows and W. T. Mellows, eds., *The Peterborough Chronicle of Hugh Candidus* (Peterborough Museum Publications, New Series, I:1; Peterborough, 1941), p. 7.

[91] *Longer Saga of Olaf Tryggvason*, c. 286; Margaret Ashdown, ed., *English and Norse Documents Relating to the Reign of Ethelred the Unready* (Cambridge, 1930), p. 153.

of sons, the health of the people'.[92] A better statement could scarcely be desired of what was expected from the divinely descended, sacrificial priest-king of Germanic heathenism; that it was written by a Christian Anglo-Saxon theologian to a Christian Anglo-Saxon king shows clearly the continuity into the new religion of English sacral kingship.

Before examining this continuity in ritual king-slaying and in offerings for peace, plenty, and victory, the transition of heathen festivals into Christian feasts may first be analysed. This shall be limited, however, to their relationship to the royal priesthood and Anglo-Saxon ruler-cult. In the first place, the three principal high feasts of English paganism—Winter's Day, Midwinter's Day, and Summer's Day—with which the king was undoubtedly associated as performer of the sacrifice are paralleled in the later high crown-wearing occasions assimilated to the Christian seasons. 'Thrice a year the king wore his royal crown', the Anglo-Saxon Chronicle reports for the year 1086 (1087); 'at Easter he wore it at Winchester, at Pentecost at Westminster, and at Midwinter at Gloucester'.[93] The crown-wearing of Edward the Confessor at Westminster, *cum gloria et honore regio*, is recorded in the Chronicle of Ramsey Abbey for the king's last Christmas on earth, and there is good evidence for the custom of crown-wearing in England on the three great festivals at least as far back as the tenth century.[94] As the heathen high days were the occa-

---

[92] *Mon. Ger. Hist., Epistolae*, IV, Ep. 18, p. 51. Cf. Pope Gregory VII's pastoral letter to King Haakon of Denmark, April 19th, A.D. 1080, in which various adverse events are blamed on the Christian clergy: 'You ascribe to your priests the inclemency of the weather, foulness of the air and certain ills of the body. How grave an offense this is . . .'; E. Emerton, ed., *The Correspondence of Pope Gregory VII* (Records of Civilization, Sources and Studies, XIV; New York, 1932), p. 153. Apparently the pope failed to appreciate the ironic justice of expecting the new priests to assume the responsibilities of the pagan priest-king when they usurped many of his privileges.

[93] MS. E; J. Earle and C. Plummer, eds., *Two of the Saxon Chronicles Parallel* (Oxford, 1892), I, p. 219. This edition will be used for the Chronicle throughout this work.

[94] The evidence, including the *Vita Oswaldi's* reference to formal royal assemblies at Easter and Whitsuntide, is gathered in G. O. Sayles and H. G.

sions *par excellence* when the sacral nature of kingship was visibly displayed, so on the high feasts of Christianity, the monarch wore the visible sign of the sovereignty of the anointed king of the New Dispensation. That the Gloucester crown-wearing was at Christmas is almost certain,[95] but the reference to it by the heathen style is not without significance.

That this crown-wearing during the principal Christian festivals was an Anglo-Saxon custom, antedating the Anglo-Saxon Chronicle's reference to William I, is indicated by Roger of Wendover's account of the visit of Kenneth, king of the Scots, to King Edgar's court in A.D. 975. Besides other gifts, the English ruler bestowed on the Scot the land of Lothian, 'on this condition, that every year at the principal festivals, when the king and his successors wore their crowns, they (the kings of the Scots) should come to the court and with the other princes of the realm joyfully celebrate the feast'.[96] The laws of the tenth century King Hywel Dda of the neighbouring Welsh also refer to 'the time when the king sits in his seat at the three principal festivals' of Christmas, Easter, and Pentecost; interestingly, 'if the Bishop is present at the three principal festivals with the King, he ought to sit at the

Richardson, *The Governance of Medieval England* (Edinburgh, 1963), Appendix I, 'Coronations and Crown-Wearings before the Conquest', pp. 405-412. E. H. Kantorowicz, *Laudes Regiae: A Study in Liturgical Acclamations and Mediaeval Ruler Worship* (Univ. of California Public. in History, XXXIII; Berkeley and Los Angeles, 1946), pp. 93-94, states that, although the origins of the custom are not known, such crown-wearings on great feast days were known in the West at least since Carolingian times and were occasions on which the *laudes in festis diebus* were sung. In Byzantium crown-wearings are found earlier.

[95] The Emperor Frederick I, probably following older custom, wore his crown only three times a year, at the same Christian feasts of Christmas, Easter, and Pentecost; P. E. Schramm, *Der König von Frankreich* (Weimar, 1939), pp. 121-122.

[96] H. O. Coxe, ed., *Rogeri de Wendover Chronica sive Flores Historiarum* (London, 1841), I, p. 416 (*sub anno* 975). Whitelock, ed., *Engl. Hist. Doc.*, p. 258. The early thirteenth century chronicler was probably using an early and now lost source for this visit; *ibid.*, p. 255. On Anglo-Saxon votive crown offerings, cf. below, pp. 139-140. Meetings of the *witan* were often held on the three Christian festivals; F. Liebermann, *National Assembly*, pp. 48-49.

right hand of the King',[97] as Christ—whom the bishop is called in at least Anglo-Saxon law—sits at the right hand of the Heavenly King. On the king's left sits the chancellor, *ut senex*. The principal festivals of both the old and the new religion called for the king to bear public witness on those special days to his oneness with divinity and the folk. The religious transition at the Conversion would in this respect, as well as others, require little politico-sociological wrenching from the old paths.

In heathen practice the feasts accompanying the sacrifices were ceremonial events of high significance. In the Scandinavian North, Ari recounts that 'the franklins held feast, to which men gathered together in the autumn. There were great drinkings ... there were Toasts of Remembrance hallowed to the Anses after the heathen fashion, slaying of cattle and horses, and reddening of the altar with blood, and sacrifices were carried on, and the proper forms for the bettering of the seasons'.[98] Drinking was thus not merely a mode of entertainment, but 'a solemn ceremonial associated with the most sacred events of human life', for 'when the cup was passed in the great hall ... divinity itself was perceptible'.[99] It is when the *bragafull* is brought out for 'the chieftain's toast' at the solemn funeral feast that a king or a jarl's successor mounts the high-seat, on the step of which he sits at the opening of the feast, and thus assumes authority.[100] After the conversion to Christianity, this *blot*-related, funeral feast continued. As Vilhelm Grönbech asserts, 'When Christian worship

[97] Haddan and Stubbs, eds., *Councils and Eccl. Doc.*, I, p. 224; cf. Melville Richards, ed., *The Laws of Hywel Dda* (Liverpool, 1954), pp. 26, 103, 123n.

[98] Ari, *Life of St. Olaf*, c. 97; C.P.B., I, p. 405. Ari was born in A.D. 1067.

[99] H. W. Splitter, 'The Relation of Germanic Folk Custom and Ritual to "ealuscerwen" ("Beowulf" 769)', *Modern Language Notes*, LXVII (1952), p. 258. The sacral element in drinking is to be seen in 'the apostles' liquor' drunk on their feast days, according to early Welsh law; M. Richards, ed., *Laws of Hywel Dda*, pp. 39, 126. The Germanic custom is recalled in Henry Wadsworth Longfellow's 'King Witlaf's Drinking Horn'.

[100] *Ynglingasaga*, c. 36; Turville-Petre, *Myth and Religion*, p. 259; discussed in connection with the royal 'sitting on the mound' in Hilda R. Ellis, *The Road to Hel* (Cambridge, 1943), p. 59. On the funeral feast in the North, *ibid.*, pp. 59–61; C.P.B., I, p. 414.

superseded the ancient *blot*, the departed were left out in the cold, or surrendered to the mercy of the church. The dying man's life was no longer insured in a clan, and he had to take measures accordingly. His care for the future then breaks out in orders for feasts to be held "to his memory" with drinking parties and in the bequest of funds for the constant continuation of the memorial feast—or we may safely say, the *blot*'.[101] The pagan sacral feasts of the Autumn, Winter, and Spring festivals were also, on occasion, carried over into Christianity. Thus, when Sigurd Thorisson in Iceland adopted the new religion, 'he continued his custom with the feasts. He then had in the Autumn a great feast for his friends, and a Yule-feast in the Winter, and still invited many people; the third feast he had at Easter-time, and then also invited many. This he continued while he lived.'[102] The conflation of heathen and Christian festivals, it has been suggested, encouraged relapses into paganism in Anglo-Saxon England, as is evidenced by the legislation of the so-called Canons of Edgar against 'heathen songs and devil's games' on Christian feast days.[103]

To the Anglo-Saxons, Heaven itself was such a celebration, 'where God's people are placed at the feast, where there is bliss unending';[104] it is in this light that we should see the ceremonial commemoration feasts provided after death in England.[105] The king also was enmeshed in these Christian parallels of the older pagan sacrificial feasts. Feasts accompanied meetings of the *witan*,

[101] V. Grönbech, *Culture of the Teutons*, II, p. 181.

[102] *St. Olaf's Saga*, c. 123; cf. Paul B. DuChaillu, *The Viking Age* (London, 1889), I, p. 465.

[103] W. Bonser, *Medical Background of Anglo-Saxon England*, p. 124.

[104] R. K. Gordon, ed., *Anglo-Saxon Poetry* (London, 1926), p. 264.

[105] E.g., F. E. Harmer, ed., *Select Historical Documents of the Ninth and Tenth Centuries* (Cambridge, 1914), pp. 1, 70, 73, on annual commemoration feasts provided for in A.D. 805–810 for Earl Oswulf and his wife. On a double funeral-feast in the Danelagh, cf. A. J. Robertson, *Anglo-Saxon Charters* (Cambridge, 1939), pp. 252–253, 502. The fact that no remains of funeral-feasts have been found at pagan Saxon barrows points not to doubt concerning their existence but to their being held elsewhere; L. V. Grinsell, *The Ancient Burial-Mounds of England* (2nd ed.; London, 1953), p. 43.

but, more important, the coronation feast of Anglo-Saxon monarchs, following the sacrifice of the coronation Mass, was a solemn occasion at which the ruler, now *a Deo coronatus*, wore his crown at the ceremonial banquet.[106] When the young King Eadwig deserted it for 'the caresses of loose women', Dunstan 'replaced the crown, and brought him with him to the royal assembly, though dragged from the women by force'.[107] The royal presence was required at the feast.

Of even greater significance than the coronation feast is the continuation of the royal role at what may be regarded as the Christian equivalent of pagan *blot* of the great festivals—the Communion. The very terms used for it in Old English—*husl* (Holy Communion) and *huslian* (to distribute the Communion) —stem from the Christianized but originally heathen word for 'sacrifice'. Related to the Gothic *hunsl* (sacrifice), it is seen in its primary meaning in the Anglo-Saxon translation of St. Matthew ix, 13, and xii, 7, *Mildheortnisse ic willo and nis husul(sacrificium)*.[108] The continuity in terminology from pagan sacrifice to the sacrifice of the Mass thus certainly supports the notion of the translation of one into the other.[109] This is particularly true, since St. Augustine introduced from Rome the primitive offertory at the Mass, in which the laity brought their own offerings of the elements for the Communion, and this usage was general in the Anglo-Saxon Church. This practice in the days of the Conversion must have been one of the many features of the new religion which facilitated the transition, for it would not seem strange to the faithful who were accustomed to bringing their own animals for the

[106] On the coronation feast as 'a kind of Messianic Banquet' in the Anonymous of Rouen, cf. George H. Williams, *The Norman Anonymous of 1100 A.D.* (Harvard Theological Studies, XVIII; Cambridge, Mass., 1951), p. 171, and on the coronation feast of Edgar *et al.*, p. 171, n. 574. On feasts at the *witenagemot*, cf. F. Liebermann, *National Assembly*, p. 52.

[107] *Vita Dunstani*, c. 21; W. Stubbs, ed., *Memorials of St. Dunstan, Archbishop of Canterbury* (Rolls Series, LXIII; London, 1874), pp. 32–33.

[108] For references, cf. R. Jente, *Mythologische Ausdrücke*, pp. 41–42; Nelius O. Halvorson, *Doctrinal Terms in Aelfric's Homilies* (Iowa City, Iowa, 1932), pp. 61–62.

[109] Halvorson, *Doctrinal Terms*, pp. 61–62.

sacrifice and food and drink for the accompanying religious meal. Although the introduction of Norman and French customs after 1066 destroyed in time this Anglo-Saxon offertory, its sole survival in the West, interestingly enough, is in the English coronation, at which the English monarch offers the bread and wine for his own coronation Mass.[110]

The king's offering to the gods, however, has even further parallels. A special coin, a *denarius oblatorius* or 'offering penny', was offered by the king at Mass on certain festivals. These Christian festivals may well, of course, have been the Easter, Pentecost, and Christmas feasts when the king, as in the three chief heathen high-days, displayed himself as the sacral ruler. A silver offering penny struck in the reign of Alfred the Great weighs more than seven pennies, obviously a ceremonial coin.[111] As the king made his special offering to the Christian God, he symbolically offered himself, since his name AELFRED REX SAXONVM was inscribed within two circles on the obverse, as the sacral kings of paganism offered themselves in emergencies to their god. The silver penny found in the grave of King Cnut the Great at Winchester may have been intended as an offering penny to God, accompanying the royal body, although it may also well be related to the 'Charon's penny' of southern Europe, which was known among the Germanic tribes of Seeland and Gotland as early as the third century A.D.[112] The *Munus Divinum* coin of Archbishop Wigmund of York (A.D. 837–854), a gold solidus which has never been explained, was perhaps also a special offering coin, although used not by the king but by a chief of the new priesthood.[113] The special minting of mancuses, the only Anglo-Saxon gold coins, for ceremonial purposes is ordered by King Eadred

[110] Dom Gregory Dix, 'The Idea of "The Church" in the Primitive Liturgies', *The Parish Communion* (A. G. Hebert, ed.; London, 1937), pp. 116–117.

[111] H. A. Grueber, *Handbook of the Coins of Great Britain and Ireland in the British Museum* (London, 1899), p. 24, no. 134.

[112] E. Philippson, *Germ. Heid.*, pp. 56–57. Until recent times a coin was placed in the mouth of the dead in Lincolnshire; *ibid.*, p. 57.

[113] H. A. Grueber, *Handbook of Coins*, plate 3, no. 91; C. F. Keary, *A Catalogue of English Coins in the British Museum: Anglo-Saxon Series* (R. S. Poole, ed.; London, 1887), I, p. 193, no. 718. The *Munus Divinum* inscription on the

(A.D. 951–955) in his will, to be distributed 'for the sake of God and the redemption of my soul'.[114] The suggestion that this coin was minted in large numbers only for such special offerings, and perhaps always a royal offering, is supported by Offa of Mercia's gift of three hundred and sixty-five mancuses annually to Rome for the support of the poor and for lights, apparently as a thank-offering to St. Peter.[115] Thus the evidence suggests that the special royal offering continued in Christian times the older royal role at the heathen festivals. The king's crown-wearing on the three festivals, his crown-offering to the Christian temples, his coronation feast, his offering with the congregation of the fruits of the earth at Mass, and his special offering coins all point to the continuation of sacral kingship in the new religion. These are often connected with the great feast-days of the latter, but all underline the special relationship between the god-descended ruler and the Divine. That some of them are related to southern European, Christian customs cannot, of course, be denied, but the northern Germanic tribes in England would see them in their own societal context and as continuation of their own ways.

The role of the sacrificial king also continues in the capacity of the ruler as the purifier of his people. As the priest-king of heathenism had to change any imbalance of nature and restore the 'luck' of the folk, so the Christian Anglo-Saxon king had to mediate for the sins of all his people. 'He ought to pray to God for the prosperity of his whole people', Alcuin concludes his list

---

reverse appears also on some solidi of Louis the Pious; H. W. C. Davis, ed., *Medieval England* (Oxford, 1924), p. 536, suggests that the term, like the Roman and Byzantine *Salus Mundi*, is a reference to the central cross on the coin.

[114] F. E. Harmer, ed., *Select Hist. Doc.*, pp. 35, 65. Whitelock, ed., *Engl. Hist. Doc.*, p. 512, n. 2, suggests that mancuses may have been minted in large numbers only for ceremonial purposes. On the mancus, a term both for a weight and for a coin, the earliest one of which is from the reign of Offa, cf. Harmer, pp. 77–78, and on the 'Arabic' inscription and origin, W. Levison, *England and the Continent in the Eighth Century* (Oxford, 1946), p. 11, n. 3; P. Grierson, 'Carolingian Europe and the Arabs: The Myth of the Mancus', *Revue Belge de Philologie et d'Histoire*, XXXII (1954), pp. 1059–1074.

[115] F. M. Stenton, *Anglo-Saxon England* (2nd ed.; Oxford, 1947), p. 215, n. 1, discusses this grant and argues against it as the origin of Peter's Pence.

F

of blessings which abide in the king's righteousness.[116] The fate of the *folc* is related to the fate of the prince; 'let us all in common urge the aforementioned king to reform himself with his people,' wrote Boniface to the priest Herefrith concerning Aethelbald of Mercia, 'that the whole nation, with its prince, may not perish here and in the future life, but that, by amending and reforming his own life, he may by his example guide his own people back to the way of salvation.'[117] If the leaders do not serve God, Aelfric preaches in one of his homilies, 'God will manifest to them their contempt of Him either by famine or by pestilence.'[118] In these Christian translations the earlier pagan 'luck' of the Anglo-Saxon king is heard in not too transposed a key. The old sacred ruler devoting himself to *blot* to assure his and the tribe's 'luck' is now seen in terms of the Christian emphasis on sin. This responsibility of the king for his people, common to both Christian and pagan Germanic concepts of kingship, is the light in which the frequent grants of land to the Church *pro expiatione nostrorum piaculorum* should be interpreted.[119]

Furthermore, as pagan priest-kings staved off tribal calamity by offering *blot*—even themselves—to the gods, so Anglo-Saxon kings of the New Dispensation ordered religious duties to be fulfilled by the *folc* for the same reason. In both cases, it was the ruler's role to put matters right with God, to purify his people. King Edgar was the first to do so in a law code, for his fourth code (A.D. 962–963) was issued as a result of a pestilence which the king related to sin and the non-payment of tithes.[120] Under the

---

[116] *Mon. Ger. Hist., Epistolae*, IV, Ep. 18, p. 51: . . . *pro totius gentis prosperitate Deum deprecari debet.*

[117] Haddan and Stubbs, eds., *Councils and Eccl. Doc.*, III, p. 358; Whitelock, ed., *Engl. Hist. Doc.*, p. 757.

[118] Whitelock, ed., *Engl. Hist. Doc.*, p. 853; cf. pp. 783 (letter of Alcuin to Offa of Mercia), 784 (letter of Alcuin to Eardwulf of Northumbria).

[119] Cf., e.g., the grant by Suebred of the East Saxons to Bishop Ingwald of London, c. A.D. 706–709, in Marion Gibbs, ed., *Early Charters of the Cathedral Church of St. Paul, London* (Camden Third Series, LVIII; London, 1939), p. 5.

[120] A. J. Robertson, ed., *The Laws of the Kings of England from Edmund to Henry I* (Cambridge, 1925), p. 29; see below, chapter VII, 'The Economics of Ruler-Cult in Anglo-Saxon Law'.

new religion the king thus legislated the equivalent of *blot* to end the anger of the deity.[121] It is as purifier of his people, finally, that the king exercised his thaumaturgic power of touching for the 'king's evil'. This cure of scrofula by the royal touch is attributed to Edward the Confessor, who cured a young woman of the disease, according to a nearly contemporary source. The 'king's evil' was the term already applied to scrofula in 1080 in England, and William of Malmesbury comments that the Confessor had this power *non ex sanctitate, sed ex regalis prosapiae haereditate*.[122] Like the cure of the ague by the touch of the royal mantle of the Frankish King Guntram, it derives from the divine power of the sacral king to purify his folk and preserve its health,[123] but if it existed before the Norman Conquest, the evidence comes only with reference to the end of the Anglo-Saxon epoch.

The sacredness of the king is also seen in the parallel of temple and palace. The temple was often a private possession of the king; Alcuin, for example, tells of Willibrord baptizing in Heligoland in 'the king's sanctuary' of Radbod, King of the Frisians,[124] and

[121] Dorothy Bethurum, ed., *The Homilies of Wulfstan* (Oxford, 1957), pp. 123–127, 287. Wulfstan preached to the people (Homily III) that national calamities were sent by God as punishment for sin.

[122] Frank Barlow, ed., *Vita Aedwardi Regis* (Nelson Medieval Texts; London, 1962), pp. 61–62; the editor dates Bk. II of the *Vita*, in which this royal cure is found, from 1067 (pp. xxvii–xxx). W. Stubbs, ed., *Willelmi Malmesbiriensis Monachi De Gestis Regum Anglorum* (Rolls Series, XC:1; London, 1887), I, p. 273 (Bk. II, c. 222). Barlow's account, as well as R. W. Southern, 'The First Life of Edward the Confessor', *English Historical Review*, LVIII (1943), pp. 389–391, must be taken as having corrected the classical account of Marc Bloch, *Les Rois Thaumaturges* (*Publications de la Faculté des Lettres de l'Université de Strasbourg*, XIX; Strasbourg, 1924), pp. 43–49. Barlow suggests (p. 123) that 'it seems that the cult was largely French in inspiration and that it had a fluctuating influence on English belief'. See also H. François Delaborde, 'Du toucher des écrouelles par les rois d'Angleterre', *Mélanges d'Histoire Offerts à M. Charles Bemont* (Paris, 1913), pp. 173–179.

[123] Gregory of Tours, *Historia Francorum*, Bk. IX, c. 21; O. M. Dalton, ed., *The History of the Franks By Gregory of Tours* (Oxford, 1927), II, p. 395. The invocation by Guntram drove out evil spirits, and he made *blot* to cure a plague affecting the groin.

[124] Alcuin, *Vita Willibrordi*, c. 10; C. H. Talbot, ed., *The Anglo-Saxon Missionaries in Germany* (London and New York, 1954), p. 10.

the northern temple has already been observed to be the sacral centre of the royal house.[125] The Germanic *Eigentempel* provides part of the politico-religious background—in parallel, if not origin—for the *Eigenkirche* of the Christian Middle Ages, with churches 'owned' by the secular nobility, and temporal power and control closely associated with ecclesiastical foundations.[126] The pagan temple, like the early Anglo-Saxon Christian church, was probably like the king's hall in appearance. The common word for the Scandinavian temple is *hof*, which means simply 'hall',[127] and there was probably little difference between the holy place of the god and the palace of the king. Excavations had never revealed the dwelling of an Anglo-Saxon ruler until the recent find at Yeavering, the royal seat of Edwin of Northumbria, of that king's palace. It not only revealed archaeological support for the *Beowulf* poet's description of the royal hall but also demonstrated the identity in plan between such a comparatively large-scale building and the early Northumbrian churches.[128] That the latter, with their essential simplicity, did not differ markedly from their pagan predecessors is indicated by the apparent fulfilling of Gregory the Great's advice that the *fana idolorum destrui . . . minime debeant* in order that they might be used for the worship of the Christian God.[129] Indeed, heathen temples were converted into Christian churches, as was done when King Aethelberht changed a temple outside Canterbury

---

[125] See above, p. 14.

[126] K. Helm, *Altgermanische Religionsgeschichte*, II:1, p. 173.

[127] *C.P.B.*, I, p. 407. For Anglo-Saxon words used for a heathen temple, cf. R. Jente, *Mythologische Ausdrücke*, pp. 6–17.

[128] On the excavation of Yeavering, its great hall, and possible identification of a converted pagan temple, cf. Peter Hunter Blair, *Roman Britain and Early England 55 B.C.–A.D. 871* (Edinburgh, 1963), pp. 28–29, 222, 258. Bertram Colgrave, *The Venerable Bede and his Times* (Jarrow Lecture, 1958; New-castle-upon-Tyne, 1958), p. 14. On the similarity between royal hall and pagan temple in Scandinavia, cf. Turville-Petre, *Myth and Religion*, pp. 240–243.

[129] Bede, *Hist. Eccl.*, I, 30; King, ed., I, p. 162. This letter to Mellitus shows a change of mind from his earlier urging of King Aethelberht, *fanorum aedificia everte*; *Hist. Eccl.*, I, 32 (King, ed., p. 170).

into the Church of St. Pancras, as was apparently done at Yeavering, and as was frequently done in Scandinavia.[130]

Further support for the physical resemblance of palace and temple-church is suggested by an early English chrismal, built in the shape of a house-shrine; the majority of such reliquaries built in the shape of houses are of Irish provenance, but the one belonging to the church of Mortain in Normandy has a runic inscription in Northumbrian and probably dates from the same time as the famous Northumbrian Franks Casket (c. A.D. 700).[131] Such chrismals may have originally been similar to the portable ark or shrine of paganism[132] and may have been miniature copies of the royal *hof* so similar to temple and church. The inconclusive nature of the evidence, however, must make any such suggestion tentative.

The sacredness of the king's residence and the parallelism of palace and temple are, however, further supported by the fact that the king's state documents are kept with his relics. The earliest surviving evidence for this is in King Aethelred's confirmation of the will of Aethelric of Bocking, dating from A.D. 995-999. 'There are three of these documents', the confirmation concludes, 'one is at Christchurch, the second is at the King's sanctuary [*aet paes cinges haligdome*, literally "with the king's relics"]; the widow has the third.'[133] The identical phrase occurs in another will, that of Leofgifu (A.D. 1035-1044), of which one

---

[130] Wilfrid Bonser, *The Medical Background of Anglo-Saxon England*, p. 122; Blair, *Roman Britain and Early England*, pp. 222, 258; Turville-Petre, *Myth and Religion*, p. 243.

[131] Erika von Erhardt-Siebold, 'Aldhelm's Chrismal', *Speculum*, X (1935), pp. 276-280, with discussion of the Mortain chrismal on p. 279. The author relates these chrismals to Aldhelm's Riddle 55. Further, the quadratic-plan buildings near the Trelleborg sanctuary in Denmark have been compared to tenth-century Anglo-Saxon lantern-covers, including the Pershore censer, which may represent pagan fire-temples; Sune Lindqvist, 'Valhal—Colosseum eller Uppsalatemplet?' *Tor*, II (1949-1951), p. 97. Cf. Sidney L. Cohen, 'The Sutton Hoo Whetstone', *Speculum*, XLI (1966), p. 468.

[132] *C.P.B.*, I, p. 407.

[133] Dorothy Whitelock, ed., *Anglo-Saxon Wills* (Cambridge, 1930), pp. 46-47; on the date, cf. p. 147.

of the three copies is *mid þise kinges halidome*,[134] in a charter of King Cnut granting land to Christchurch, Canterbury, the third copy of which is *inne mid þaes kynges haligdome*,[135] and in an endowment by Earl Leofric and his wife, the first document of which is also *mid þaes kyngces haligdome*.[136] Symbolic of the union of politics and religion in Anglo-Saxon England, the preservation of these and of course other documents with the sacred relics belonging to the monarch makes of his palace both archive and shrine.[137]

A much more decisive parallel, however, is the concept of pagan temple, Christian church, and royal palace as places of peace and asylum. 'The house inside was a place of great peace [asylum],' says Ari of the temple built by Thorwolf of Most,[138] and we have already noted that weapons desecrated the pagan temple both in Anglo-Saxon Northumbria and in the Scandinavian North.[139] Icelandic saga informs us that an outlaw was not permitted by the god Frey even in the vicinity of his temple.[140] This temple-peace becomes the church-peace of the New Dispensation. Consequently, the Christian *Law of the Northumbrian Priests*, in the same area of the North in which Coifi broke his temple's sacral peace, commands: 'If a priest comes with weapons into the church, he is to compensate for it.'[141] The king's palace as well was a place of peace and asylum. Although this shall be

[134] Whitelock, ed., *Anglo-Saxon Wills*, p. 78; for date, cf. p. 187.

[135] A. J. Robertson, ed., *Anglo-Saxon Charters*, p. 170; for date, c. 1024-1032, cf. p. 417.

[136] Robertson, ed., *Anglo-Saxon Charters*, p. 216; for date, c. 1053-1055, cf. p. 465.

[137] King Athelstan was a particularly assiduous collector of relics. For the cult of relics in Anglo-Saxon England, cf. Max Förster, 'Zur Geschichte des Reliquienkultus in Altengland', *Sitzungsberichte der Bayerischen Akademie der Wissenschaften, Phil.-hist. Abteilung*, 1943, no. 8.

[138] 'þar fyrir innan var frið-staðr mikill'; quoted in the *Eyrbyggia Saga* from the lost *Islendingabok* of Ari. *C.P.B.*, I, p. 403.

[139] See above, p. 62. Cf. H. M. Chadwick, *Origin*, pp. 302-303; O. Henssler, *Formen des Asylrechts*, p. 74.

[140] Bertha Phillpotts, 'Germanic Heathenism', *Cambridge Mediaeval History* (New York, 1913), II, p. 493.

[141] D. Whitelock, ed., *Engl. Hist. Doc.*, p. 437.

examined more thoroughly in the analysis of ruler-cult in the Anglo-Saxon *dooms*, it may be sufficient now to cite that special penalties were inflicted for breaking the peace in the king's dwelling and the asylum of nine days, equal to that of 'a holy church of God', which the king's presence affords.[142] Thus, temple, church, and palace are all *mikill grithastathr* (a place of great peace), and one who enters a sacred area comes under this divine and royal peace.[143] In the North images of the heathen gods were carved in the throne of the tribal ruler and not on other seats, but there is no evidence for this practice in England.[144] That the Anglo-Saxon term *'gifstol'*, however, has meanings of both king's throne and God's altar lends even greater support to this parallelism of temple and palace and its continuation into the new religion.[145] And the spread of this religion from the English royal centre, which was almost always the bulwark of the Conversion, strengthened the age-old alliance of sacral powers.

The royal role in mediatorship with the divine continues in the special role assigned many kings in the new religion—the bestowal on them of sainthood. So in England kings such as Edwin and Ecgfrith of Northumbria and Edmund of East Anglia, who fell in battle against the heathen, Oswini of Deira, who was murdered by King Oswiu, Aethelberht of East Anglia, beheaded by Offa of Mercia, and others who died unjust and violent deaths became popular saints.[146] When King Aelfwold of Northumbria

---

[142] Peace and asylum are discussed below in chapter VII, 'The Economics of Ruler-Cult in Anglo-Saxon Law'. On the significance of nine, see my 'Aethelberht's Code and the King's Number', *American Journal of Legal History*, VI (1962), pp. 151–177.

[143] See below, pp. 107–109.

[144] Hans Naumann, 'Die Magische Seite des Altgermanischen Königtums und Ihr Fortwirken in Christlicher Zeit', *Wirtschaft und Kultur: Festschrift zum 70. Geburtstag von Alfons Dopsch* (Baden bei Wien, 1938), p. 4.

[145] See below, pp. 135–137.

[146] Anglo-Saxon Chronicle, *sub anno* 633; Bede, *Hist. Eccl.*, IV, 26; Anglo-Saxon Chronicle *sub annis* 870, 650/651, and 792 (794), respectively. H. A. Wilson, ed., *The Calendar of St. Willibrord from MS Paris. Lat. 10837* (Henry Bradshaw Society, LV; London, 1918), dating from the first quarter of the eighth century, commemorates Edwin, Egfrid, and Oswini, besides Oswald; cf. introd., p. xxii. Another early eighth-century calendar, in P. Romuald

was treacherously slain by his *patricius* Sicga, 'a heavenly light was often seen where he was killed', and his body was brought with ceremony to Hexham.[147] The seven-year-old Kenelm of Mercia, murdered at the instigation of his sister by his guardian, became an Anglo-Saxon saint,[148] as did Queen Osthryth, niece of Oswald of Northumbria and wife of King Aethelred of Mercia, after she was killed by the Mercians in A.D. 697.[149] Of King Edward the Martyr, stabbed to death at Corfe in 978 (979), the Anglo-Saxon Chronicle says that *men hine of myðrodon ac God hine maersode*,[150]

Bauerreiss, 'Ein Angelsächsisches Kalendarfragment des Bayrischen Hauptstaatsarchivs in München', *Studien und Mitteilungen zur Geschichte des Benediktinerordens und Seiner Zweige*, LI (1933), p. 179, commemorates Egfrid and King Osric of Deira, the latter remarkable in view of his excision from the king-lists as an apostate, slain by Cadwallon. This will be discussed below. On Aethelberht of East Anglia, cf. M. R. James, 'Two Lives of St. Ethelbert, King and Martyr', *English Historical Review*, XXXII (1917), pp. 214–244; C. E. Wright, *The Cultivation of Saga in Anglo-Saxon England* (Edinburgh, 1939), pp. 95–106.

[147] Anglo-Saxon Chronicle, *sub anno* 789 (788); Earle and Plummer, eds., I, p. 55. Simeon of Durham, *Historia Regum*, *sub anno* 788, in T. Arnold, ed., *Symeonis Monachi Opera Omnia. Historia Regum* (Rolls Series, LXXV:2; London, 1885), p. 52. Sicga committed suicide in A.D. 793; Simeon of Durham, *sub anno* 793 (*ibid.*, p. 54). The pillars of light may have special significance for Anglo-Saxon royal saints, carrying a reminiscence of pagan pillar cults. Cf. below, p. 117. The murder of the king-saint Kenelm was revealed by a *columna lucis* (Florence of Worcester, *sub anno* 819), and a pillar of light also shone over Oswald's bones when they were left overnight outside Bardney Abbey (Bede, *Hist. Eccl.*, III, 11).

[148] B. Thorpe, ed., *Florentii Wigorniensis Monachi Chronicon ex Chronicis* (London, 1848), I, p. 65 (*sub anno* 819). A white dove with golden wings is said to have soared to heaven from his head as he fell. Kenelm is not mentioned in the Anglo-Saxon Chronicle, in which (*sub annis* 819, 821) his father Kenwulf is said to have been succeeded by Ceolwulf, omitting Kenelm's reign of a few months; Earle and Plummer, eds., I, pp. 60–61. The story of his murder does not appear before the eleventh century (*ibid.*, II, p. 69), but he is listed as a saint and martyr in the Anglo-Saxon *Þa halgan on Angelcynnes*, in which Winchcombe is given as the place of his burial; F. Liebermann, *Die Heiligen*, p. 18.

[149] Anglo-Saxon Chronicle (MSS. D, E), *sub anno* 697; Earle and Plummer, eds., I, p. 41. F. Liebermann, *Die Heiligen*, p. 12.

[150] Anglo-Saxon Chronicle (MS. E), *sub anno* 979 (978); Earle and Plummer, I, p. 123. On his murder, cf. the anonymous *Life of St. Oswald, Archbishop of York*; D. Whitelock, ed., *Engl. Hist. Doc.*, pp. 841–843. On his early *cultus*, cf.

and he became a saint much honoured in the Anglo-Saxon calendars. It is not without importance in parallel with ritual king-slayings in time of dearth, that the slaying of this king took place soon after the great famine of A.D. 976.

Thus, there are numerous examples of English kings who died violent deaths and were translated into sainthood. Indeed, an unjust and violent death seems to have been sufficient reason for a canonization by the folk.[151] Dorothy Whitelock believes that the early cult of St. Edmund of East Anglia 'is understandable only on the assumption that something other than his death in battle took place'.[152] However, in the light of the evidence concerning Ecgfrith of Northumbria, whom Bede considered justly cursed,[153] Kenelm, whose only qualification for canonization was his extreme youth, and even Edward the Martyr, who 'inspired in all not only fear but even terror',[154] I see no difficulty in his cult. It is understandable on his death in battle alone.

This is strengthened, furthermore, by the most remarkable

B. Fehr, 'Altenglische Ritualtexte für Krankenbesuch, Heilige Ölung und Begräbnis', *Texte und Forschungen zur Englischen Kulturgeschichte. Festgabe für Felix Liebermann* (Halle, 1921), p. 38.

[151] Even ignoring the growth of popular cults, the folk played a role even in more formal canonizations. Thus Dunstan's name was placed in the calendar of saints by order of the *witan* during King Cnut's reign: 1 Cnut 17 §1. F. E. Harmer, *Anglo-Saxon Writs* (Manchester, 1952), p. 509. Consequently, there was good English precedent for the creation of saints—e.g., Charles I and Archbishop Laud—by act of Parliament after the Restoration of 1660.

[152] Whitelock, ed., *Engl. Hist. Doc.*, p. 31. On King Edmund's death, besides the Anglo-Saxon Chronicle, *sub anno* 870, cf. Simeon of Durham in T. Arnold, ed., II, pp. 76–77. For hymns of the Anglo-Saxon period on this king (from MS. Cotton Vespasian D. xii, fol. 116–117), cf. J. Stevenson, ed., *The Latin Hymns of the Anglo-Saxon Church* (Surtees Society Publications, XXIII; Durham, 1851), pp. 148–150. For parallel of his death with martyrdom of St. Sebastian, cf. C. E. Wright, *Cultivation of Saga*, p. 55. On the St. Edmund Memorial Coinage, cf. Philip Grierson, *Sylloge of Coins of the British Isles. Fitzwilliam Museum, Cambridge, Part 1. Ancient British and Anglo-Saxon Coins* (London, 1958,) coins 457–471; C. F. Keary, *Cat. of Engl. Coins*, pp. 98–137, coins 106–697.

[153] *Hist. Eccl.*, IV, 26; King, ed., p. 160.

[154] Anonymous, *Life of St. Oswald, Archbishop of York*, which also records the king's dying words, hardly a model of Christian emotion: 'What are you doing—breaking my right arm?' Whitelock, ed., *Engl. Hist. Doc.*, pp. 841–842.

example of all. In an early eighth century calendar there is commemorated on May 8th the very Osric of Deira (d. A.D. 634) who
was excised from the king-lists of Northumbria for returning to
the old gods.[155] Both Bede and the Anglo-Saxon Chronicle
assign an extra year to King Oswald's reign 'on account of the
heathen practices which had been performed by those who had
reigned the one year between him and Edwin', i.e., Eanfrid of the
Bernicians and Osric of Deira.[156] Osric's violent slaying by
Cadwallon placed him, heathen though he was, among the
commemorations of Christianized royal sacrificial victims, the
saints. Here indeed we see the enshrinement in the new religion
of kings 'sacrificed' by violence and the continuation of earlier
attitudes toward ritual king-slaying.

Over and beyond these king-saints who died such deaths and
were thus accorded the rank of Christian martyrs, the royal nature
of mediatorship with the divine is seen in Christian accommodation in the fact that a large percentage of, if not most, Anglo-
Saxon saints belong to royal families.[157] The god-descended,
mana-filled dynasty was the richest source of sanctity for the new
religion as well as for the old; just as the pagan *heil*-renowned
king was culturally venerated after death,[158] so a Christian king
known for his holiness, his victories, or the prosperity of his reign,
received cult honours as a saint. As the burial mound of the pagan
ruler was a holy place and a tribal centre, used for the assembly of

---

[155] See above, n. 146. This Osric of Deira, father of Oswin, is not to be
confused with the later Osric of Northumbria. The strangeness of this commemoration has not, to my knowledge, been pointed out previously except in my
'Paganism to Christianity in Anglo-Saxon England', *Harvard Theological
Review*, LIII (1960), p. 213. The necrological additions to this calendar in the
first ms. hand are, besides Osric, King Egfrid of Northumbria (d. 655);
Etiltrud, an often-honoured member of Anglo-Saxon royalty though not yet
canonized; Abbot-bishop Eadberth of Lindisfarne (d. 698 or 700); and Bishop
John of Beverley (d. 721). All of these additions show north English provenance
for the calendar, and all are May and June commemorations.

[156] Anglo-Saxon Chronicle, *sub anno* 634 (MS. E); Earle and Plummer, eds.,
I, p. 27. Bede, *Hist. Eccl.*, III, 1; King, ed., p. 326.

[157] F. Liebermann, *Die Heiligen, passim.*

[158] See below, pp. 94–95.

the folk,[159] so also the burial place of a Christian English monarch noted for his *heil* was a sacred shrine. 'The person of the ruler,' as Heinrich Fichtenau declares, 'was sacred *ex officio*.' And though he correctly adds that 'this did not mean that the ruler as a human being was a saint, still less that he was more sacred than the saints',[160] the sacral nature of kingship, pagan and Christian, would lead the folk to expect God to honour the *stirps regia*. The recognized form of this in the new religion was sainthood. Thus of Anna, King of the East Angles, it was said not only that he was *swyðe cristen man* but that 'his whole family was honoured by God'.[161] One of the fullest lists of saints commemorated by the Anglo-Saxon Church, *þa halgan on Angelcynne*, written shortly before A.D. 1000, was united between 1013 and 1030 with a work treating of royal lineages, particularly of Kent, as though kings and saints were a natural combination.[162]

Saints of the royal stock abound in Anglo-Saxon England. Among them, besides those already mentioned, are Aelhmund, a Northumbrian prince;[163] Aelfgifu, wife of Edmund I;[164] Princes Aethelred and Aethelberht and their sisters Earmengyth and Eormenburg, children of Eormenred of Kent;[165] Cyneburga, daughter of Penda of Mercia and wife of King Oswy's son Alfrid;[166] Cyneswitha, another daughter of Penda;[167] Osgyth,

---

[159] The Anglo-Saxon *gemot* often met at a burial mound. See below, pp. 104–105.

[160] Heinrich Fichtenau, *The Carolingian Empire* (Peter Munz, transl.; Oxford, 1957), p. 56.

[161] Aelfric, Homily XX, ll. 5–7; W. W. Skeat, ed., *Aelfric's Lives of the Saints* (Early English Text Society, LXXXII; London, 1885), pp. 432–433.

[162] This ms., frequently referred to above, has been edited by F. Liebermann, *Die Heiligen*, pp. 1 ff., with the second part, on Anglo-Saxon hagiology, on pp. 10 ff; on the date of the work and of its union, cf. pp. iv, xiii.

[163] *þa halgan on Angelcynne*, c. 11; *Die Heiligen*, p. 12.

[164] *þa halgan . . .*, c. 36; *Die Heiligen*, p. 18. For her canonization and miracles at her tomb at Shaftesbury, cf. Aethelweard, Bk. IV, c. 6, in J. Stevenson, ed., *The Church Historians of England* (London, 1854), II:2, p. 439.

[165] First mentioned in *þa Halgan . . .*; cf. Liebermann, *Die Heiligen*, pp. iv–v, ix.

[166] *þa halgan . . .*, c. 26; *Die Heiligen*, p. 14.

[167] *þa halgan . . .*, c. 26; *Die Heiligen*, p. 14.

daughter of Fridwold, sub-king of Surrey;[168] Cuthburh and Cwenburg, sisters of Ine of Wessex;[169] and Eadgytha, daughter of King Edgar and abbess of Wilton.[170] These are all mentioned in a late tenth century Anglo-Saxon hagiological account. Other commemorations of English royal saints include Aelfgifa, daughter of Alfred the Great and a nun at Shaftesbury; Aethelthryth, daughter of King Anna of East Anglia and wife of King Ecgifrh, of Northumbria, the first abbess of Ely; Eadburga, wife of King Edward the Elder, a nun in Nunnaminster, Winchester; Eadgyth sister of King Athelstan and wife of Sihtric of Northumberland; Edward the Confessor; Eormenhilda, widow of King Wulfhere of Mercia and abbess of Ely; King Erdulf, buried in Breedon in Leicestershire; Milburga, Mildred, Mildgyth, and Merewine, children of Merewald, son of King Penda; King Regenhere, buried in Southampton; Seaxburga, another daughter of King Anna and the wife of Eorconberht of Kent; and Withburgh, yet another daughter of Anna.[171]

There are, then, at least a score of saints of Anglo-Saxon royal dynasties. That this has a parallel among their non-Germanic neighbours, the Welsh, is demonstrated in the fifth century history of Brecknock. Its ruling house was 'the most sanctified in

---

[168] *Þa halgan . . .*, c. 22; *Die Heiligen*, p. 14.

[169] *Þa halgan . . .*, c. 45; *Die Heiligen*, p. 20.

[170] *Þa halgan . . .*, c. 35; *Die Heiligen*, p. 18.

[171] Cf. the list of Anglo-Saxon, Irish, Breton, British, and Frankish saints in Karl Wildhagen, 'Das Kalendarium der Handschrift Vitellius E XVIII', *Texte und Forschungen*, pp. 108–113. On Anglo-Saxon saints and their resting-places, cf. C. Mellows and W. T. Mellows, ed., *Peterborough Chronicle*, pp. 29–32. On Queen Aethelthryth, King Anna's daughter, cf. Bede, *Hist. Eccl.*, IV, 19–20, including a hymn; King, ed., II, pp. 102–116. Aelfric's Homily XX (cited above, n. 161) is in honour of this saint. Cf. Eddius Stephanus, *Vita Wilfridi*, c. 19; B. Colgrave, ed., p. 40. Roger of Wendover, *sub anno 925*, tells of Queen Eadgyth's marriage to Sihtric, who became a Christian convert for love of her but later apostacized, and of the miracles at her tomb; H. O. Coxe, ed., I, pp. 385–386. In addition to the Eadburga of Winchester, a similarly named daughter of King Aethelberht was honoured at Lyminge. Her body was removed from Lyminge to St. Gregory's, Canterbury, by Lanfranc in A.D. 1085; G. H. Doble, ed., *Ordinale Exon.* (Henry Bradshaw Society Publications, LXXIX; London, 1940), IV, p. 56, n. 1.

British history', for its king and queen and all their many children, including the famous St. Ninnoc, were considered saints.[172] As among the English, so here too we hear of no non-royal families which fill so consistently the calendars of the Church. The thaumaturgic powers of these Anglo-Saxon king-saints, like the magical power of their pagan ancestors, stirred the imagination of the folk. Bede, for example, tells story after story which must have been current in his day of King Oswald's miracles, particularly of healing, at the site of the cross he erected near Rowley Water, on the battlefield where he met his death, at the translation of his relics, and at the latter's shrines.[173] He inserts a hymn he wrote in honour of another royal saint, Aethelthryth, in which her miracles of healing are mentioned,[174] as Aethelweard tells of the miracles at Queen Aelfgifu's tomb.[175] The many thaumaturgic miracles of kingship are in the tradition not only of the *vitae* of Christian hagiology but, like the power of touching for the king's evil, also of the *salus*-giving responsibility of heathen priest-kingship.

It is interesting, however, that on the one occasion when an actual Christian priest sat on an Anglo-Saxon throne, the Church was bitter in its opposition to him. In A.D. 796, Eadbert Praen, a priest, with the support of the Kentish nobles, overthrew the Mercian overlordship and assumed the crown of Kent.[176] Archbishop Aethelheard of Canterbury supported Mercia, and, at his instigation, Pope Leo III, in a letter to King Kenwulf of Mercia, anathematized the priest-king *qui ascendat in regnum* as like Julian the Apostate himself.[177] Church and Mercian state combined to

[172] Nora Chadwick, ed., *Studies*, pp. 44, 226–227.

[173] *Hist. Eccl.*, III, 2, 9–13; King, ed., I, pp. 330–332, 368–390. Cf. Wilfrid Bonser, 'The Magic of Saint Oswald', *Antiquity*, IX (1935), pp. 418–423, on his miracles.   [174] *Hist. Eccl.*, IV, 20; King, ed., II, pp. 112–116.

[175] See above, n. 164. On the incorruption of royal bodies after death—including Edmund of East Anglia, Edward the Martyr, Aethelberht of East Anglia, Edgar, Edward the Confessor, and others—cf. Bonser, *Medical Background*, pp. 191–197.

[176] Anglo-Saxon Chronicle, *sub annis* 794 (796), 798, (796F); Earle and Plummer, eds., I, pp. 56, 57.

[177] Haddan and Stubbs, eds., *Councils and Eccl. Doc.*, III, p. 524. For the

suppress the rebellion, and Eadbert was seized, chained, blinded and had his hands cut off. The Church's opposition to a king whose priestly powers were institutionalized by ordination was surely based not simply on Archbishop Aethelheard's dependence on Mercian support but on its recognition of the genuine danger to it from so firm a linking of the two sacral offices. No miracles flowed from Eadbert Praen, and the threat in that form did not rise again.

Ecclesiastical wariness of sacral kingship can also be seen in the Church's attitude toward the cult of the saint-kings. Although the cult of royal saints was obviously popular,[178] on the other hand the early English king-saints were not represented in the early dedications of churches. These were predominantly Roman in character, except for a single example, the church of St. Cuthbert and St. Oswald, near the spot where King Aelfwald of Northumbria was murdered.[179] I suggest that the Church regarded it as dangerous to strengthen royal cults by official dedications of churches, in spite of its apparent blessing of these saints and their popular cult, since their localization might lead analogously to the local 'high places' and royal sanctuaries of heathenism. In spite of the general obedience of Pope Gregory's advice concerning the adaptation of local custom, the ecclesiastical organization, wary of royal saints, preferred Roman dedications.[180] The pagan traditions of royal *mana* and their continuation in Christian terms

---

episode of Eadbert Praen, cf. *ibid.*, p. 496; W. Levison, *England and the Continent,* p. 18. For a Scottish parallel, cf. the Cistercian Bishop of Man and the Isles, Wymund, who abandoned his see to claim the crown of Scotland, A.D. 1130–1139; Haddan and Stubbs, eds., II:1, pp. 189–190.

[178] Cf., e.g., their frequent appearance in Anglo-Saxon liturgical observances, as attested by the pre-Norman Conquest calendars; Francis Wormald, ed., *English Kalendars Before A.D. 1100* (Henry Branshaw Society Publications, LXXII; London, 1934), I, *passim.*

[179] Simeon of Durham, *sub anno* 788, in T. Arnold, ed., II, p. 52. Cf. W. Levison, *England and the Continent,* p. 36.

[180] In the later Anglo-Saxon period, when the danger was less great than in the Age of Conversion, one finds occasional royal dedications. Cf. Florence of Worcester, *sub anno* 1032: 'The Church of St. Edmund, king and martyr, was

might well make the priests of the new religion hostile to the cult of the 'sacrificed' king. It is to this royal role as sacrificer for peace, plenty, and victory for his folk that we must now turn. 'Just within the shadow at which the records of English history fail,' as Jolliffe has written, 'stands the sacrificial king.'[181]

---

dedicated in this year'; B. Thorpe, ed., *Florentii Wigorniensis* . . ., I, p. 189. When the danger had passed, such dedications were even popular. Thus 67 churches were dedicated to King Oswald and 61 to Edmund before A.D. 1700; Bonser, *Medical Background*, p. 197.

[181] J. E. A. Jolliffe, *The Constitutional History of Medieval England* (New York, 1947), p. 42.

CHAPTER III

The sacrificial king

Belief in the dependence of the fruits of the earth on the king's right relationship with the divine is common to many cultures. The Homeric *Odyssey*, for example, declares that 'when a blameless king fears the gods and upholds right judgment, then the dark earth yields wheat and barley, and the trees are laden with fruit, the young of his flocks are strong, and the sea gives abundance of fish, all from his good leading'.[1] It is in such a role that heathen Germanic belief casts the tribal ruler of the North. Harvests depend on the king's 'luck', and the fruitfulness of his kingdom on the vitality of his own *mana*. Fertility flows from the king's person, even from the royal touch; King Waldemar I of Denmark touched the seed of the future harvest, as well as children and both sick and well among his folk.[2] King Olaf, the son of Charlemagne's enemy, Godfrid, was worshipped after his death for good seasons, and bad harvests brought about the ritual king-slaying of the Ynglingar Domaldi and Olaf Tretelgia and of King Harald in Reithgotaland.[3] King Haakon the Good, the

---

[1] *Odyssey*, XIX, ll. 109-114. Cf. the control over crops and weather by chiefs in Africa and the South Pacific in Sir James Frazer, *Lectures on the Early History of the Kingship* (London, 1905), pp. 110-111, 116-117, 133-134.

[2] A. Holder, ed., *Saxonis Grammatici Gesta Danorum* (Strassburg, 1886), p. 537 (Bk. XIV, c. 779). H. Naumann, 'Die Magische Seite des Altgermanischen Königtums und Ihr Fortwirken in Christlicher Zeit', *Wirtschaft und Kultur. Festschrift zum 70. Geburtstag von Alfons Dopsch* (Baden bei Wien, 1938), p. 5. On the sacral hand, see below, p. 116 and n. 130-131, and O. Höfler, 'Der Sakralcharacter des Germanischen Königtums', *The Sacral Kingship: Contributions To The Central Theme Of The VIIIth International Congress For The History Of Religions (Rome, April, 1955)* (Leiden, 1959), pp. 680-681. On harvest in the North, cf. V. Grönbech, *The Culture of the Teutons* (London, 1931), II, ch. 11, 'For Harvest and Peace', pp. 176-188.

[3] Fritz Kern, *Kingship and Law in the Middle Ages* (S. B. Chrimes, transl.; Oxford, 1948), p. 86, in his well-known discussion of the Germanic right of

foster-son of Athelstan of England, in A.D. 952 was advised to continue the rites of his father and 'sacrifice for good seasons and peace'.[4] The old religion gives way to the new, but the age-old beliefs are continued; the health-giving quality of the pagan priest-king is especially easily transferred to a saint-king. 'He is a man of God,' sings Thorarin Praise-Tongue of King Olaf the Holy, as he urges Sweyn, Aelfgifu's son, to pray to him, 'and he can get good seasons and peace (*ar ok frið*) for every man of God himself, when thou puttest forth thy prayers before the mighty pillar of the Scriptures.'[5] Fertility, good seasons, and peace are the responsibility of the sacral king.

In Scandinavia these blessings are peculiarly identified with the god Frey. 'He rules over the rain and the shining of the sun, and therewithal the fruit of the earth,' *Gylfaginning* tells us, 'and it is good to call on him for fruitful seasons and peace.'[6] This 'God of the Fertile Season'[7] originally was, according to the *Ynglingasaga*

---

resistance, points out that violent removal of the ruler 'was not entirely devoid of justification in legal theory. The "lawlessness" of a monarch above all, but also bodily or mental incapacity, cowardice or political ineptitude, defective kin-right or the lack of other legitimation, and even the anger of the gods as manifested in bad harvests or military failures, all these demerits could suffice, in the common conviction, to justify or even to require the abandonment of the king.' On the larger problem of the Germanic right of resistance, cf. *ibid.*, pp. 85–97. On ritual king-slaying, see below, pp. 113–115.

[4] At the Frostathing; *Fornmanna Sögur*, I, c. 22, quoted in Paul DuChaillu, *The Viking Age* (London, 1889), I, p. 465. A. Rugg-Gunn, *Osiris and Odin: The Origin of Kingship* (London, 1940), p. 117.

[5] Thorarin Praise-Tongue, *Glaelogns-kviða*, ll. 36–39, in *C.P.B.*, II, p. 161. The poem is dated by its editors (p. 158) between A.D. 1032 and 1034, shortly after Olaf's death in battle, A.D. 1030. For the ancient northern pillarcult, which may have inspired the description of King Olaf as 'the mighty pillar of Scriptures', see below, n. 132. Olaf, whose hair and nails are described in this poem (ll. 18–19) as growing on him 'as on a living man', was *perpetuus rex Norwegiae*, later rulers being regarded as governing the kingdom in his name; Peter Paulsen, *Axt und Kreuz bei den Nordgermanen* (Berlin, 1939), p. 226. The growth of Olaf's hair and nails after death is also attested by Sighvat the Poet in his *Olafs Drapa* (c. A.D. 1031); *C.P.B.*, II, p. 142.

[6] *Gylfaginning*, c. 24; A. G. Brodeur, ed., *The Prose Edda by Snorri Sturluson* (New York, 1916), p. 38.

[7] *Skaldskaparmal*, c. 7; Brodeur, ed., *The Prose Edda*, p. 112.

G

and *Olafs Saga Tryggvasonar*, a Swedish king whose reign was one filled with these gifts; when he died and was buried in a large howe, this fact was kept secret, and the king's tribute-money, which was still collected, was placed in his barrow. 'When the Swedes saw that Frey was dead, and that yet good seasons and peace continued, then they believed that it would be so as long as Frey remained in Sweden, and they would not burn him. And they called him *veraldar goð* (God of the World), and sacrificed especially to him for good seasons and peace ever afterwards.'[8] Further, we have already noted that in Ari's account of the feast accompanying heathen sacrifice, the second toast was to Frey and his father Njörd for good seasons and peace, and that his festival and procession for these blessings were an Autumn celebration.[9] Fertility and peace in Scandinavia were thus associated with both the king, whose 'luck' assured them, and Frey, the god who granted them and whose representative the Swedish kings, at least, were.

Did Anglo-Saxon England parallel this northern dependence of peace and plenty on the person of the god-descended sacral ruler? In the first place, we might be led to expect this by the evidence for a cult similar to that of Frey. Frey's father in northern mythology was Njörd, also a god of good seasons and peace; his cult is apparently descended from that of Nerthus, the *Terra Mater* of Tacitus, with whose name Njörd (Njörðr) is phonetically equivalent. The ritual procession of this early earth-goddess, as we have seen, was a time of peace when *non bella ineunt, non arma sumunt*. The Continental Angli, ancestors of the Anglian tribes of England, were among her worshippers, and, as H. M. Chadwick has demonstrated, the evidence points to the continuation of her cult in both the Danish goddess Gefion on Sjaelland and Scyld Scefing, ancestor of the royal House of Wessex and husband of Gefion of the ox-plough.[10] The complications of these early

---

[8] *Olafs Saga Tryggvasonar*, I, c. 322; *C.P.B.*, I, p. 414. *Ynglingasaga*, c. 10 (12); E. Wessen, ed., *Snorri Sturluson. Ynglingasaga* (Nordisk Filologi, Series A, no. 6; Copenhagen, 1952), p. 14.   [9] See above, p. 57.

[10] *Germania*, c. 40, on Nerthus cult. On the cults and interrelationships of Nerthus, Njörðr, Frey, Freyja, Gefion, Scyld Scefing, and Ing (of the *Inguaeones*

agricultural and fertility cults need not envelop us here except for one conclusion. The traditional descent of at least West Saxon royalty from Scyld and Sceaf, and the connection between these and the sheaf as a religious symbol among the pagan Anglo-Saxons, apparently bearing the chief role in a ritual in which it was regarded as the child of the grain-deity,[11] ties in English monarchs with the fertility and good seasons it was their role to further.

This is supported, we have noted, by the Christian Alcuin in his assertion that *aeris temperies, terrae habundantia, filiorum benedictio, sanitas plebis* all rest in the king's person.[12] It is precisely these that depend on the *mana* of the northern pagan king, and Alcuin's statement, like Waldemar of Denmark's touching of seed and of children, cannot be unrelated to the heathen past of his people and its belief in precisely the same royal power. This interdependence of fertility and the king is to be witnessed in legends of Anglo-Saxon kings, even though these are often known to us only from later sources. Thus, when King Edmund of East Anglia fell on his knees and interceded for his folk, twelve springs came forth from the spot as he rose.[13] An ecclesiastical document of the

---

of Tacitus and Pliny, probably to be identified with the worshippers of Nerthus and later found in Yngvi-Frey), cf. the seminal chapters 10 (The Cult of Nerthus) and 11 (King Aethelwulf's Mythical Ancestors) in H. M. Chadwick, *The Origin of the English Nation* (Cambridge, 1924), pp. 220–283. Also Elliott Van Kirk Dobbie, ed., *The Anglo-Saxon Minor Poems* (Anglo-Saxon Poetic Records, VI; New York, 1942), p. 158 (on the Ing stanza of the Anglo-Saxon Rune Poem and Ing's relation to Frey and Nerthus). Karl Helm's claim in *Altgermanische Religionsgeschichte* (Heidelberg, 1913), p. 277, that Frey was unknown to the West Germans cannot be supported; cf. discussion below, pp. 124–126; Chadwick, *Origin*, and the widespread cult of the boar, Frey's animal, among the West Germanic tribes.

[11] H. M. Chadwick, *Origin*, pp. 254–276. On Scyld and Sceaf, cf. also *Beowulf*, ll. 4–52; E. Philippson, *Germanisches Heidentum bei den Angelsachsen* (*Kölner Anglistische Arbeiten*, IV; Leipzig, 1929), pp. 95–98, whose disagreement with Chadwick on the interpretation of the Abingdon monks' use of a floating shield does not affect our use of the source; and on Sceaf born in Noah's Ark, above, p. 41.

[12] *Mon. Ger. Hist., Epistolae*, IV, Ep. 18, p. 51. See above, pp. 64–65.

[13] C. E. Wright, *The Cultivation of Saga in Anglo-Saxon England* (Edinburgh, 1939), p. 119.

twelfth century relates that King Ine of Wessex (A.D. 688–725) was found by hearing a ploughman call to him to bring oxen.[14] Although this is a fabrication inasmuch as Ine was of royal stock and not a commoner, it could well be a late reminiscence of the king's responsibility for agricultural plenty and even of the ox-drawn ceremonial *Umritt* by which the pagan king, like the goddess Nerthus, brought well-being to his land.[15] Its similarity to a legend of the Visigothic King Wamba suggests that it is not an isolated legend. On more historical evidence, King Aethelwulf, Alfred the Great's father, is disturbed by the report of a vision of crop failure caused by the sins of the people,[16] and although a king would well be concerned with a vision which was distressing many of his people, it serves to underline his responsibility for plenty.

Peace and plenty, it has been observed, are intertwined in early Germanic ruler-cult. Sacred peace-kings are recorded in Scandinavian legend as ruling lands showered with a fertile abundance, as riches were an attribute of the 'luck'-crowned Anglo-Saxon monarch. Both *eadig* and *saelig*, as has been seen, have the meaning sometimes of 'rich' and sometimes of 'lucky'. Riches were a sign of 'luck' and to be 'lucky' was to be blessed.[17] The great peace-king of the Danish past was Frothi, who established that peace which the Swedes attributed to Frey, the contemporary of Frothi, the *Ynglingasaga* records.[18] Saxo Grammaticus writes that Frothi

[14] Alexander H. Krappe, 'An English Version of the Ploughman King', *Journal of English and Germanic Philology*, XLVIII (1949), pp. 108–111. The document, written by a canon of Wells, is now in the library of Lincoln's Inn.

[15] Frey made his ceremonial journey to cause plenty, as did 'Berecynthia', who was carried around at Autun *pro saluatione agrorum ac uinearum*; Chadwick, *Origin*, p. 229. Cf. the ceremonial procession in ox-cart around his realms by the Merovingian king.

[16] Aethelwulf related the vision to the Emperor Charles the Bald in a letter requesting safe passage through the Frankish kingdom. *Annals of St. Bertin*, *sub anno* 839; D. Whitelock, ed., *English Historical Documents c. 500–1042* (London, 1955), pp. 314, 806.

[17] Ernst Leisi, 'Gold und Manneswert im "Beowulf",' *Anglia*, LXXI (1953), pp. 259–260.

[18] *Ynglingasaga*, c. 10 (12); E. Wessen, ed., p. 13.

had gold rings placed on the public highways on Jaellinge Heath, and no one dared to steal them.[19] 'No man injured any other, even though he met face to face his father's slayer or his brother's, loose or bound. Neither was there any thief nor robber then.'[20] Plenty and peace went hand in hand. 'Plenty is a boon to men; I say that Frothi was generous', says the Old Norse Runic Poem.[21] Gold was known to northern skalds as *Fróða mjöl*, 'Frothi's meal', because his quern, Grotti, would grind gold for him;[22] Egill Skallagrimsson, for example, whose encomium to the Anglo-Saxon King Athelstan has survived in part, in his *drapa* on Erik Bloodaxe at York sings, 'Many he'll dower / With Frothi's flour'.[23] Thus the holy peace-king Frothi becomes a model of that prosperous and beneficent reign which the sacral king was to provide.

In Anglo-Saxon England a *rex pacificus* would draw, then, not only on the Christian ideal of peace but on the ancient associations of peace and plenty as the golden age and model rule among the Germanic peoples.[24] England would flourish under a peace-king, as it did in the early years of Edward the Confessor, '*quiescente in pacis quiete universali Britannia*'.[25] The great example of the Anglo-

[19] *Gesta Danorum*, Bk. V, in A. Holder, ed., pp. 169–171; when Frothi was very old, the son of a sorceress at his mother's instigation stole one, and the king was slain in his pursuit by the sea-cow into which the mother had changed herself. The *Skiöldungasaga*, c. 3 (*Skaldskaparmal* 43), however, reports that Frothi III, with whom the peace-king is usually identified, was slain by a stag. On the stag cult, see below, pp. 130–132. The *Skiöldungasaga* tells the story of the gold rings of King Frothi I of Denmark and Saxo of Frothi III. The two, both of whom are associated with peace, may originally have been identical; cf. H. M. Chadwick, *Origin*, p. 242.

[20] *Skaldskaparmal*, c. 42; A. G. Brodeur, ed., p.161.

[21] *Ar er gumna góðe*; / *get ek at ǫrr var Fróðe*; Bruce Dickins, *Runic and Heroic Poems of the Old Teutonic Peoples* (Cambridge, 1915), pp. 26–27.

[22] *Skaldskaparmal*, c. 42.

[23] Gwyn Jones, 'Egill Skallagrimsson in England' (Sir Israel Gollancz Memorial Lecture), *Proceedings of the British Academy*, XXXVIII (1952), p. 140.

[24] Cf. Tacitus on the Swedes (*Suiones*) in *Germania*, c. 44; M. Hutton, ed., *Tacitus. Germania* (Loeb Classical Library; London, 1946), p. 326.

[25] From an eleventh century *vita* of the Confessor; H. R. Luard, ed., *Lives of Edward the Confessor* (Rolls Series, III; London, 1858), p. 396. Cf. *ego Eadgar*

Saxon peace-king, however, was King Edgar the Peaceable (A.D. 959–975), whom his own and later reigns united in hailing as *rex pacificus*. This was already foretold at the moment of his birth in a divine revelation to Dunstan, who, while in his cell, meditating, heard voices on high, singing, *Pax Anglorum ecclesiae exorti nunc pueri et Dunstani nostri tempore*.[26] Success attended the peace-king like those of old: 'God granted him that he lived in peace as long as he lived ... and he improved the peace of the people more than the kings who were before him in the memory of man. And God also supported him so that kings and earls willingly submitted to him and were subjected to whatever he wished. And without battle he brought under his sway all that he wished.'[27] As 'Frothi was generous', so Edgar is praised as 'dispenser of treasure to warriors';[28] as peace and plenty accompanied one another in Frothi's realm, so the *rex Anglorum pacificus* 'ruled

---

gratia Dei Anglorum rex pacificus in an apparently genuine charter of Edgar, dated A.D. 968; J. Stevenson, ed., *Chronicon Monasterii de Abingdon* (Rolls Series, II:1; London, 1858), I, p. 311. This was prior to his consecration in 973. Cf. the *pacis securitas*, also of the Confessor's reign, in the eleventh century *Miracula Sancti Eadmundi* of Heremann the Archdeacon, c. 26; F. Liebermann, *Ungedruckte Anglo-Normannische Geschichtsquellen* (Strassburg, 1879), p. 239.

[26] *Epistola Adelardi ad Elfegum Archiepiscopum De Vita Sancti Dunstani, Lectio III*, which also refers to him as *rex pacificus*; W. Stubbs, ed., *Memorials of St. Dunstan, Archbishop of Canterbury* (Rolls Series, LXIII; London, 1874), p. 56. It is repeated *sub anno* 943 by Florence of Worcester; B. Thorpe, ed., *Florentii Wigorniensis Monachi Chronicon ex Chronicis* (London, 1848), I, p. 133. In contrast, Dunstan forecast evil days for Aethelred the Redeless because the latter polluted the font during his baptism; C. Grant Loomis, *White Magic: An Introduction to the Folklore of Christian Legend* (Mediaeval Academy of America, Publication No. LII; Cambridge, Mass., 1948), p. 71.

[27] Anglo-Saxon Chronicle (MSS. D, E, F) *sub anno* 959; Earle and Plummer, eds., I, p. 114. D. Whitelock, ed., *Engl. Hist. Doc.*, pp. 205–206. On the accounts in the Anglo-Saxon Chronicle (in which the number is given as six), Florence of Worcester, and Aelfric of the eight subject kings rowing Edgar on the river Dee, as the helmsman of the state steered, cf. *ibid.*, pp. 208, 853; also W. H. Stevenson, 'The Great Commendation to King Edgar in 973', *English Historical Review*, XIII (1898), pp. 505–507.

[28] *beorna beah gifa*; Anglo-Saxon Chronicle (MS. A, B, C) *sub anno* 975. Earle and Plummer, eds., I, p. 120.

everything so prosperously [*gesundlice*] that those who had lived in former times . . . wondered very greatly'. It was as if God had said to him that for defending God's cause, 'as a recompense to you I will . . . increase and advance your kingdom *in gode*'.[29] As the deities Nerthus and Frey and the Merovingian sacral kings made ceremonial progresses through the realm, establishing good seasons by their coming, so Florence of Worcester reports a tradition that King Edgar made progresses through his lands to correct wrongs and establish a *tempus laetitiae*.[30] The English monarch did not leave gold rings on the public roads to demonstrate the safety of treasure, but in a less legendary mode of establishing its security, he 'ordered new money to be made throughout the whole of England', because of the debasing of the older coins.[31] Indeed, he so 'justly struck down the unjust with the imperial rod, but peacefully guarded the good under the same rod of equity',[32] that the words of Simeon of Durham on Alfred the Great might well be applied to the peace-king Edgar: *magnificatus est rex pacificus super omnes reges terrae*.[33] This is, of course, not at all to imply that the subjects of this staunchly Christian king thought of him only as a parallel to the peace-kings of the North, even less as Frey returned; rather, the Christian emphasis on *pax et justitia* as ideals of kingly government well expressed a continuity with the priestly royal role of the *rex pacificus* of the

[29] From a fragmentary text surviving only in B.M. MS. Cotton Faust. A. x, of which Bishop Aethelwold was perhaps the author. O. Cockayne, ed.. *Leechdoms, Wortcunning and Starcraft of Early England* (Rolls Series, XXXV:3; London, 1866), III, pp. 436 (Anglo-Saxon) and 437 (transl.); also transl. in Whitelock, ed., *Engl. Hist. Doc.*, p. 847. In the opening, of which the first words have been lost, the text, probably referring to God's favour to Edgar, relates that 'he gave to him manifold and plentiful possessions and power'; Cockayne, ed., p. 432. For *rex anglorum pacificus*, cf., e.g., Florence of Worcester, *sub anno* 973, in B. Thorpe, ed., I, p. 142.

[30] B. Thorpe, ed., p. 144.

[31] H. O. Coxe, ed., *Rogeri de Wendover Chronica sive Flores Historiarum*, (London, 1841), I, p. 416 (*sub anno* 975).

[32] From the nearly contemporary *Vita Sancti Dunstani Auctore B*, c. 24; W. Stubbs, ed., *Memorials*, p. 36.

[33] T. Arnold, ed., *Symeonis Monachi Opera Omnia. Historia Regum* (Rolls Series, LXXV; London, 1885), II, p. 88 (*sub anno* 885).

Germanic pagan *Weltanschauung*. Supported by a folk against whose pagan beliefs and practices even his own reign had to legislate,[34] King Edgar could well draw on whatever pagan tradition survived which enhanced the reign of the great Woden-sprung peace-king with belief in his divine support. When the king of peace and plenty was gone—*corpus vero illius Glaestoniam delatum, regio more est tumulatum*[35]—signs appeared at once of the loss of the realm's 'luck'. 'Soon in the same year in harvest time there appeared the star comet, and in the next year there came a very great famine and very many disturbances throughout England.'[36] Peace and plenty had departed with the *rex pacificus*.

The relation of peace and plenty with the person of the king did not necessarily end with the ruler's death. His *mana* could follow him into his grave and bless the site of his burial. When Frey was placed in his howe, offerings were poured into it, and good seasons and peace still continued; as a result, the Swedes 'sacrificed especially to him for good seasons and peace ever afterwards'.[37] Olaf of Geirstaðr, King of Vestfold, was also worshipped after his death for good seasons, following his burial in a great mound.[38] A notable example of the continuing veneration of the king for his ability to bring abundance to his realm is to be found in the Saga of Halfdan the Black.[39] The father of Harald Fairhair and brother of Olaf of Geirstaðr, Halfdan *svarti* was a Norwegian king whose reign was so crowned with plenty that it was believed the division of his kingdom in which he was buried would continue in the prosperity brought by the king's *heil*. Consequently, when he was to be buried in Hringariki, the three other sections of the realm—Vestfold, Heiðmörk, and

---

[34] See below, chapter VII, 'The Economics of Ruler-Cult in Anglo-Saxon Law', on legislation against heathenism.

[35] Florence of Worcester, *sub anno* 975, in B. Thorpe, ed., I, p. 143.

[36] Anglo-Saxon Chronicle (MS. D, E), *sub anno* 975; Earle and Plummer, eds., I, p. 120.

[37] See above, pp. 87–88.

[38] See below, p. 114.

[39] *Heimskringla*, c. 9; C.P.B., I, p. 417. His saga is translated in S. Laing, *Heimskringla: The Norse King Sagas by Snorre Sturlason* (Everyman's Library; London, 1930), pp. 44–50.

Raumariki—sent men, 'all begging to have the body'; the eventual solution was to divide the *mana*-filled body of the king into four parts. 'The head was laid in a howe at Stein in Hringariki, and each man bore home a part of the body and laid it in a howe; these howes are called "the howes of Halfdan"'.[40]

Is there any influence of such pagan practice to be detected in Anglo-Saxon England? The answer must lie in the assimilation of king-cult to the saint-cult of the new religion. The cult of saints was one of the features of Christianity which was easily 'naturalized' in the Age of Conversion. This is seen not only in the cult-honouring of the *stirpes regiae* and the assimilation of royal saints to the ritual king-slaying of pagan days, which have been examined. The elevation into sainthood of kings whose 'luck' was strong was a natural product of Germanic religious thought, and the possession of the relics of these sacred rulers was an object of rivalry. When King Edwin's head was brought to York after his death in battle in A.D. 633 and placed in a temple of the new faith, his folk undoubtedly saw this in terms of the 'luck'-bringing sacral head.[41] Edwin and his folk had been converted only six years previously, and his successors in both Deira and Bernicia apostacized to the old faith. The cult of relics of the new religion could be seen so soon after the Conversion only in context of the old, and the burial of the king's head in York probably had closer kinship in the minds of its witnesses with the veneration after death of such kings as Olaf and Halfdan the Black than with anything else. Similarly, King Oswald's body, divided after *Maserfelth* by the pagan Penda, probably as an offering to Woden,[42] remained divided instead of being buried in one place,

[40] Transl. in H. R. Ellis, *The Road to Hel* (Cambridge, 1943), p. 100.

[41] Bede, *Hist. Eccl.*, II, 20; King, ed., I, p. 316. On the head as a fertility centre, see R. B. Onians, *The Origins of European Thought* (Cambridge, 1951), pp. 109–127. Cf. A. W. Smith, 'The Luck in the Head: A Problem in English Folklore', *Folklore*, LXXIII (1962), pp. 13–24, and 'The Luck in the Head: Some Further Observations', *Folklore*, LXXIV (1963), pp. 396–398; in the second article the burial of Edwin's head is related to the concept of 'luck' in the head, a conclusion to which I had come independently, before the appearance of these articles.

[42] See below, pp. 117–119.

after its recovery by his people. His head was buried on Lindisfarne, his uncorrupted hands and arms at Bamburgh, and his body first at Bardney and later at Gloucester.[43] To the Northumbrians, so recently converted and in part by the actions of Oswald himself, this *rex victoriosissimus*, as Bede calls him, would continue to impart his 'luck' through his divided body even after his death. The many miracles performed by him after his death vouch for this continuing sacral power of the king's person.

Further, both Scandinavian and Anglo-Saxon evidence points to an original ruler-cult in the veneration of the royal burial mound. 'Man', as Sir Thomas Browne said, 'is a noble animal, splendid in ashes and pompous in the grave'. As the king powerful in *mana* was given cult honours after his death, so his howe or burial mound was a holy place. Once again pagan Scandinavia may shed light on Anglo-Saxon England. The Scandinavian king's grave mound often became a sanctuary of the folk, as we have already seen, and a central gathering point of the tribe. The royal residence was frequently in the vicinity of a royal howe which was regarded as the grave of the dynasty's ancestral founder.[44] Sacrifice to mounds was, of course, related to the veneration of the dead chieftain buried within, as the stories of Halfdan the Black and Olaf Geirstaðaalfr testify, but it is not surprising to find a shift in worship from the howe-dweller to the burial mound itself.[45] Thus King Framarr in *Ketils Saga Haengs*,

[43] Bede, *Hist. Eccl.*, III, 6, 12; King, ed., I, pp. 352, 386. Anglo-Saxon Chronicle (MS. E), *sub anno* 641; Earle and Plummer, eds., I, p. 27. See above, p. 83 and n. 173.

[44] On the royal howe, cf. esp. Karl Lehmann, 'Grabhügel und Königshügel in Nordischer Heidenzeit', *Zeitschrift für Deutsche Philologie*, XLII (1910), pp. 1–15; Wilhelm Jordans, *Der Germanische Volksglaube von den Toten und Dämonen im Berg und Ihrer Beschwichtigung (Bonner Studien zur Englischen Philologie*, XVII; Bonn, 1933); H. R. Ellis, *Road to Hel*, esp. pp. 34–39, 61–62, 100–111, 191–194; Birger Pering, *Heimdall* (Lund, 1941), pp. 196–201.

[45] H. R. Ellis, *Road to Hel*, pp. 102–105. On the burial mound, cf. Karl Helm, *Altgermanische Religionsgeschichte* (Heidelberg, 1953), II:2, pp. 29–30. On burial mounds and veneration of the dead, cf. also *C.P.B.*, I, p. 415. On sacrifice to mounds, cf. Mary W. Williams, *Social Scandinavia in the Viking Age* (New York, 1920), p. 365.

whose son dwells near the 'howe of plenty', together with 'all the people of the land sacrificed to it for plenty',[46] and of Halfdan the Black's howes the *Flateyjarbok* records that 'men sacrificed and believed in them'.[47] Behind this, however, must have been a belief in the habitation of the mound. The *Ynglingasaga* parallels the spirits of howes with those dwelling in mountains and stones, over all of whom the god Othin has power.[48] The existence in England of belief in the occupation of the howe and the association with the old religion is shown in Felix's *vita* of St. Guthlac, dating from the first half of the eighth century. When the saint built his hermitage on top of a pillaged tumulus, demons attacked him constantly, a reflection of the opposition of the heathen holy place he had chosen to live.[49] The identification of the howe with the heathen is reflected in Charlemagne's Saxon Capitulary (c. 22), which states that Christian Saxons should be buried in church-graveyards and not in 'the mounds of the heathen'.[50]

In Anglo-Saxon England not only were earlier existing burial mounds used for English burials—as in White Horse Hill (Berkshire), in which 46 graves were intruded, and the Uncleby (Yorkshire) mound, with its 68 later graves—but the erection of great tumuli was also well known.[51] The large number of formerly existing barrows is suggested by the 150 examples of them which Kemble discovered as landmarks in Anglo-Saxon

[46] Ellis, *Road to Hel*, p. 104.

[47] Ellis, *Road to Hel*, p. 102.

[48] *Ynglingasaga*, c. 7; E. Wessen, ed., p. 10. Cf. King Svegðir, who disappeared into a rock when told that he would meet Othin there (*Ynglingasaga*, cc. 11–12), and Barðr of Snjofell, who entered into the mountains and was seen no more; Ellis, *Road to Hel*, p. 194. On the widespread legends of the king in the mountain, cf. A. H. Krappe, 'Die Sage vom König im Berge', *Mitteilungen der Schlesischen Gesellschaft für Volkskunde*, XXXV (1935), pp. 76–102.

[49] Bertram Colgrave, ed., *Felix's Life of St. Guthlac* (Cambridge, 1956), pp. 92–94 (c. 28), 100–110 (cc. 31–34).

[50] *Capitulare de partibus Saxoniae*, c. 22; *Mon. Ger. Hist.*, *Leges*, II:1, p. 69. K. Helm, *Altgermanische Religionsgeschichte*, pp. 29–30.

[51] Hilda R. Ellis Davidson, 'The Hill of the Dragon: Anglo-Saxon Burial Mounds in Literature and Archaeology', *Folk-Lore*, LXI (1950), pp. 169–172. The quotation from Sir Thomas Browne, given above, is cited by Mrs. Davidson (p. 169).

boundary charters.[52] The ancient terms for these burial mounds survive in English place-names to the present day, as the Saxon *hlaew* or *hlaw* is incorporated in Taplow (Bucks.) and Bartlow Hills (Cambs.) and *beorg* in many others.[53] The most important of all Anglo-Saxon royal mounds was the famous Sutton Hoo find in Suffolk, but others are also extant. The grave-goods of the Anglo-Saxon Taplow barrow (Taplow = the *hlaew* of Taeppa) in Buckinghamshire—including two spears, a sword, a gold buckle with garnets and lapis lazuli, glass drinking horns, two shield bosses, and two buckets—would suggest an important chief. Other such barrows, if not as rich in grave-goods as Taeppa's, include those at Asthall (Oxon.), Benty Grange (Derbyshire), whose boar helmet will be discussed later, Broomfield (Essex), and on Salisbury racecourse (Wilts.).[54] *Cerdices beorg*, the 'barrow of Cerdic', in northern Hampshire may or may not mark the burial of the leader of the invading Saxons,[55] but the howe-burial of non-chieftains and non-royal personages is witnessed by the intrusive interment in Anglian times which undoubtedly gave the present name of Lilla Howe to an earlier barrow on Goathland Moor. The name and the grave-goods make it most likely that this secondary burial was that of Lilla, the loyal thegn of King Edwin of Northumbria who sacrificed his own life to save his royal master.[56] At least two known examples of the ritual breaking of grave-goods indicate pagan Saxon ceremonial at the howe, at Sutton Hoo, where the harp was purposely broken, and at Alvediston (Wilts.).[57] The

[52] H. Ellis Davidson, 'Hill of the Dragon', pp. 173–174, citing *Archaeological Journal*, XIV (1857), pp. 119–120.

[53] L. V. Grinsell, *The Ancient Burial Mounds of England* (2nd ed., London, 1953), p. 62. Since the common meaning of *beorg* is simply 'hill', it is often impossible to distinguish from place-name evidence alone whether the name refers to a natural hill or artificial tumulus; cf. A. H. Smith, *English Place-Names, Part I* (English Place-Names Society, XXV; Cambridge, 1956), p. 29.

[54] Grinsell, *Ancient Burial Mounds*, p. 27.

[55] G. Copley, *The Conquest of Wessex in the Sixth Century* (London, 1954), p. 126. The name Cerdic is British.

[56] *Hist. Eccl.*, II, 9; King, ed., I, p. 250. Grinsell, *Ancient Burial Mounds*, p. 234.

[57] Grinsell, *Ancient Burial Mounds*, pp. 42–43.

deposit of grave-goods themselves, however, is no proof of pagan interment. After the Conversion, grave-goods continue to accompany the now Christian burials, sometimes on a lavish scale.[58] At Sutton Hoo, for example, the find contained family treasures dating over a period of three generations.[59] The continuity of pagan practice in the new religion is clear, here as elsewhere.

The richest Anglo-Saxon archaeological find ever made is that of the royal ship-burial in the howe of Sutton Hoo.[60] The identity of the East Anglian chief honoured by this magnificent deposit of grave-goods in a type of burial reserved in the North for the great is still controversial. The earlier scholarly view that it was probably King Aethelhere was based primarily on two facts: the absence of a body, which supported the opinion that it was a cenotaph for that king, who was killed at *Winwaed*, in Yorkshire, in A.D. 655, and the apparently pagan custom of depositing grave-goods, since Aethelhere was probably heathen.[61] However, the possibilities have broadened with the now generally accepted view that the deposition of grave-goods continued into Christian times and can no longer be regarded as confined to pagan rulers;[62]

---

[58] T. C. Lethbridge, *Merlin's Island* (London, 1948), pp. 130–146. The difficulty of identifying Christian Viking graves because of the continuation in Scandinavia of this custom is pointed out by H. R. Ellis, *Road to Hel*, p. 12.

[59] See below, chapter IV, on royal insignia among the treasures, and below, on the problem of its purpose as cenotaph or burial and on the identity of its royal 'occupant'.

[60] R. L. S. Bruce-Mitford, *The Sutton Hoo Ship Burial: A Handbook* (London, 1968). Charles Green, *Sutton Hoo: The Excavation of a Royal Ship-Burial* (London, 1963).

[61] Bruce-Mitford, *Sutton Hoo Ship Burial*, p. 56.

[62] This makes improbable Bruce-Mitford's dramatic conjecture, in support of his earlier suggestion of Aethelhere as the object of honour, 'that the old heirlooms and treasures were felt to have a pagan taint, and that Aethelbald, burying them with his brother, felt himself presiding at the winding-up of the pagan age'; R. L. S. Bruce-Mitford, *The Sutton Hoo Ship Burial: A Provisional Guide* (London, 1947), p. 43. In the discussion of Sutton Hoo here and in the next chapter the reference to Bruce-Mitford's work on it will be to the 1968 *Handbook* unless specific reference is made to the 1947 *Provisional Guide*. Bruce-Mitford, after suggesting Aethelhere, later tended to support Anna as

it has even been suggested that Sutton Hoo may well have marked not a cenotaph but an actual burial, with all remains of the interred body having disintegrated.[63] There is, however, no evidence for any body having been interred with the ship, although chemical analysis has demonstrated that cremated bone, either animal or human, once was present on or near the great silver Anastasius dish in the ship. If an East Anglian king, cremated in the old pagan manner, were placed in an unburned burial-ship, this would further support, as he notes, R. L. S. Bruce-Mitford's suggestion of Redwald as the monarch honoured. 'His conversion in Kent, at Aethelbert's court, could easily explain the Christian objects, no doubt gifts, in the grave. His subsequent relapse could account for his burial in the pagan tradition in a burial ground with pagan associations, and not, as became the rule immediately with converted royalty, in a church. Indeed, Redwald's attempt to get the best of both worlds, by scandalously setting up altars to Christ and to the devil [i.e., pagan gods] side by side . . . might explain any mixture of Christian and pagan features in the burial. The pre-eminence of the burial seems to match perfectly the pre-eminence of Redwald. The standard and whetstone-sceptre could well be symbols of his high office as Bretwalda, an office which on his death left the Wuffinga family and passed to King Edwin of Northumbria,' who was accustomed to having a standard (*tuuf*) carried before him. The most recent numismatic evidence for dating the burial, with c. A.D. 625 'as the latest date for the coming together of the coins found in the purse', would fit in with the possibility of Redwald, who died in A.D. 624 or 625.[64] Nonetheless, whether for Redwald, Aethelhere, the Christian Anna, or another of the East Anglian royal house, and whatever the still-debated dating of the ship-burial, it must have honoured an Anglo-Saxon king of considerable wealth and distinction.

The Sutton Hoo ship, it has been suggested, may have been

---

the king honoured; for his present view, based on the most recent studies of the evidence, see below. C. Green, *Sutton Hoo*, ch. 6 (The King-Burial: Which King?), advocates Anna or, more probably, Aethelhere.

[63] S. Lindqvist, 'Sutton Hoo and *Beowulf*', p. 132.

[64] Bruce-Mitford, *Sutton Hoo Ship Burial*, pp. 52–56, with quotations on p. 53.

of Swedish construction and indeed that which brought the founder of the East Anglian dynasty to British shores c. A.D. 550.[65] Since the ship in Scandinavia was a cult object apparently connected with Nerthus, who emerged from the sea, and with Freyja, a Swedish ship-burial in England connects even more firmly with the latter country the continuity with northern paganism.[66] That ship-burials of rulers at sea were known to the Anglo-Saxons is evidenced in the *Beowulf* in the famous treasure-enriched funeral of Scyld.[67]

As in Scandinavia, Anglo-Saxon veneration for the dead chieftain of the howe and for the howe itself existed in heathen times, but the evidence for it, except in the archaeology of the interments themselves, depends, of course, on sources entirely from the Christian period. However, as early as the first half of the eighth century, as we have noted, demons in a burial mound attacked St. Guthlac, who had built his hut on its top. Silbury Hill, the largest artificial mound in Europe, was until modern times visited on Palm Sunday by villagers of the neighbouring countryside who feasted there, a reminiscence of the feasting at northern burial mounds on pagan high festivals. In Norway, in parallel, as late as 1827 the custom survived of pouring beer over the roots of a birch tree growing on a particular burial mound.[68] That earlier beliefs about such tumuli continued in Christian

[65] N. E. Lee, 'The Sutton Hoo Ship Built in Sweden?' *Antiquity*, XXXI (1957), pp. 40–41. The ship in the smaller Sutton Hoo mound, however, like that of the forty-two foot boat from Snape Common, had a square stern, previously unknown in Germanic boat-building; T. C. Lethbridge, *Merlin's Island*, p. 106, n. 1, suggests an origin in vessels of Irish pirates.

[66] B. Pering, *Heimdall*, pp. 182–184. Nerthus may well have been the deity which Tacitus (*Germania*, c. 9) says the Suebi worshipped under the sign of a ship. On the Virgin Mary living in the sea and the concept of Mary as *stella maris*, cf. *ibid.*, p. 186.

[67] *Beowulf*, ll. 26–52. On Scyld and his relation to England, cf. H. M. Chadwick, *Origin*, pp. 264–267.

[68] B. Pering, *Heimdall*, p. 150. The lack of remains of funeral feasts at English howes indicates this part of the funeral observance was held elsewhere; L. V. Grinsell, *Ancient Burial Mounds*, p. 43, which also suggests that Anglo-Saxon measures against songs and laments by clergy at funeral feasts indicate that pagan funeral ritual included such practices.

times is also seen in an Anglo-Saxon charm against rheumatism, which was regarded as caused by the shot of elves, of hags, or of the Aesir themselves. 'Loud were they, lo loud, *ða hy ofer þone hlaew ridan* (when they rode over the mound)', it opens.[69] The riding of the old gods, of 'mighty women', or of elves, tradition-ally associated with Frey, over a burial mound harks back to pagan ritual or belief now lost but obviously associated with these howes.

The Christianization of burial mounds is seen first of all in their continued erection in memory of the great, whether of kings as at Sutton Hoo or of non-royal personages such as Edwin's minister, Lilla. The Christian practice of burying the great in churches, however, soon ended the use of burial mounds, but early Christian churches were located on occasion on or near a tumulus. Thus, the famous Taplow mound is in the old parish churchyard, the church at Ludlow was built on the site of an earlier mound, and in Yorkshire the church at Fimber was built on a barrow.[70] Indications of the use of mounds are also occasion-ally found. When a prioress of Wimborne died, for example, 'a mound was raised over her grave with the earth piled up according to custom'. However, the young nuns, who disliked her because of her severity, 'mounted the mound' and, with something less than Christian charity, trampled on it 'as if it were the dead corpse'. Soon after, 'in a wonderful manner the earth which had lately been heaped up had subsided and sunk to a distance of half a foot below the top of the grave'. The royal abbess of Wimborne, Tette, the sister of Ine of Wessex, 'realized from the disappearance of the earth the punishment of the woman buried there' and united the nuns with her in prayer. As a result, the earth rose again to show the absolution of the prioress.[71]

[69] G. Storms, *Anglo-Saxon Magic* (The Hague, 1948), pp. 140 (text), 142, 145 (comment). On the Aesir, see above on *Os-*, pp. 22–23. On the relation-ship of Frey and elves, see above, p.50 n.30.

[70] H. Ellis Davidson, 'Hill of the Dragon', p. 175. Continental examples are also cited.

[71] Rudolf of Fulda, *Life of Leofgyth*, c. 4. The *vita* is edited by G. Waitz in *Mon. Ger. Hist.*, *SS.*, XV:1, pp. 118 ff. and translated in part by D. Whitelock, ed., *Engl. Hist. Doc.*, pp. 719–724, with the above account on pp. 720–721.

The use of burial mounds, small no doubt in this case, belief in them as indicating the glorified state of their inhabitants, and the desecration of the mound affecting the buried are all contained in this miraculous tale.

The most notable example of their Christian adaptation is their assimilation to the cult of saints. Showing the ancient veneration of the pagan great in howes, skeletons were removed from them and 'translated' to monasteries and into saints' bones, used to work miracles.[72] Specific examples of this date from the twelfth century, when about A.D. 1178, the monks of St. Alban's excavated barrows called the Hills of the Banners to find a skeleton which could be regarded as St. Amphibalus. In A.D. 1199 three skeletons were found in a barrow at Ludlow when it was being removed to enlarge the church; they were proclaimed as three Irish saints, and the clergy 'buried them devoutly in their church, with the confidence that their holiness would be soon evinced in numerous miracles'.[73] That this assimilation of the venerated dead of the old and new religions reaches back into Anglo-Saxon times is shown, however, by a canon attributed to Archbishop Theodore of Canterbury: 'Dead pagans shall be cast out from the places of saints'.[74] The presence of the dead pagan great had merged them with the *saelig* of Christianity. Although the evidence does not allow us to assert that this was true only of the royal stock, it would be at least unsurprising to assume that the 'luck'-giving kings, often worshipped in the Germanic North and themselves called *saelig*, were once again among the chief objects translated into terms of the new religion. This is supported by a letter to Edward the Elder c. A.D. 900 in which a thief is referred to as having 'sought your father's (i.e. King Alfred's)

[72] L. V. Grinsell, *Ancient Burial Mounds*, p. 80.

[73] Grinsell, *Ancient Burial Mounds*, p. 110. On the vitality-restoring quality of a sepulchre on top of a hill near Cardigan, in western Wales, cf. Nennius, *The Marvels of Britain*, c. 74; A. W. Wade-Evans, ed., *Nennius's 'History of the Britons'* (London, 1938), p. 121.

[74] Canon 5; J. T. McNeill and H. M. Gamer, eds., *Medieval Handbooks of Penance* (Records of Civilization, no. 29; New York, 1938), p. 216. For dating of canons, cf. p. 215.

H

body' and taken an oath there. When King Edward saw the sealed document of the oath, he removed the thief's outlawry. This oath-taking at the king's grave suggests a continuity with the sacral nature of the king's mound.[75]

The burial mound is also a tribal centre with its sacral site giving increased religious authority to official acts of the realm. Thus Axel Olrik has demonstrated that the frequent allusions to 'sitting on a howe' in Norse sagas and other poems refer to kings acting in their official role and depend on the priestly, mantic origin and functions of the ruler. Hilda Ellis has extended this by emphasizing the importance of the fact that it was a burial mound on which the king sat and its relationship to the cult of the dead.[76] There seems to be no parallel for this royal practice in Anglo-Saxon England, although the heathen who from his high mound cursed the company of Christians with St. Wilfrid seems to be directly related to the prophesying from a high place by the Scandinavian *völva* (seeress), which Olrik has connected with the king on his howe.[77] Besides the varied epic sources for the king 'sitting on a howe', it is known that the Swedish king made his public declarations from a mound-throne, such as the Inglingehögen in Värend (Schonen),[78] and howes were often the sites for Scandinavian *things* or assemblies. The Anglo-Saxon *gemot* also often met at a burial mound, and the king may well have made his pronouncements and issued his dooms from it when the *witan* assembled there. One burial mound in Schleswig was a cult-centre of the Angles and assembly site of their *thing* for four hundred years,[79] and one of the major categories of names for meeting places of the Anglo-Saxon hundreds derives from the

[75] With Professor Whitelock, I take the phrase, 'and brought a seal to me', as a reference to a document authenticated in that manner to prove the thief had taken the oath; Whitelock, ed., *Engl. Hist. Doc.*, p. 503.

[76] H. R. Ellis, *Road to Hel*, pp. 105–111, with discussion of Olrik's thesis and parallel Welsh and Irish material.

[77] See above, p. 63. Ellis, *Road to Hel*, pp. 105–106.

[78] Jan De Vries, 'Das Königtum bei den Germanen', *Saeculum*, VII (1956), p. 295.

[79] Ortwin Henssler, *Formen des Asylrechts und Ihre Verbreitung bei den Germanen* (Frankfurt-am-Main, 1954), pp. 88–89.

mounds where they assembled.[80] The Danelagh bears witness to the same custom, as at Thinghoe (mound of the *thing*) in Suffolk, where the hundred-court met at a tumulus north-west of the town.[81]

Thus the burial mound was a tribal centre and cult centre among the Germanic peoples, and the Anglo-Saxons shared in this mode of honouring the dead. 'Bid my renowned warriors raise a noble barrow after the burning, on a headland by the sea. It shall be a memorial to my people,' says the dying Beowulf.[82] Such a cenotaph would be understood by the audience of the *Beowulf* poet, for the mound as a sign of the king who had brought plenty to his folk was clearly known among them. The peace- and plenty-producing 'luck' which was the mark of the great ruler accompanied him into his howe and led to the veneration both of him and the mound into which he had descended.

Another survival of the peace-cult of the Germanic king is in the offerings for peace and plenty. The heathen sacrifices for these blessings are well attested, as we have observed. Under Christianity, Anglo-Saxon England also bears witness to parallel rites for their acquisition. Among the religious obligations enforced by royal *dooms*, for example, is that of *cyrisceat* (church-shot, church dues). Distinct from tithes and probably even older than regular parish organization, this payment was apparently the

[80] Olof S. Anderson, *The English Hundred-Names* (Lunds Universitets Årsskrift. N.F. Avd. 1, XXX:1; Lund, 1934), I, pp. xxxiii–xxxiv. Again there is difficulty in distinguishing natural from artificial hills, but 'many hundred-names in O.E. *hlaw* and *beorg* that have place-names for their first elements no doubt . . . refer to meeting-places at burial mounds' (p. xxxiv). See also *ibid.*, III, pp. 164–166. Cf. the *Gemot beorh* in the Isle of Wight in Anglo-Saxon land-charter Birch 392; Grinsell, *Ancient Burial Mounds*, p. 78. Howes are sometimes used in boundary descriptions, as in a Latin charter of Cnut restoring land to the New Minster, Winchester (A.D. 1019): '. . . from Leofwine's boundary to the heathen barrow, and from the heathen barrow back into Drayton'; Whitelock, ed., *Engl. Hist. Doc.*, p. 554.

[81] O. Anderson, *English Hundred-Names*, I, pp. 95–96. On Norse hundred-names in England with the element *haugr* (mound, hill), cf. Anderson, III, pp. 189–190.

[82] *Beowulf*, ll. 2802–2807.

offering of the first fruits of the seed-harvest.[83] When it makes its first appearance in law, under Ine of Wessex, its payment is called for at Martinmas, the great feast day closest to the old Winter's Day festival, on which the king sacrificed for a good year. Now given to the God who triumphed over the old deities, offering of the first crops of the harvest is made to the Church and probably replaced the old feasting of the pagan sacrifice. When in the eleventh century Domesday survey we find the citizens of Derby paying twelve thraves of grain to the king every Michaelmas, this apparently secularized church-shot, as Sir Frank Stenton interprets it, is understandable in the old terms of the king's connection with the harvest and plenty.[84] Offerings are still made, related in mode to the harvested crops, in time to the old festival of the beginning of Winter, and to the king both in his laws directing their payment and in the occasional payment to the ruler himself.

Similarly, the union of king and peace, the accompaniment of plenty in the pagan past, continues. Ecclesiastical prayers for peace, needless to say, do not derive from the Germanic North, but the sacred quality bestowed on it by the Church would be understandable to a recently heathen people who had themselves sacrificed for peace, led by a king whose function originated in a mantic peace-king. Thus, Christian and pagan precedents would merge when an early tenth century Anglo-Saxon coronation rite prayed, *pretende famulo tuo regi nostro arma celestia ut pax eclesię tuę nulla turbetur tempestate bellorum.*[85] It is also in this light of peace as the responsibility of the God-favoured king that we should interpret the PAX coinage of the late Anglo-Saxon period.[86] Coins

[83] This is discussed below in chapter VII, 'The Economics of Ruler-Cult in Anglo-Saxon Law'.

[84] F. M. Stenton, *Anglo-Saxon England* (2nd ed.; Oxford, 1947), p. 154.

[85] G. H. Doble, ed., *Pontificale Lanaletense* (Henry Branshaw Society Publications, LXXIV; London, 1937), p. 63, in the Post-Communion of the Mass. The editor comments (p. xvii) on the 'special interest' of this prayer. This Coronation *ordo* is based on the Leofric Missal and, according to P. E. Schramm, follows the 'Egbert' recension of the Dunstan *ordo*.

[86] H. Grueber, *Handbook of the Coins of Great Britain and Ireland in the British Museum* (London, 1899), pp. 31–33. They may be related to the LVX coins of

with the legend PACX and PAX appear first in the reign of Cnut and have been taken as a commemoration of the peace made in 1016 between that monarch and Edmund Ironside. They continue under Harold I and Harthacnut, but the type is not a monopoly of the Scandinavian house, for it occurs frequently among the coins of Edward the Confessor and is the only one known for Harold II's brief rule. Thus, as the old pagan rulers made *blot* for peace and plenty, so their Christian successors made their oblations also. With the harvest offering, with prayers for peace in the temples, and with the desired *pax* inscribed on their coins—and offered to God with every such monetary gift—the sacrifices of the king for peace and plenty displayed his ancient involvement in his responsibility for these blessings.

Finally, the close relation of sacral peace and the king's person is reflected in sanctuary and asylum associated with the ruler. Since these are primarily dependent on a study of the laws, a thorough examination of the problem must be postponed, but a summary of it will shed light on peace and the king. The 'peace' of certain places and the right of asylum, so common in Anglo-Saxon law, stem not from constitutional but from sacral realms.[87] We have already noted the forbidding of arms to the priests of the Angles and the banning of weapons from their temples, as in Scandinavia, a cult feature probably descended from the cult of Nerthus. It has also been seen that this continued in Christian times in the same area in the *Law of the Northumbrian Priests*, which decreed that 'if a priest comes with weapons into the church, he is to compensate for it'.[88] This and the early northern notion that the area surrounding the king was *mikill grithastathr* (a place of great peace) are based on the premise that one who enters a sacred area

---

Egfrith of Northumbria, *rex piisimus*, which, unless they derive from the $^{VOT}_{XX}$ inscription, are the only example of a religious inscription in Anglo-Saxon numismatics until the coins of the early Viking settlers in Northumbria. Cf. *ibid.*, p. 14.

[87] O. Henssler, *Formen des Asylrechts*, pp. 54–55. Sanctuary was sought at the shrine of Edward the Confessor even before he was canonized; F. E. Harmer, ed., *Anglo-Saxon Writs* (Manchester, 1952), p. 13, n. 2.

[88] See above, p. 62, 76.

becomes himself *heilerfüllt*.[89] Certain words for 'prince'—O.N. *jaðarr*, O.E. *eodor*—may even derive from the primary meaning of 'protective boundary'.[90] The neighbourhood of the peace-king is itself devoted to peace, in order not to break the royal power to bring *grith* to his folk nor to desecrate the sacral area. This is seen in the right of asylum which the *mana*-filled person of the ruler grants. 'If (a thief) seeks the king, or the archbishop, or a holy church of God, he shall have respite for nine nights', declares a law of Athelstan the Glorious.[91] This royal asylum is granted also in the eleventh century laws *Be grithe and be munde*, although here this right, which is granted also to an archbishop or a prince, can be extended beyond the nine nights by the king and the king alone.[92] In yet another law, the king's peace is said to extend from his *burh*-gate 'three miles and three furlongs and three linear acres and nine feet and nine *scaeftamunda* and nine barleycorns'.[93] Here the pagan North breaks through even more; the length of a grain of barley as one of the measures of the plenty-bringing king's *grith* combines with the number nine, which is the magic number of the North, found also in the other two laws of royal asylum and related to fertility, magic, and royal cult.[94] The barley-grain, which later becomes a regular measure of length, aids in the establishment of the jurisdictional sacred area of peace, as symbols of peace and plenty once more unite.

The area of the king's person as one covered by that peace for which his forebears sacrificed is even more notably seen in Anglo-

---

[89] O. Henssler, *Formen des Asylrechts*, pp. 71–73.

[90] J. Sahlgren in *Eddica et Scaldica* (1927–1928), pp. 225–239; E. O. G. Turville-Petre, *Myth and Religion of the North: The Religion of Ancient Scandinavia* (New York, 1964), p. 308.

[91] IV Athelstan 6; F. L. Attenborough, ed., *The Laws of the Earliest English Kings* (Cambridge, 1922), p. 149. See above p. 77.

[92] Felix Liebermann, *Die Gesetze der Angelsachsen* (Halle a. S., 1903), I, p. 470.

[93] From *Pax*, dating c. A.D. 910–c. 1060, in Liebermann, *Gesetze*, I, p. 390 (with Latin text of Quadripartitus, p. 391). This is discussed below in chapter VII, 'The Economics of Ruler-Cult in Anglo-Saxon Law'.

[94] W. A. Chaney, 'Aethelberht's Code and the King's Number', *American Journal of Legal History*, VI (1962), pp. 151–177.

Saxon law. Four laws—two of King Edmund and two of Aethelred the Redeless—forbid anyone polluted by homicide from approaching the king, unless he has been absolved by the bishop.[95] The vicinity of the Woden-sprung monarch is not to be polluted, as outlaws are not permitted in the neighbourhood of Frey's temple; only after the ritual cleansing by the new religion could the criminal enter the area of peace, the region of the king.

The king as bringer of victory is another royal role which continues in Anglo-Saxon England. Whether or not descended in function from the Tacitean *dux* or war-chief, the Germanic king of the Age of Migrations is leader of the war-hosts. He intercedes with the gods, particularly Woden, for victory, and this ancient concept of the king 'lucky' in war is maintained in England as well. Oswald, for example, prays for his army with his dying breath.[96] The Christian God, 'Lord of Victories' (*sigora frean*) as the Anglo-Saxon Chronicle calls Him,[97] gave triumph to the earthly rulers who served Him, as Edwin, for example, 'in omen of his receiving the faith and the heavenly kingdom, received increased power also in his earthly dominion'.[98] Aelfric relates that 'in England also kings were often victorious through God', paralleling Alfred, Athelstan, and Edgar with the judges of Israel.[99]

Many battles are won by Christian kings, 'Christ aiding'.[100]

[95] I Edmund 3, II Edmund 4, V Aethelred 29, VI Aethelred 36; these are discussed in chapter VII.

[96] See below, p. 117.

[97] Anglo-Saxon Chronicle (MSS. A, B, C), *sub anno* 973 (974 in C); Earle and Plummer, eds., I, p. 118. On parallels of this 'Frey of Victories', see below, pp. 50–51. Cf. *sub anno* 975 for God as *sigora Waldend*; Earle and Plummer, eds., I, p. 120.

[98] Bede, *Hist. Eccl.*, II, 9; King, ed., I, p. 244.

[99] From Judges; S. J. Crawford, ed., *The Old English Version of the Heptateuch, Aelfric's Treatise on the Old and New Testament and his Preface to Genesis* (Early English Text Society, CLX; London, 1922), pp. 416–417. In the case of Edgar the Peaceable, 'God subdued for him his adversaries, kings and earls, so that they came to him without any fighting'.

[100] E.g., at the Battle of *Brunanburh* in A.D. 937, when Athelstan and his brother, 'Christ aiding, had victory'; Anglo-Saxon Chronicle (MS. F), *sub anno* 937. Earle and Plummer, eds., I, p. 107. Bede, *Hist. Eccl.*, III, 24, reports

On the other hand, the Devil helped the heathen; in a British source, Nennius reports that the pagan Penda of Mercia 'was victorious (at *Maserfelth*) by diabolical agency'.[101] Thus, as Aelfric says of the kings of Israel, 'some believed in the living God, some in idols to their own destruction'.[102] The true faith brings victory to its royal supporters. So much is the royal person associated with victory in battle and royal devotion to God or the gods a part of maintaining the kingdom's 'luck' that Sigbert, King of the East Angles, who had retired to a monastery, was forced against his will to come forth to lead the *fyrd* into battle against Penda; however, *ipse professionis suae non immemor*, he—like the priests of Anglo-Saxon paganism and the peace-kings of the North—refused to carry a weapon but, with only a little staff (*virga*) in his hand, went into battle and was slain. The mere presence of the victory-bringing king, it was thought, would serve *ad confirmandum militem secum venire in praelium*.[103]

It has already been observed that victory in battle was one of the major blessings for which the kings of the North sacrificed for divine aid. The Summer sacrifice to Woden marked the war-year and was *Sigr-blot*, while in Ari's account of the pagan sacrificial feast, the first toast was to Woden for victory. Thus, dedication of armies to Woden for victory should also be recalled, as well as

---

that King Oswiu and his son Alchfrid at their defeat of Penda in 655, 'trusting in Christ as their leader', met the larger Mercian host and were triumphant; King, ed., I, p. 450. Florence of Worcester, following Bede, says that Oswiu was *unam tantum legionem habens, sed Christo duce confisus*; B. Thorpe, ed., I, p. 23. *Christo auxiliante* or its equivalent is, of course, common in the Middle Ages. Cf. Annals of St. Bertin, *sub anno* 850, when the Danes were defeated by the English with the 'help of our Lord Jesus Christ'; Whitelock, ed., *Engl. Hist. Doc.*, p. 315.

[101] A. W. Wade-Evans, ed., *Nennius's History*, p. 83.

[102] Homily XVIII (*Sermo Excerptus De Libro Regum*), ll. 39-44; W. W. Skeat, ed., *Aelfric's Lives of Saints* (Early English Text Society, LXXXII; London, 1885), p. 386. The genealogies in Nennius drop the name of Wulfhere, probably the ruler who lost the Battle of *Mons Badonicus*; Wade-Evans, ed., *op. cit.*, p. 78. Is the omission of an unvictorious king related to the dropping of apostate kings from the king-lists by Bede and the Anglo-Saxon Chronicle? See above, pp. 79-80.

[103] Bede, *Hist. Eccl.*, III, 18; King, ed., I, pp. 412-414.

the Merovingian King Theudebert's human sacrifice in A.D. 539 at the Po bridge as 'the first offering of the war'.[104] 'Choosers of the slain', paralleling the Valkyrie daughters of the northern Othin, were known to English paganism and by the tenth century are counted among the enemies of the conquering God.[105] But is there any evidence for parallel royal intercessions in Anglo-Saxon England? Did the English king make special offerings to God, in terms of Christianity, for the victory of his folk?

Perhaps the most noteworthy Christian translation of royal intercession for divine aid from the 'Ruler of Victory' is in King Aethelred's action at the Battle of Ashdown (*Aescesdun*) in A.D. 871. While his younger brother Alfred prepared to give battle, Aethelred remained in his tent *in oratione positus*, occupying himself with *blot*, and refused to leave for the fight until the sacrifice of the Mass was concluded. He would not abandon *divinum pro humano . . . servitium*, since the offering of Mass and prayer to God was a necessary aid for victory. Asser attributes the latter as much to the royal intercession as to Alfred's more bellicose role; *quae regis Christiani fides multum apud Dominum valuit*.[106] Like the Tacitean division between sacral king and war-chief, the two brothers gained the God-given victory, and Aethelred was the *rex praecinctus armis et orationibus*.[107]

There has survived what purport to be the very words of the prayer of King Athelstan the Glorious before he went into battle in A.D. 926.[108] Praying that the Lord's hand may strengthen his

---

[104] See above, p. 39.

[105] H. R. Ellis, *Road to Hel*, pp. 71–72, 77.

[106] Asser, *De Rebus Gestis Alfredi*, c. 37; W. H. Stevenson, ed., *Asser's Life of King Alfred* (Oxford, 1904), pp. 28–29.

[107] Simeon of Durham, in T. Arnold, ed., p. 79. Similarly, the anonymous Monk of Ramsey, in the *vita* of St. Oswald, Archbishop of York, written between A.D. 995 and 1005, tells of the famous Ealdorman Brihtnoth at the Battle of Maldon being strengthened on his right hand 'by alms-deeds and holy Masses' and on his left by 'prayers and good deeds'; Whitelock, ed., *Engl. Hist. Doc.*, p. 843.

[108] W. Birch, ed., *An Ancient Manuscript of the Eighth or Ninth Century: Formerly Belonging to St. Mary's Abbey, or Nunnaminster, Winchester* (London, 1889), p. 116. On the importance of the hand, see below, p. 116 and nn. 130–131.

heart, he asks that God grant him to fight well 'that my enemies may fall in my sight'. We may hear here in the voice of the king raised to God, making his *blot* before battle, the echoes of the king's sacrifice for victory when it was Woden instead of Christ who was believed to be aiding his worshipper. A third example of a royal prayer for victory is found in one of the several poems composed by King Aethelwald of Mercia. Written in the fanciful style of the *Hisperica Famina* and, so far as is known, not for any specific emergency, the Mercian ruler's *Oratio ad Deum* concludes with a plea for protection from the enemy and Christ's aid for the faithful: *Hostium a ferocibus / Protegens arundinibus / Concertantes agonibus / Christo semper fidelibus!*[109]

Not only did the sacral monarch himself offer intercessions to the new God for victory, however. Christianity presents direct parallels to the old pagan sacrifices for the war-year in the Church's Masses and Benedictions *in tempore belli siue contra paganos*. The *Missa contra paganos* mentioned in Anglo-Saxon law (VII Aethelred 2) and by the homilist Aelfric is contained in the Missal of Robert of Jumieges,[110] and such liturgies of the Anglo-Saxon period as the Benedictional of Archbishop Robert (late tenth century), the Pontifical of St. Dunstan (tenth century), and the Canterbury Benedictional (early eleventh century) all contain prayers for victory against the Danes, the enemies of folk and faith.[111] Asking God to grant triumph to his faithful, their *orationes* often compare the armies of the Christian king with the hosts of Israel and invoke the image of David and Goliath.[112]

---

[109] *Aethelwaldi Oratio Ad Deum*, ll. 43–46; *Mon. Ger. Hist., Auct. Ant.,* XV, p. 534, and, for comment, p. 533, note.

[110] This is discussed by Bernhard Fehr, 'Altenglisches Ritualtexte für Krankenbesuch, Heilige Ölum und Begräbnis', *Texte und Forschungen zur Englischen Kulturgeschichte* (Halle, 1921), pp. 27–28. On *missae contra paganos*, cf. Gerd Tellenbach, 'Römische und Christliche Reichsgedanke in der Liturgie des Frühen Mittelalters', *Sitzungsberichte der Heidelberger Akademie der Wissenschaften, Philosophisch-historische Klasse* (1934–1935), pp. 36–37.

[111] For references and dating, cf. Carl Erdmann, 'Der Heidenkrieg in der Liturgie und die Kaiserkrönung Ottos I', *Mitteilungen des Österreichischen Instituts für Geschichtsforschung*, XLVI (1932), pp. 133–134.

[112] Cf. Reginald M. Woolley, ed., *The Canterbury Benedictional* (British

However, derived as they are from Christian and Continental sources, they integrate with features of the Germanic past and facilitate the transition from one religion to the other. For king and faith to beseech the divine for victory continues the practice of the Germanic tribes who expected their war-chief to open the way for their deity-favoured arms to triumph. Thus, the priests of the new religion intercede even during battle, as is witnessed by the death at the Battle of *Assandun* in A.D. 1016 of Bishop Eadnoth of Dorchester and Abbot Wulsy of Ramsey, *qui ad exorandum Deum pro milite bellum agente convenerant.*[113] The offering, whether to Woden or of prayers and Masses, was the chief insurance for triumph and brought victory and peace to the cultivators of the faith: *Pax et victoria apostolicae fidei cultoribus in perpetuum!*[114]

The sacrificial kingship is visible, however, in even more startling form in Anglo-Saxon England. It has already been observed briefly that, in the royal responsibility for the tribe's temporal prosperity, when the heathen king lost his 'luck', he himself might be sacrificed to maintain the *mana* of his house. Ritual king-slaying is well attested in the legendary history of the early North. The Yngling King Domaldi of Sweden, for example, was sacrificed by his people because of a great famine; the first year oxen were offered to bring the dearth to an end, the second year human sacrifice was made, but, when these were not successful, in the third year of the famine, the folk 'all agreed that the time of dearth was on account of their king Domaldi, and they resolved to offer him for good seasons [*til ars*]'.[115] To stop a famine in Reithgotaland King Harald and his son Halfdan were

---

Museum, Harl. MS. 2892) (Henry Bradshaw Society Publications, LI; London, 1917), p. 127; *et qui per angelorum presidia. israhelis protexisti agmina. angelicam huic plebi opem tribuas. hostiumque illi terga prebeas. . . . Et sicut dudum dauid in golia. persoluisti triumphanti spolia . . .* This Benedictional probably dates from the second quarter of the eleventh century; *ibid.*, p. xiii.

[113] B. Thorpe, ed., *Florentii Wigorniensis . . .*, I, p. 178, in which Eadnoth is referred to as Bishop of Lincoln.

[114] Opening formula in charter of King Aethelred, A.D. 1000; J. Stevenson, ed., *Chronicon Monasterii de Abingdon*, I, p. 406.

[115] *Ynglingasaga*, c. 15 (18); E. Wessen, ed., p. 18. *Ynglingatal*, c. 5; C.P.B., I, p. 245.

slain as an offering to Othin,[116] and the last of the Ynglings, King Olaf Tretelgia, was burned in his house by his subject Swedes as a sacrifice to Othin because of bad harvests.[117] The *Gautrekssaga* tells of the legendary King Vikar, who was selected by the casting of lots as an offering to Othin for a fair wind; the god demanded and even arranged the carrying out of the sacrifice, and the king was dedicated to him by both stabbing with a spear and hanging from a tree, the traditional modes of offerings to that deity.[118] In a legend attaching to the historical King Eric of Sweden, when the tide of battle appeared to be against him at the fight at the Fyris-field, the king offered himself to Othin in exchange for ten years of victory, and the god accepted.[119] King Olaf or Anlaf 'the Garstead Elf', son of Charlemagne's Viking adversary, God-frid, prophesied during a famine and plague that these would not abate until he had died; a great howe was prepared to receive him, and although he was not sacrificed—indeed he outlived his warriors—when he himself had succumbed to the pestilence and was placed in his mound, the plague ceased. He was later worshipped for good seasons.[120]

[116] *Haraldasaga Graumantel*, c. 16; *Hervarar saga ok Heiðreks konungs*, cc. 11–12. H. M. Chadwick, *The Cult of Othin* (London, 1899), p. 5.

[117] *Ynglingasaga*, c. 43 (47) (*Heimskringla*, I, 75–76); E. Wessen, ed., pp. 45–46.

[118] *Gautrekssaga*, c. 7; C.P.B., I, pp. 466–467. A. Holder, ed., *Saxonis Grammatici Gesta Danorum* (Strassburg, 1886), pp. 184–185 (Bk. VI, cc. 276–277). O. Höfler, *Germanisches Sakralkönigtum* (Tübingen, 1952), pp. 153–161.

[119] *Flateybok*, II, c. 72; C.P.B., I, p. 410.

[120] Theodwulf, however, after giving the account says somewhat shatteringly that Olaf died of gout; C.P.B., I, pp. 414–415. He was later thought to be re-born as King Olaf the Holy, to the embarrassment of that Christian monarch. One day Olaf the Holy 'rode with his bodyguard past the howe of Olaf Geirstaðaalfr. "Tell me, lord" (says one of his men), "were you buried here?" The king replied to him: "My soul has never had two bodies; it cannot have them, either now or on the Resurrection Day; if I spoke otherwise there would be no common truth or honesty in me." Then the man said: "They say that when you came to this place before you spoke so, and said 'We have been here before also'." "I have never said this," said the king, "and never will I say it." And the king was much moved, and clapped spurs to his horse immediately, and fled from the place as swiftly as he might'. *Flateyjarbok: Olafs Saga Helga*, II, c. 106, in H. R. Ellis, *Road to Hel*, p. 139.

Substitute victims are also sometimes encountered in ritual king-slaying. The legendary Swedish king, Aun or Ani of Uppsala, for example, dedicated nine of his sons to Othin, one after the other, every ten years, for a long life for himself; this ruler is a primary example of the early sacral ruler, for 'he was a wise man and much given to *blot*; he took no part in military expeditions, but governed his territories'. When the folk prevented the senile 'sacrificer of his sons', who had not the strength even to lift a drinking-horn but drank from its small end, from killing his tenth son, Aun died of old age.[121] That he was known in Anglo-Saxon England is demonstrated in the appearance in an Old English leechbook of *Anaþyrm* (On's Worm), 'when a man died of old age without agony', a reference to King Aun or Ani.[122] Another son-substitute appears when Jarl Haakon of Norway sacrificed his son Erling for victory in battle against the Jomsvikings at Hjorungavagr,[123] and a saga of the Netherlands tells of a king offering his oldest son to Mars (= Othin) for victory.[124] In contrast, King Heidrek the Wise offered the sacrifice of King Harald's army to Othin as a substitute for his own son.[125] When defeat in war or the failure of crops faced the Burgundians, however, deposition of the kings instead of sacrifice was the practice.[126] The point, however, is clear. Ritual king-slaying was a common custom in the North as a means of meeting tribal calamities when the 'luck' of the king and folk had deserted them; to restore the favour of Woden-Othin the king, whose responsibility that favour was, was offered to him.

In Anglo-Saxon England non-royal sacrifices to Woden have

[121] *Ynglingasaga*, c. 25 (29); E. Wessen, ed., p. 28. *Ynglingatal.* c, 13; C.P.B., I, p. 247.

[122] Frederik Grön, 'Remarks on the Earliest Medical Conditions in Norway and Iceland with Special Reference to British Influence', *Science, Medicine and History: Essays on the Evolution of Scientific Thought and Medical Practice written in honour of Charles Singer* (E. Ashworth Underwood, ed.; London, 1953), I, p. 152.

[123] *Heimskringla*, I, c. 337; Jan de Vries, 'Das Königtum', p. 294.

[124] J. de Vries, 'Das Königtum', p. 294.

[125] Christopher Tolkien, ed., *Saga Heiðreks Konungs ins Vitra* (London, 1960), pp. 25–26.

[126] Ammianus Marcellinus, Bk. XXVIII, c. 5 §14; see above, p. 15 and n. 31.

already been suggested.[127] However, the most dramatic, if problematic, royal offering to Woden is that of King Oswald of Northumbria by the great pagan warrior, Penda of Mercia. This Northumbrian ruler sheds some interesting light on a god-sprung king of the Conversion period. The *mana*-filled Oswald, *sanctissimus ac victoriosissimus rex*,[128] was much given to *blot*, for Bede tells us that he often remained in prayer from matins until day, *ubicumque sedens, supinas super genua sua manus habere solitus sit*.[129] The praying position of sitting with the palms of his hands turned upward on his knees suggests not the customary Christian posture for prayer but a ritual attitude perhaps used by his pagan predecessors in offering intercessions for the folk, particularly in view of the hand and knee as sacral objects associated with fertility.[130] Oswald's sacral hands were themselves undecayed after his death.[131] This king, noted for bringing victory to his folk, was a Christian of renowned devotion, but his father was the pagan Ethelfrith, who had slaughtered the monks of Bangor because they made *blot* to their God for his defeat, and his brother was the apostate Eanfrid. A Christian of such recent vintage might well have prayed in an ancestral manner and have associated himself with tribal notions on his responsibility for bringing victory

[127] See above, pp. 38–39.

[128] Bede, *Hist. Eccl.*, III, 7; King, ed., I, p. 354.

[129] *Hist. Eccl.*, III, 12; King, ed., I, p. 384.

[130] Dom Louis Gougaud, *Devotional and Ascetic Practices in the Middle Ages* (London, 1927), p. 32, n. 3, mentions this *modus orandi* of King Oswald, but it is not included in, or a parallel of, any of the seven attitudes of prayer analysed by Gougaud (pp. 2–31), nor does he give any other examples of it. On the hand and knee as sacral objects in the North, cf. O. Henssler, *Formen des Asylrechts*, pp. 100–101 (including references to Anglo-Saxon royal *handgrið*), 107–108 (on relation established between Athelstan of England and King Harald Fairhair's natural son, when the Anglo-Saxon ruler takes the latter on his knee). On the Last Judgement 'before the knee of Christ', cf. *Phoenix*, ll. 510–520.

[131] Bede, *Hist. Eccl.*, III, 6, in which his right hand is blessed for its generosity by Bishop Aidan and remains incorruptible after death; King, ed., I, p. 352. Anglo-Saxon Chronicle, *sub anno* 641 (MS. E); Earle and Plummer, eds., I, p. 27. The majority of Oswald's miracles after death were wrought by his uncorrupted right hand and arm; Wilfrid Bonser, *The Medical Background of Anglo-Saxon England* (London, 1963), pp. 185–186.

through his own relationship with the new God of battles. Thus, he had already, before his victory over the British Cadwallon at *Hefenfelth*, erected a cross with his own hands, perhaps in Christian *imitatio* of the cult-pillars, judgement pillars, and tree-cult of Germanic heathenism.[132] And even as he met his own death, he prayed *pro animabus exercitus sui*—not for the souls of his enemies, as might be expected of the model Christian, but for his own army, for whose victory the Woden-sprung king may have regarded himself as sacrificed. The fact that his dying words became a proverb—*Unde dicunt in proverbio: 'Deus miserere animabus, dixit Osuald cadens in terram'*,[133]—among his folk suggests they fitted in with the folk-beliefs of that recently pagan people.

It was at *Maserfelth* on August 5th, A.D. 642, that this king was slain, *pro patria dimicans*, by Penda of Mercia.[134] The pagan victor's treatment of the body of the dead monarch is of high interest: *caput et manus cum brachiis a corpore praecisas, iussit rex qui occiderat, in stipitibus suspendi*.[135] In this hanging of parts of the king's body we can almost undoubtedly detect a ritual offering to Woden the god of war and himself known as the Hanging God. The implications of Woden hanging on a tree need not be discussed here,[136] but we may observe that this form of offering was

---

[132] *Hist. Eccl.*, III, 2; King, ed., I, pp. 328–330. Heretofore *nullum fidei Christianae signum* had been erected among the Bernicians (pp. 330–332). On cult-pillars, etc., and the stone crosses in England as possible Christian variants, cf. O. Henssler, *Formen des Asylrechts*, pp. 67–68. The use of chips of wood from Oswald's cross, placed in water, as cures for sick men and animals relates to the sacral touch of the king in restoring the folk to health. B. Colgrave, *The Venerable Bede and his Times* (Jarrow Lecture, 1958; Newcastle-upon-Tyne, 1958), p. 12, suggests a native English derivation for the erection of these standing-crosses, beginning with wooden ones, such as Oswald's.

[133] *Hist. Eccl.*, III, 12; King, ed., I, p. 386.

[134] *Hist. Eccl.*, III, 9 (p. 368). *Maserfelth* has been identified with Oswestry (Oswald's Tree), although it is perhaps an unexpected site for the Northumbrians and Mercians to meet. If, however, Oswald were returning from another expedition against the Welsh, Penda might well have attacked him from the east. Oswald's victory over Cadwallon was, after all, at Chester.

[135] Bede, *Hist. Eccl.*, III, 12; King, ed., p. 386.

[136] See below, n. 137. On Othin (= Woden) as 'Lord of the Gallows', cf. Turville-Petre, *Myth and Religion of the North*, pp. 42–50.

apparently traditional for that deity. In Leire and Uppsala bodies of the dead were hung from trees as sacrifices to him,[137] and it has already been seen that King Vikar, in a ritual king-slaying arranged by the god himself, was suspended in the crown of a tree. Further, Procopius records that 'the noblest of sacrifices' in Thule—northern Scandinavia or Iceland—is the sacrifice to Ares (= Woden) of the first human to be captured in a war, and hanging the victim to a tree is, besides sacrificing on an altar, the first mode of execution mentioned.[138] Saxo Grammaticus notes that the northern Othin possessed magic pillars.[139] Further, a reminiscence of this cult of Woden and the possibility of the princely dead being hung on gallows may lie behind both Ongentheow's treatment of Haethcyn and the criminal on the gallows in *Beowulf*.[140] Oswald's decapitation has parallels in 'head-hunting' in the North, witnessed in England by the carrying away of the heads of Edwin of Northumbria and Earl Byrhtnoth after their deaths in battle.[141] The later burial of

[137] *Corpora autem suspenduntur in lucum, qui proximus est templo. . . . Ibi etiam canes et equi pendent cum hominibus, quorum corpora mixtim suspensa narravit mihi aliquis christianorum 72 vidisse*; Adam of Bremen, *Gesta Hammaburgensis Ecclesiae Pontificum*, Bk. IV, c. 27. A. G. van Hamel, 'Oðinn Hanging On a Tree', *Acta Philologica Scandinavica*, VII (1932–1933), p. 263. Cf. H. M. Chadwick, *The Cult of Othin*, pp. 3–4, 16–20, on sacrificial hangings to Woden.

[138] Procopius, *The Gothic War*, Bk. II (VI of the *History*), c. 15; H. B. Dewing, ed., *Procopius* (Loeb Classical Library; London, 1919), III, p. 420.

[139] On Othin as 'pillar-king', cf. E. Philippson, *Germ. Heid.*, p. 44. There is a possibility that overtones of northern pillar-cult remain in Christian references to 'pillars' of the Church. Cf., e.g., Alcuin to Archbishop Eanbald II of York, A.D. 796: *Esto columna firmissima in domo Dei*; *Mon. Ger. Hist., Epistolae*, IV, Ep. 116, p. 171. Of the recently discovered, impressive buildings at the Northumbrian *villa regia* of Yeavering, only one—significantly, the pagan temple, later converted to Christian use—had a double row of inner pillars; Rosemary J. Cramp, '*Beowulf* and Archaeology', *Medieval Archaeology*, I (1957), p. 71.

[140] *Beowulf*, ll. 2940 and 2444–2471, respectively. On the former, cf. Philippson, *Germ. Heid.*, p. 150, and on the latter, A. R. Taylor, 'Two Notes on *Beowulf*', *Leeds Studies in English*, VII–VIII (1952), pp. 5–13.

[141] The former by his friends, who buried it at York, the latter by his enemies, who carried it away with them after the Battle of Maldon; cf. H. M. and N. K. Chadwick, *The Growth of Literature* (Cambridge, 1932), I, pp. 93–94,

Oswald's divided body, like that of the Scandinavian Halfdan the Black and Edwin of Northumbria, may have been a ritual interment to provide good seasons in different sections of the realm he had ruled so notably.[142] Indeed, the very water in which his bones were washed gave to the earth on which it was poured *gratiae salutaris ... effectum.*[143]

There are, of course, difficulties in this interpretation of Penda's act. All other human sacrifices to Woden are of living men whose death becomes an oblation to the god; we know of no other hanging or other sacrifice of one already dead. Nonetheless, it may have been the completion of a dedicatory vow made before the battle by the Woden-worshipping Mercian king. Certainly, Penda ordered the king's head and hands with the arms placed *in stipitibus* for some reason, and no more plausible explanation has, I believe, been offered. Such an early connection between Woden and Oswald, finally, would help explain King Oswald's later role in folklore as a Christian Woden, both as a *Wetter-herr* in the Tyrol and in the assumption of Woden's sacral bird, the raven, as his own emblem.[144]

The role of the sacrificial king of heathenism thus continued in Anglo-Saxon England. Enmeshed in the folk's expectation of fertility and plenty, peace, and victory in battle, the monarch drew on ancient traditions of the Germanic peace-king, royal responsibility for the harvest, veneration for the body and mound

---

for these as well as examples among Scandinavians, Lombards, Gauls, and Celts. See above, p. 95.

[142] On division of the king's body, see above, pp. 95–96. Oswald's head was buried on Lindisfarne, his hands and arms in Bamburgh, and the rest of his body, translated from Bardney into Mercia (Anglo-Saxon Chronicle, *sub anno* 909), in St. Oswald's, Gloucester. Bede, *Hist. Eccl.*, III, 12; King, ed., p. 386; F. Liebermann, *Die Heiligen Englands* (Hanover, 1889), p. 10 (from text of *Þa halgan on Angelcynne*).

[143] *Hist. Eccl.*, III, 11; King, ed., p. 378.

[144] Carl A. Bernoulli, *Die Heiligen der Merowinger* (Tübingen, 1900), pp. 199–203. It is not known whether this union of Oswald and Woden occurred in England or only after Oswald's move, in folk-superstitions, to Bavaria and the Tyrol. On belief in 'royal weather', cf. Turville-Petre, *Myth and Religion*, p. 193.

I

of the *heil*-bringing king, sacrifice, ritual king-slaying, sanctuary and asylum associated with his sacral person, and divine intervention for victory obtained by the ruler. A religion which could absorb these prime features of the old politico-religious structure would meet with little open hostility when the king, the pivot of Germanic heathenism, was converted to it and led his folk to a more powerful God.

CHAPTER IV

The survival of royal cult-objects

The sacral king-cult of the deity-descended monarchs was also vested in cult-objects and symbols which served as another link tying the rulers into the two worlds. The association of such objects with rulership, like divine descent, enhanced its religious power. To understand this cult of kingship more fully, therefore, these cult-objects now need analysis. They were symbols not in the sense of a mere sign of the sacred king but rather as the touchstones of a dynamic relationship uniting the monarch to the divine sphere from which his *mana* flowed into him. The vitality of the gods and of the whole world of awe with which the ruler served as mediator for his folk was made palpable in the cult-objects and hence in him. Several of these were animals associated with that world.

The animals of sacral kingship may indeed be seen behind the Anglo-Saxon prophecy that 'to see any four-footed beast betokens a king's friendship'.[1] However, certain animals are peculiarly associated with the king, and of these one of the most important was the boar. In the magnificent ship-burial find of Sutton Hoo, for example, there are ten representations of boars among the grave-goods.[2] On the iron helmet, each of the bronze eyebrows ends above the cheek-guard in a small, stylized, gilt-bronze head of a boar;[3] further, on the beautifully worked clasps,

[1] Cotton MS. Tiberius A iii, fol. 29a; ed. by Oswald Cockayne, *Leechdoms, Wortcunning and Starcraft of Early England* (Rolls Series, Vol. XXXV:3; London, 1866), III, p. 211.

[2] On Sutton Hoo, see above, pp. 99-100.

[3] R. L. S. Bruce-Mitford, *The Sutton Hoo Ship Burial: A Handbook* (London, 1968), p. 27 and plate 16. Charles Green, *Sutton Hoo: The Excavation of a Royal Ship Burial* (London, 1963), plate X.

at each end of each clasp are two interlinked boars with tusks and crested backs, their bodies and haunches formed of plate-garnets. R. L. Bruce-Mitford points out that 'the crested spines on the animals and the lowered heads forcibly suggest a comparison with the late Saxon (eleventh century) boar on a tympanum at St. Nicholas Church, Ipswich'.[4] The boars on the Sutton Hoo royal helmet are particularly interesting for the parallel they present for both archaeological and literary evidence of Anglo-Saxon warrior helmets. The only other Anglo-Saxon helmet ever found in England, discovered at Benty Grange in 1848 and dating probably from the sixth century, is crowned by a free-standing model of a boar.[5] Scandinavian helmets of similar construction have been discovered but without the boar, so that the only boar-helmet of this type actually known is Anglo-Saxon. Swedish parallels exist, however, in the well-known boar-crested helmet portrayed on the Torslunda plates and the animal-headed

[4] Bruce-Mitford, *Sutton Hoo Ship Burial*, p. 65, plate D, and fig. 26. C. Green, *Sutton Hoo*, p. 81 and plate XXV. A boar's head appears also on a silver bracelet from Faversham, Kent (in British Museum tablecase, Bay XI).

[5] Rosemary J. Cramp, '*Beowulf* and Archaeology', *Medieval Archaeology*, I (1957), p. 59 and plate 10, A. The Sutton Hoo helmet is illustrated on plate 9, A. She correctly says of these two that 'their dating makes nonsense of the sort of chronology Stjerna attempted, whereby he takes the Celtic boar-helmet from the Gundestrup vessel of about the second century B.C. calling it "before A.D. 500" and then attempts to show the animal subsiding into the helmet after Benty Grange through the stage of losing its legs in the Öland plates until by the early seventh century it had become the terminal of a comb, such as one finds in the Vendel helmets, and at the close of the century had been lost altogether' (p. 59). On the Benty Grange helmet, cf. R. W. Chambers, *Beowulf: An Introduction to the Study of the Poem* (3rd ed., Cambridge, 1959), pp. 358-360; G. Baldwin Brown, *The Arts in Early England* (London, 1915), III, plate 21; L. V. Grinsell, *The Ancient Burial-Mounds of England* (2nd ed.; London, 1953), p. 228 (where an interment of c. A.D. 650 is suggested). The Benty Grange boar was at first thought to have been enamelled, but this notion was abandoned after further laboratory investigation; Françoise Henry, 'Irish Enamels of the Dark Ages and Their Relation to Cloisonné Techniques', *Dark Age Britain: Studies presented to E. T. Leeds* (D. B. Harden, ed.; London, 1956), p. 75. However, its eyes are of garnet in gold mountings, its shoulders and buttocks are covered by silver plates, and its flanks are surmounted by gilded silver studs.

helmet depicted on the Vendel helmet-plates.[6] Further, King Athal's helmet, taken from King Ali, in *Skaldskaparmal* is named Hildigölt ('battle-boar').[7]

Boar-helmets are familiar to the *Beowulf* poet as well, for he mentions the helmet-boar five times. He tells us *sofor-lic scionon / ofer hleor-ber(g)an: gehroden golde / fah ond fyr-heard, ferh-wearde heold: / guð-mod grummon*.[8] These gold boar-crests stood guard over the lives of the warriors who wore them not only because they may have warded off sword strokes, but, as shall be seen, because of the sacral nature of that animal. 'The swine all golden, the boar iron-hard' (*swyn eal-gylden, / eofer iren-heard*) appears again in *Beowulf* (ll. 1111–1112) on the funeral pyre of Hnaef the Scylding, and the helmet of Beowulf himself is *besette swin-licum*. This suggests more than one boar on the helmet and may refer to the Sutton Hoo type of boar-topped cheek-guards.[9] However, when the poet says *sweord swate fah swin ofer helme* (the sword stained with gore the swine above the helmet),[10] the parallel summoned is the freestanding boar on top of the Benty Grange helm. The Old English *Elene* also speaks of the *eofor-cumbol*, once as a boar-shaped helmet-badge and once as a boar-banner.[11] But the point is clear: Anglo-Saxon warriors wore boar-helmets, both crowned and decorated with representations of that animal, and both archaeology and literature of pre-Norman England testify

[6] H. Shetelig and H. Falk, *Scandinavian Archaeology* (E. V. Gordon, transl.; Oxford, 1937), p. 259 and plate 243. Cf. the older Gundestrup bowl; H. M. Chadwick, *The Origin of the English Nation* (Cambridge, 1924), p. 233.

[7] *Skaldskaparmal*, c. 43; A. G. Brodeur, ed., *The Prose Edda by Snorri Sturluson* (Scandinavian Classics, Vol. V; New York, 1916), p. 171.

[8] Beowulf, ll. 303–306; for textual problems and meaning, cf. C. L. Wrenn, ed., *Beowulf* (London, 1953), pp. 191–192. If the boar-images are over the cheek-guards (*ofer hleorberan*), they are probably like the Sutton Hoo helmet-boars.

[9] *Beowulf*, l. 1453. R. J. Cramp, '*Beowulf* and Archaeology', p. 62.

[10] *Beowulf*, l. 1286.

[11] *Elene*, ll. 76 (*eofurcumble*), 259; G. P. Krapp, ed., *The Vercelli Book* (Anglo-Saxon Poetic Records, Vol. II; London, 1932), pp. 68, 73. For the meaning of O.E. *cumbol*, cf. Otto Springer, 'Old Norse Kumbla-Smiðr "Helmet-Smith": The Story of a Kenning', *Journal of English and Germanic Philology*, L (1951), p. 237.

to these. The *Beowulf* poet makes clear that this animal served as protection for the wearer.

The boar is also associated with banners by the Anglo-Saxons. A boar banner is one of the gifts of Hrothgar to Beowulf,[12] and in *Elene* the Emperor Constantine sleeps under his boar-banner (*He of slaepe onbraegd, eofurcumble bepeaht*).[13] A military emblem decorated with a boar parallels this type of standard on a Roman triumphal relief in the Vatican Museum, where the boar insigne is next to a captive Germanic tribesman.[14] The oldest Germanic banners were the *effigies et signa* taken from the sacred groves and carried before the tribal armies, and some of these were no doubt animal fetishes.[15]

Why, then, does the boar occur on helmets and banners of the Anglo-Saxons in particular and of Germanic tribes generally? The answer is to be found in the ancient cult of the Teutonic mother-goddess and its later derivatives. Tacitus reports that the Aestii, on the shore of the Suebic Sea, worship a mother-goddess and 'as an emblem of that superstition they wear the figures of wild boars: this boar takes the place of arms or of any other protection, and guarantees to the votary of the goddess a mind at rest even in the midst of foes'.[16] The Aestii are said to have the same religion and general customs as the Suebi, and the common cult of many of the Suebic tribes was that of the mother-goddess Nerthus, whose festive procession has been discussed.[17] The procession of Frey in the later Scandinavian North, like that of Nerthus and derived from it, was a fertility rite bringing plenty to the regions it visited, and the sacred animal of Frey was the boar. Both Frey and the goddess Freyja, who may represent an intermediate stage between Nerthus and Frey, rode on boars. Frey rode on his boar, Gullinbursti ('Gold bristles') or Sliðrugtanni ('Fearful tusk'), to

---

[12] *Beowulf*, l. 2152: *Het ða in beran eafor, heafodsegn.*

[13] *Elene*, l. 259.

[14] O. Springer, 'Old Norse Kumbla-Smiðr', p. 237; it is illustrated in L. Stacke, *Deutsche Geschichte* (Bielefeld and Leipzig, 1880), I, pp. 56–57.

[15] Tacitus, *Germania*, c. 7; M. Hutton, ed., *Tacitus: Germania* (Loeb Classical Library; London, 1946), p. 274. See below on the boar of the Aestii.

[16] *Germania*, c. 45; M. Hutton, ed., p. 329.

[17] *Germania*, c. 40. See above, p. 88.

Baldur's funeral, according to the late-tenth-century *Husdrapa* of Ulf Uggason,[18] and in the *Hyndluljoð* Freyja rides her gold-bristled boar, Hildisvini ('Battle-swine'), which is really her protege Ottarr in the form of Frey's boar.[19] Furthermore, after Yule Eve the greatest boar was sacrificed to Frey as the *sonargoltr*, the 'atonement boar',[20] to persuade the god to grant a good year, and it was on the head and bristles of this sacral animal that King Heidrek and his followers placed their hands and took their most solemn oaths.[21] In Valhöll, *Grimnismal* and *Gylfaginning* tell us, the warriors feed on the boar Saehrimnir, which never diminishes no matter how much is consumed.[22]

The boar thus stands out clearly as the animal *par excellence* of the mother-goddess of the Aestii, of Frey and Freyja, and of the fertility cult which all of these represent.[23] Like the pig, it is a form

---

[18] *Husdrapa* in *Skaldskaparmal*, cc. 7, 35; *C.P.B.*, II, p. 23. Cf. *Skaldskaparmal*, c. 44. Cf. Lee M. Hollander, *The Skalds* (Princeton, N.J., 1947), pp. 52–53; M. Mallet, *Northern Antiquities* (Bishop Percy, transl.; new ed. by I. A. Blackwell; London, 1859), p. 448.

[19] *C.P.B.*, I, pp. 227, 233; G. N. Garmonsway, 'Old Norse Jarðarmen', *The Early Cultures of North-West Europe: H. M. Chadwick Memorial Studies* (Sir Cyril Fox and Bruce Dickins, eds.; Cambridge, 1950), p. 424.

[20] *C.P.B.*, I, pp. 405–406. On boar-sacrifice among the Franks, cf. K. Helm, *Altgermanische Religionsgeschichte* (Heidelberg, 1953), II:1, p. 197. Cf. the boar's head procession at Christmas in medieval England and still today at Queen's College, Oxford.

[21] *C.P.B.*, I, pp. 405–406. Swearing on the head of an animal *ut est gentilium consuetudo* is condemned by the Synod of Orleans, A.D. 511; K. Helm, *Altgermanische Religionsgeschichte*, II:1, p. 204. Cf. bristles of swine falling out as prophecy of loss in 'experiment' by Theodatus the Goth; Procopius, *The Gothic War*, II (Bk. V of the *History*), c. 9; H. Dewing, ed., III, pp. 82–84. On Heiðrek's oath, cited in *C.P.B.*, etc., above, cf. *Heiðreks konungssaga (Hauksbok)*, c. 10; C. Tolkien, ed., *Saga Heiðreks Konungs ins Vitra* (London, 1960), pp. 30–31. Judgement at Heiðrek's court was to be given by twelve counsellors who tended the boar.

[22] *Grimnismal*, appendix 2; *C.P.B.*, I, p. 75. *Gylfaginning*, c. 38; A. G. Brodeur, ed., *Prose Edda*, p. 50.

[23] The most complete study of the Germanic boar is Heinrich Beck, *Das Ebersignum im Germanischen: Ein Beitrag Zur Germanischen Tier-Symbolik* (Quellen und Forschungen zur Sprach- und Kulturgeschichte der Germanischen Völker, N.F., Vol. XVI (CXL); Berlin, 1955). For good surveys of the boar

of the grain-spirit in Europe and the animal primarily associated with harvest and fertility, a role it may have come to play by its own reputation for fertility and reproduction.[24] Although its associations are not limited to the monarch, its close identification with king-cult demands special emphasis. It is associated with fertility and plenty, for which the Germanic king sacrificed and with which his own cult was so closely enmeshed. The Swedish king was credited with the same powers over good seasons which were held by Frey, whose representative every Uppsala king was. To Woden, ancestor of the Anglo-Saxon royal houses, the boar's head is ascribed as an emblem by Saxo Grammaticus,[25] which may well relate to the boar as protector of warriors and consequently to the king as war-chief and bringer of victory. In England boars appear on the helmet buried in the royal cenotaph at Sutton Hoo; since the identity of the Benty Grange interment is unknown, it may be conjectured that he also was of royal stock. The boar-banner of *Elene* marks the emperor, as the *Beowulf*'s boar-banner was the gift of one chieftain to another. The Old Norse *jöfurr*, the equivalent of the Anglo-Saxon *eofor* ('boar') survived only in poetic language as a word for a chief.[26] The royal house of the Merovingians was reputed to have bristles on its spine, like boars, probably a reminiscence of the primitive ritual battle in which the king slew his predecessor, impersonating the god during the struggle in the guise of the deity's sacral animal.[27]

---

and its role, cf. Chadwick, *Origin*, pp. 232–234; K. Helm, *Altgermanische Religionsgeschichte*, pp. 73–76; O. Höfler, *Germanisches Sakralkönigtum* (Tübingen, 1952), I, pp. 95–99, 139.

[24] James Hastings, ed., *Encyclopaedia of Religion and Ethics* (Edinburgh, 1908), I, pp. 524–525 (under 'Animals').

[25] Oliver and F. York Powell, eds., *The Nine Books of the Danish History of Saxo Grammaticus* (London, 1905), I, p. xlix. On the relation of head of cult-animals to 'luck', sacrifice, and surviving folk customs, cf. A. W. Smith, 'The Luck in the Head: A Problem in English Folklore', *Folklore*, LXXIII (1962), pp. 13–24, which includes the Hornchurch, Essex, boar's head procession and wrestling for the head.

[26] Shetelig and Falk, *Scandinavian Archaeology*, p. 305.

[27] The Merovingians as χριστάται go back to Theophanes, although independent traditions seem to exist. J. Grimm, *Deutsche Mythologie* (2nd ed.;

Indeed the boar is so identified with Germanic sacral kingship that its appearance in Anglo-Saxon England with royal graves and banners and with boar-helmeted warriors led by the royal war-chief leads one to conclude that knowledge of its magical, god- and king-associated role continued into Christian times.

The same can be said of the dragon, although with less certainty. The so-called 'dragon of Wessex' makes its first appearance in surviving written records in Henry of Huntingdon's twelfth century account of the Battle of Burford in A.D. 752. There the forces of Cuthred of Wessex were preceded into battle against Aethelbald of Mercia by the *ealdorman* Edelhun *regis insigne draconem scilicet aureum gerens*.[28] Although this does not appear in the Anglo-Saxon Chronicle nor later accounts such as Florence of Worcester and William of Malmesbury, Professor J. S. P. Tatlock regards it as the sort of detail, especially considering its connection with the otherwise known *ealdorman*, which is pro-bably derived from a no longer extant source.[29] It is also Henry of Huntingdon who reports of the Battle of Assandun in A.D. 1016 that Edmund Ironside dashed into the struggle against Cnut, *loco regio relicto, quod erat ex more inter draconem et insigne quod vocatur* Standard.[30] The dragon banner as a royal emblem serving

Göttingen, 1844), p. 364. George L. Hamilton, 'The Royal Mark of the Merovingians and Kindred Phenomena', *Medieval Studies in Memory of Gertrude Schoepperle Loomis* (New York, 1927), pp. 301–316. Cf. Beck, *Ebersignum*, pp. 148–153. On the marriage of Ottarr, who was disguised as a boar, with the king's widow, cf. A. Ohlmarks, *Heimdalls Horn und Odins Auge* (Lund and Copenhagen, 1937), I, pp. 104–105, 109. The long hair of the Merovingians is a possible survival of the boar-king's embodiment of the fertility deity. On boar-sacrifice among the Franks, suggested by higher penalty in the *Lex Salica* (2, 12) for theft of the *majalis sacrivus* or *votivus*, cf. K. Helm, *Alt-germanische Religionsgeschichte*, II:1, p. 197.

[28] T. Arnold, ed., *History of the English, by Henry, Archdeacon of Huntingdon* (Rolls Series, Vol. LXXIV; London, 1879), p. 121 (Bk. IV, c. 19). J. S. P. Tatlock, 'The Dragons of Wessex and Wales', *Speculum*, VIII (1933), p. 225.

[29] Tatlock, 'Dragons', p. 225.

[30] T. Arnold, ed., *History of the English, by Henry, Archdeacon of Huntingdon*, p. 184; Tatlock, 'Dragons', p. 225. Friedrich Wild, 'Das Drachenfeldzeichen als "Königstandarte" in England', *Moderne Sprachen*, VII (1963), pp. 133–160. For the Anglo-Saxon royal standard, see below.

as a rallying point in battle is confirmed by the scene of the Battle of Hastings on the Bayeux Tapestry. There Harold II is seen fighting under a pennant-style standard which clearly is a dragon.

Although it has been demonstrated that the term 'dragon of Wessex' is entirely modern, stemming probably from Freeman,[31] two things are clear. Each reference shows that the dragon was the mark of the king, locating his position in battle and serving as the emblem of the monarch himself, the *regis insigne*. Secondly, the late term 'dragon of Wessex' has confused the problem, since there is no indication it was used in that kingdom alone. It was not Wessex the dragon was peculiar to but the king. Indeed, at Burford, Ealdorman Edelhun, who bore the West Saxon golden dragon, stabbed the standard-bearer of Mercia; no information survives of its description, but it is at least possible that Aethelbald of Mercia also flew the same animal figure.

The earliest Germanic 'literary' dragons—those of *Beowulf* and the *Finnsburg Fragment*[32]—are both in Anglo-Saxon poems, whatever their original residence. Indeed, Knut Stjerna, whose *Beowulf* studies have usually underlined the Scandinavian features of the poem, nonetheless regarded the hero's fight with the dragon as of Anglo-Saxon origin.[33] Early English familiarity with this common Germanic beast is verified in place-name investigations. Anglo-Saxon charters place locations *to þes dracon horde* (Birch 817, c. A.D. 940) and *aet dracan hlawan* (Birch 772, A.D. 942), the modern Drakelow in Derbyshire, while the dragon has also insinuated himself into Drakelow and Drake's Cross (both in Worcestershire), Drakenedge (Warwickshire), Drakestone (Gloucestershire), Dragley Beck (Lancashire), Drake's Island (Devonshire), and Drakeholes (Nottinghamshire).[34] Surely their presence

---

[31] Tatlock, 'Dragons', p. 227.

[32] *Beowulf*, ll. 2200 ff.; *Finnsburg Fragment*, ll. 3 ff.

[33] K. Stjerna, *Essays on Questions connected with the O.E. Poem of Beowulf* (J. R. Clark Hall, transl.; Coventry, 1912), p. 39.

[34] For these as well as Scottish and Irish place-names, cf. E. Philippson, *Germanisches Heidentum bei den Angelsachsen* (*Kölner Anglistische Arbeiten*, Vol. IV; Leipzig, 1929), p. 88; C. H. Whitman, 'The Old English Animal Names', *Anglia*, XXX (1907), pp. 389-390, has collected Anglo-Saxon dragon references. The burial-mound Dragon Hill, below the White Horse and Uffington

was believed in by a people who located them geographically and who saw *fyrene dracan on þam lyfte fleogende* (fiery dragons flying through the air) as a portent of coming famine, as the Anglo-Saxon Chronicle reports *sub anno* 793.[35]

Without entering into the celebrated controversy over the significance of the *Beowulf* dragon and its possible role as a symbol of evil,[36] one may affirm that it shares its primary function with other dragons of the North. They have one of their principal *raisons d'etre* as protectors of treasure-hoards in burial mounds. As Beowulf's adversary 'for three hundred years held the vast treasure-hall under the earth',[37] and as a self-respecting dragon did not sally forth against humans until his hoard was disturbed, so one of their principal tasks is to guard the ancestral treasure buried in cairns and to ravage the countryside when their permanent occupation is interrupted. Thus the dragon of Old English lore proverbially is a hoard-protector; *draca sceal on hlaewe, frod, fraetwum wlanc*, as a gnomic verse asserts.[38]

This role as the guardian of gold is as old as Herodotus, who tells of 'gold-guarding griffins' (χρυσοφύλακες γρύπες) occupying the extreme north of Europe or Asia.[39] The evidence of folk-lore

Castle in Berkshire, is the legendary site of St. George's slaying the dragon. Undoubtedly the dragon was there first, as the mound-dwelling guardian of the hoard, and St. George was a later comer, added by accretion to local lore. Cf. Wilhelm Jordans, *Der Germanische Volksglaube von den Toten und Dämonen im Berg und Ihrer Beschwichtigung* (*Bonner Studien zur Englischen Philologie*, Vol. XVII; Bonn, 1933), pp. 45-47, on dragons in Burford, Northleigh, Strathmartin (in Scotland), and Wharncliff.

[35] MSS. D, E, F; Earle and Plummer, eds., I, pp. 55-57.

[36] Cf., e.g., J. R. R. Tolkien, 'Beowulf: The Monsters and the Critics', *Proceedings of the British Academy*, XXII (1936), pp. 245-295; Adrien Bonjour, 'Monsters Crouching and Critics Rampant: Or the *Beowulf* Dragon Debated', *PMLA*, LXVIII (1953), pp. 304-312.   [37] *Beowulf*, ll. 2278-2280.

[38] *Maxims* II, ll. 26-27; Elliott Van Kirk Dobbie, ed., *The Anglo-Saxon Minor Poems* (Anglo-Saxon Poetic Records, Vol. VI; New York, 1942), p. 56. On dragons and mounds, cf. H. R. Ellis Davidson, 'The Hill of the Dragon: Anglo-Saxon Burial Mounds in Literature and Archaeology', *Folk-Lore*, LXI (1950), pp. 179-182.

[39] Herodotus, *The Histories*, III, 116; IV, 13, 27. H. M. Chadwick, *The Heroic Age* (Cambridge, 1912), p. 127, n. 2. On the Germanic dragon, cf. K. Helm, *Altgermanische Religionsgeschichte*, II:1, pp. 70-73.

and legend points to the dragon as the inhabitant of tombs and perhaps the incarnation of the spirit of the great man interred in the mound.[40] The princely dead guards his hoard against any who breaks into the cairn, and to do so he takes the monstrous form of the dragon. Its treasure was the princely treasure of the howe, its residence was the howe of the great departed, and its presence was associated with death.[41] Thus when the dragon, related as it is to burial mounds, death, heroes, and the spirits of the great departed, fluttered over the Anglo-Saxon monarch, marking the king as his *regis insigne*, 'who knows', in the words of Professor Tatlock, 'what primitivenesses may have been in the Anglo-Saxon mind?'[42]

There is also evidence for the stag as a cult-animal of Anglo-Saxon sacral kingship. On top of the iron 'standard', generally recognized as a royal insigne, found in the Sutton Hoo ship-burial stands a bronze stag with widespread antlers.[43] This stag emblem in a royal cenotaph brings to mind the great hall of King Hrothgar, known as Heorot (Hart-Hall) in *Beowulf*.[44] It has been suggested that the Celtic deity Kerunnos ('horn-god'), to whom stags were sacrificed, was known to the Germans under the guise of Frey, who used a stag-horn to slay the giant Beli, but the

[40] Chadwick, *Heroic Age*, p. 127, n. 2; E. Salin, *La Civilisation Mérovingienne* (Paris, 1949), II, p. 233. The dragons of the *Gull-Thoris Saga* were once Vikings but had changed themselves into dragons to guard their gold; R. W. Chambers, *Beowulf*, p. 458. Cf. Fafnir in the Siegfried story.

[41] R. B. Onians, *The Origins of European Thought* (Cambridge, 1951), pp. 155–156, n. 4.

[42] Tatlock, 'Dragons', p. 227, although he does not make these associations. On the possible relationship of the dragon, connected with rain and lightning, and the guardian spirits of the fields and crops, cf. Ladislaus Mittner, *Wurd. Das Sakrale in der Altgermanischen Epik* (Bern, 1955), p. 57; this is another link with the sacral king. In the beast's Christianization, he is sometimes the form taken by the Devil; thus in Aelfric, II, 176, 23–25; *þa mynster-munceas urnon to, and swa-ðeah nateshwon þone dracan ne gesawon, forðan þaet waes se ungesewenlica deofol*; Nelius O. Halvorson, *Doctrinal Terms in Aelfric's Homilies* (Iowa City, Iowa, 1932), p. 30.

[43] Bruce-Mitford, *Sutton Hoo Ship Burial*, p. 20 and plate 2 a, b; C. Green, *Sutton Hoo*, pp. 66–68 and plate VIII. On the 'standard', see below, pp. 142–143.

[44] *Beowulf*, l. 78.

evidence is too slim for this to be more than conjecture.[45] The same holds for Philippson's connection of Heorot with the Ing cult of the Ingvaeones and consequently of the Angles and Saxons,[46] but it may not be without significance that in northern mythology four harts gnaw the high shoots of the tree Yggdrasil.[47] The hart may well have been the divine ancestor of the tribe of the Cherusci, and that animal is associated in many ways with the hero Sigurð.[48] The reminiscence of an early stag cult is probably still to be seen in the antlers used in stag-impersonation by Morris Dancers in England, but an Anglo-Saxon origin for these dances is uncertain. Certainly such impersonation was a heathen practice on the Continent, where the horns and hide of the stag were donned for heathen festivities at the New Year. The Church preached against the custom *in cervulo ambulare* and *cervulum facere*, and Caesarius of Arles forbade stags and other *portenta* to go in procession.[49] The stag as guide appears in Frankish and Germanic legends.[50] It is Christianized in the cult of St. Hubert, but the *Corrector* of Burchard of Worms (d. A.D. 1025) still asks, 'Hast thou done anything like what the pagans did, and still do, on the first of January, in (the guise of) a stag or a calf?'[51] Further, on a seventh-century Lombard sarcophagus

---

[45] *Gylfaginning*, c. 37; Brodeur, ed., p. 49. Philippson, *Germ. Heid.*, pp. 90–91.

[46] Philippson, *Germ. Heid.*, p. 91.

[47] *Grimnismal*, cc. 27, 29; *C.P.B.*, I, p. 73.

[48] E. O. G. Turville-Petre, *Myth and Religion of the North: The Religion of Ancient Scandinavia* (New York, 1964), pp. 199, 204–205.

[49] For references and discussion, cf. K. Helm, *Altgermanische Religionsgeschichte*, II:1, pp. 82–85. The first source for Germanic regions is Eligius of Noyon (d. A.D. 659) for northern France. However, the Council of Auxerre of A.D. 578 forbade dressing up as a stag or calf on the kalends of January; cf. M. Deanesly and P. Grosjean, 'The Canterbury Edition of the Answers of Pope Gregory I to St. Augustine', *Journal of Ecclesiastical History*, X (1959), pp. 21, 22 n. 3, 23 n. 3.

[50] K. Helm, *Altgermanische Religionsgeschichte*, II:1, p. 82.

[51] *Corrector*, c. 99. The best single guide to pagan practices in the Middle Ages, the *Corrector* is Bk. 19 of Burchard's *Decretum*; it is edited by John T. McNeill and Helena M. Gamer, eds., *Medieval Handbooks of Penance* (Records of Civilization, no. 29; New York, 1938), pp. 321–345; above reference, p. 334. The calf reference is reminiscent of the bull's heads on the Sutton Hoo 'standard';

from Civezzano, now in the Tiroler Landesmuseum in Innsbruck, an iron stag-head with horns stands erect at each end of the sarcophagus.[52] Whatever the association of the stag or hart with fertility and the new year, with Frey, with dedicated deaths, or with primitive animal-gods cannot now be determined with any certainty. What is certain, however, is that the two stags most prominent from Anglo-Saxon times are both connected with kings, the emblem surmounting the unique 'standard' in the royal cenotaph of Sutton Hoo and the great hall of Heorot in *Beowulf*.

To the Woden-descended Anglo-Saxon monarch the raven of his divine ancestor might be thought to be of special symbolic significance. It is in Scandinavia primarily, however, and not England that the raven as a sacral bird is found.[53] The capture of the Danish flag called the Raven is recorded in the Anglo-Saxon Chronicle *sub anno* A.D. 878;[54] it was said to have been woven by the two daughters of Ragnar Lothbrok, whose death, as we have seen, may itself have been modelled after dedications to Woden.[55] When it flapped in the wind, victory was believed in the offing, but when it hung lifeless, the omen was for evil.[56] The Saga of Olaf Tryggvason tells of a raven flag made by Eithne, Jarl Hlödver's wife, which flew above the Viking invaders of Ireland. When it was carried at the Battle of Clontarf in A.D. 1014, Hrafn the Red called it the devil because all who carried it were

cf. Bruce-Mitford, *Sutton Hoo Ship Burial*, p. 20 and fig. 5. On Merovingian steer-cult, cf. K. Helm, *Altgermanische Religionsgeschichte*, II:1, pp. 77–78.

[52] Illustrated in Percy Ernst Schramm, *Herrschaftszeichen und Staatssymbolik* (*Schriften der Monumenta Germaniae Historica*, Vol. XIII:1; Stuttgart, 1954), I, plate 16, fig. 21 a, b.

[53] On the *hravnblots goði* (the priest of the raven-*blot*), cf. Ake V. Ström, 'The King God and his Connection with Sacrifice in Old Norse Religion', *The Sacral Kingship* (Leiden, 1959), p. 711, n. 71.

[54] Earle and Plummer, eds., I, p. 77; only MS. A omits reference to it. A. H. Krappe, 'Arturus Cosmocrator', *Speculum*, XX (1945), pp. 408–409, where references to the Raven banner are collected.

[55] See above, p. 40.

[56] An interpolation in Asser, *De Rebus Gestis Aelfredi*, c. 54b; W. Stevenson, ed., *Asser's Life of King Alfred* (Oxford, 1904), p. 44. *Annals of St. Neot sub anno* 878; *ibid.*, p. 138.

slain.[57] Cnut the Great was also accompanied by a raven banner.[58] The raven was an emblem of Othin—known as *Hrafnass* (the raven god)—who was accompanied by two of these birds, Huginn and Muninn, 'Thought' and 'Mind'.[59] A bird generally identified as Othin's raven replaces the Roman winged Victory on sixth- and seventh-century Scandinavian golden bracteates, which were derived from Roman imperial medallions.[60] Thus the battle-bird of the divine victory-bringer of the North is a Germanic parallel and translation of the *Victoria* of the South.

Thus in Anglo-Saxon poetic references to the raven as the bird of battle, one must be careful before assuming it is there merely as a carrion-bird. To Woden belong the dead of battle, and the raven is probably there in reminiscence of his cult-bird, as it also may have been present at the Wild Hunt, to whose leadership legend has assigned Woden.[61] 'The raven screamed aloft, black and greedy for corpses. . . . The raven rejoiced in the work,' says the Anglo-Saxon *Elene*,[62] and *Judith* speaks of 'the dark raven, the bird greedy for slaughter'.[63] As the sign of death it is seen in the *Soul's Address to the Body:* 'Thou art not more dear as a comrade to any living man . . . than the dark raven.'[64] Its peculiar character

[57] Krappe, 'Arturus Cosmocrator', p. 408; Joseph Anderson, *The Orkneyinga Saga* (Edinburgh, 1873), p. 210.

[58] A. Campbell, ed., *Encomium Emmae Reginae* (Camden Third Series, Vol. LXXII; London, 1949), pp. 24 (Bk. II, c. 9), 96–97 (Appendix Vb).

[59] *Grimnismal*, c. 3; *C.P.B.*, I, p. 75. *Ynglingasaga*, c. 7; E. Wesen, ed., p. 10. On the raven as Othin's bird, cf. Turville-Petre, *Myth and Religion*, pp. 57–60, 249, 258.

[60] N. Lukman, 'The Raven Banner and the Changing Ravens', *Classica et Mediaevalia*, XIX (1958), p. 133.

[61] Krappe, 'Arturus Cosmocrator', pp. 410–411.

[62] *Elene*, ll. 52–53, 110; G. P. Krapp, ed., pp. 67–69.

[63] *Judith*, ll. 206–207; Dobbie, ed., *Beowulf and Judith* (Anglo-Saxon Poetic Records, Vol. IV; London, 1954), p. 105.

[64] *Soul and Body* I, ll. 52–54; G. P. Krapp, ed., p. 56. *Soul and Body* II, ll. 49–51; G. P. Krapp and E. V. K. Dobbie, *The Exeter Book* (Anglo-Saxon Poetic Records, Vol. III; London, 1936), p. 176. For these and other references to ravens (and their associations with Woden) in Old English Poetry, cf. J. S. Ryan, 'Othin in England: Evidence from the Poetry for a Cult of Woden in Anglo-Saxon England', *Folklore*, LXXXIV (1963), pp. 468–472.

as a more than natural associate of death and battle is seen in its role as prophet of the old religion. In the early *Life of St. Gregory*, written between A.D. 680 and 714 by an anonymous monk of Whitby and one of the very earliest pieces of literature in England, it is narrated that when King Edwin of Northumbria was on his way to Church one Sunday, for the catechizing of those still heathen, a crow 'sang with an evil omen'. The whole company with the king stopped in the street to listen to it, until Bishop Paulinus gave the order to a servant, 'Shoot an arrow carefully into the bird'. He later brought the bird and arrows into the hall and, showing them to the heathen catechumens, 'proved that they should know by so clear a sign that the ancient evil of idolatry was worthless to anybody', since the bird 'did not know that it sang of death for itself' and so could not prophecy anything for those 'baptized in the image of God'.[65] Obviously a heathen Anglo-Saxon belief existed that a crow or raven, which is of the crow family, had the gift of foretelling the future and was one of the 'idolatries' which Paulinus had to combat. In parallel among other Germanic tribes, a crow sitting on a tree prophesied to Hermigisel, king of the Warni, who died c. A.D. 500, that the king would die after forty days.[66] Gregory of Tours refers to observation of birds for prophetic signs as a custom of the Franks.[67]

Further, a raven (*corvus*), obviously an enemy of the faith, stole a page of writing from Wilfrid, when he was St. Guthlac's guest, but it was found again by a miracle.[68] These two early sources, both written at the time of the transition from paganism to Christianity, support the notion of the pagan role of the raven.

[65] *Life of St. Gregory*, c. 15; translated in Whitelock, ed., *Engl. Hist. Doc.*, p. 688. For date, *ibid.*, p. 687.

[66] Procopius, *De Bello Gothico*, IV, 20; for this and other prophetic birds, cf. K. Helm, *Altgermanische Religionsgeschichte*, II:1, p. 161.

[67] *Historia Francorum*, VII, 29; Helm, *Altgermanische Religionsgeschichte*, II:1, p. 162.

[68] B. Colgrave, ed., *Felix's Life of St. Guthlac* (Cambridge, 1956), pp. 116–118 (c. 37). This *Vita* was probably written between A.D. 730 and 740; *ibid.*, p. 19. A raven was also among the animals, including the boar, stag, wolf, and horse (the latter two also Othin's sacral animals), which troubled St. Guthlac (c. 36).

When it is recalled that Woden was god of magic and prophecy and that the raven was his sacral agent, the Anglo-Saxon raven indeed suggests a survival of an older cult-object of Woden-sprung kingship. The ruler who sacrificed to that god for victory on the field of battle recognized the cult-bird as it flew overhead, and the knowledge may well have permeated the literature of Christian times.

Among the cult-objects of Anglo-Saxon kingship royal insignia other than animals demand consideration: the throne, the crown and helmet, the standard and banner, the sceptre and staff, the shield, the harp, and the ring. In early England the throne plays little role in the remaining sources. When the German coronation *ordo* was revised for King Edgar's rite in A.D. 973, the earlier formula, *Sta et retine locum*, was changed so that *locum* was replaced with the even less precise *statum*; it was not until the so-called 'Anselm-Ordo' of A.D. 1100 that *locum* was reinserted and a reference to the *regale solium* added.[69] An Anglo-Saxon throne is shown on no royal seal before Edward the Confessor, who is seated on a cushioned but backless throne-bench on a seal imitated from that of Cnut the Great, which in its turn was influenced by that of the Emperor Conrad II.[70] Nonetheless, the Anglo-Saxon throne is enhanced by a special character which can only be related to the sacred nature of its occupant.

The role of the throne in Early English literature supports this. Grendel, in *Beowulf*, for example, could not approach the royal throne 'because of God', undoubtedly, as shall be seen later, a reminiscence of sacral regalia related to the sanctuary of the royal presence itself, which no homicide could approach.[71] A *heahsetl* is

[69] P. E. Schramm, *Herrschaftszeichen*, III, p. 929.

[70] Schramm, *Herrschaftszeichen*, pp. 929-930; F. E. Harmer, ed., *Anglo-Saxon Writs* (Manchester, 1952), pp. 94-101. The Confessor's seal is illustrated in A. B. Wyon and Allan Wyon, *The Great Seals of England from the Earliest Period to the Present Times* (London, 1887), plate 1 and description on pp. 3-4. Cf. also Reginald Lane Poole, *Studies in Chronology and History* (Oxford, 1934), pp. 107-108.

[71] William A. Chaney, 'Grendel and the Gifstol: A Legal View of Monsters', *PMLA*, LXXVII (1962), pp. 513-520; Robert M. Estrich, 'The Throne of Hrothgar—*Beowulf*, ll. 168-169', *Journal of English and Germanic Philology*, XLIII

the one thing bestowed specifically by Finn on Hengest and the Danes in his peace with them, other than control of half his land and a hall,[72] as a house and *bregostol* are granted with lands to Beowulf by Hygelac upon the hero's return.[73] After the death of Heardred, he *let ðone bregostol Biowulf healdan*,[74] as though holding the *bregostol* was the formal entry into rulership, as later King Cnut 'entered the city (London) and sat on the throne of the kingdom'.[75] When Hygd had offered the realm to Beowulf, the *bregostol* and the treasure were the only specific prizes to be mentioned as accompanying the *rice*.[76] As Professor Estrich has pointed out, it is the throne, the *gifstol*, which is the centre of the formal ceremonies binding the war-band to the lord in the Exeter *Gnomes*, as it is the homage to the gifstol and rewards from it of which the Wanderer dreams.[77] This 'gift-stool' in pagan times was a kind of altar of the chief who made gifts to the gods he served, so that in the Christian age as well the connotations of

---

(1944), pp. 384–389, is the only commentator with whom I am familiar in the vast *Beowulf* scholarship who has understood these lines, which Wrenn describes as 'one of the greater unsolved cruces of the poem'. The following references to the throne in *Beowulf*, *Wanderer*, and the Exeter *Gnomes* have been collected by Estrich, pp. 386–387. For the problem of asylum and the king, see below, chapter VI, 'Sacral Kingship in Anglo-Saxon Law'.

[72] *Beowulf*, l. 1087.

[73] *Beowulf*, l. 2196.

[74] *Beowulf*, l. 2389.

[75] *Cnuto autem ciuitatem intrauit, et in solio regni resedit*; Alistair Campbell, ed., *Encomium Emmae Reginae*, p. 22. I cannot agree with the view of the Encomiast's editor (p. lviii) that this is 'a mere rhetorical flourish', especially since Cnut at the time had not been elected. To sit on the throne would itself invest the claimant with some right, if the throne possessed qualities of a sacred *regalium*. So, on Cnut's death, Harald, before his election as king, tried in vain to persuade Archbishop Aethelnoth to lead him *in sublime regni solium* and give him the crown and sceptre; *ibid.*, p. 40. In Norway a dead ruler did not succeed his predecessor until he sat on the high-seat; *C.P.B.*, I, pp. 404–405. On the Scandinavian high-seat, cf. Schramm, *Herrschaftszeichen*, III, pp. 792–802. On the holding of a feast and sitting on the high-seat as the sign of a king or jarl coming into his inheritance, cf. Turville-Petre, *Myth and Religion*, p. 259.

[76] *Beowulf*, ll. 2369–2370.

[77] Exeter *Gnomes*, l. 69; *Wanderer*, ll. 41–44.

'altar' and 'throne' may well have been associated with it.[78] Reflecting these sacred attributes of the throne, the *Christ*, in its Christianized use of the image, reverses it so that 'holy Jerusalem . . . city of Christ' is described as the *cynestola cyst*, the sacred in terms of the royal throne instead of the throne in terms of the sacred.[79] And the cosmic, supernatural element of the royal throne perhaps accounts for Byrhtferth's description of the *quadrans* of a day as proceeding *uelut rex a solio suo*.[80] In spite of the fact that, as usual, no single Anglo-Saxon work gives a succinct account of the term, the varied sources give to the Old English throne the character of a royal insigne displaying the survival of sacral rulership.

The crown is another badge of kingship, but it cannot be dissociated from the helmet which itself was the early Germanic crown. Anglo-Saxon homilies translate the Latin *corona* of Biblical texts with *cynehelm*, and the common Anglo-Saxon word for *coronare* is *cynehelmian*. The crown of thorns of Christ, for example, becomes a thorn-*helm*.[81] In the oldest English coronation *ordo* a helmet is bestowed on the king, and the liturgy at the place in which the Continental *ordines* speak of the crown reads: *Hinc omnes pontifices sumant galeam et ponant super caput ipsius*.[82] Contemporary coins also show the English king with a helmet. The helmet of Sutton Hoo has a protective face-mask but no crown, and on the battle-field King Harold II, according to the Bayeux Tapestry, wears only the helmet with protective nose-guard that all of his warriors have and no crown. It is only a later century which will tell of an English crown being picked up from a thorn-bush after a monarch's death in battle. Harold

---

[78] Arthur E. Dubois, 'Gifstol', *Modern Language Notes*, LXIX (1954), p. 547, who also suggests that Toller's gloss of *gifu* as connoting God's grace or favour might increase the concept of the throne's altar-like nature.

[79] *Christ*, ll. 50-51; Krapp and Dobbie, eds., p. 4.

[80] S. J. Crawford, ed., *Byrhtferth's Manual (A.D. 1011)* (Early English Text Society, Original Series, no. 177; London, 1929), p. 4.

[81] W. Schücking, *Der Regierungsantritt* (Leipzig, 1899), p. 193. The *cynehelm* in the sense of 'crown', 'kingship', is employed, but it was probably not in general use in Anglo-Saxon times; F. E. Harmer, *Anglo-Saxon Writs*, p. 477.

[82] Schramm, *Herrschaftszeichen*, II, p. 392.

apparently wore none, and his rank was marked instead by the dragon-banner under which he fought.

That a crown existed, however, is indicated by considerable evidence, including the use of the word *beag* ('ring'). Thus, some translations of Christ's crown of thorns make it a thorn-*beag*,[83] and *Beowulf* (l. 1163) speaks of Wealhtheow as *under gyldnum beage*. *Wuldor-beag* (ring of glory) and *coren-beag* (ring of the elect) also occur in Anglo-Saxon texts. A *corona* or *diadema* makes its first appearance in the chronicles in Simeon of Durham *sub annis* 794, 796, 798, and 802, but these passages of his history are apparently of later date than the Northumbrian annals which he uses elsewhere.[84] King Athelstan (925-939) is shown on some of his coins wearing a simple, pronged metal-ring crown.[85] In the coronation liturgy the *corona* is first mentioned in the *ordo* for King Edgar's coronation of A.D. 973,[86] and the description of that monarch in his anonymous *Vita* as *coronatus lauro* probably indicates a *beag* which was lighter than the formal *diadema*.[87] A coin of Edgar portrays him wearing a crown surmounted by three staff-shaped decorations and the bands of the *diadema* hanging down in the back.[88] Edward the Confessor and Harold II wore the lily-crown when they were enthroned, the Bayeux Tapestry reveals, although Harold, as we have noted, wore only the helmet at Hastings. The great change in the English crown comes only with William the Conqueror, who, dissatisfied with the Anglo-Saxon tradition in this respect, modelled his own *corona* after the Continental imperial diadem.[89]

The growth in importance of the crown, however, can be

---

[83] Schücking, *Regierungsantritt*, p. 193.

[84] T. Arnold, ed., *Symeonis Monachi Opera Omnia. Historia Regum* (Rolls Series, Vol. LXXV:2; London, 1885), pp. 57, 58, 59, 68; Schücking, *Regierungsantritt*, p. 193.

[85] Christopher Brooke, *The Saxon and Norman Kings* (London, 1963), p. 77.

[86] P. E. Schramm, 'Die Krönung bei den Westfranken und Angelsachsen von 878 bis um 1000', *Zeitschrift der Savigny-Stiftung für Rechtsgeschichte, Kanonistische Abteilung*, XXIII (1934), pp. 163-164, 217, 226.

[87] Schramm, 'Krönung', p. 180.

[88] Schramm, *Herrschaftszeichen*, II, p. 394.

[89] Schramm, *Herrschaftszeichen*, pp. 393-395.

regarded as a Christian influence. It is with the *rex Christianissimus* Edgar that the Church elevates its importance in the blessing of the monarch at his coronation, and in the late Anglo-Saxon period only that it plays a considerable role as a sign of kingship. The older Germanic tradition for the king was the gold helmet, the sign of his leadership as the war-chief. Thus kennings often refer to the prince as the helmet of his people—he is the *aeðelinga helm*,[90] *heriga helm*,[91] *lidmanna helm*,[92] *weoruda helm*,[93] *helm Scyldinga*,[94] and *Wedra helm*[95]—but I know of no kenning which makes of him the 'crown' of his folk or even its *beag*. The growing importance of the crown and its Christianization can be well seen, however, in the offering of it to the Church. In the tradition of Roman *aurum coronarium* and in parallel with both the votive crowns which the Lombard kings dedicated to God and hung in the cathedral at Monza and the rich Visigothic *coronae votivae* of Guarrazar,[96] King Cnut in A.D. 1023 placed his golden *kinehelm* 'with my own hands upon the altar of Christ in Canterbury' for Christ Church Cathedral and there it was kept *in capite crucis majoris in navi ejusdem ecclesiae*.[97] This is no doubt related to the famous story of that ruler's command to the waves, first recorded by Henry of Huntingdon, who concludes his tale with the assertion 'Cnut never afterwards wore his gold crown, *sed super*

[90] *Genesis*, ll. 1858, 2146, 2657, 2722; these and the following kennings are collected in Hertha Marquardt, *Die Altenglischen Kenningar* (*Schriften der Königsberger Gelehrten Gesellschaft, Geisteswissenschaftliche Klasse*, 14 Jahr., 3 Heft; Halle, a. S., 1938), p. 253.

[91] *Elene*, l. 148.   [92] *Beowulf*, l. 1623.   [93] *Elene*, l. 223.

[94] *Beowulf*, l. 371 *inter alia*.

[95] *Beowulf*, l. 2462 *inter alia*.

[96] On votive crowns, cf. Schramm, *Herrschaftszeichen*, III, pp. 910–911. Also Schramm, 'Vom Kronenbrauch des Mittelalters', *Festschrift für Will-Erich Peuckert* (Helmut Dölker, ed.; E. Schmid Verlag, 1955), pp. 69–70. On the offering of these votive crowns (called *regna*) to saints, cf. A. Marignan, *Études sur la Civilisation Française* (Paris, 1899), II, p. 84, with sources in n. 3–4.

[97] The crown-offering is recorded in Cnut's charter to Christ Church and, also with his grant of Sandwich to the latter, in a late Canterbury list of benefactors; A. J. Robertson, ed., *Anglo-Saxon Charters* (Cambridge, 1939), pp. 158, 407. Charles Cotton, *The Saxon Cathedral at Canterbury and the Saxon Saints Buried Therein* (Manchester, 1929), p. 95.

imaginem Domini, quae cruci affixa erat, posuit eam in aeternum, in laudem Dei Regis magni.'[98] This gift of the *corona aurea* by the earthly king to the Eternal King has not, I believe, been associated with a pictorial representation which reflects both crown-offering and the divine blessing bestowed on the ruler; this is the well-known Winchester School drawing in the New Minster (Winchester) Register of 1016–1020, showing Cnut with his hand on an altar cross and, above, an angel touching with its left hand the crown on the king's head and with its right hand pointing aloft to Christ in Majesty, Who is enthroned above the cross.[99] The helmet, symbol of the Germanic warrior-king, has thus given way to the Church-blessed royal crown which the king, *a Deo coronatus*, returns to God. When a crown was placed in the tomb of Edward the Confessor in Westminster Abbey,[100] the process of change is complete from the Sutton Hoo burial, in which a helmet but no crown bore witness to the *helm* of his folk.

More important than the crown as a sign of Anglo-Saxon kingship is the standard or banner. We have already noted the *eafor-heafod-segn* in *Beowulf* and the similar banners in *Elene*. *Beowulf*, ll. 47, 1021, 1022, 1204, 2152, 2505, and 2767 all speak of banners under forms of the words *segn* (from Latin *signum*) and *cumbol*. A golden standard was elevated above King Scyld *heah ofer heafod*, for example, and Wiglaf sees in the dragon's hoard a *segn eall-gylden / heah ofer horde, hond-wundra maest, / gelocen leoðo-craeftum*.[101] The dragon-banner as an Anglo-Saxon royal

---

[98] T. Arnold, ed., *History of the English*, p. 189 (Bk. VI §17).

[99] In Stowe MS. 944, the *Liber Vitae* of Hyde Abbey, reproduced frequently, including *British Museum: A Guide to the Anglo-Saxon and Foreign Teutonic Antiquities* (Oxford, 1923), p. 94, fig. 114; T. D. Kendrick, *A History of the Vikings* (London, 1930), plate 9 (facing pp. 270–271); C. Dawson, *Religion and the Rise of Western Culture* (London, 1950), plate 4 (facing p. 112). It has been interpreted (e.g., Dawson, p. xiii) as an angel placing the crown on Cnut's head, but if the drawing, usually dated c. A.D. 1020, can be dated 1023, it may reflect the actual crown-offering to Christ in that year. The latter and Cnut's God-given Christian kingship are not, however, mutually exclusive but rather mutually supporting.

[100] Found when his grave was opened in A.D. 1102; Schramm, *Herrschafts-zeichen*, III, p. 911.   [101] *Beowulf*, ll. 47–48, 2767–2769.

emblem has also already been discussed. But the evidence for the relation of banner or standard and English kingship is much richer.

In the Old English *Exodus* the banner is again associated with royalty, not only in the golden lion on the banner of the tribe of Judah but in the *segncyning* (banner-king) who rides *wið þone segn*.[102] The Venerable Bede recounts of King Edwin of Northumbria that 'he had such excellency of glory in the kingdom that not only in battle were banners (*vexilla*) borne before him, but in time of peace too a standard-bearer was accustomed to go before him whensoever he rode about the cities, townships or shires with his thanes; yea, even when he passed through the streets to any place there was wont to be carried before him that kind of banner which the Romans call *Tufa* but the English *Tuuf*.'[103]

In spite of efforts to trace Edwin's *tuuf* to Roman origins,[104] the strongest probability ties it to a northern, Germanic background. The *tufa*, which first appears as one of several terms for military *signa* in the *Epitoma rei militaris* of Vegetius (A.D. 383–450), probably stemmed from Germanic warriors in the legions; John Lydos, an author of the age of Justinian, asserts that *tufae* were used by the barbarians, among whom, including the Anglo-Saxons, the word also had the meaning of 'bush' or 'tuft'.[105] The *tuuf* borne before the newly converted Edwin and the relation of the word with 'burial-mound', its only meaning in Norse, point to a tribal image or standard borne before the northern king. It must not be forgotten that this relation between banners and burial-mounds, which will be discussed shortly, is supported by the erection of a purple and gold *vexillum* on the grave of King

[102] *Exodus*, l. 172. On the use in battle by King Athelstan of a banner from a church, cf. Carl Erdmann, *Die Entstehung des Kreuzzugsgedankens* (Stuttgart, 1935), p. 46.

[103] Bede, *Hist. Eccl.*, II, 16; King, ed., I, p. 299. The word is also used for a banner in Anglo-Saxon poetry.

[104] Margaret Deanesly, 'Roman Traditionalist Influence Among the Anglo-Saxons', *English Historical Review*, LVIII (1943), pp. 136–142, which hypothesizes a misreading of *tufae* for *rufae*, so that Vegetius' list, . . . *vexilla, flammulae, tufae* . . ., would read, . . . *vexilla, flammulae rufae*, . . .

[105] Schramm, *Herrschaftszeichen*, I, pp. 248–249.

Oswald in Bardney.[106] The conclusion of Percy Schramm that *derlei Brauchtum bildete sich, als die Feldzeichen Sippen-oder Stammes-zeichen waren*[107] is really more convincing than Miss Deanesly's 'Roman' hypothesis that Bede's *tufa* is the result of 'a hole in the papyrus'.[108]

Miss Deanesly, in dismissing this *signum* of King Edwin, asserts that 'the study of Roman sculpture and monuments, which has thrown so much light on the equipment of the imperial armies, has failed to produce a single *tufa*'.[109] The reason she has searched in vain is that her Roman theory led her to investigate in the wrong direction. The *tufa* should have been sought four miles from Rendlesham, the palace of the royal house of the Wuffingas of East Anglia, where King Edwin lived as an exile at the court of King Redwald.[110] There, at Sutton Hoo, the excavation of 1939 uncovered above where the corpse's head would have been in a burial, an iron-standard which probably is the *tufa* of the North.[111] In the words of Miss Martin-Clarke, 'it is a long iron object, five feet three inches or five feet six inches long, in the form of a bar with its lower end pointed like a rail-way spike. At the top end is an equal-armed cross at right angles to the bar, each end of which is decorated with the head and horns of a bull. Eleven inches farther down, the bar passes through an almost square iron frame also at right angles. Again the four corners are decorated with bulls' heads and the frame is filled in with iron bars parallel to its edges on all four sides. . . . A small figure of a stag (with large antlers) mounted on an iron ring and hitherto unclassified, is now known to belong to it.'[112] The

---

[106] Bede, *Hist. Eccl.*, III, 11; King, ed., I, p. 378.

[107] Schramm, *Herrschaftszeichen*, I, p. 249. Cf. the *sige-þufas* of *Judith*, l. 201.

[108] Deanesly, 'Roman Traditionalist Influence', p. 139, the hole in a Vegetius MS. producing *tufae* for *rufae*.

[109] Deanesly, 'Roman Traditionalist Influence', p. 142.

[110] Bede, *Hist. Eccl.*, II, 12, and (on Rendlesham) III, 22; King, ed., I, pp. 270–272, 440.

[111] Bruce-Mitford, *Sutton Hoo Ship Burial*, plate 2 and figs. 4, 5. The earlier view that it might be a lampstand has little support now.

[112] D. Elizabeth Martin-Clarke, 'Significant Objects at Sutton Hoo', *The Early Cultures of North-West Europe*, pp. 112–113.

animal effigy, shaft, and cross-bar all are paralleled in Roman *signa*, but the grid-iron frame, which may have had supports, and the general structure are derived from no known Roman source. No similar objects have been found in Anglo-Saxon or Scandinavian remains,[113] but it suits the requirements of a royal standard more than it does anything else. It could be carried by one person and also could, with its end spike, be stuck in the ground as a rallying point during a battle. Any cloth-banner attached to the upper bar has disintegrated, but the stag surmounting the standard has parallels in military *vexilla*, including the boar-headed banner of *Beowulf* and perhaps the boar banner of *Elene*. The close association of banners, often decorated with cult-animals, and royalty in the North has already been verified, and the consequent placing of a standard among the grave-goods of a person almost certainly of royal rank might even be expected. The use of a standard in both peace and war by King Edwin is stated by Bede, and the term *tufa* used for it as well as for 'banner' in Anglo-Saxon verse tempts one to identify the Sutton Hoo standard not only with a royal *vexillum* but with 'that kind of banner which the Romans call *Tufa* but the English *Tuuf.*' Under the protective stag, it marked the sacred king in peace and war and was buried in the commemorative funeral-ship of a royal scion of the Wuffingas near where that East Anglian House had given shelter to the exiled Northumbrian ruler.

One last step needs to be taken to lead us to the Sutton Hoo banner in the burial-mound—the Anglo-Saxon association of the banner with the noble dead. Two words used for the former unite it with the howes which marked the graves of kings. The word *tuuf*, used for Edwin's *vexillum*, is found in Old Norse as *þufa*, but there its primary meaning is 'burial-mound'.[114] Also the Old English *cumbol* is employed for both 'banner' and 'helmet-badge',

---

[113] Its similarities to the 'Standard of Ur', Central Anatolian stag-rings and sundisc-rings, and other Near Eastern finds, as well as other parallels particularly associated with sun-cults, do not concern us here. Cf. Schramm, *Herrschaftszeichen*, I, pp. 251–255; Martin-Clarke, 'Significant Objects', pp. 113, 117–119.

[114] R. Cleasby and G. Vigfusson, *An Icelandic-English Dictionary* (Oxford, 1874), p. 750; Schramm, *Herrschaftszeichen*, I, p. 249; Martin-Clarke, 'Significant Objects', pp. 116–117.

with the former meaning dominating in the more than twenty combinations in which *cumbol-* occurs in Anglo-Saxon.[115] In its Old Norse cognates (*Kumbl*, *Kuml*, *Kubl*), it is occasionally used as 'badge' or 'emblem' but the most frequent meaning is 'mound' or 'howe'.[116] The word occurs both for the howe itself and for the *brautar kuml* (road monuments) or *bautar steinar,* such as Othin ordered to be erected for all who had distinguished themselves.[117] These stones, sometimes carved with magic runes, were placed on the burial-mound or even in it. It will be seen later that the veneration of stones, probably connected with the veneration of the dead, was one of the heathen practices most difficult to eradicate in England.[118] Thus this etymological link between banners and the dead supports the hypothesis of the iron standard of Sutton Hoo as a royal emblem placed in the king's cairn as a symbol of that sacral kingship which united the worlds of the living and the dead. As the golden banner of King Scyld was elevated above him at his ship-funeral, and as the *segn eallgylden* was found by Wiglaf among the dragon-guarded hoard of the burial-mound, so the standard of the Wuffingas was placed in the howe of Sutton Hoo to accompany its dweller as he sailed into the realm of the dead.[119] In the earliest Anglo-Saxon coronation *ordo,* among the symbols of sovereignty which are bestowed on the monarch, no banner appears, even though it was one of the ancient symbols of English royal authority. It may well have been this heathenism-associated antiquity of the royal standard that barred its acceptance

[115] Cf. the *eafor-cumbol* of *Elene,* ll. 76, 259. O. Springer, 'Old Norse Kumbla-Smiðr', pp. 237–238.

[116] Springer, 'Old Norse Kumbla-Smiðr', pp. 218, 220–221. Cf. also the non-West Saxon *becn* (banner) in the poetic *becn beadurofes* for a tumulus in *Beowulf,* l. 3160; Martin-Clarke, 'Significant Objects', p. 115.

[117] *Ynglingasaga,* c. 8: Othin ordained that 'a howe should be raised as a memorial to noblemen, and for all such persons as had achieved any distinction *bauta*-stones should be set up'; E. Wessen, ed., p. 11. Martin-Clarke, 'Significant Objects', pp. 112, 116.

[118] See below, chapter VI, 'Sacral Kingship in Anglo-Saxon Law'.

[119] On ship-funeral and the journey to the land of the dead, cf. H. R. Ellis, *The Road to Hel* (Cambridge, 1943), pp. 39–50, 170–197. Although probably a cenotaph, Sutton Hoo may well have marked an actual burial; see above, p. 100.

by the Church when it substituted an ecclesiastically blessed Christian kingship for the sacral king-cult of paganism of which the banner was an emblem.

Next to the standard of Sutton Hoo lay another object which all evidence suggests must be taken as another cult-emblem of kingship—the so-called 'whetstone'.[120] A four-sided staff, two feet long and six and one-quarter pounds in weight, it tapers at each end, culminating in a lobed knob, formerly painted red. Each knob had a small, flat bronze vessel attached to it by bronze bands, and under the knobs, on all four sides are human faces, some with beard and moustache and some feminine. This great sandstone 'sceptre' indicates no trace of use, and its elaborate end-decorations would militate against such practical employment. Small whetstones have been found in other graves, especially in Wales and Ireland, although a fragment of one was discovered in Lincolnshire in 1956, but none of such size, decoration, and weight as the Sutton Hoo find is known.[121]

Germanic royal insignia were not originally acquainted with the short Roman-style sceptre. Art-historical and literary sources combine to show the early Teutonic ruler either with the spear or with the long staff. There is no evidence for the use of the short *sceptrum* prior to its appearance at the turn of the ninth to tenth century in the representations of the Carolingian emperors.[122] The Germanic royal long-staff was itself probably a variant of the spear, the weapon of Woden, which appears in the king's hand.[123] It was this sacred character of Woden's spear which may have led to the reception of the 'lance of Charlemagne' among the

[120] Bruce-Mitford, *Sutton Hoo Ship Burial*, p. 21 and plate 3. C. Green, *Sutton Hoo*, pp. 68–69 and plate IX a, b.

[121] For other whetstones, cf. Schramm, *Herrschaftszeichen*, I, pp. 260–261, although his statement that English finds are confined to Yorkshire must be changed in view of the Lincolnshire discovery at Hough-on-the-Hill; C. Green, *Sutton Hoo*, p. 69 and plate IX c.

[122] Schramm, *Herrschaftszeichen*, I, pp. 263–264, and P. E. Schramm, *Die Deutschen Kaiser und Könige in Bildern Ihrer Zeit* (Leipzig, 1928), pp. 39, 51.

[123] Schramm, *Herrschaftszeichen*, I, pp. 263–264; for the spear as the special weapon of Woden, not mentioned by Schramm, cf. Chadwick, *The Cult of Othin*, pp. 4, 7, 15–16.

relics received by King Athelstan from Hugh Capet and the lance's ready identification with that which pierced the side of Christ.[124] The Christianization of the 'holy' spear is seen further in the lance of St. Maurice with which the legendary hero Guy of Warwick fought for King Athelstan against the giant Colibrand—giants being often associated with the old faith.[125] The long *baculus* was distinguished in coronation liturgies from the shorter *sceptrum*,[126] the dual presence probably representing the two traditions, Germanic and Roman-Christian. The Anglo-Saxon homilies speak only of the *cyne-gyrd* as the translation of sceptre.[127] The Germanic lance, as Schramm says, *ist nicht nur Waffe, sondern auch 'Zeichen' des wehrhaften Mannes*, and in the hand of the king it displays *die Führung von Stamm und Heer*.[128] An enthroned Anglo-Saxon king is shown with banner-lance in hand in a mid-eleventh century Benedictional, but this Germanic symbol of the Woden-descended leader of the host is not taken over by the Church and never appears in the ecclesiastical coronation *ordines* of the West.[129]

The whetstone of Sutton Hoo, however, is another Germanic tradition. It is perhaps related to the staff with a silver knob and

[124] William of Malmesbury, *Gesta Regum Anglorum*, Bk. II, c. 135; *Mon. Ger. Hist.*, SS., X, p. 460. Adolf Hofmeister, *Die Heilige Lanze. Ein Abzeichen des Alten Reiches* (*Untersuchungen zur Deutschen Staats- und Rechtsgeschichte*, Vol. XCVI; Breslau, 1908), pp. 54, 67–69. William derived his information from a mid-tenth century Latin poem. The lance as a gift of King Athelstan is mentioned twice in the eleventh century among the relics of the monastery of Exeter. Cf. Schramm, *Herrschaftszeichen*, II, pp. 522–523.

[125] Hofmeister, *Die Heilige Lanze*, p. 68. The two lances may have originally been identical, since the *vexillum* of St. Maurice was another of the relics given by Hugh to Athelstan. On the relationship of St. Maurice and the Holy Lance, cf. Laura H. Loomis, 'The Holy Relics of Charlemagne and King Athelstan: the Lances of Longinus and St. Mauricius', *Speculum*, XXV (1950), pp. 437–456.

[126] Schücking, *Regierungsantritt*, pp. 193–194.

[127] Schücking, *Regierungsantritt*, p. 194.

[128] Schramm, *Herrschaftszeichen*, II, pp. 493–494; on the significance of the Germanic royal lance, pp. 493–501.

[129] Schramm, *Herrschaftszeichen*, II, p. 523; the Benedictional illustration is reproduced in the *Propyläen-Weltgeschichte* (Berlin, 1932), III, p. 380.

ring carried by King Sigurd Sau,[130] to the gold-decorated staff with which King Olaf Tryggvason smashed an idol of Thor,[131] and to the one with a stone-adorned knob used by the Greenland prophetess Thorbjörg.[132] The human visages of the Sutton Hoo 'sceptre' recall the staff with an incised human figure with which Duke Tassilo handed over his duchy to Charlemagne.[133] There are thus analogies, but none is a complete parallel for the great unused whetstone. In that form perhaps to display the king's role as 'giver and master of the swords of his war band',[134] it may well have drawn also both on the magical properties believed to invest stone in the Germanic North and the supernatural role of the northern smith.[135] Still unique in an Anglo-Saxon or any other find, however, its full significance must remain concealed along with the identity of the Wuffing whom Sutton Hoo honoured.

Three less significant but possible cult-objects of rulership

---

[130] *Heimskringla, Saga of Olaf the Holy*, c. 33; this and the following parallels to the Sutton Hoo whetstone have been collected by Schramm, *Herrschaftszeichen*, I, p. 266.

[131] *Heimskringla, Saga of Olaf Tryggvason*, c. 69.

[132] *Eiriks Saga Rauða*, c. 4.

[133] *Annales Guelferbytani, sub anno* 787; *Mon. Ger. Hist., SS.*, I, p. 43. For a Danish staff decorated with a human face, cf. also Schramm, *Herrschaftszeichen*, I, pp. 266–267. Because of the deity-related torque which surrounds each face on the Sutton Hoo whetstone, the latter has been related to the cult of Woden; *ibid.*, pp. 199–210. However, Sidney L. Cohen, 'The Sutton Hoo Whetstone', *Speculum*, XLI (1966), pp. 466–470, has argued persuasively that it is associated with Thor, connecting the four faces with the quadratic-plan sanctuaries of the Trelleborg type, the three bearded faces and the red-painted knob with Thor's red beard, the torques with the ring of Thor, and the whetstone itself with sacrifices to Thor. The Danish bishop Absalon destroyed in 1169 at Arkona an idol of the god Svantowit which had four heads facing in the four directions, and Svantowit had other attributes of Thor; *ibid.*, p. 469. St. Olaf of Norway (d. 1030) destroyed an idol of Thor to which four loaves of bread were offered each day; *ibid.*

[134] Bruce-Mitford, *Sutton Hoo Ship Burial*, p. 21: 'It is an impressive, savage object, which seems to symbolize in a striking manner the pagan Saxon king in the role of a Wayland the Smith—the forger, giver, and master of the swords of his following.'

[135] On supernatural smiths and their relation to the dead, cf. H. R. Ellis Davidson, 'Weland the Smith', *Folklore*, LXIX (1958), pp. 145–159.

remain to be discussed briefly—the shield, the harp, and the ring. The ancient custom of elevating the *dux* or king on the shield as leader of his war-band, which is mentioned by classical authors and in time infiltrated Roman imperial custom, has no foundation in England or Scandinavia.[136] It may have had no significance beyond the proclamation of the war-chief. Nonetheless, the legend of Scyld Scefing, known to the Anglo-Saxons, and the use of a floating shield by the monks of Abingdon to prove their ownership of certain lands suggest a possible original cult significance to this object; indeed Chadwick suggests that the Germanic goddess Gefion, known apparently also to the Anglo-Saxons, may have been a 'shield-maiden', with this as her symbol.[137] A large shield was found at Sutton Hoo decorated with figures of an eagle and dragon.[138]

That the iron ring which the stag of the Sutton Hoo standard surmounts has religious significance is a possibility. The *stallahringr* or altar-ring was commonly used in Scandinavian practice for confirming oaths.[139] Icelandic literature of the late ninth and early tenth centuries provides our only written descriptions of them and their use, but that they were known to the Danish Vikings in England we know from the Anglo-Saxon Chronicle *sub anno* 876. They swore oaths for King Alfred that they would evacuate his kingdom '*on þaem halgan beage*, something they had done for no other people'.[140] The high seriousness of this kind of oath is seen when Othin himself swears a ring-oath: *Baugeið Oðinn*

[136] Chadwick, *Origin*, p. 266. Tacitus, *Histories*, IV, c. 15, reports the custom among the Batavians; C. H. Moore, ed., *Tacitus: The Histories* (Loeb Classical Library; London, 1956), II, p. 28. On the shield-elevation, cf. W. Ensslin, 'Zur Torqueskrönung und Schilderhebung bei der Kaiserwahl', *Klio*, XXXV (1942), pp. 293–298, and bibl. in Schramm, *Herrschaftszeichen*, I, p. 337, n. 2, and II, p. 495, n. 2.

[137] Chadwick, *Origin*, pp. 260–267. On the creation of Scyld as an eponymous ancestor of the Scyldings, cf. E. Philippson, *Die Genealogie*, p. 13.

[138] Bruce-Mitford, *Sutton Hoo Ship Burial*, pp. 21–24 and plates 4–6; C. Green, *Sutton Hoo*, pp. 70–71 and plates XI, XII.

[139] Francis P. Magoun, Jr., 'On the Old-Germanic Altar- or Oath-Ring (Stallahringr)', *Acta Philologica Scandinavica*, XX (1947–1949), pp. 277–293, with references on p. 277, n. 1.

[140] Earle and Plummer, eds., I, pp. 74, 75. The text occurs in all Mss.

hygg-ek at unnit hafi.[141] That its sacred nature is related to royal power seems evident from Simeon of Durham's report of the Viking Guthred's coronation as king of Northumbria: *posita in brachio eius dextro armilla in regnum constituatur.*[142] The famous necklace of the Brosings, known to the *Beowulf* poet, may well have been a Gautish *stallahringr*, Professor Magoun claims.[143] There is no evidence that the ring-oath existed among the Anglo-Saxons, although as Magoun states, it 'is ... not to be automatically ruled out'.[144] Certainly, as pagan Icelandic ring-oaths were Christianized by swearing on relics or the Gospel, similar sacred oaths among the Christian Anglo-Saxons—such as the peace between Eardwulf of Northumbria and Cenwulf of Mercia, sworn on the Gospel in A.D. 801[145]—may well have had pagan precedent which would give such oaths the support of tradition. That earlier oaths were sworn on rings, however, is unsubstantiated.[146] The English king is *beaggifa*, nonetheless, which may reflect a sacral, irrational element in ring-giving, harking back to these concepts.[147]

[141] 'I think that Odin swore a ring-oath:' *Havamal*, l. 110; *C.P.B.*, I, p. 22.

[142] In directions given by St. Cuthbert in a vision; T. Arnold, ed., *Symeonis Monachi Opera Omnia. Historia Ecclesiae Dunhelmensis* (Rolls Series, Vol. LXXV:1; London, 1882), I, p. 69 (Bk. II, c. 13). Magoun, 'On the Old-Germanic Altar- or Oath-Ring', p. 285.

[143] Magoun, 'On the Old-Germanic Altar- or Oath-Ring', pp. 286-287. This *healsbeah* appears, under various terms, in *Beowulf*, ll. 1195-1211, 2172.

[144] Magoun 'On the Old-Germanic Altar- or Oath-Ring', p. 293. However, when the German coronation *ordo* was introduced into England in A.D. 973, the section concerning the *armilla* was omitted; it did not appear until the 'Anselm-Ordo' of c. 1100; Schramm, *Herrschaftszeichen*, II, p. 550. That this omission was caused by ecclesiastical opposition to a practice which might be interpreted in a pagan light would be difficult to maintain without more specific evidence for its existence in England.

[145] Simeon of Durham, *Historia Regum, sub anno* 801; T. Arnold, ed., II, p. 65. Cf. oaths sworn on relics provided for in the *dooms*: e.g., III Aethelred 2 §1, 3 §1; VII Aethelred 2 §5; II Cnut 36.

[146] The weapon-oath (*on anum waepne*) survived for some time; Magoun, 'On the Old-Germanic Altar- or Oath-Ring', pp. 292-293.

[147] Ernst Leisi, 'Gold und Manneswert in "*Beowulf*",' *Anglia*, LXXI (1953), pp. 264-268; the monarch is referred to as *beaggifa* by the Anglo-Saxon Chronicle into the tenth century (p. 268).

The broken fragments of the small harp discovered in the hanging-bowl of Sutton Hoo raises questions about its significance for a royal mound.[148] Germanic royalty is known to have played the harp. Thus, King Hrothgar of the Danes himself 'at times would lay his hands on the joyous harp, the wood of mirth', says the *Beowulf* poet.[149] Gelimir, the last king of the Vandals, accompanied himself on the harp as he sang songs of his own composing; at the siege of Mount Papua in A.D. 534 he wrote to the Herulian chief, Pharas, who was besieging him, and requested that a harp be sent, since, 'being a skilful harpist, he had composed an ode relating to his present misfortune, which he was eager to chant to the accompaniment of a lyre while he wept out his soul'.[150] Another royal harper was Olaf Sihtricsson, who, disguised as a harper, gained entrance to King Athelstan's camp to spy by 'singing before the entrance and now and then touching the resounding strings with a sweet loud sound . . . He captivated the king and the companions at his board . . . with the musical harmony'.[151] Even more famous is the tale which William of Malmesbury also recounts of King Alfred entering the Viking camp as a harper.[152] Thus skill on the harp was not infrequently an attribute of the Germanic king, but whether this has any relationship to the chanting which accompanied the old religion must remain unknown. It may not be without significance, however, that the bards, perhaps simply as the vessels of much pagan lore, often clashed with the Church and made special efforts on

[148] Bruce-Mitford, *Sutton Hoo Ship Burial*, p. 26 and plate 12. The harp has been reconstructed at the British Museum; although small, the instrument was usable, since its reconstruction has been played, accompanying Anglo-Saxon chanted lays. C. Green, *Sutton Hoo*, p. 73 and plate XVI a.

[149] *Beowulf*, ll. 2107–2108.

[150] Procopius, *The Vandalic War*, II (Bk. IV of the *History*), c. 6; H. B. Dewing, ed., II, p. 262 (trans., p. 263).

[151] W. Stubbs, ed., *Willelmi Malmesbiriensis Monachi De Gestis Regum Anglorum* (Rolls Series, Vol. XC:1; London, 1887), I, pp. 142–143 (Bk. II § 131); Whitelock, ed., *Engl. Hist. Doc.*, p. 278. In the attack which Olaf and his ally King Constantine the Scot then launched, King Athelstan, losing his sword, gained another miraculously by invoking God and St. Aldhelm.

[152] *De Gestis Regum Anglorum*, Bk. II §121; W. Stubbs, ed., I, p. 126.

occasion to show their devotion to the new faith.[153] The question of whether the deliberately shattered harp of Sutton Hoo represents a ritual 'death' of a royal symbol or the burial of a prized possession of its user remains, nonetheless, unanswered.

Not only is Anglo-Saxon sacral kingship evident in the cult-animals and cult-objects associated with it but in both the popular superstitions and prophecies which so readily accrued around the royal person. We have already noted the suggestion of the ancient animal-cult relationships with rulership in the prediction that 'to see any four-footed beast speak betokens a king's friendship'.[154] Further, popular superstition, as might be expected in view of the role of the king and his mound in the veneration of the dead, associated the ruler with death in the belief that 'to see kings betokens departure from this world'.[155] Another set of Anglo-Saxon prognostications relates thunder to three things in succession which have been demonstrated to be closely integrated—national calamity, king-slaying, and the failure of the harvest: 'In the present year, if it thunders on a Sunday, then that betokeneth a great bloodshed in some nation. If on the next day, Monday, that storm betokeneth that a royal child shall be put to death. If it thunders on Tuesday, then that betokeneth failure of crops.'[156] Another prophecy in the same manuscript foretells the

---

[153] C. M. Bowra, *Heroic Poetry* (London, 1952), pp. 422–423. The Anglo-Saxon bard seems not to have held the high position of the Welsh court-bard; cf. John J. Parry, 'The Court Poets of the Welsh Princes', *PMLA*, LXVII (1952), pp. 511–520. The Welsh bard's role in divine and royal cult is seen in the ninth century laws of Hywel the Good: 'When the king desires to listen to songs, let the chief poet sing two songs to him in the upper hall, one of God and another of the kings'; Melville Richards, ed., *The Laws of Hywel Dda* (Liverpool, 1954), p. 41.

[154] See above, p. 121. From the Anglo-Saxon MS. Cotton Tiberius A iii.

[155] From same MS. More obviously, 'to receive a royal messenger is a great token'.

[156] Thunder on Wednesday foretells the death of tillers of the land, on Thursday the death of women. Bodleian MS. Junius 23, fol. 148, dating from c. A.D. 1120 but containing old superstitions; O. Cockayne, ed., *Leechdoms, Wortcunning and Starcraft*, pp. 166–168 (trans., pp. 167–169). On integration of kingship and king-slaying with national calamity and crop failure, see above, pp. 113–115.

L

death of kings—closely related in paganism to crop failure—if the Midwinter Day Mass falls on the same day, Tuesday.[157]

Another strange prediction of the death of kings is found in the taboo against Anglo-Saxon monarchs visiting or even seeing Congresbury in Somerset, named for the British St. Cyngar (Cungar) ab Geraint, who had settled there. Although King Ine gave the saint all the land he wanted, if *reges aut viderent aut visitarent a beato Cungaro incultum, aut graviter et continuo inciperent infirmari, aut viso loco non haberent longius spacium vivendi.*[158] It may, however, simply reflect the antipathy of the British Church for the Anglo-Saxon invaders, in spite of the generosity of the English king, so that a cult-centre of the former would be desecrated by the leaders of the enemy, for whom it was *unheil*.

As well as these general vaticinatory superstitions, prophecies were made in Anglo-Saxon England concerning specific kings. Although these parallel well the prophecies in the *vitae* of Christian saints and Continental rulers, they served to place the monarch in a special God-related role, as did the heathen religion, showing him in a peculiar and sacral relationship with the divine. Several English kings were themselves seers, although none suffered the fate of the northern King Vanlande, who died from a night-

---

[157] Cockayne, *Leechdoms, Wortcunning and Starcraft*, pp. 162–164; an evil Winter, a windy Spring, a rainy Summer, the death of many women, and danger to sheep are also prophesied on such an occasion. Cf. letter of Alcuin to Archbishop Eanbald II of York, A.D. 796: *Tempora periculosa sunt in Brittania; et mors regum miseriae signum est*; Mon. Ger. Hist., Epistolae, Ep. 116, p. 171.

[158] Although this occurs in the late *Vita* of St. Cyngar, probably by John of Tynemouth (Capgrave, ed., *Nova Legenda Angliae*, p. 250), it has ear-marks of old superstition; S. Baring-Gould and John Fisher, *The Lives of the British Saints* (Hon. Society of Cymmrodorion; London, 1908), II, pp. 249–250. C. Grant Loomis, *White Magic* (Mediaeval Academy of America, no. 52; Cambridge, Mass., 1948), p. 101. The King Ine of Wessex in the *Vita* is probably an error for the Anglian King Ine. Congresbury was one of the monasteries given by King Alfred to Asser, but the latter mentions nothing of this; Asser, *De Rebus Gestis Aelfredi*, c. 81, edited by W. Stevenson, p. 68. V. H. Galbraith, *An Introduction to the Study of History* (London, 1964), pp. 95–98, uses the passage on Congresbury in the latter work to argue that 'the Life was written at some date after the tenth century revival' (p. 97), but the dating of 'Asser' does not affect the superstition concerning Congresbury.

mare.[159] Thus both Bede and the Monk of Whitby's early *Vita* of Gregory the Great recount the vision of King Edwin of Northumbria which not only foretold his escape from the threat of death at King Redwald's court and his restoration to the throne but arranged the sign by which the king recognized that his 'luck' was improved by the Christian God.[160] Similarly, St. Guthlac appeared after his death to Aethelbald of Mercia to prophecy the latter's attainment of the kingship, how long he should live, and the end of his life.[161] King Oswald's vision of St. Columba prior to his battle with Cadwallon resulted not only in the victory predicted by the saint but in the conversion of Oswald's *folc*.[162] Another saint appeared in a prophetic vision when St. Cuthbert foretold to Alfred his triumph and the establishment of his family's rule over *tota Albion* by the aid of God and the saint.[163] Further, a vision appeared to King Harthacnut, while he 'was at rest in his bed', telling of the approaching death

---

[159] *Ynglingasaga*, c. 13 (16); E. Wessen, ed., p. 17. Cf. Frederik Grön, 'Remarks on the Earliest Medical Conditions in Norway and Iceland with Special Reference to British Influence', *Science, Medicine and History. Essays on the Evolution of Scientific Thought and Medical Practice written in honour of Charles Singer* (E. Ashworth Underwood, ed.; London, 1953), I, p. 145.

[160] Bede, *Hist. Eccl.*, II, 12; King, ed., I, pp. 270–280. *Life of St. Gregory*, c. 16; D. Whitelock, ed., *Engl. Hist. Doc.*, pp. 688–689.

[161] B. Colgrave, ed., *Felix's Life of St. Guthlac*, pp. 164–166 (c. 52 of Felix's *Vita* of Guthlac). D. Whitelock, ed., *Engl. Hist. Doc.*, pp. 712–713, who comments shrewdly that 'if he had foretold that he should be murdered by his own guards Aethelbald would have found it poor comfort'. Felix dedicated this *Vita* to King Aelfwald of East Anglia, who reigned A.D. 713–749, so the author is a contemporary of Bede.

[162] Adamnan, who records this in his *Vita* of St. Columba (Bk. I, ch. 1), heard the account of the vision from Abbot Failbhe of Iona, who was told it by Oswald himself; Whitelock, *Engl. Hist. Doc.*, p. 691.

[163] The earliest version is in the eleventh-century *Historia de Sancto Cuthberto*, cc. 15–16; T. Arnold, ed., *Symeonis Monachi Opera . . .*, I, pp. 204–205. It is found also in William of Malmesbury, but absent from the Anglo-Saxon Chronicle, Asser, and Florence of Worcester; the *Historia's* editor, although believing it to be an interpolation, places it in the Anglo-Saxon period, in the age of Cnut: *ibid.*, pp. 62, 207. In comparing it with Edwin's vision, the *Historia* makes the unknown man of Bede's version introduce himself as St. Peter.

of his rival, Harald, and the king's succession *iusto heredi iustissima successione*.[164]

Besides the king-seers, there are more frequent prophecies concerning kings revealed to others. The location of the bones of King Edwin, for example, was revealed by a man who appeared in a vision to the priest Trimma, directing the latter to find the bones at Hatfield and bring them to *Streoneshealh* (Whitby); after much encouragement in three visits, the priest obeyed the vision.[165] Guthlac of Crowland prophesied future success to the exiled Aethelbald of Mercia, when the latter went to see the saint, 'as was his custom'. And 'all these things which the man of God had prophesied about him happened in this very way ... as the actual outcome of present events proves'.[166] Guthlac's concern for the king did not end with the saint's death, for, as we have seen, he later appeared in a vision to encourage Aethelbald once again. Another saintly visionary who was a royal favourite was the famous seer Drythelm, who told his visions to the learned King Aldfrith of Northumbria, who very often went to hear him at Melrose.[167] Cuthbert, who later came in a vision to Alfred the Great, during his own lifetime prophesied the approaching death of King Ecgfrith, when the latter's sister, the Abbess Aelflaed, questioned him concerning the length of her brother's reign.[168] Later, the same saint, in a vision to Abbot Edred in A.D. 883, directed that Guthred be made king of Northumbria and, the vision containing its own reward, ordered that the new king then give the saint all the land between the Tyne and the Wear.[169] Surely the busiest prophet and recipient of forecasts of royal fates, however, was St. Dunstan. His first vision, in which

[164] Alistair Campbell, ed., *Encomium Emmae Reginae*, p. 48 (Bk. 3, c. 9). Soon afterwards, according to the Encomiast (c. 10), the 'glad tidings' of Harald's death reached Harthacnut.

[165] *Life of St. Gregory* by the Monk of Whitby, cc. 18–19; Whitelock, ed., *Engl. Hist. Doc.*, pp. 689–690.

[166] B. Colgrave, ed., pp. 148–150 (c. 49 of the *Vita* of Guthlac).

[167] Bede, *Hist. Eccl.*, V, 12; King, ed., II, p. 266.

[168] Aelfric's sermon for March 20th, the Deposition of St. Cuthbert; B. Thorpe, ed., *The Homilies of Aelfric* (London, 1846), II, p. 147.

[169] T. Arnold, ed., I, p. 203 (c. 13).

St. Peter, St. Paul, and St. Andrew came to him after his refusal to be a bishop under King Eadred, concerned himself, but it provided the rare occasion of the king himself, *ut erat divina eruditione praeditus*, serving as the vision's interpreter.[170] When that king was on his death-bed, a *vox coelitus emissa*, declaring, *Ecce nunc Eadraedus obiit in pace*, came to Dunstan, who was on the road with the royal treasure. The message was particularly hard on Dunstan's horse, which died on the spot.[171] Another heavenly voice came to Dunstan when Edgar the Peaceable was born, proclaiming, *Pax Anglorum ecclesiae nati nunc pueri, et nostri Dunstani tempore*.[172] Finally, at the coronation of Aethelred in A.D. 978, Dunstan himself prophesied the *magnos labores et multas vitae suae tribulationes* which were to come during the reign and attributed them to the murder of the king's brother.

Thus in an entirely Christian setting the king is made an object of heavenly voices and prophesies, continuing the special character of his relationship with the divine under paganism. A folk turning from one religion to another—indeed, led by the ruler from one to the other—would not only adjust to it more readily if it found parallels and continuities with the old, but to see the new in terms of the folk's own socio-political, tribal context would be unavoidable. To preserve many of the features of that sacral rulership which was so integral a part of Germanic heathenism was, then, also natural. The divinely descended king, surrounded by the cult-objects with which that rulership was associated and integrated by popular belief with the heavenly powers, was, as we have seen in this chapter, a vital factor for both the old and new faiths in Anglo-Saxon England. And, as we shall see, it was indeed this *mana*-charged monarch who led his people from the old to the new faith.

[170] *Epistola Adelardi ad Elfegum Archiepiscopum De Vita Sancti Dunstani, Lectio IV*, in W. Stubbs, ed., *Memorials of St. Dunstan* (Rolls Series, Vol. LXIII; London, 1874), p. 57.

[171] *Vita Sancti Dunstani Auctore B*, in W. Stubbs, ed., *Memorials*, p. 31. Cf. the *Epistola Adelardi, Lectio V*; *ibid.*, p. 58.

[172] *Epistola Adelardi, Lectio IV*; W. Stubbs, ed., *Memorials*, pp. 56, 446, 449–450.

CHAPTER V

The royal role in the conversion of England

As Sir Frank Stenton has said, 'throughout the country in which Augustine and his companions laboured, heathenism was still a living religion when it met the Christian challenge'.[1] The binding elements in that pagan faith, as has been observed, were the kin-group and the head of the tribe who bound the folk to the gods and the gods to the folk. The less, therefore, that a new religion attempted to isolate the converted from their group and to arouse a combined political-religious opposition, the less difficult would it be to effect a conversion to a new and more powerful God. When religious and political opposition were combined, as in King Olaf the Holy's attempted conversion of Norway, during the apostasy of Eadbald of Kent, or among the East Saxons under the sons of King Saberht, Christianity met formidable hostility; when there was little political opposition, on the other hand, the reception of the new faith was even undramatic in its lack of tension and high events.[2] The crucial figure, consequently, in any conversion was the sacral king, and the fact that in Anglo-Saxon England the paths of the new religion were made smooth was in every kingdom due to the role played by its ruler.

The story of the English Conversion opens in Kent with the arrival in Thanet of St. Augustine and about forty companions.[3]

[1] F. Stenton, *Anglo-Saxon England* (2nd ed.; Oxford, 1947), p. 102.

[2] These elements of kin-group, Germanic religious concepts, and conversion are well discussed, without application to Anglo-Saxon England, in Helmut de Boor, 'Germanische und Christliche Religiosität', *Mitteilungen der Schlesischen Gesellschaft für Volkskunde*, XXXIII (1933), pp. 26–51. On the relation of cult and culture in the conversion of England, cf. my 'Paganism to Christianity in Anglo-Saxon England', *Harvard Theological Review*, LIII (1960), pp. 197–217.

[3] Bede and the letters of Gregory the Great are the basic sources for the conversion of Kent under Augustine; cf. A. W. Haddan and W. Stubbs, eds., *Councils and Ecclesiastical Documents relating to Great Britain and Ireland* (Oxford,

The mission had left Rome probably early in A.D. 596 and landed early the next year in the realms of the *bretwalda* Aethelberht, the most powerful ruler in southern Britain.[4] Its reception was not unfriendly. The king ordered it to be provided with *necessaria*, and after some days went himself into Thanet to hear the *nuntium optimum* which the Roman had claimed to bring. Since for at least nine years Christian services had been held in the royal capital, celebrated for Queen Bertha, the Christian daughter of the Merovingian King Charibert, by her chaplain, Bishop Liudhard, the *fama ... Christianae religionis* had, as Bede says, come to the king before, and modern historians may have under-estimated his knowledge of the faith.[5] When Pope Gregory writes that 'the news had reached him that the English people wished to become Christians',[6] the possibility is at least open that Aethelberht himself or Bertha may have acted to instigate the mission. Certainly he acknowledged in terms of his own religion (*vetere usus augurio*) the possible power of Augustine's band, 'for

---

1871), III, pp. 5–38, where they are collected. Gregory's correspondence is edited by Ewald and Hartmann in *Mon. Ger. Hist., Epistolae*, I–II. Augustine's landing and the early establishment of his mission are recounted in Bede, *Historia Ecclesiastica*, I, 25–26; J. E. King, ed., *Baedae Opera Historica. Historia Ecclesiastica Gentis Anglorum* (Loeb Classical Library; London, 1930), I, pp. 106–114. Cf. Anglo-Saxon Chronicle (MS. E), *sub annis* 565 (560), 596; John Earle and Charles Plummer, eds., *Two of the Saxon Chronicles Parallel* (Oxford, 1892), I, pp. 18, 19, 21.

[4] On the dating, cf. Bede, *Hist. Eccl.*, I, 23–24; Stenton, *Anglo-Saxon England*, pp. 104–105. The following account stems from *Hist. Eccl.*, I, 25–26; King, ed., I, pp. 106–114. For a recent defence of Bede's accuracy and argument against Dom Suso Brechter's view that Aethelberht, contrary to Bede's account, was still pagan in A.D. 601, cf. R. A. Markus, 'The Chronology of the Gregorian Mission to England: Bede's Narrative and Gregory's Correspondence', *Journal of Ecclesiastical History*, XIV (1963), pp. 16–25.

[5] Cf., e.g., Stenton, *Anglo-Saxon England*, p. 105.

[6] Letter of Gregory to Theoderic and Theodebert, kings of the Franks; Haddan and Stubbs, eds., *Councils and Eccl. Doc.*, III, p. 10. Gilbert Sheldon, *The Transition from Roman Britain to Christian Britain A.D. 368–664* (London, 1932), pp. 120–121, suggests that Aethelberht may have considered the advantages of removing a religious obstacle to his being recognized as overlord by British princes.

he would not permit them to come to him in any house, lest . . . if they practiced any magical arts, they might deceive him by surprise, prevailing against him'.[7] Nonetheless, the Gospel impressed him as *nova . . . et incerta*, so that, as he declared, he could not abandon the faith which he and his people had observed for so long. However, he not only welcomed Augustine with all courtesy and provided for his wants but gave permission for him to 'win unto the faith of your religion with your preaching as many as you may'. Some (*nonnulli*) were baptized before Aethelberht, but it was only after the royal conversion that many (*plures*) turned to Christianity, so that on Christmas, A.D. 597, Gregory reports in a letter to Patriarch Eulogius of Alexandria, more than ten thousand of the king's subjects were baptized.[8]

The dependence of the Kentish mission on the royal role is seen with equal clarity after the death of the converted Aethelberht on February 24th, A.D. 616.[9] His and Bertha's son, the new king Eadbald, was openly heathen and, following pagan practice, married his father's widow, the second and probably heathen wife of Aethelberht.[10] When their king moved to the worship of the old gods, so did the superficially converted folk. The very

---

[7] *Hist. Eccl.*, I, 25; King, ed., I, p. 110.

[8] *Ep.* viii, 29; discussed in Markus, 'Chronology of the Gregorian Mission', p. 24. H. G. Richardson and G. O. Sayles, *Law and Legislation from Aethelberht to Magna Carta* (Edinburgh, 1966), pp. 162–166, question both Aethelberht's conversion and Bede's account. Their views, stimulating as always, need careful analysis, but problems largely of dating need not lead us to discard the fact of the conversion itself. Further, Aethelberht's second marriage, probably to a pagan, and his son Eadbald's paganism do not necessarily 'tell very strongly against Bede's assumption that Aethelberht was baptized or was ever indeed a true convert', as the authors maintain (p. 163), any more than Bertha's marriage to a pagan king should count against her being a Christian, or the fact that the three sons of King Saberht of the East Saxons were still heathen when their father died become evidence for rejecting Bede's account of Saberht's conversion.

[9] *Hist. Eccl.*, II, 5; King, ed., I, p. 224. In the several following references to Bede, the page number of this edition will be placed parenthetically immediately after the citation of the *Hist. Eccl.*

[10] *Hist. Eccl.*, II, 5 (p. 228). On marriage with the father's widow, see above pp. 25–28.

life of the Christian mission was threatened when Augustine's successor, Laurentius, agreed with the fugitive bishops, Mellitus of London and Justin of Rochester, that 'it were better for them all to return to their own country and there to serve the Lord with a free mind, than to abide without profit amongst barbarous men that were rebels of the faith'.[11] It was only the conversion and baptism of Eadbald and the strong royal support for the Church thereafter which brought his people once more into the Christian fold. His son and successor, King Eorcenberht, was the 'first of the kings of the English who by his princely authority ordered that idols in his whole realm should be abandoned and destroyed', and with this visible sign of the king's allegiance to the new religion, we never hear of popular apostasy in Kent again.[12]

The loose hegemony which the *bretwalda* Aethelberht exercised over the entire territory south of the Humber facilitated the advance of Christianity. Although none of the kings who acknowledged his overlordship was forced to change his religion when the king of Kent did, yet the latter's influence on these monarchs aided the adoption of the faith by them and consequently by their people. The first kingdom to be affected was that of the East Saxons, ruled by Saberht, the son of Aethelberht's sister, Ricula. When, in A.D. 604, Augustine consecrated his follower Mellitus as bishop to preach in Essex, not only were the king and, as Bede says, the *provincia* converted, but Aethelberht himself built the church of St. Paul in Saberht's capital city, London.[13] Again, however, royal faith and popular faith moved together, for upon the death of the East Saxon monarch his three sons, still heathen, 'gave free license to the people subject to them to worship idols'; so strong was the return to paganism that not only was Mellitus driven out, but when he had returned and Eadbald had restored the faith in Kent, Essex remained true to its 'idolatrous high priests'.

[11] *Hist. Eccl.*, II, 5 (p. 230; transl., p. 231).
[12] *Hist. Eccl.*, III, 8 (p. 362).
[13] *Hist. Eccl.*, II, 3 (p. 214). Anglo-Saxon Chronicle (MS. E), *sub anno* 604; Earle and Plummer, eds., I, pp. 21-23.

It was not for almost half a century (A.D. 653) that a Christian
mission entered Essex, when once again the baptism of its king
preceded its conversion. The East Saxon king, Sigbert the Good, a
friend and frequent visitor at the court of Oswiu of Northumbria,
was persuaded in the North that 'such could not be gods which
had been made with men's hands'.[14] Following his baptism and
return to Essex, the mission of Cedd was invited to his kingdom
and there, since the cult-leader of the folk was now favourable
to the mission, it was a success, and a 'great church', increasing
daily, was brought into existence. After the murder of Sigbert
the Good, his successor, Swidhelm, son of Sexbald, was a Christian, having been baptized in East Anglia, and his subjects stayed
firm in the faith of their monarch. However, when Sighere
followed him to the throne, the great plague of 664 swept through
the land, and the king himself, in his old role as guardian of the
health of his folk, restored the pagan temples and returned *cum
sua parte populi* to the worship of idols, 'as though they could
thereby be protected from the mortal sickness'.[15] It was, thus,
a national calamity such as paganism had called upon the king to
cure, which caused King Sighere to offer *blot* to the offended
gods, and 'his part of the people' apostacized with him. Wulfhere
of Mercia, overlord of Sighere, however, sent a mission under
Bishop Jaruman to re-christianize the country, and it turned
populum et regem together again to Christ.[16] Essex remained firm
thereafter, but the powerful role of the king in determining the
religion of his people is obvious in the long history of its conversion. When Saberht was converted, so were the East Saxons;
when his sons worshipped the old gods, their subjects followed
their lead; when Sigbert turned to the new religion, the conversion was again successful; when the panic of the plague swept
Essex, one king and his people alike reverted to the old gods;

[14] *Hist. Eccl.*, III, 22 (p. 434; transl., p. 435).

[15] *Hist. Eccl.*, III, 30 (p. 502; transl., p. 503). Sighere shared the rule with
Sebbi, who remained a Christian, as did apparently 'his part of the people',
confirming the strength of the royal role in establishing which faith was to be
both the official and popular cult.

[16] Bede (III, 30), was told of this mission and its discreet tactics by a priest
who participated in it.

and, finally, both together returned to Christianity. The pagan Germanic notion that the gods are primarily the gods of the king, who mediates with them for his folk, is clearly witnessed in Anglo-Saxon England.

Christianity also first entered East Anglia through the over-lordship of Kent. King Redwald, the outstanding member of the House of the Wuffings in the early years of the seventh century, and the fourth in the Anglo-Saxon Chronicle's list of *bretwaldas*, was converted on a visit to the Kentish court. However, upon his return to his own realm he served both Christ and the old gods, setting up two altars in one temple, one *ad sacrificium Christi* and the other *ad victimas daemoniorum*.[17] The Germanic king was willing to worship the new God but continued to make *blot* to the gods of his folk, as was his tribal duty. Under these circumstances we do not hear, of course, of the conversion of his subjects. His son and successor, Eorpwald, however, was persuaded by Edwin of Northumbria to abandon pagan worship, and as a result he embraced Christianity *cum sua provincia*.[18] Slain soon after by a heathen, he was succeeded by his brother, Sigeberht the Learned, in A.D. 631. This monarch, *homo bonus ac religiosus*, had received baptism as an exile in France, and it was to the archbishopric in Kent that he turned 'to make all his realm partaker' in the faith.[19] East Anglia was converted, and the Burgundian missionary Felix established his see at Dunwich. The scholarly Sigeberht laid down his crown to retire to a monastery, but, as we have seen, was forced to come out to serve as 'bringer of victory' for his folk. When he was slain in battle by the heathen Penda, along with his brother King Egric, the throne went to the devout King Anna, whose whole family was noted for its loyalty to the Christian faith. It was this apparently

---

[17] *Hist. Eccl.*, II, 15 (p. 292). King Aldwulf of East Anglia, who lived in Bede's day, saw the temple in his childhood.

[18] *Hist. Eccl.*, II, 15 (p. 292). Cf. Anglo-Saxon Chronicle, *sub anno* 632 (627–628); Earle and Plummer, eds., I, pp. 24, 25. Eorpwald is one of the few kings to whom the seventh-century silver coinage, the *sceattas*, has been ascribed, 'though this is now regarded as unlikely'; H. R. Loyn, *Anglo-Saxon England and the Norman Conquest* (London, 1962), p. 119.

[19] *Hist. Eccl.*, III, 18–19 (pp. 412–428).

firmly converted kingdom, however, that, perhaps under the strain of national calamity in the loss of King Aethelhere and his army in the North, buried in the old heathen fashion the rich funeral ship of Sutton Hoo.[20]

Again it was through Kent that Roman Christianity made its appearance in Northumbria. There King Edwin (A.D. 617–633), brought to the rule of a united Deira and Bernicia by his alliance with Redwald of East Anglia, ruled as the most powerful Anglo-Saxon monarch to that time, as Bede tells us,[21] and the head of a confederation of English kingdoms which omitted only Kent. It was with the marriage of this king, whom Stenton has well portrayed as primarily an epic monarch of the Heroic Age,[22] with Aethelburga, daughter of Aethelberht of Kent, that Christianity was able to enter his lands. Her brother Eadbald had at first refused the suit, saying it was not allowed for a Christian maiden to marry a pagan, but Edwin promised not only that she and all her companions might practice their faith but that he himself would consider it if it proved to be *sanctior ac Deo dignior*. The result was the mission of Paulinus from Canterbury to Northumbria and the subsequent conversion of the king as the result of the vision previously discussed and perhaps of the papal letters he had received. Following the famous council called to consider the new faith and the action of the heathen priest Coifi in defiling the temple he had served, Edwin was baptized *mid his theode* on Easter Eve, A.D. 627.[23] Like Aethelberht of Kent, Edwin adopted the religion of his queen.

When this powerful *bretwalda* was slain at Heathfield a scant

[20] Françoise Henry, 'Irish Enamels of the Dark Ages and their Relation to Cloisonné Techniques', *Dark Age Britain: Studies presented to E. T. Leeds* (D. B. Harden, ed.; London, 1956), pp. 81–82, explains the presence of Irish-style hanging bowls in Saxon graves, especially at Sutton Hoo, by the mission of the Irish Fursey, friend of King Sigeberht, to East Anglia.

[21] *Hist. Eccl.*, II, 9 (p. 244).   [22] Stenton, *Anglo-Saxon England*, pp. 79–80.

[23] The vision, council, and baptism are recounted in Bede, *Hist. Eccl.*, II, 12–14 (pp. 270–292). Cf. Anglo-Saxon Chronicle, *sub anno* 627, for his baptism; Earle and Plummer, eds., I, pp. 24–25. His daughter had been baptized the preceding Pentecost. For a clear account of the four stories of Edwin's conversion—(1) conversion after victory over Wessex, (2) Edwin's dream and

six years later, Christianity's strength in Northumbria was diminished. Paulinus fled with Queen Aethelburga and the royal family, and the new rulers of the separated states of Deira and Bernicia—Osric and Eanfrid—both abjured the Christian religion.[24] The cause of their action is unknown, although it may have been a loss of faith in the religion of Edwin, who had lost his 'luck' as 'bringer of victory'. Slain by Cadwallon within the year, however, the apostate kings were removed from the king-lists of Northumbria and their reign, as we have noted, assigned as a ninth year to King Oswald 'because of the heathenism practiced by those who reigned the one year between him and Edwin'.[25] With the succession of Eanfrid's brother, Oswald, to the throne of a united Northumbria, Christianity became again victorious with the *rex sanctissimus ac victoriosissimus*. 'Desiring that the whole folk whom he began to rule should be filled with the grace of the Christian faith, of which he had already had very great proofs in defeating the barbarians', he sent to the Dalriadic Scots, with whom he had lived in exile, for a missionary. With royal support, the mission of Aidan brought Northumbria into the Christian fold. Indeed, Bede records that, when Aidan, *qui Anglorum linguam perfecte non noverat*, preached the Gospel, 'the king himself was interpreter of the heavenly word to his aldermen and thegns'.[26]

---

the later role of Paulinus, (3) the debate in the council, and (4) his baptism by a Celtic churchman (the latter not in Bede)—cf. C. Brooke, *The Saxon and Norman Kings* (London, 1963), pp. 106–108.

[24] *Hist. Eccl.*, II, 20–III, 1 (pp. 314–328). Cf. Anglo-Saxon Chronicle (esp. MS. E), *sub annis* 633–634; Earle and Plummer, eds., I, pp. 24–27.

[25] Anglo-Saxon Chronicle (MS. E), *sub anno* 634; Earle and Plummer, eds., p. 27. Cf. *Hist. Eccl.*, III, 1 (p. 326), which adds that Cadwallon slew them without delay *iusta ultione*. Peter Hunter Blair, 'The Moore Memoranda on Northumbrian History', *The Early Cultures of North-West Europe*: *H. M. Chadwick Memorial Studies* (Sir Cyril Fox and Bruce Dickins, eds.; Cambridge, 1950), pp. 248–249, discusses this and suggests Anglo-Saxon familiarity with the Roman custom of *damnatio memoriae*. However, see above, pp. 78 n. 146, 80, on Osric's commemoration in an eighth century calendar. Osric's son, Oswini, was, on the contrary, a man *eximiae pietatis et religionis* (*Hist. Eccl.*, III, 14).

[26] *Hist. Eccl.*, III, 3 (pp. 336–337).

After Oswald's death in battle against Penda of Mercia, his brother King Oswiu held Bernicia in the faith as well as sending Cedd's mission to the East Saxons. At the crucial Synod of *Streoneshalh* (Whitby) in A.D. 664, Oswiu presided, spoke first, as did the pagan kings at the ancient assemblies of the folk, and gave the judgement.[27] The debate, which was apparently confined to the dating of the Easter celebration, would not be without interest, contrary to some modern writers,[28] to a king and people in whose recently pagan past high feast days and the proper observance of *blot* were of such crucial importance to their well-being. Further, the royal house itself was divided, since Oswiu and his queen observed different Easter festivals, the former according to the Celtic rite, the latter according to the Roman. What remains certain is that in Northumbria as in the other Anglo-Saxon kingdoms, it was the king who led his folk into the new religion.

Wessex, unlike Essex, East Anglia, and Northumbria, was not influenced toward Christianity by the royal house of Kent. Bishop Birinus, coming 'by the counsel of Pope Honorius', had planned to penetrate inland, but finding the Gewissae, among whom he landed, to be *paganissimi*, he preached the Gospel there. As a result, the West Saxon king, Cynegils, was baptized in A.D. 635 *cum sua gente*, with Oswald of Northumbria, who was to become the monarch's son-in-law, acting as godfather.[29] Cyne-

---

[27] *Hist. Eccl.*, III, 25 (pp. 456–476). Eddi, *Vita Wilfridi*, c. 10, reports that the king asked his question concerning the relative greatness of Peter and Columba *subridens*; B. Colgrave, ed., *The Life of Bishop Wilfrid by Eddius Stephanus* (Cambridge, 1927), p. 22. This has been interpreted as suggesting the king was not newly convinced by the debate but had made up his mind before it began; Stenton, *Anglo-Saxon England*, p. 123.

[28] Cf. R. H. Hodgkin, *A History of the Anglo-Saxons* (3rd ed.; London, 1952), I, p. 299: 'Oswy no doubt failed to follow the abstruse arguments as closely as he might.'

[29] *Hist. Eccl.*, III, 7 (pp. 354–356). Anglo-Saxon Chronicle, *sub anno* 635; Earle and Plummer, eds., I, pp. 26–27. On this kingdom, cf. T. S. Holmes, 'The Conversion of Wessex', *English Historical Review*, VII (1892), pp. 437–443. D. P. Kirby, 'Problems of Early West Saxon History', *English Historical Review*, LXXX (1965), p. 12, contends the baptism of Cynegils could not have occurred before A.D. 636, since Oswald could not have gone to Wessex earlier.

gil's eldest son, Cwichelm, was baptized the next year, and Cwichelm's son, Cuthred, in A.D. 639.[30] However, Cenwalh, Cynegil's second son and successor, 'refused to receive the faith and sacraments', and was converted only at the East Anglian court of the devout Anna after Penda had driven him from Wessex in 645.[31] Stenton concludes that 'if an important member of the royal house delayed so long before accepting Christianity it is unlikely that Birinus secured any general conversion of the West Saxon people'.[32] This is especially true in the light of Cenwalh's later quarrels with his bishops Agilbert and Wini, so that 'the province of the West Saxons was without a bishop for no small time'.[33] Finally, convinced that his defeats were due to God's displeasure over the absence of a prelate in his realms, the king recalled Agilbert to Wessex. Agilbert refused to return but sent his nephew, Leutherius.[34]

For nearly a generation after the death of Edwin of Northumbria in A.D. 632, the centre of the Anglo-Saxon historical stage was held by a warrior-king of the Germanic epic style, the pagan Penda of Mercia. The slayer of Edwin and his sons Osfrid and Eadfrid, of King Oswald, and of the East Anglian monarchs Sigeberht the Learned, Egric, and Anna, the powerful Mercian was still heathen when he was struck down in battle against Oswiu in A.D. 654. However, Penda was not hostile to Christianity itself, allowing the Gospel to be preached in his realm and despising only the converted who did not live up to the teachings of their faith. His son Peada became a Christian during his father's lifetime, largely through the persuasion of Alchfrid, Oswiu's son, who had married Peada's sister.[35] On his return from Northumbria, where he was baptized in A.D. 653, Peada brought four priests with him, who preached not only in the East Midlands

[30] Anglo-Saxon Chronicle, *sub annis* 636, 639; Earle and Plummer, eds., I, pp. 26–27.

[31] *Hist. Eccl.*, III, 7. Anglo-Saxon Chronicle, *sub annis* 645, 646; Earle and Plummer, eds., I, pp. 26–27.

[32] Stenton, *Anglo-Saxon England*, p. 118.

[33] *Hist. Eccl.*, III, 7 (p. 358).

[34] *Hist. Eccl.*, III, 7 (pp. 358–360).

[35] *Hist. Eccl.*, III, 21, tells of the conversion of Mercia (pp. 430–434).

which Penda had assigned to his son but without opposition in central Mercia as well. Upon Penda's death, the conversion of Mercia continued with royal support and without dramatic incident, *desecto capite perfido*.

The last heathen Anglo-Saxon kingdom was Sussex. About A.D. 680 it was ruled by the Christian Aethelwalh, who with his chief nobles had been baptized in Mercia at the instigation of its king, Wulfhere, who served as godfather to the South Saxon monarch.[36] Although Bede informs us that, following the royal conversion, others of the realm were baptized *vel tunc vel tempore sequente* by four priests, yet there were sections of Sussex where the Gospel had not been preached. It was these areas which were converted by Wilfrid after his flight from Northumbria about A.D. 681. The immediate success of Wilfrid's mission was aided not only by the king's earlier conversion but by the desertion of the South Saxons by their old gods. For three years prior to Wilfrid's arrival there had been no rain, and the resulting famine caused widespread suffering and mass suicidal leaping from cliffs, which, as we have noted, may have been offerings to Woden for the return of his favour.[37] However, on the very day on which the folk were baptized into Christianity 'there fell a mild but plentiful rain, wherewith the earth flourished again, a joyful and plentiful year returned, and the fields were clothed with green'.[38] The blessings with which the old religion was associated were brought by Christ after the ancestral gods had failed and the more powerful one, worshipped by their king, now held their allegiance. Indeed, it may not be too much to suggest that the conversion of Aethelwalh himself may have been stimulated by a desire to seek relief from the famine by turning to a God more effective than the tribal deities who had failed to alleviate it. After the king's death at the hands of the exiled Caedwalla of Wessex, a mission begun by Wilfrid soon converted the last stronghold of Anglo-Saxon heathenism, the Isle of Wight.

Clearly, then, the history of the coming of Christianity displays

[36] *Hist. Eccl.*, IV, 13, tells of the conversion of Sussex (II, pp. 72–78).
[37] See above, p. 38.
[38] *Hist. Eccl.*, IV, 13 (II, p. 74; transl. p. 75).

the role of the English king as the converter of his people. In no kingdom did the conversion occur without royal support, and in none do we hear of the conversion of the folk without that of the monarch previously. Even in Mercia, it was only after Peada, who ruled as sub-king under his father, became a Christian and with the permission of the great pagan war-lord himself that the Gospel was preached; the major work of the mission was done nonetheless only after Penda's death. The tribal relation with the divine still was dependent on the king's relation with the divine, and the proper *blot* was primarily the ruler's affair. Consequently, the conversion of the *folc* stemmed from the conversion of the king to the more powerful deity, since it was the king's relationship with the gods which 'saved' his people as much as did the gods themselves. When the king turned to Christ, it was done *cum sua gente*.

Further, in most of the kingdoms—Kent, Essex, East Anglia, Deira, and Bernicia—royal apostasy occurred, a fact which can best be explained by the long tradition of performing essential rites for the folk. In Deira and Bernicia the one year rule of the apostate kings was so brief that we are told nothing of popular reaction. However, when Redwald of East Anglia offered sacrifice to the former gods, it would certainly have had popular support for him to have done it in the face of his conversion. In Kent, King Eadbald led his people *ad priorem vomitum*, and in the realm of the East Saxons, Bede tells us, the apostate folk could not be recalled to faith in Christ even after Saberht's heathen sons had been killed in battle against the West Saxons. Converted again under Sigbert the Good, they apostacized once more when Sighere returned to his ancestral gods during the great plague of A.D. 664–665. Thus, as conversion of the subjects depends on that of the ruler, so also royal and popular apostasy are closely related.

In addition, as in the pagan North improper observance of the rituals was the cause of royal deposition and even king-slaying, so apostasy from the Christian faith was regarded as bringing about the loss of kingdom and on occasion the deletion from the line of Woden-sprung monarchs who had made the proper sacrifices.

M

Thus, when Cenwalh succeeded his father, Cynegils of the West Saxons, Bede reports that he 'refused to accept the faith and sacraments of the heavenly kingdom and not long after lost even the power over his earthly kingdom'. When he was converted in East Anglia, however, he was restored to his realm.[39] We have also noted that Osric of Deira and Eanfrid of Bernicia were removed from the king-lists because of their apostasy. However, when Eadbald of Kent apostacized after the death of his father Aethelberht, he was not stripped of his place in the line of monarchs, even though his subjects followed him, nor was Sighere of Essex. In both cases, however, they returned to the Christian faith. This cannot be said, though, of Redwald of East Anglia, who worshipped at two altars in one temple and who was nonetheless listed as a *bretwalda*. Thus, while the tribal culture was still strong enough after the Conversion to bring royal apostasy, both the old and the new religions related the fate of the kingdom to the cult of the king.

Christianity, however, even linked the destiny of king and kingdom not only with worship of God but with obedience to his priesthood. Consequently, *pax et gaudium in populis et anni frugiferi victoriaeque in hostes*—the traditional rewards to rulers for pagan *blot*—were given 'by the aid of God' to King Egfrith and Queen Aethelthryth, rulers of Deira and Bernicia, as long as they were obedient to Bishop Wilfrid; however, when the king was no longer at one with the bishop, his 'luck' left him.[40] Here, of course, unlike the old religion in which there was no powerful priesthood to be equated with the Divine Will and the *principes* themselves performed priestly functions, the possibility of division between two functions of the pagan Anglo-Saxon royal *persona mixta* appears. This division was to become crucial for the later concept of Christian kingship.

A final element in the royal role during the Conversion is the spiritual fatherhood of Anglo-Saxon kings over pagan rulers

[39] *Hist. Eccl.*, III, 7 (I, p. 356). Later also, when his kingdom lacked a bishop, 'he understood that a province forsaken by its prelate was rightfully forsaken also by divine help'.

[40] Eddius Stephanus, *Life of Bishop Wilfrid*, c. 19; B. Colgrave, ed., p. 40.

whose submission to Christianity they had procured. The adoption of rulers by Roman emperors was, of course, not unknown, as in the adoption by the latter of Gothic kings through the symbolic handing over of weapons.[41] The reception by a noble foster-father was, however, a feature of pagan baptism in the North, and it was most probably from this source that the Anglo-Saxon royal custom was derived. Thus Guthorm the Earl, for example, set the eldest son of King Harald Fair-Hair of Norway on his knee and became his foster-father.[42] This spiritual relationship occurs as early as A.D. 635 in England, when the Christian Oswald of Northumbria received his future father-in-law, King Cynegils of the West Saxons, as his son upon the latter's conversion.[43] When Cynegil's grandson, Cuthred, was baptized four years later, Bishop Birinus 'received him for son', in a prelude to the later expansion of this custom of the adoption of rulers. Thus, in a letter of A.D. 798 to Pope Leo III concerning the see of Lichfield, King Cenwulf of Mercia, ruling those 'who dwell at the end of the world', requests 'that you will especially receive me as your son by adoption, just as I love you in the person of a father, and always honour you with obedience with all my strength. For it is meet that holy faith be kept among such great persons, and inviolate love be guarded.'[44] As pagan chieftains were received as foster-sons at the hands of other rulers, so Anglo-Saxon

[41] E. Eichmann, 'Die Adoption des Deutschen Königs durch den Papst', *Zeitschrift der Savigny-Stiftung für Rechtsgeschichte, Germanistische Abteilung,* XXXVII (1916), pp. 294–295; cf. p. 294 for *filius* as *defensor.* A letter of Cassiodorus informs a king of the Heruli that Theodorich the Ostrogoth has created the Herulian his *filius per arma: Variae,* IV, 2; Chadwick, *The Heroic Age* (Cambridge, 1912). p, 374.

[42] *Harald Haarfagrs Saga,* c. 21; Eleanor Hull, 'Pagan Baptism in the West', *Folklore,* XLIII (1932), p. 411, for this and for sources for pagan Scandinavian lay baptism by sprinkling with water at the naming of the child. On the sacral nature of the knee, see above, p. 116.

[43] Anglo-Saxon Chronicle, *sub anno* 635; Earle and Plummer, eds., I, pp. 26–27.

[44] Extant only in William of Malmesbury; Haddan and Stubbs, eds., *Councils and Eccl. Doc.,* III, pp. 521–523. The extract is given in translation in Dorothy Whitelock, ed., *English Historical Documents c. 500–1042* (English Historical Documents, I; London, 1955), p. 791.

kings desired the prestige that would come from entering into this traditional spiritual sonship with the great chief of the new religion in far-off Rome. Such personal relationships 'among great persons' were honourable and customary. Indicating the cautious reception of this apparently unfamiliar custom in Rome, however, Pope Leo does not even mention the matter in his reply to Cenwulf. He speaks to the problem of the see of Lichfield but confines his suggestions for a closer relationship to exhorting the Mercian monarch to continue Offa's annual payment of three hundred and sixty-five mancuses to Rome.[45]

The first such papal adoption of royalty occurs under Leo IV, when Alfred, the five-year-old son of Aethelwulf of Wessex, came to Rome, where the pope *Aelfredum oppido ordinans unxit in regem, et in filium adoptionis sibimet accipiens confirmavit.*[46] The bestowal of the *cingulum* and consul's garb on Alfred, in the honorary act of making him Roman consul, was unfamiliar in Anglo-Saxon England and misinterpreted as a royal consecration;[47] indeed, if Matthew Paris is right, this Roman coronation—or rather its misinterpretation as a coronation—was one of the reasons for the conspiracy against Aethelwulf.[48] However, the pope's spiritual fatherhood is mentioned by both Asser and the Chronicle as separate from the 'coronation' and as important enough for parallel account. It was a well known relationship and

[45] B.M. MS. Cotton Vespasian A. xiv; Haddan and Stubbs, eds., *Councils and Eccl. Doc.*, pp. 523–525.

[46] Asser, *De Rebus Gestis Aelfredi*, c. 8; W. H. Stevenson, ed., *Asser's Life of King Alfred* (Oxford, 1904), p. 7. Anglo-Saxon Chronicle (MS. A), *sub anno* 853 (854): *ond hiene him to biscep sune nam*; Earle and Plummer, eds., I, p. 64. *Epistola Leonis IV in Mon. Ger. Hist., Ep.*, V, p. 602: *eo quod in suis se tradiderit manibus*. Cf. E. Eichmann, 'Adoption des Deutschen Königs', p. 300.

[47] W. Stevenson, ed., *Asser's Life of King Alfred*, pp. 180 (for letter of Leo IV to Aethelwulf of Wessex, explaining the ceremony), 180–185 (for commentary); D. Whitelock, ed., *Engl. Hist. Doc.*, pp. 115, 174, 810.

[48] Henry R. Luard, ed., *Matthaei Parisiensi Monachi Sancti Albani Chronica Majora* (Rolls Series, LVII:1; London, 1872), I, p. 385: *Causa autem bifaria erat, una, quod filium juniorem Afredum, quasi aliis a sorte regni exclusis, in regem Romae fecerat coronari*. This is found only in Matthew as a cause of the conspiracy but is of particular interest for the opposition it indicates to what was taken as an attempt at securing the succession for the boy in Aethelwulf's lifetime.

was not misinterpreted. Alfred's own spiritual fatherhood over a ruler is recorded by both of these same sources in the conversion of the Danish Guthrum. After the defeat of his army, Guthrum came to the king with the great men of his host 'at Aller, which is near Athelney', and the king, says the Chronicle *sub anno* 878, 'stood sponsor to him at his baptism there; and the unbinding of his chrism [*crism lising*] took place at Wedmore'.[49] Alfred, further, was god-father to a son of the Viking Hasting,[50] and the Welsh ruler Anarawd ap Rhodri was also a god-son of Alfred the Great. Deserting his Northumbrian alliance, Anarawd requested King Alfred's friendship. 'And when he had been honourably received by the king, and been accepted by him as his son from the hands of the bishop at confirmation, and been enriched with great gifts, he submitted with all his followers to the king's overlordship, on such terms that he would be obedient to the king in all things.'[51]

That this spiritual fatherhood of the Anglo-Saxon ruler was not confined to baptismal occasions, however, is indicated in the reception by King Constantine II of Scotland and several other northern princes—Scottish, English, and Viking—of Edward the Elder as their 'father and lord'.[52] This is, I suggest, more than a formal phrase, when taken in conjunction with the tradition of the spiritual relationship of rulers; as Alfred became god-father and overlord to Anarawd, it places the princes as foster-sons of the Anglo-Saxon monarch, as well as making them 'co-operator both by sea and by land', as was Constantine's successor, Malcolm I, to King Edmund.[53] In A.D. 943 the latter ruler also, the

[49] Earle and Plummer, eds., I, pp. 76, 77. For Asser, cf. Stevenson, ed., p. 47. The 'chrism-loosing' marked the removal of the fillet which was tied around the head to cover the baptismal chrism. Guthrum, the Anglo-Saxon Chronicle tells us *sub anno* 890, took the baptismal name of Aethelstan.

[50] Another son had Ealdorman Aethelred as his godfather. Anglo-Saxon Chronicle (MS. A), *sub anno* 894 (893); Earle and Plummer, eds., I, p. 86.

[51] Asser, *De Rebus Gestis Aelfredi*, c. 80; W. Stevenson, ed., pp. 66–67.

[52] The Viking Raegnald and the son of the Anglo-Saxon Eadwulf, both of Northumbria, and the king of the Strathclyde Welsh were the others who, with all their subjects, accepted Edward. Anglo-Saxon Chronicle (MS. A), *sub anno* 924 (923); Earle and Plummer, eds., I, p. 104.

[53] Earle and Plummer, eds., I, p. 110, in MS. A *sub anno* 945. H. M. Chadwick, *The Heroic Age*, p. 374, suggests such obligations were entailed by the

Chronicle states, 'received King Olaf at baptism, and in the same year, after a fairly long interval, he received King Ragnald at his confirmation'.[54] Similarly, Athelstan the Glorious became the spiritual father to the Scottish King Constantine's son, after he had ordered his baptism,[55] as did King Aethelred to King Olaf Tryggvason of Norway, after peace had been made between them.[56] Thus the English monarch not only had a definitive role in the conversion of his own folk but brought pagan rulers to the worship of the Christian God, an act through which a spiritual tie was formed 'among such great persons' which accords with what we know of pagan baptism. Political allegiance and peace were strengthened by vows to the same God, and the lordship of the Anglo-Saxon king by his acceptance as father.[57]

The king's role in conversion in England is thus well established. The theological content of the old religion, as well as its integration into the social and political background of the Germanic tribes, helped cast the mould into which Christian doctrine was poured and affected the interpretation of the finished work. As the change was more palatable to the folk if the new God were worshipped in the temples of the old, as Gregory the Great realized, so Christianity was the more readily accepted if the tribes were able to follow the sacrificial king of the old religion into the new.

---

*bretwalda*ship which the Anglo-Saxon Chronicle and Bede (the latter without using the title) ascribe to certain Anglo-Saxon kings.

[54] Anglo-Saxon Chronicle, without date but in A.D. 943; Earle and Plummer, eds., I, p. 110. Cf. B. Thorpe, ed., *Florentii Wigorniensis Monachi Chronicon ex Chronicis* (London, 1848), I, p. 133, in which Edmund *Anlafum regem . . . de lavacro sanctae regenerationis suscepit, regioque munere donavit: et parvo post tempore Reignoldum Northanhymbrorum regem, dum ab episcopo confirmaretur, tenuit, sibique in filium adoptavit.*

[55] W. Stubbs, ed. *Willelmi Malmesburiensis Monachi De Gestis Regum Anglorum* (Rolls Series, XC:1; London, 1887), p. 147 (Bk. II, §134).

[56] Anglo-Saxon Chronicle (MS. A), *sub anno* 993 (991) and (MSS. C, D, E) *sub anno* 994 (991); Earle and Plummer, eds., I, pp. 126, 129.

[57] Edmund and Cnut, however, as equals without either submitting to the other, 'became fellows and sworn brothers, and confirmed it both with pledge and also with oaths'. Earle and Plummer, eds., I, p. 152, in MS. D, *sub anno* 1016.

The totality of life and worlds made impossible the later duality of Church and State, and the interweaving of cult and culture enhanced the sacral strand of kingship which knit together the tapestry of tribal life.

CHAPTER VI

Sacral kingship in Anglo-Saxon law

J. M. Wallace-Hadrill is correct when he claims that 'behind the barbarian laws lies the Book of Deuteronomy'.[1] The Anglo-Saxon tribes of the New Dispensation often found their prototype in the tribes of Israel, and, as they turned their paraphrases of Old Testament Scripture into reflections of their own Germanic society, so their laws often reflect those of the warlike tribes of Israel more than they do the generalized legal principles of a Roman universal state. Occasionally, of course, we find specific Old Testament influence on Anglo-Saxon laws.[2] Alfred the Great, in his law code, even prefaces his own decrees with the Mosaic law of Exodus,[3] thus placing his ensuing dooms, or laws, in the tradition of law emanating from and continuing the dooms of Israel. A kingship reflected against such a background, as well as that which we have been examining, although Christian, may well be expected to be absorbed in a God-centred concept of monarch, heavenly and earthly, and in a ruler balanced between the tribal society he rules and the God who gives him and his people their 'luck'.

However, the two greatest influences on the actual codification of Anglo-Saxon law must be sought elsewhere; they are Roman and ecclesiastical. Before the introduction of Christianity we know of no Germanic written code, and the written formulation of law is largely stimulated by an attempt to cope with the new religion and with the status of its institution, the Church, in terms of

[1] J. M. Wallace-Hadrill, *The Barbarian West 400–1000* (2nd ed.; London, 1957), p. 56.

[2] Cf., e.g., A. J. Robertson, *The Laws of the Kings of England from Edmund to Henry I* (Cambridge, 1925), p. 335, notes to VI Aethelred 47, 48.

[3] Felix Liebermann, *Die Gesetze der Angelsachsen* (Halle a. S., 1903), I, p. 26–43. Cf. the reference to Mosaic Law in Alfred's preface to his translation of the *Cura Pastoralis*; F. Liebermann, 'King Alfred and Mosaic Law', *Transactions of the Jewish Historical Society of England*, VI (1908–1910), pp. 21–31.

Germanic society. In Kentish law, for example, dooms concerning the Church show less alliteration and consequently may be taken as newer.[4] The Anglo-Saxon laws which have survived are due to ecclesiastical scribes,[5] just as the use of written documents to record the gift of land or privileges was introduced because of the Church and indeed perhaps through the specific influence of the archbishop from out of the East, Theodore of Tarsus.[6] 'What the memory of man lets slip', as a charter of King Aethelred I asserts, 'the circumscription in letters preserves';[7] the Roman Church, unaccustomed to trust in an oral tradition, brought with it to the island realms its knowledge of preservation in written laws.

The Venerable Bede states specifically that the earliest Anglo-Saxon laws were drawn up *iuxta exempla Romanorum*.[8] The study of Roman law in the time of Aldhelm of Malmesbury is certainly clear.[9] But combined with this Roman and Christian influence on

[4] Dorothy Bethurum, 'Stylistic Features of the Old English Laws', *Modern Language Review*, XXVII (1932), p. 271. It is pointed out, however (p. 270), that although the weight of scholarly opinion tends to equate alliteration and *Sagvers* with antiquity and pre-Christian influence, the early laws of Kent are singularly short and less alliterative than the more extended forms of later codes.

[5] Dorothy Whitelock, ed., *English Historical Documents c. 500–1042* (English Historical Documents, I; London, 1955), pp. 327–328.

[6] Whitelock, ed., *Engl. Hist. Doc.*, pp. 342–343. Cf. p. 443 for the earliest authentic charter, that of Hlothhere of Kent, A.D. 679. The pre-Christian and pre-written form of transfer is probably reflected in an actual symbolic act of exchange in the earliest charters of land grants; J. M. Kemble, ed., *Codex Diplomaticus Aevi Saxonici* (London, 1847), V, no. 1019, p. 58. Whitelock, ed., *Engl. Hist. Doc.*, p. 343. On knowledge of Roman law in the Canterbury school of Theodore of Tarsus, and on the existence of a copy of the Breviary of Alaric in his library, cf. Frank Stenton, *Anglo-Saxon England* (2nd ed.; Oxford, 1947), p. 181 and note. His teaching may perhaps be seen in Greek influence on Old English; cf. Robertson, ed., *Laws of the Kings of England*, pp. 306–307, n. 2 to IV Edgar 1 §5a.

[7] Kemble, *Codex Diplomaticus*, III, no. 692, p. 291; Whitelock, ed., *Engl. Hist. Doc.*, p. 530.

[8] *Historia Ecclesiastica*, II, 5; J. E. King, ed., *Baedae Historia Ecclesiastica Gentis Anglorum* (Loeb Classical Library; London, 1930), I, p. 226.

[9] Stenton, *Anglo-Saxon England*, p. 181. Cf. also Paul Vinogradoff, 'Romanistische Einflüsse im Angelsächsischen Recht: das Buchland' *Mélanges Fitting: LXXVe Anniversaire de M. le Prof. Hermann Fitting* (Montpellier, 1908), II, p. 499–522.

law—and on the concept of kingship reflected in that law—is the Germanic society whose customs this new instrument of writing was to record. In contrast to the general legal principles characteristic of Roman law and the work of its jurisconsults, the principal features of the first Anglo-Saxon codes are the concrete and specific nature of their dooms and the elliptical, unelaborated method of recording what the tribal practice has been.[10] The laws did what it was their job to do—to state specific customary law, particularly with the changes necessary to integrate the new religion into the old, established societal structure—and it has consequently been suggested that this task necessitated the use of the vernacular;[11] the legal terminology was technical in that it applied to specific Anglo-Saxon practice, and consequently the Romans, not having the practice, did not have the terms to describe the practice.

In these laws, combining then the three great formative elements of the early Middle Ages—Roman, Christian, and Germanic—both Church and State, both ecclesiastical and lay authority, are intermeshed. Sometimes they are shown uniting in legal transactions;[12] sometimes the king, becoming a homilist,[13] pursues his role of protector of ecclesiastical rights even more vigorously than does Rome itself;[14] sometimes a high statement of the vision of co-operating sacred and secular spheres is achieved.

[10] Ernst Levy, 'Reflections on the First "Reception" of Roman Law in Germanic States', *American Historical Review*, XLVIII (1942), p. 23, attributing statements of general legal principles to Roman influence, declares that 'no primitive people has, on its own account, ever arrived at such generalizations'.

[11] Peter Hunter Blair, *An Introduction to Anglo-Saxon England* (Cambridge, 1956), p. 329.

[12] Whitelock, ed., *Engl. Hist. Doc.*, pp. 80, 328, 387–391 (VI Athelstan, ordinance of bishops and reeves of the London district).

[13] See below, pp. 185–187, 200–203, e.g.

[14] In relation to excommunication, cf. Rosalind Hill, 'The Theory and Practice of Excommunication in Medieval England', *History*, XLII (1957), p. 4; here also lapses into heathenism are acutely seen as a stumbling in the difficult path between common and ecclesiastical law. The twelve-fold compensation for theft from a church in Aethelberht 1 is in contrast to the repayment of the simple value of the object, suggested by Pope Gregory I to Augustine; Bede, *Hist. Eccl.*, I, 27; King, ed., I, p. 122.

Thus Aethelred in his tenth code, in impressive Anglo-Saxon alliteration, declares that 'frequently and often it has come into my mind that sacred precepts and wise secular decrees promote Christianity and strengthen royal authority, further public interests and are the source of honour, bring about peace and reconciliation, put an end to strife and improve the whole character of the nation'.[15] Throughout the laws, certainly, as would be expected, the king as embodiment of the state[16] is prominently seen. As in a Norse kenning the king is called 'Justice',[17] so in Anglo-Saxon law he reflects still the ancient Germanic royal role of the judge the breaking of whose decrees looses the wrath of God upon the offender. His word is incontrovertible,[18] and he has the gift of *raed*, the 'power that comes from within and flows out in counsels, orders, plans; it is the wisdom that fills words and thoughts, the justice that inspires them, the authority which makes people obey the order'.[19] Its loss, as in the case of Aethelred *Unraed*, makes the ruler unable to give wise council, 'unlucky' for himself and his folk.[20]

Of Anglo-Saxon, only Kentish and West Saxon codes survive.[21] No royal laws from early Mercia or Northumbria have come down to us, although we know that the most powerful

---

[15] *Mearn to gemynde oft 7 gelome þe godcunde lara 7 wislice woroldlaga Cristendom fyrðriað 7 cynedom micliað, folce gefremiað 7 weorðscypes wealdað, sibbiað 7 sehtað 7 sace twaemað 7 þeode þeawas ealle gebetað:* X Aethelred §1; Robertson, ed., p. 130.

[16] On the king as 'state' in Anglo-Saxon law, cf. F. Liebermann, ed., *Gesetze*, II:2, p. 548, article *König*, sec. 1a.

[17] Gudbrand Vigfusson and F. York Powell, eds., *Corpus Poeticum Boreale* (Oxford, 1883), II, p. 480. This work is referred to here as *C.P.B.*

[18] Wihtred 16; F. L. Attenborough, ed., *The Laws of the Earliest English Kings* (Cambridge, 1922), p. 27.

[19] Vilhelm Grönbech, *The Culture of the Teutons* (London, 1931), III, p. 12.

[20] On *unraed* as 'counsel-less' not in the sense of counsel from others but from himself, and on concept of *raed*, cf. Grönbech, *Culture of the Teutons*, III, pp. 12–14, '*Rad*, Anglo-Saxon *Raed*'.

[21] References to the laws throughout this chapter are made to the most convenient and generally accessible scholarly editions, by F. L. Attenborough and A. J. Robertson, as cited above. References to them will be to author only in these notes and, except for special purposes, will be made to the pages of the

English ruler of the second half of the eighth century, Offa of Mercia, issued laws.[22] In the late references to the customary laws of Mercia, which appear as an administrative division in the dooms of Cnut and in greater detail in the early Norman code attributed to the Conqueror, few distinctions between Mercia and Wessex are reflected, and those are minor.[23] What early sources would show for the period before the kingdoms were knit under one rule, however, it is, of course, impossible to say. The earliest English laws, although surviving only in post-Conquest manuscripts, are those of Kent. The code of the first royal Anglo-Saxon convert to Christianity, Aethelberht of Kent, shows primarily an attempt to integrate the Church into a Germanic society which is hierarchic but based on a free, non-noble, land-holding peasantry subject directly to the king.[24] The other two remaining Kentish codes stem from the chaotic time of Hlothhere and Eadric (c. A.D. 673-685) and from the reign a decade later of King Wihtred. The former shows an all-powerful king or aristocracy as little as does Aethelberht's collection but is of little significance in our problem of the king in his religious aspect; Wihtred's dooms are above all of value for their evidence of royal jurisdiction in ecclesiastical matters and of a Church which has grown powerful in the century since Aethelberht's conversion.

The West Saxon series begins with Ine of Wessex (A.D. 688–

English translations in these editions, when these translations are cited in my text; the Anglo-Saxon text, however, will always be found on the preceding page of these parallel editions. Felix Liebermann, ed., *Die Gesetze der Angelsachsen* (Halle, a. S., 1903-1916), I-III, already cited, has still not been replaced as the best commentary and complete edition, and reference will be made to it when useful. For a good introduction to Anglo-Saxon laws, their Mss., and problems, cf. D. Whitelock, ed., *Engl. Hist. Doc.*, pp. 327-337. For dating of codes, see the introductions to them in Attenborough, Robertson, and Whitelock.

[22] From King Alfred's reference to them in the introduction to his own code. Introd. 49 §9; Liebermann, ed., *Gesetze*, I, p. 46.

[23] Stenton, *Anglo-Saxon England*, pp. 498-499. The eleventh century *Northleoda Laga* and *Mircna Laga*, perhaps collected by Archbishop Wulfstan, contain material which seems to be much earlier; see below, pp. 222-223.

[24] Stenton, *Anglo-Saxon England*, p. 274.

726), who perhaps followed the example of his contemporary, the law-giver Wihtred. Ine's code, as Sir Frank Stenton remarks, 'stands for a new conception of kingship' and is 'the work of a responsible statesman, capable of bringing his clergy and nobles into deliberation on the blending of ancient custom and new enactment in an elaborate body of law'.[25] From the next two centuries no Anglo-Saxon code has survived, although Offa's lost laws fall in this period, but when the next does appear, it is for Kent and Mercia as well as Wessex. This sign of the growing political cohesiveness of the English, developed under the impact of the Scandinavian onslaught, is the famous code of Alfred the Great. Prefaced by excerpts from Old Testament law, a history of Christian councils in the early Church and in England, and reference to the law-giving of Ine, Offa, and Aethelberht, his laws give a sense of the continuity of law but display an even higher view of Christian monarchy and of its role in relation to the Church than the earlier English dooms.[26] The reign of Edward the Elder, Alfred's son and successor, gives us two short codes, and from his and his father's period come in all probability most of the contents of the law-including treaties with the Danes, the so-called Laws of Alfred and Guthrum and of Edward and Guthrum.[27]

The century that follows—that from King Athelstan to Cnut the Great—provides the largest bulk of the surviving codes. Six

[25] Stenton, *Anglo-Saxon England*, p. 71. Cf. F. Liebermann, 'Ueber die Gesetze Ines von Wessex', *Mélanges d'Histoire offerts á M. Charles Bemont* (Paris, 1913), pp. 21–42.

[26] Stenton, *Anglo-Saxon England*, pp. 272–273; Whitelock, ed., *Engl. Hist. Doc.*, pp. 331–332. On the relation of Alfred's laws to the Continent, cf. J. M. Wallace-Hadrill, 'The Franks and the English in the Ninth Century', *History*, XXXV (1950), p. 216.

[27] The laws of Edward and Guthrum have been attributed to Archbishop Wulfstan; cf. Dorothy Whitelock, 'Wulfstan and the So-Called Laws of Edward and Guthrum', *English Historical Review*, LVI (1941), pp. 1–21. On Wulfstan as legislator, cf. Whitelock, ed., *Engl. Hist. Doc.*, p. 854, and her articles, 'A Note on the Career of Wulfstan the Homilist', *English Historical Review*, LII (1937), pp. 460–465; 'Wulfstan and the Laws of Cnut', *ibid.*, LXIII (1948), pp. 433–452; 'Wulfstan's Authorship of Cnut's Laws', *ibid.*, LXX (1955), pp. 72–85; also Dorothy Bethurum, ed., *The Homilies of Wulfstan*

codes, most of them dealing at length with theft, and an ordinance on alms-giving come from the reign of Athelstan (A.D. 925–939), while three date from King Edmund (A.D. 939–946), one of which treats exclusively of ecclesiastical matters. The four codes of Edgar (A.D. 959–975), one of which is nameless but attributed to him,[28] give ample evidence of that ruler's concern for religious well-being, but one of them, IV Edgar, also recognizes the legal

---

(Oxford, 1957), pp. 62, 70, 72–83 (where his authorship of Edward and Guthrum's laws is assumed); D. Bethurum, 'Six Anonymous Old English Codes', *Journal of English and Germanic Philology*, XLIX (1950), pp. 449–463. Between them Miss Whitelock and Miss Bethurum have claimed almost every law code of the early eleventh century for Wulfstan on the grounds of style. The noted Wulfstan authority Karl Jost rejected the archbishop's authorship of both codes of Cnut and excluded Edward and Guthrum as well from his *Wulfstankanon*, warning of the dangers of ascribing works to Wulfstan because they have his style; K. Jost, *Wulfstanstudien* (Swiss Studies in English, XXIII; Bern, 1950), pp. 102–103. However, I am indebted to Professor Whitelock for the information that, in a personal letter to her before his death, Jost accepted Wulfstan's authorship of Edward and Guthrum. For his arguments against Whitelock's attribution of Cnut's laws to Wulfstan, cf. pp. 94–103. Jost's *Wulfstankanon* includes, besides the homilies, V–X Aethelred, I and II Polity, the Pseudo-Edgar Canons, the poem in the Anglo-Saxon Chronicle *sub anno* 975, and Wulfstan's letter to Cnut; *ibid.*, p. 116. Cf. R. R. Darlington's review of Miss Bethurum's edition of the *Homilies* in *Journal of Ecclesiastical History*, X (1959), p. 104. One must, of course, distinguish here the content of the laws from the form in which they are now cast. I myself regard Professor Whitelock, certainly one of the greatest Anglo-Saxonists of our day, as having made a virtually conclusive case for Wulfstan's authorship of the existing form of the laws. However, no one would claim that he himself created their contents. Although an early eleventh century dating of Edward and Guthrum would not be fatal to any use I have made of that code, the contents often bespeak an earlier date, as will be seen, even though the form in which it has survived may, on stylistic grounds, be ascribed to Wulfstan. Miss Whitelock, 'Wulfstan and the So-Called Laws of Edward and Guthrum', after giving her arguments (pp. 11–17) against Liebermann's dating of the code between 921 and 939, admits (p. 18) both that II Edward 5 §2 shows the existence of treaties with the Danes which gave laws and that 'it is more than probable that in general the code represents regulations of considerable antiquity, or otherwise the author's claim that they went back to Alfred and Guthrum would have been too demonstrably false'.

[28] Robertson, p. 4.

independence of districts under the Danes by this time. Ten codes or portions of codes, six of them generally attributed to Archbishop Wulfstan's authorship, date from the turbulent reign of Aethelred the Redeless, and the last laws of the Anglo-Saxon period are the two codes of King Cnut. The post-Conquest laws attributed to William I are not treated here except in rare cases, although 'there is little . . . which might not have been prescribed by an Anglo-Saxon king';[29] even though the laws of the Conqueror were largely 'the same as King Edward his cousin observed before him',[30] the kingdom of the Anglo-Saxon monarchs ended at Senlac, and except where his *leis e custumes* shed new light on earlier English kingship, they will not enter our consideration. Non-royal laws, primarily of status, surviving from the late Anglo-Saxon period, will, however, be discussed when they treat of our problem. A detailed analysis of all these sources for kingship in the laws is now needed.

The earliest of all English laws come from the Jutish kingdom of Kent. The *bretwalda* Aethelberht was the most prominent ruler in England in the late sixth and early seventh centuries, but, as Stenton rightly claims, 'it is through the laws which he issued for his own kingdom of Kent that Aethelberht enters into general history'.[31] Even on first examination the position of the ruler in these dooms and those of his successors is far from that of an omnipotent autocrat acting independently as lord over his folk. There is, first of all, the *consilium sapientium* which participated in their promulgation. 'One can in the council of sages', as the Anglo-Saxon poem *The Arts of Man* affirms, 'devise a decree for the people, where the *witan* is gathered together'.[32] Unlike its

[29] Stenton, *Anglo-Saxon England*, p. 676. No written laws of William or his predecessors are known for Normandy; *ibid.*, p. 547.

[30] Preface to so-called Laws of William I; Robertson, p. 253.

[31] Stenton, *Anglo-Saxon England*, p. 60. H. G. Richardson and G. O. Sayles, *Law and Legislation from Aethelberht to Magna Carta* (Edinburgh, 1966), pp. 1–11, hold that the first clause of Aethelberht's code is an interpolation and that the code might date from any year of his reign, since, they suggest, his conversion to Christianity can itself be questioned. On the latter, *ibid.*, pp. 162–166.

[32] *Arts of Man*, ll. 41–43; G. P. Krapp and E. V. K. Dobbie, eds., *The Exeter Book* (Anglo-Saxon Poetic Records, III; New York, 1936), p. 138.

specific role in the issuing of Wihtred's code, this *witan* is not mentioned in Aethelberht's laws as sharing in them, but Bede says they were issued by its advice,[33] and Felix Liebermann may be correct in suggesting a lost prologue to the code as the basis of Bede's comment.[34] In the next Kentish code, that attributed to Hlothhere, grandson of Aethelberht's successor Eadbald, and Eadric, the nobles in charge of pleas in the assemblies appear as 'judges of the Kentish people' and as more than judicial advisers to the king.[35] However, their more powerful role may be attributed to the less stable times in which the throne was occupied by Hlothhere and his nephew Eadric, who invaded his uncle's realm, fought a battle which resulted in the latter's death, and died himself the following year (A.D. 686).[36] The royal council appears again in the promulgation of the last Kentish dooms, those issued by Wihtred at Barham in A.D. 695, in which co-operation of lay and ecclesiastical is well seen.[37] This customary function of the *witan* is seen in the issuing of the contemporary code of Ine of Wessex, and when Alfred rejects earlier laws which displeased him he does so *mid minra witena geðeahte*.[38] The preamble of the so-called Laws of Edward and Guthrum[39] testifies

[33] *Hist. Eccl.*, II, 5; King, ed., I, p. 226.

[34] F. Liebermann, *The National Assembly in the Anglo-Saxon Period* (Halle, 1913), p. 2.

[35] In Alfred the Great's translation of Mosaic law he substitutes *witan* for 'judges'; F. Liebermann, 'King Alfred and Mosaic Law', p. 25.

[36] Hlothhere and Eadric 8; Attenborough, p. 21. *Hist. Eccl.*, IV, 26; King, ed., II, p. 164.

[37] 'During the sovereignty of Wihtred, the most gracious king of Kent, in the fifth year of his reign, the ninth Indiction, the sixth day of Rugern, in a place which is called Barham, there was assembled a deliberative council of notables. There were present there Berhtwald, the chief bishop of Britain, and the above mentioned king; the bishop of Rochester, who was called Gefmund; and every order of the Church province expressed itself in unanimity with the loyal laity (assembled there). There the notables, with the consent of all, drew up these decrees, and added to the legal usages of the people of Kent.' Attenborough, p. 25. On variant locations of *Berghamstyde*, cf. *ibid.*, p. 180, n. 4.

[38] Alfred, Introd. 49 §9; Liebermann, ed., *Gesetze*, I, p. 46.

[39] Attenborough, p. 103.

to the *witan*'s frequent re-enactment of and additions to this code, and III and IV Athelstan are even issued as the decrees of the councillors themselves.[40]

However, royal power in the laws is less than absolute not only because of the well known principle that the Anglo-Saxon monarch governed with the advice of his council.[41] The elevation in law of king and Church seems to create a duality of powers. The double compensation paid for breaking the peace of assembly, or paid to a liege of the king when summoned by his royal lord, or again for breaking the peace when the king is feasting at a man's house, is matched by the double compensation for breach of the peace of a church.[42] The king's *mundbyrd* of fifty shillings is matched by that of the Church which 'shall be fifty shillings like the king's'.[43] The incontrovertibleness of the king's word, whether or not supported by an oath, is paralleled by that of the unsupported word of a bishop.[44] Furthermore, an abbot, priest, or deacon in the code of Wihtred has the same right as a king's thegn of clearing himself by his own oath at the altar,[45] and servants of the king or of a bishop, when accused, are subject to the same procedure, the hand of the reeve, the king's representative, serving as the instrument of clearance.[46] The Church is immune from taxation, and indeed in case of theft recompense to the king—nine-fold—is less than the Church's twelve-fold or a Bishop's eleven-fold compensation and is equal only to that of a priest.[47]

[40] Attenborough, e.g., pp. 37, 63, 119; 143, 147, for III and IV Athelstan.

[41] Cf. Stenton, *Latin Charters of the Anglo-Saxon Period* (Oxford, 1955), pp. 34–35, for cartulary evidence that in this period in Kent assent of the nobles was also essential for making a privileged estate.

[42] Aethelberht 1, 2, 3, and (for the Church) 1, respectively; Attenborough, p. 5.

[43] Aethelberht 8, Wihtred 2; Attenborough, pp. 5, 25.

[44] Wihtred 16; Attenborough, p. 27.

[45] Wihtred 17–18; Attenborough, p. 29.

[46] 'If a servant of a bishop or of the king is accused, he shall clear himself by the hand of the reeve': Wihtred 22; Attenborough, p. 29.

[47] Aethelberht 1, 4; Attenborough, p. 5. On the significance of the king's nine-fold compensation, cf. W. A. Chaney, 'Aethelberht's Code and the King's Number', *American Journal of Legal History*, VI (1962), pp. 151–177.

This evidence for the lack of uniqueness in royal prerogatives, as witnessed in the dooms, and the absence—or apparent absence —of exaltation of the Woden-sprung Kentish king must, however, be counterbalanced by two factors. In the first place, underlying these limitations are the positive features of royal authority: the king's peace is double that of his subjects; his word is incontrovertible; his thegn and servant have special privileges. The ancient right of the king to be entertained as he passed through the countryside, the custom underlying the later royal *feorm*, is to be seen in the double penalty for the breach of peace 'if the king is feasting at anyone's house'.[48] Further, no noble is seen in the laws between the free peasant and the king, who appears as possibly the personal lord of every free man.[49] Moreover, the royal prerogative is emphasized when, in the words of the code of Aethelberht, 'the king calls his lieges to him'.[50] Bede underscores this prerogative when, whatever the role of the *witan*, he writes that 'he (Aethelberht) ... ordained what amends he ought to make, which had by theft taken away anything from the churches, bishops, or the other orders, wishing doubtless to provide a safeguard for them whom and whose doctrine he had received'.[51] That laws are indeed the king's decrees is seen in the preambles to many codes: 'These are the decrees which King Aethelberht established.' 'These are the decrees which Hlothhere and Eadric, Kings of Kent, established. Hlothhere and Eadric, Kings of Kent, extended the laws which their predecessors had made by the decrees which are stated below.' 'These are the decrees of Wihtred, King of Kent.' 'I, Ine, by the grace of God king of Wessex ... that no *ealdorman* nor subject of ours may from henceforth pervert these decrees.' 'Now I, King Alfred, have collected these laws.'[52] As the pre-migration Germanic king

---

[48] Aethelberht 3; Attenborough, p. 5.

[49] Attenborough, p. 175, n. 1 to Aethelberht 6.

[50] Aethelberht 2; Attenborough, p. 5.

[51] *Hist. Eccl.*, II, 5; King, ed., I, p. 227.

[52] Attenborough, pp. 5, 19, 25, 37, 63; cf. pp. 115, 119, 123, 127, 153. A council issued III Athelstan as its decrees but besought the king 'if this document contains either too much, or too little, to command alterations to be made according to your wishes'; *ibid.*, p. 147.

spoke first in the assembly, to exercise his *auctoritas suadendi*, so the prominent role of the king in assembly in England appears in the attribution of its decrees to his authority. But the royal position is demonstrated by the laws not only in these manifest statements of authority. It appears as well even in the royal assertion of ecclesiastical rights and power, too often misinterpreted as evidence of limitations on the king.

Bede's statement of the purpose of Aethelberht's decrees notes once more the purpose of the first written laws of the English: to integrate the new religion into the already existing societal structure. These brief, laconic laws do not, unhappily for our purposes, portray that structure in its fullness, but their very brevity demonstrates that much is assumed—including the basic and ancient role of the tribal king. The necessity of the Church has called the laws into being—Wihtred's code, for example, 'apart from four final clauses . . . relates exclusively to matters of ecclesiastical interest', as Stenton has pointed out[53]—but in their Church-centredness, these codes at the same time present the parallel of the sacred character of the royal person. The sacrificial priest-king of ancient Germanic heathenism has his successor in the Christian tribal king, who is shown as the counterpart of the new high priests and with parallel privileges. Among the pre-Christian tribes, 'kingship was less a matter of political authority than of descent from ancient gods',[54] as we have seen, and this holiness of monarchy is reflected in the laws even when that 'political authority' is not revealed in detail. This second factor—the exaltation of royal cult in the very parallel, too often interpreted as a rival authority, of the Church—necessitates a fuller examination of the relation of king and Church in the laws. The accommodation of the old religion in terms of the new will be seen to play its role here too.

The relation of heathen king with heathen religion continues in the relation of Christian king with Christian Church. 'A Christian king is Christ's deputy [*Cristes gespelia*] among Christian people,' as Aethelred II declares in his eighth code, 'and he must

[53] Stenton, *Anglo-Saxon England*, p. 62.
[54] Stenton, *Anglo-Saxon England*, p. 37.

avenge with the utmost diligence offences against Christ'.[55] This premise and this conclusion underlie the entire body of Anglo-Saxon law. Offences against the Church[56] are thus a necessary and legitimate area of royal legislation, as *Cristes gespelia* on earth, the king, must needs punish offences against Christ, not in the sense of offences against royalty alone but in the sense of sin, offences against Heaven. As the heathen king, the representative of the gods among the folk, was responsible for the tribe's right relationship with the divine, so his Christian successor continues the same function in later terms.

This assertion of royal duty in the dooms, repeated, for example, in the preambles to II Edmund and X Aethelred,[57] occurs again explicitly in the laws of Cnut: 'It is the duty most incumbent upon a Christian king that he should avenge to the uttermost offences against God.'[58] This conclusion concerning the royal role of avenger for sin is supported in Anglo-Saxon homiletic writing; thus, the *Institutes of Polity, Civil and Ecclesiastical*, written by Archbishop Wulfstan of York, asserts: 'Of a King.—It is very rightly the duty of a Christian king to be in the place of a father to a Christian nation, and in watch and in ward Christ's vice-gerent, so as he is accounted. And it is also his duty, with all his mind, to love Christianity, and shun heathenism, and everywhere to honour and protect God's church.'[59] And again: 'Lo! through

[55] Robertson, p. 119. For parallel statements to this law, VIII Aethelred 2 §1, in the so-called Laws of Edward the Confessor and in the Homilies of Wulfstan, cf. Liebermann, *Gesetze*, II:1, p. 549. The Benedictines considered the abbot as *Cristes gespelia*: ibid., II:2, p. 314, article *König*, sect. 6e.

[56] On the use of the term 'Christ' as the Church, cf. Liebermann, *Gesetze*, II:2, p. 340, article *Christus*, sect. 1, and p. 535, article, *Kirche*, sect. 2.

[57] Robertson, pp. 9, 131. Cf. VIII Aethelred 36: 'And secular councillors showed wisdom in appointing civil laws to uphold the privileges of religion, for the governance of the people, and in assigning the compensation to Christ and the king, so that thereby many are forced of necessity to submit to justice'; ibid., p. 127. For parallels, ibid., p. 341, n. 1. For significance of 'Christ and the king', see below, pp. 197–200.

[58] II Cnut 40 §2; Robertson, p. 197. Cf. V Aethelred 1, VII Aethelred 1; ibid., pp. 79, 109.

[59] Benjamin Thorpe, ed., *Ancient Laws and Institutes of England* (London, 1840), II, p. 305; Karl Jost, ed., *Die 'Institutes of Polity, Civil and Ecclesiastical'*

what shall peace and support come to God's servants and to God's poor, save through Christ, and through a Christian king?'[60]

In spite of the change in the official religion with the conversion of the king,[61] it was still necessary to legislate against the old religion, which lingered on. This has been noted previously, and it is only with reference to the laws that the problem shall now be evidenced briefly once more. King Eorcenberht, Aethelberht's grandson, we have seen, 'was the first of the kings of the English who ordered by his supreme authority that the idols in his whole realm be abandoned and destroyed',[62] but these laws, if this royal action was expressed in legal form, have not survived. At the end of the seventh century, Wihtred, in the last surviving Kentish law code, forbids both freemen and slaves from making offerings to 'devils'.[63] The earliest West Saxon law code, on the other hand, that of Wihtred's contemporary, Ine, does not legislate against heathenism, but, as Professor Whitelock has pointed out, this does not mean that paganism did not survive in the West Saxon realms, since Ine's laws have come down to us only in Alfred's edition of them.[64] With the resurgence of paganism on the heels of the Viking invasions, the problem recurs in the laws, but this cannot be taken as evidence that heathen practices perished between Wihtred and the invasions, especially since the laws of the greatest English ruler of the interim period of the late eighth century, Offa of Mercia, have not survived. Although Alfred's code proper contains no legislation on the subject, it is significant that in the preamble containing laws from the Old Testament and New Testament, he deviates from the Vulgate and substitutes the

(Swiss Studies in English, vol. XLVII; Bern, 1959), p. 40. See below, pp. 257–259.

[60] Thorpe, Ancient Laws and Institutes, II, p. 307; Jost, Institutes of Polity, p. 46.

[61] See above, chapter V, 'The Royal Role in the Conversion of England'.

[62] Bede, Hist. Eccl., III, 8. See above, p. 159. This is treated here only as evidenced in the laws.

[63] Wihtred 12–13; Attenborough, p. 26. Wilfrid Bonser, The Medical Background of Anglo-Saxon England (London, 1963), p. 118, notes that 'devil' often has the meaning 'pagan deity', in Anglo-Saxon England, rather than 'spirit of evil'.

[64] Whitelock, ed., Engl. Hist. Doc., p. 331.

forbidding of idol-worship for the original inhibition against eating the meat of sacrifices.[65] He furthermore not only includes the Mosaic injunction not to swear by heathen gods but adds that they should not be invoked,[66] and in the Decalogue, while omitting the commandment against the worship of images, he adds to the Decalogue a later verse from Exodus against idols.[67] Thus Alfred's concern with a revived heathenism in the face of the invasions is perfectly clear. Its omission from his own legislation is no indication of a lessening of the problem, in view of the detailed changes in Biblical laws on the subject.

After the coming of the Vikings, the joint legislation attributed to Edward the Elder and the Danish Guthrum renounces *aelcne haethendom* and fixes money penalties 'according to the nature of the offence'.[68] The existence of 'wizards and sorcerers', who are to be 'driven from the land' or killed, also testifies to the survival of the old beliefs.[69] Those who encompass a death by witchcraft are to be killed themselves, the next king, Athelstan, also rules, but he provides for trial by ordeal.[70] The laws of King Edmund generalize—or 'spiritualize'—the penalty, providing that sorcerers 'shall be cast out forever from any portion in God'.[71] The general injunction to shun heathen practices is often repeated in the laws of the troubled times of Aethelred the Redeless,[72] and King Cnut

[65] Alfred, Introd. 49 §5, based on Acts 15:29; Liebermann, *Gesetze*, I, p. 44, and III, p. 48.

[66] Alfred, Introd. 48, based on Exodus 23:13; Liebermann, *Gesetze*, I, p. 42.

[67] The Latin version of the laws, the *Quadripartitus*, reintroduces the second Commandment, although keeping Alfred's addition. The latter is omitted in a twelfth century transcription of the *Quadripartitus*. The customary Roman Catholic Decalogue fills up the gap caused by its omission of the second Commandment by dividing the tenth into two. F. Liebermann, 'King Alfred and Mosaic Law', pp. 25–26.

[68] Edward and Guthrum, Preamble §2 and c. 2; Attenborough, pp. 102–103.

[69] Edward and Guthrum 11; Attenborough, p. 109.

[70] II Athelstan 6–6 §1; Attenborough, p. 131.

[71] I Edmund 6; Robertson, pp. 7, 296, n. 3 to c. 6.

[72] V Aethelred 1, 34, VI Aethelred 1, 6, VIII Aethelred 44, IX Aethelred 1, X Aethelred 1; Robertson, pp. 79, 89, 91, 93, 129, 131, 133. VI Aethelred 7 repeats Edward and Guthrum's law against wizards and sorcerers; Robertson, p. 93.

enumerates these more specifically: 'namely, the worship of idols, heathen gods, and the sun or the moon, fire or water, springs or stones or any kind of forest trees, or indulgence in witchcraft, or the compassing of death in any way, either by sacrifice or by divination or by the practice of any such delusions.'[73] Thus these royal laws from Wihtred—and indeed perhaps Eorcenberht—to the last code of the Anglo-Saxon period attest to the presence of heathenism and to the king's role in extirpating it. The kings who in Christian times still traced their descent from Woden also issued their dooms against their ancestor and his religion.

Not only is the old religion condemned but the new one is upheld. The legal protection of the Christian clergy will be discussed later. As early as the protection of the Christian clergy appear royal decrees to maintain ecclesiastical discipline and to exhort the clergy to the responsibilities of their calling. The favour of God depends on the makers of *blot*, and they must not neglect it. Already in the late-seventh-century laws of Wihtred of Kent are found provisions that a priest neglecting his duty by consenting to an illicit union, by failing to provide baptism for a sick man, or by drunkenness, is to be removed from his priestly functions until his bishop makes a judgement in the case; severe limits are also placed on hospitality to wandering 'tonsured' not under ecclesiastical discipline.[74] In the contemporary code of Ine of Wessex, a priest who works on Sunday is subject to a double fine, the equivalent of the 120 shilling fine for insubordination to the king, since that for a freeman working on Sunday is sixty shillings.[75] Thus again rebellion against God's law is equated in earthly compensation with insubordination to the terrestrial king. Later dooms concern murder by a priest,[76] stealing, fighting,

[73] II Cnut 5 §1; Robertson, p. 177; cf. 4a (p. 177) for repetition of Edward and Guthrum 11. The Northumbrian Priest's Law, probably contemporary with Cnut, also legislates against heathen practices (47-48, 54, 67); Whitelock, ed., *Engl. Hist. Doc.*, pp. 437-439.
[74] Wihtred 6, 7; Attenborough, p. 27.
[75] Ine 3 §2; Attenborough, p. 37.
[76] Alfred 21; Attenborough, p. 75. The priest with 'all the share of the monastic property which he has bought for himself shall be given up; and the bishop shall unfrock him when he is ejected from the monastery and given up', unless

committing perjury or adultery,[77] the misdirecting of the people by a *maessepreost* about a festival or a fast, and the withholding of baptism from one needing it or the neglect of bringing the chrism on Maundy Thursday.[78]

The multiplication of royal laws on ecclesiastical discipline comes, however, from the mid-tenth century, following the monastic reforms associated with King Edgar, *Salomon secundus*.[79] The concern for the responsibilities of the clergy and for the imposition of a monastic discipline on secular as well as ecclesiastical clergy becomes more and more extensive in the laws of the English monarchs, particularly in the ecclesiastical codes (V–X) of Aethelred II. 'The servants of God, bishops and abbots, monks and nuns, priests and women under religious vows, shall submit to their duty, and live according to their rule, and zealously intercede for all Christian people,' exhorts V Aethelred 4, an injunction which is repeated both in substance and with regard to specific deeds.[80] For the first time, after the monastic reform not only are priests and lower clergy involved in these regulations, as in the earlier laws and in King Edgar's decree that 'I and my thegns shall enforce upon our priests the duties prescribed for us by the guardians of our souls, namely our bishops.'[81] The lower clergy are still not neglected, but here bishops and abbots as well are called on to 'submit to their duty'.[82]

---

the lord of the monastery pays the slain man's *wergeld*. Cf. Edward and Guthrum 4 §2: 'If a man in orders [*gehadod man*] places his life in jeopardy by committing a capital crime, he shall be arrested, and his case shall be reserved for the bishop's decision'; *ibid.*, p. 105.

[77] Edward and Guthrum 3; Attenborough, p. 103. A distinction is again made between the ecclesiastical and civil natures of the offence, since a *gehadod man* who commits these crimes must 'pay either *wergeld* or fine or *lahslit*, according to the nature of the offence; and in any case shall he make compensation to God as the canon directs'.

[78] Edward and Guthrum 3 §1, 2; Attenborough, pp. 103–105.

[79] T. Arnold, ed., *The History of the English, by Henry, Archdeacon of Huntingdon* (Rolls Series, LXXIV; London, 1879), p. 166 (Bk. V, c. 26).

[80] Robertson, *Laws*, p. 81.

[81] IV Edgar 1 §8; Robertson, p. 33.

[82] Cf. VI Aethelred 2, VIII Aethelred 31 §1, and I Cnut 6a; Robertson, pp. 91, 127, 163.

One of the most repeated reforms now attempted in the laws, the enforcement of clerical celibacy, reflects, of course, the reforms of Edgar and Dunstan and the extension of rules for the regular to the secular clergy. Concern for illicit lay unions had troubled the Church as long before as Augustine's question to Pope Gregory concerning marriage with relations[83] and is reflected in the early ecclesiastical opposition to the heathen practice of marriage with the father's widow.[84] With the increased emphasis of the reform movement on clerical celibacy, it is this ecclesiastical type of illicit union that appears with greater frequency in the dooms. The first law to deal with it dates from the council which King Edmund held at London on an Easter in A.D. 942 or 944–946: 'Those in holy orders whose duty it is to teach God's people by the example of their life,' reads the first injunction, 'should observe the celibacy befitting their estate, whether they be men or women'.[85] Edgar also enjoins *claenan life* on *Godes theowas*,[86] and Aethelred decrees it not only for all clergy—'and priests above all'—but specifically for monks without a monastery and for canons whose property allows a refectory and dormitory.[87] A priest who is celibate is accorded the rank of a thegn.[88]

Other laws of clerical discipline in these late codes concern the return of monks outside a monastery to their house,[89] the participation of priests in processions and the performance of Services,[90] accusations brought against the clergy,[91] participation

---

[83] *Hist. Eccl.*, I, 27, quaestiones 4–5.

[84] See above, pp. 26–28.

[85] I Edmund 1; Robertson, pp. 7, 3 (for dating).

[86] IV Edgar 1 §7; Robertson, p. 30.

[87] V Aethelred 9, VI Aethelred 5, 41, VIII Aethelred 30, I Cnut 6a §1, 2; Robertson, pp. 83, 93, 127, 163. V Aethelred 6, VI Aethelred 3 §1; *ibid.*, pp. 81, 93. V Aethelred 7, VI Aethelred 4; *ibid.*, pp. 81, 93.

[88] V Aethelred 9 §1, VI Aethelred 5 §3; VIII Aethelred 28, I Cnut 6a §2a; Robertson, pp. 83, 93, 125, 163.

[89] V Aethelred 5, VI Aethelred 3; Robertson, pp. 81, 91.

[90] VII Aethelred 2 §2, 2a; Robertson, p. 109. Prayers for the king are discussed below, pp. 203–205.

[91] VIII Aethelred 19–24, I Cnut 5–5a §2a; Robertson, pp. 123–125, 159–161.

in vendetta,[92] homicide,[93] false witness, perjury, and the aiding of thieves,[94] apostasy of a priest or monk.[95] Thus the king's concern for the spiritual well-being of his kingdom's clergy—and so of his realm itself—is much in evidence in Anglo-Saxon law. Once again there is no separation of spheres, but rather the laws are given a *character mixtus* in which secular and religious are both areas of royal jurisdiction. And since 'great and wonderful are the things which a priest is able to do for the benefit of the people, if he is duly pleasing to his Lord',[96] to maintain the *salus* of the kingdom the responsibilities of the clergy are a natural object of juridical concern.

The 'mixed character' of the dooms and of the king's role in them has certainly emerged. It is not that the Anglo-Saxon legal world is divided into purely secular and purely religious compartments, with the ruler having an interest in each. Rather, the world is unitary, with what later times would distinguish as secular and religious bound into one world-view. The result is often a paralleling of divine and human rule, for as the Christian God created and then became Man and thereby enmeshed human history in theology, so the human realms of the Anglo-Saxon monarch depend for their *salus* on their relationship with the divine. The ruler, therefore, as 'Christ's deputy among Christian people', must legislate on ecclesiastical as well as on secular matters—that is, on the totality of his kingdom's well-being under God and the king. Thus, 'considering first of all how I could best promote Christianity and the just interests of the royal authority', King Aethelred reflects, 'frequently and often it has come into my mind that sacred precepts and wise secular decrees promote Christianity and strengthen royal authority, further public interests and are the source of honour, bring about peace and

92 VIII Aethelred 25, I Cnut 5a §2b, d; Robertson, pp. 125, 161.

93 VIII Aethelred 26, I Cnut 5a §2b, II Cnut 41; cf. II Cnut 42; Robertson, pp. 125, 161, 197.

94 VIII Aethelred 27, I Cnut 5a §3; Robertson, pp. 125, 161. Cf. Edward and Guthrum 3; Attenborough, p. 103.

95 VIII Aethelred 41; Robertson, p. 129.

96 I Cnut 4 §1; Robertson, p. 159.

reconciliation, put an end to strife and improve the whole character of the nation'.[97] This touching faith in the efficacy of law at the same time gives a more than earthly support, of course, to royal dooms. Athelstan the Glorious, for example, after urging the payment of ecclesiastical dues to be used by those who 'wish to gain the favour of God and me', warns that 'ye must guard against the anger of God and insubordination to me'.[98] And again: 'It is the duty of all,' Aethelred II and his councillors state, 'to love and honour one God, and zealously uphold one Christian faith, and wholly renounce all heathen practices. And let us loyally support one royal lord.' The doom ends, 'Blessed be the name of the Lord,' at least by implication drawing both God and king into its scope.[99] So also the Northumbrian Priests' Law concludes with a parallel reference to the unity of 'above all ever one Christianity and one royal authority in the nation', and then adds the immediate epilogue: 'Blessed be the name of the Lord from now and into eternity.'[100]

Similar utterances emphasizing *unus Deus, unus rex* are found in VI Aethelred 1, VII Aethelred 1 (one God shall be loved and honoured above all, and all men shall show obedience to their king), VIII Aethelred 44, and IX Aethelred 1, probably to emphasize the kingdom's unity under *Cristes gespelia* Aethelred at a time when his rule was threatened by Sweyn Fork-beard.[101] These

[97] X Aethelred Preamble and §1; Robertson, p. 131. The editor calls attention to the significant alliteration; *ibid.*, p. 342, n. to §1.

[98] I Athelstan 4, 5; Attenborough, p. 125. Cf. Edward and Guthrum 6 §7, in which no compensation is to be paid for anyone who is killed 'by setting himself against the laws of God and the king'; *ibid.*, p. 107. Cf. VI Aethelred 38, 'the law of Christ or the king': Robertson, p. 103.

[99] V Aethelred 34-35 §1; Robertson, pp. 89-91. The code opens with the confirmation of 'our firm intention of observing one Christian faith under the authority of one king'; the editor relates this phrase to the threat from Sweyn Fork-beard; *ibid.*, pp. 48, 79 (c. 1), 327, n. 5 to c. 1. This same king's second code marks the first occurrence in the dooms of the term *Englaland*; *ibid.*, p. 315, n. 1 to II Aethelred 1 §1.

[100] Whitelock, ed., *Engl. Hist. Doc.*, p. 439.

[101] Robertson, *Laws*, pp. 91, 109, 129, 131. Cf. above, n. 99. These codes are attributed to Wulfstan. Cf. Wulfstan's Homily 51; K. Jost, *Wulfstanstudien*, pp. 104-105.

generalized paraphrases of the Biblical injunction to 'Fear God, honour the king' find a parallel in King Alfred's juxtaposition of God and king as he quotes, 'Thou shalt not revile thy God, nor curse the rulers of thy people.'[102] Cnut substitutes his own name for the earlier general demand for loyalty: 'The first provision is, that above all else they would ever love and honour one God, and unanimously uphold one Christian faith, and love King Cnut with due fidelity.'[103] Faithfulness to this earthly lord would bring its reward from the Heavenly Lord, the same code promises: 'Let us ever be faithful and true to our Lord [hlaforde], and always, with all our might, promote his honour and carry out his will. For all that we ever do, through just fidelity to our lord, we do to our own great advantage, for truly God shall be gracious to him who is justly faithful to his lord.'[104]

Perhaps the most striking exposition of the idea that the earthly kings of the Anglo-Saxons should be obeyed, however, is the earlier translation of this recurring notion into direct divine injunction. Alfred the Great states that Christ ordered that everyone should love his lord [hlaford] as He Himself did.[105] As Liebermann has pointed out, no such command of Christ is known, and he suggests that Alfred is probably conflating St. Matthew 22:37 (Jesus said unto him, Thou shalt love the Lord thy God with all thy heart, and with all thy soul, and with all thy mind) and St. Matthew 22:39 (Thou shalt love thy neighbour as thyself) and misinterpreting the second passage.[106] This fairly feeble explanation fails to underline the emphasis on the parallelism of rulership, however. Even in the unlikely 'misinterpreting' of 'neighbour' as king or lord, Alfred does not say that one should

[102] Exodus 22: 28 (in Vulgate), quoted in Alfred, Introd. 37; Liebermann, Gesetze, I, p. 40. Hlaford often has the meaning of 'king' or 'lord of the people'; ibid., III, p. 47, n. to this law, and II, p. 556, article Königstitel, sect. 1c.

[103] I Canute 1; Robertson, p. 155.

[104] I Canute 20–20 §1; Robertson, p. 171. Hans Würdinger, 'Einwirkungen des Christentums auf das Angelsächsische Recht', Zeitschrift der Savigny-Stiftung für Rechtsgeschichte, Germanistische Abteilung, LV (1935), pp. 123–125, on Treuversprechen and Christian influence on it. On hlaford, see above, n. 102.

[105] Alfred, Introd. El. 49 §7; Liebermann, ed., Gesetze, I, p. 47.

[106] Liebermann, Gesetze, III, p. 49, n. 25.

love his lord as himself, but that as Christ loved God, so everyone should love the earthly, God-paralleled lord who is over him. The relationship is vertical, as in loving one above, and not a horizontal one of equality, as in loving someone 'as thyself'. Whatever the reason for the virtual creation of Scripture,[107] its meaning is clear; this *mimesis* parallels the Anglo-Saxon monarch with God the Father, as it was the Father whom Christ loved as his 'lord'. The warping of Scripture to fit the demands of the English societal and governmental *Weltanschauung* is comparable to the accommodation of Christian theology to pagan belief and tribal custom that we have already examined.

Support for this parallel between God and the king, both as personal lord, is given by the fact that in Kentish law the word *dryhten* is employed as a term for a personal lord and for the king, inasmuch as he is a personal lord.[108] In other prose works, however, the word *dryhten* is used only for God, and, although the term in law is not used solely for the king, it designates an earthly personal lord.[109] In poetry, on the other hand, the earthly ruler frequently appears as *dryhten*.[110]

Thus, throughout the dooms the king is placed in parallel with God. As in more rhapsodic and less legal language Thorarin Praise-Tongue lauded Cnut with the words, 'Cnut guards his land as the King of Greekland (God) keeps the kingdom of Heaven!'

[107] Cf. the inaccurate quotation from the Bible to support the payment of tithes; see below, p. 201 and n. 136.

[108] See especially Aethelberht 6; Attenborough, pp. 5, 175, n. 1 (*to drihtinbeage*) to c. 6. The word is used for 'lord' in Kentish laws of Wihtred 5, 9, 10, 23, 24 (*ibid.*, pp. 24, 26, 28) and then drops from the laws; *hlaford* is the customary term in West Saxon law. In the latter *Dryhten* is used for God as the Lord; cf. IV Edgar 1 §3, V Aethelred 6, VI Aethelred 3 §1, 53, VIII Aethelred 7, I Cnut 4 §1, 6 §3, II Cnut 84, 84 §3, 84 §4b. Robertson, pp. 30, 80, 92, 106, 120, 158, 162, 216, 218.

[109] Attenborough, *Laws*, p. 3; Liebermann, ed., *Gesetze*, II:1, pp. 55–56, *Dryhten*, and II:2, p. 556, *Königstitel* (*Dryhtenbeag*).

[110] For ruler as *freadryhten, gumdryhten, hleodryhten, mandryhten, sigedryhten, winedryhten*, etc., cf. H. Van der Merwe Scholtz, *The Kenning in Anglo-Saxon and Old Norse Poetry* (Utrecht and Nijmegen, 1927), p. 90; Hertha Marquardt, *Die Altenglischen Kenningar* (*Schriften der Königsberger Gelehrten Gesellschaft, Geisteswissenschaftliche Klasse*, 14 Jahr, Heft 3; Halle a. S., 1938), pp. 249–250.

and again as the poet Hallward Harek's Blesi sang, 'Cnut defends his land as the Lord of all does the glorious hall of the mountains (Heaven),'[111] so the same Cnut in his laws was to speak in conjunction of 'the law of God and my royal authority or secular law'[112]—which indeed helped him guard his land—and of the *fidem quam Deo et mihi debetis*.[113] The recent editor of the homilies of Wulfstan interprets such passages in Cnut's dooms in the light of a greater awareness that secular and ecclesiastical 'are two and not one' in the late tenth and early eleventh centuries, 'a recognition probably enforced by the presence of the Danes in England'. This growing 'distinction between secular and ecclesiastical realms', Professor Bethurum claims, is evidenced by the appearances of such phrases as *for Gode and for worolde* in legal literature.[114] To see either the preceding age of King Edgar—its secular guardianship of the Church and the consequent enhancing of the spiritual aspect of Christian kingship—or the frequency of such phrases, which not accidentally appear most often in the century following these Edgarian reforms, as a separation between the two spheres is surely unnecessary. Rather is such phraseology a more explicit statement of suppositions implicit in Anglo-Saxon law since the earliest codes: a paralleling of spiritual and secular spheres in one world under God, and the duty of royal authority to legislate support of the Church. It is not that 'God and the world' any more than 'Christ and the king' embody above all a distinction between 'those who recognize the church's authority and those nominal Christians who because of their barbarian background did not'.[115] Instead, the very statement from the decrees of Edward and Guthrum taken by Miss Bethurum as the most explicit recognition of the distinction between the two realms is primarily a recognition of the royal obligation to enforce the rule of God in the king's realm: after fixing 'secular penalties because they knew that otherwise there would be many people whom

[111] *C.P.B.*, II, pp. 160, 161.
[112] Proclamation of 1020, c. 9; Robertson, p. 143.
[113] Proclamation of 1027, c. 16; Robertson, p. 152.
[114] D. Bethurum, ed., *Homilies*, pp. 72–76.
[115] Bethurum, ed., *Homilies*, p. 72.

they would not be able to control, and that otherwise many men would not be willing to submit as they ought to do, to the amends required by the church, ... they fixed secular amends which should be divided between Christ and the king, wheresoever people would not legally submit to the amends required by the church and determined by the bishops'.[116] To view this as a Christianization of the religious functions of the pagan Germanic king and as the royal duty to maintain the right tribal relations with deity would be to see here, as elsewhere, a continuity between present and past and the working within a tradition while accommodating to the Christian faith, instead of a radical break with the past and the casting off of deeply embedded tribal-centred processes of thought. Even beyond this, however, this law of Edward and Guthrum contains a significant specific parallel of the divine and earthly rulers—'Christ and the king.'

This formula of 'Christ and the king' is repeated many times in the dooms of Aethelred and Cnut, representing the parallelism of authority. Compensation for attempting to kill or rob a man in orders or a stranger is to be 'promptly paid to Christ and the king';[117] the legal right to offer compensation for the violation of a church's protection (by committing homicide within its walls) is to be obtained on the condition that the offender 'shall give his own *wergeld* to the king and to Christ';[118] the civil penalty for refusing to render God's dues is to be divided 'between Christ and the king'.[119] Nor is this phrase confined to the dooms of the kings. In the eleventh century Northumbrian Priests' Law from York the penalty for participating in heathen sacrifices, prophecies, or magical practices is paid 'half to Christ and half to

[116] Edward and Guthrum, Preamble §2; Attenborough, p. 103.

[117] Edward and Guthrum 12; Attenborough, p. 109. In II Cnut 40 §1, this payment is made to the king alone, and in VIII Aethelred 33 the king alone acts as 'kinsman and protector', both laws reflecting the growth of the king's peace; Robertson, pp. 127, 197.

[118] VIII Aethelred 2; repeated in I Cnut 2 §4, except that *tham cyninge 7 Christe* here reads *Criste 7 tham cyningce*; Robertson, pp. 119, 157 (Anglo-Saxon on preceding pages).

[119] VIII Aethelred 15; Robertson, p. 123. 'In accordance with former custom' indicates that this division is earlier than Aethelred.

the king',[120] who are also to be compensated for failure of payment of Peter's Pence.[121] This division of compensation and consequent co-jurisdiction of the King of Heaven and the king of the English is generalized and, in effect, summarized in VIII Aethelred 36: 'And secular councillors showed wisdom in appointing civil laws to uphold the privileges of religion for the governance of the people, and in assigning the compensation to Christ and the king, so that thereby many are forced of necessity to submit to justice.'[122] However, the code continues, 'in the assemblies since the days of Edgar ... the laws of Christ have been neglected and the laws of the king disregarded [*Cristes laga wanodan and cyninges laga litledon*]. And then the (dues from) civil penalties which had previously been shared between Christ and the king were separated, and things have continuously gone from bad to worse both in religious and in secular affairs. God grant that there may now be improvement!'[123]

This interdependence of the two realms and the observance of the laws of Christ and the king may give rise to the problem of determining to whom Christ's portion of these payments was actually made. Indeed, as the king had his agents for collecting fines due to him, so Christ had his agents through whom treasures were laid up on earth. The effective comptroller on earth of these funds is shown in VI Aethelred 51: 'And if monetary compensation is paid as amends for religious offences, in accordance with the penalties fixed by wise secular authorities, it is proper that this should be applied, *in accordance with the direction of the bishops* [*be biscpa dihte*], to paying for prayers, and to the maintenance of the indigent, and to the repair of churches, and to education, and

---

[120] C. 48; cf. 49, 54, 54 §1. Liebermann, ed., *Gesetze*, I, p. 383.

[121] C. 59; Liebermann, ed., *Gesetze*, I, p. 384.

[122] Robertson, ed., *Laws*, p. 127. The beginning is remarkable for its alliteration: *And wise waeran worldwitan the to godcundan rihtlagan woroldlaga settan*, ...; pp. 126, 341, n. 1 to c. 36.

[123] VIII Aethelred 37–38; Robertson, pp. 127–129. V Aethelred 31: 'If anyone is guilty of offering obstruction or open opposition anywhere to the law of Christ or of the king, he shall pay either *wergeld* or fine or *lahslit* according to the nature of the offence'; ibid., p. 89. Cf. VI Aethelred 38; ibid., p. 103.

to clothing and feeding those who serve God, and to the purchase of books and bells and ecclesiastical vestments.'[124]

This general principle is reflected in specific laws providing for payments to bishops. In the same law of Edward and Guthrum providing that compensation for attempting to kill or rob a stranger or man in holy orders should be paid 'to Christ and the king', the king and bishop are the victim's 'kinsmen and protectors', implying their role in rights of compensation as well;[125] Cnut's second code states specifically that payments for binding or beating a man in orders shall be 'the fine due to the bishop for sacrilege . . . and to his lord or to the king the full fine for breach of his *mund*'.[126] That the bishop is indeed the recipient of payments to Christ is also shown by the fact that penalties for failure to pay *ciricsceat*, Church-dues, to be divided between 'Christ and the king', go actually to the bishop and the king; 'and he who holds them [Church dues] beyond that date [Martinmas] shall give them up to the bishop, and repeat the payment eleven times, and [pay] 120 shillings to the king'.[127] So also failure to pay Peter's Pence, to be compensated to 'Christ and the king' in the Northumbrian Priests' Law, is according to Cnut to be recompensed by giving 'the bishop the penny and thirty pence in addition, and 120 shillings to the king'.[128] Other religious offences—such as taking a nun from a nunnery and swearing a false oath on relics—are compensated half to the bishop and half to the king (or lord), the former again referred to by his office and not designated by 'Christ'.[129]

[124] Robertson, pp. 105–107. Italics mine.

[125] Edward and Guthrum 12; Attenborough, p. 109.

[126] II Cnut 42; Robertson, p. 196.

[127] I Cnut 10 §1; Robertson, p. 165. Cf. William A. Chaney, 'Anglo-Saxon Church Dues: A Study in Historical Continuity', *Church History*, XXXII (1963), pp. 271–273, on the pagan background of Martinmas payment.

[128] I Cnut 9 §1; Robertson, p. 165. According to the so-called Laws of William I, 17b §3, one arraigned in the King's Court for failure to pay Peter's Pence is fined '30 pence to the bishop and 40 shillings [i.e. 120 Mercian shillings] to the King'; *ibid.*, pp. 263, 368, n. 1 to 17b §3.

[129] Alfred 8; Attenborough, p. 69. II Cnut 36; Robertson, p. 195. Liebermann also judges payments to 'Christ' to be made to the bishop; Liebermann, ed., *Gesetze*, II:2, pp. 313 ff., *Bischof*, esp. sect. 6; also p. 340, *Christus*, sect. 1.

o

Consequently the parallel of Christ and the king in law as recipients for these amends is also one between the bishop, the shepherd of the divine flock,[130] and the king, 'Christ's deputy among Christian people'.[131] Both alike share in the divinely appointed task of directing the *folc*. The Anglo-Saxon poem *Widsith* says that it was God who gave government to men,[132] and the king and bishop are both His agents in that government. So as the bishop appears as 'Christ' in the dooms, the king, also 'Christ's deputy', is again in earthly parallel with the divine.[133] The legal structure of the king's position is analogous to the Anglo-Saxon comparison of the Cross of Christ with the throne of the king, both the dwelling-place of majesty and of God's election.[134]

This divine agency embodied in the king, the character of which we have been analysing in the laws, has already been examined in some detail. The priestly character of Christian kingship was, for the Anglo-Saxons, largely a translation into terms of the new religion of the sacral kingship of Germanic heathenism. This role of priest-king we also see in the dooms in the capacity of the king as homilist, exhorting the folk on their road to salvation. Not only, as we have noted, is there a mixture of spiritual and secular matters in law, since a firm boundary line between them did not exist, but short homilies are preached in the codes themselves. These are not found in the elliptical early codes. In spite of the lengthy introduction to Alfred's laws, making use both of the Old and New Testaments and of Church history to place his own

---

[130] I Cnut 26 §3; Robertson, p. 175.

[131] See above, p. 185.

[132] *Widsith*, ll. 133–134.

[133] On the relation of this to the later parallelism of *Christus* and *fiscus*, cf. Ernst H. Kantorowicz, *The King's Two Bodies* (Princeton, 1957), pp. 173–192.

[134] Peter H. Brieger, 'England's Contribution to the Origin and Development of the Triumphal Cross', *Mediaeval Studies*, IV (1942), pp. 87–88. In the *Dream of the Rood*, from the school of Cynewulf, 'Christ mounted the cross as a king would mount his throne.' Cf. the Welsh triadic law, 'Three timbers which are free in a king's forest: timber for the roof of a church, and the timber of shafts applied to the use of the king, and wood for a bier'; Melville Richards, *The Laws of Hywel Dda* (Liverpool, 1954), p. 106.

dooms in the continuity of Hebraic and Christian law,[135] the first truly homiletic framework for a code is Athelstan's series of decrees on the tithing of his property. 'Let us remember,' he exhorts, 'how Jacob the Patriarch declared "*Decimas et hostias pacificas offeram tibi*", and how Moses declared in God's Law "*Decimas et primitias non tardabis offerre Domino*". It behooves us to remember how terrible is the declaration stated in books' that God shall 'deprive us of the nine [remaining] parts' if we withhold the tenth from Him. He reminds his reeves that 'divine teaching instructs us that we gain the things of heaven by those of the earth, and the eternal by the temporal', and concludes by warning against 'the anger of God and insubordination to me'.[136] The tone continues, if not so explicitly, in the ecclesiastical character of Edmund's legislation,[137] but it is with the religious reforms of King Edgar and Archbishop Dunstan that the royal codes lengthen their exhortations and present the king most thoroughly in his homiletic role. IV Edgar, for example, opens with a sermon complete with *exemplum*,[138] and 'the last codes of Aethelred's reign', as their editor correctly claims, 'are thoroughly ecclesiastical in tone and homiletic in style, full of tiresome repetitions and injunctions'.[139] 'Tiresome' many of these sermonettes may be, but they have their moments. The collapse of law and the disorders of a weak reign break through time and again,[140] and

---

[135] See above, p. 174 and n. 3. For the parallel use in Ireland of canon laws 'taken directly from the Bible and particularly from the Old Testament', cf. Wilhelm Levison, *England and the Continent in the Eighth Century* (Oxford, 1946), p. 100.

[136] I Athelstan 2–5; Attenborough, pp. 123–125. See above, p. 193. The quotations from Jacob and Moses are both inaccurate.

[137] See especially II Edmund, Preamble and §1; Robertson, p. 9.

[138] See above, pp. 190–191.

[139] Robertson, *Laws*, p. 49, where Archbishop Wulfstan's influence on them is also noted. See above, n. 27. Aelfric's role in drawing up Aethelred's later laws has been suggested by Stenton, *Anglo-Saxon England*, p. 453. Whether either of these great homilists is behind these passages is, of course, impossible to conclude with certainty.

[140] E.g., VIII Aethelred 37–38, 43; Robertson, pp. 127–129. Cf. the measures *contra paganos* in VII Aethelred; *ibid.*, pp. 109–113.

elsewhere sound principles of justice for any age may be found in them. 'The strong and the weak are not alike,' as Aethelred the Redeless could well testify, 'nor can they bear a like burden, any more than the sick can be treated like the sound. And therefore, in forming a judgement, careful discrimination must be made between age and youth, wealth and poverty, health and sickness, and the various ranks of life ... And if it happens that a man commits a misdeed, involuntarily or unintentionally, the case is different from that of one who offends of his own freewill, voluntarily and intentionally ... Careful discrimination shall be ordered with justice, according to the nature of the deed, and meted out with proportion, in affairs both religious and secular; and, through the fear of God, mercy and leniency and some measure of forbearance shall be shown towards those who have need of them.'[141] The homiletic style is continued by Cnut the Great not only in both of his codes but in his Proclamations of 1020 and 1027.[142] Thus in the last century of Anglo-Saxon law—from the first code of Athelstan to the last code before the Norman Conquest—this feature of the style of the royal codes occurs frequently, asserting in its essence the hortatory role of the monarch, whose 'mixed character' places him as *populi Dei*

[141] VI Aethelred 52–53; Robertson, p. 107. In the same code he repeats the older injunction 'that henceforth all men, both rich and poor, shall be allowed the benefit of the law'; VI Aethelred 8 §1; *ibid.*, p. 95. But cf. the conclusion to this notion in the poem *Doomsday*: 'There (at the Last Day) the poor and the wealthy shall have one law; therefore they shall all together feel fear'; *Judgment Day* II, ll. 164–165; E. V. K. Dobbie, ed., *The Anglo-Saxon Minor Poems* (Anglo-Saxon Poetic Records, VI; New York, 1942), p. 62.

[142] E.g., Proclamation of 1020, especially opening and conclusion, Proclamation of 1027, cc. 9–13, I Cnut 1–2, 4, 19–26, II Cnut 1–2, 11, 68, 84. Stenton, *Anglo-Saxon England*, pp. 403–404 on Cnut's ecclesiastical interests and on king as homilist. I Cnut 26 is derived from II Polity; cf. K. Jost, *Wulfstanstudien*, p. 78. The editor of the *Encomium Emmae Reginae* notes that the Encomiast includes with Cnut's generosity to the Church 'his suppression of unjust laws, a point which would have come more fittingly in the course of his preceding remarks on the king's secular affairs'; Alistair Campbell, ed., *Encomium Emmae Reginae* (Camden 3rd Series, LXXII; London, 1949), p. lxii. It is, of course, just as fitting where it is, since only a later age would expect a neat and marked division.

gubernator and *aecclesiae Christi ut pater, sacerdotibus ut frater.*[143] This kingship is thoroughly Christianized and occurs most in the period of strongest ecclesiastical influence, but its expositors are direct descendants of those sacral kings of Germanic heathenism whose *auctoritas suadendi* swayed the folk to obey the gods whose representatives the rulers were.

This cult of kingship as evidenced by the laws also encompasses prayers and masses *pro rege*, a subject which shall be treated here only insofar as it is illuminated by the laws.[144] The first legal provision for them occurs as early as the dooms of Wihtred of Kent; after decreeing in his first law that 'the Church shall enjoy immunity from taxation,' he adds in the same decree: 'The king shall be prayed for, and they [the clergy] shall honour him freely and without compulsion.'[145] The next doom requiring inter-cession for the ruler is not found for almost two and a half centuries, in the fifth code of King Athelstan, the first King of all Britain; for the two centuries between the codes of Wihtred and Alfred the Great, however, no codes have been preserved, except that of Ine, and there is no reason to think that such intercessions ceased or were neglected. The liturgies of the Anglo-Saxon Church, on the contrary, show the vigorous continuity of these prayers, and in this interim period of no surviving codes the Council of *Clovesho* of A.D. 747 and other synods also sanctified prayers *pro regibus ac ducibus.*[146]

When Athelstan legislates on the subject, prayers *pro rege* are elaborated in greater detail than in Wihtred's simple statement. 'And in every monastery, all the servants of God[147] shall sing

---

[143] Alcuin to Offa of Mercia, A.D. 796; *Mon. Ger. Hist., Ep.,* IV, p. 147. Gerd Tellenbach, *Church, State and Christian Society at the Time of the Investiture Contest* (Oxford, 1940), p. 59, n. 1.

[144] See above, n. 90.

[145] Wihtred 1–1 §1; Attenborough, p. 25.

[146] A. W. Haddan and W. Stubbs, eds., *Councils and Ecclesiastical Documents Relating to Great Britain and Ireland* (Oxford, 1871), III, p. 375. These, however, valuable as they are for the light shed upon liturgical kingship, are not to be considered here, in which the strand of these prayers will be traced in the dooms alone.

[147] The whole of the clergy, both secular and regular; cf. Attenborough,

every Friday fifty psalms[148] for the king, and for all who are minded to carry out his wishes. And (they shall sing psalms) for these others according to their merits.'[149] Friday, the day appointed for these intercessions, is the day both on which Christ the King ended his earthly life and on which rulers are traditionally prayed for in the Roman Church. More frequent intercessions and a mass for the king in time of war were added by Aethelred later in the tenth century during the invasions of the Northmen: 'And we decree that in every religious foundation a mass entitled "Against the heathen" shall be sung daily at matins, by the whole community, on behalf of the king and all his people. And at the various hours, all members of the foundation, prostrate on the ground, shall chant the psalm: "O Lord, how are they multiplied", and the Collect against the heathen, and this shall be done as long as the present need continues. And in every foundation and college of monks every priest severally shall celebrate thirty masses for the king and the whole nation, and every monk shall repeat [the psalms from] his psalter thirty times.'[150] The Anglo-Saxon manuscript of this code (VII) provides also for prayers and mass but on the Monday, Tuesday, and Wednesday before Michaelmas, as well as a daily mass with special reference to the contemporary plight 'until an improvement takes place'.[151]

Here the pagan king who offers intercessions to the gods for his people has indeed become the Christian king for whom the new institution, the Church, intercedes with God. The priest-king of paganism making *blot* for victory is still enmeshed with the divine in his new form of Christ's deputy for whose victory *contra*

Laws, p. 183, n. 3, to Ine, Preamble. In V Aethelred 4 *Godes theowas* are defined as *biscopas and abbudas, munecas and myncena, preostas and nunnan*; Attenborough, p. 183.

[148] One of the three sections of the psalter; cf. Charles Plummer, ed., *Venerabilis Bedae Historiam Ecclesiasticam Gentis Anglorum* (Oxford, 1896), II, p. 137; Attenborough, *Laws*, p. 212, n. 2 to V Athelstan 3.

[149] V Athelstan 3; Attenborough, pp. 155, 212, n. 4, which suggests concerning the last clause that 'their merits (are) measured by their benefactions to the Church'.

[150] VII Aethelred 3–3 §2; Robertson, p. 111.

[151] VII Aethelred A.–S. 6–6 §3; Robertson, p. 117.

paganos mass is now offered. Interceder and object of intercession, once joined, have now been separated, but the God of battles and the earthly ruler are still linked in the crises of the *folc*. In the emergency of Aethelred's crisis-strewn reign, moreover, the weekly fifty psalms of Aethelstan's doom have multiplied with the heathen, and a daily mass *pro rege et populo*, prayer, and Psalm 3 in all the monastic offices are required for the duration of the emergency, as well as a thirty-fold repetition of an intercessory mass by each priest and the reading of the psalter by each monk. This is typical Aethelredian application of crisis-theology, but that the principle is nothing new is evidenced not only by Wihtred's and Athelstan's codes but by a doom of the last king to issue laws before Aethelred, Edgar the Peaceable, and by the canonical collection of Aelfric. 'The servants of God who receive the dues which we render to Him,' King Edgar rules, 'shall live a pure life, so that, by virtue of their purity, they may intercede for us with God'.[152] And the same general principle of intercession for the ruler is found in extended form in Aelfric's twentieth canon, which provides that all mass-priests and all of God's servants 'shall fervently pray for the king, and for their bishop, and for those who do good to them, and for all Christian people'.[153] The Anglo-Saxon king is thus given a special liturgical role in the dooms.

The 'peace' of the king—his person and his residence—is an outstanding feature of Anglo-Saxon law,[154] and is to be seen not only in the constitutional-political aspects of a later age but in the succession from the sacrificial priest-king of a not far distant Germanic past. Religion and law cannot be separated here. In the

[152] IV Edgar 1 §7; Robertson, p. 31. If the intercession referred to is general, the king is at least included.

[153] B. Thorpe, ed., *Ancient Laws and Institutes*, p. 444.

[154] Cf., e.g., W. Stubbs, *The Constitutional History of England* (5th ed.; Oxford, 1891), I, pp. 198–206; F. Pollock and F. W. Maitland, *The History of English Law before the Time of Edward I* (2nd ed.; Cambridge, 1923), I, pp. 44–45. I am not concerned here with the often discussed extension of the king's peace in its legal-constitutional development. Payments to the king for breaking his peace other than in his residence or when he is present in person are consequently not treated.

earliest code, that of Aethelberht of Kent, a double compensation is assessed against an offence committed at a gathering of the ruler's *leod* summoned by the king or at a feast if the king is present.[155] In general, early West Saxon laws relating to violence against the king's person treat of fighting in the king's house or hall, while later laws, reflecting an extension of jurisdiction, are less localized and concern plotting against the ruler. Thus both Ine and Alfred decree that if anyone fights in the King's residence—*huse* in Ine's law, *healle* in Alfred's—'it shall be for the king to decide whether he shall be put to death or not'.[156] To fight or draw a weapon in the presence of the archbishop or of a bishop or *ealdorman* invokes a lesser penalty of 150 and 100 shillings respectively in Alfred's code.[157] With the single exception of a doom of Cnut, which repeats the provision that anyone fighting at the king's residence (*hird*, court) 'shall lose his life, unless the king is willing to pardon him',[158] none of the later laws,

---

[155] Aethelberht 2–3; Attenborough, p. 5. In the former case, fifty shillings, the amount of the king's *mundbyrd* and the compensation to be paid for slaying a man in the king's *tun* (Aethelberht 8, 5), is also to be paid to the king. For double compensation due for breach of the *frith* of a church or meeting-place, cf. Aethelberht 1.

[156] Ine 6, Alfred 7; Attenborough, pp. 39, 69. The former provides for loss of all property in addition. The lesser penalties for fighting in a monastery (120 shillings), the house of an *ealdorman* (60 shillings), the house of a taxpayer (120 shillings, but see p. 183, n. 1 to Ine 6 §2), in the open (120 shillings), and in a tavern (30 shillings), are provided in the same law, Ine 6 §1–§5.

[157] Alfred 15; Attenborough, p. 73. Cf. Alfred 38–38 §2 for fighting or drawing a sword at a meeting in the presence of the king's *ealdorman* or of an official subordinate to the king's *ealdorman*; *ibid.*, p. 81. These represent the king's peace. For the status of the ninth century *ealdorman*, cf. H. R. Loyn, 'The Term "Ealdorman" in the Translations Prepared at the time of King Alfred', *English Historical Review*, LXVIII (1953), pp. 513–525.

[158] II Cnut 59; Robertson, p. 205. Cf. in Welsh law, the first of 'the four persons for whom there is no protection, either in court or in church, against the King: one is, a person who shall violate the King's protection, in one of the three principal festivals in the palace; the second is, a person who is delivered with his own consent as a hostage to the King; the third is, a person to whom the King is a supper guest, who ought to supply him with food that night and who does not supply him; the fourth is, the King's bondman': Haddan and

except those concerning asylum, concerns fighting in the king's presence or in the royal residence. This is not to say that this disappeared as a crime, since not all valid laws were repeated in each new code. However, as the personal rulership of the early English kingdoms gave way in time to a more institutionalized framework of government, two developments occurred: the king's peace spread beyond the monarch's immediate vicinity to larger areas of jurisdiction, embracing the whole realm, and, secondly, the re-emphasis in the tenth century on the sanctity of kingship still expressed the personal quality in laws demonstrating the sacral character of the ruler, still in continuity with pagan precedent. The second of these we shall note in the dooms concerning asylum. The first is seen now in a translation of laws against violence in the king's presence into laws against plotting against the king, wherever in the realm such plots occurred.

The first of these laws dates from the time of Alfred: 'If anyone plots against the life of the king, either on his own account, or by harbouring outlaws, or men belonging to [the king] himself, he shall forfeit his life and all he possesses.'[159] Loss of life, unless the accused is cleared 'by the most solemn oath determined upon by the authorities', is also the penalty in V Aethelred 30 for plotting against the king,[160] as it is, along with forfeiture of all goods, in VI Aethelred 37 and II Cnut 57.[161] This treachery to the lord was one of the greatest of crimes and sins, of course, in Anglo-Saxon

---

Stubbs, eds., *Councils and Eccl. Doc.*, I, p. 237 (Bk. II, c. 8 §13 of Dimetian Code); cf. Bk. II, c. 39 of Gwentian Code: *loc. cit.*

[159] Alfred 4; Attenborough, p. 65. An oath equal to the king's *wergeld* is necessary to clear the accused of the charge (4 §1), an amount which, while never found in the laws for the West Saxon monarch, was apparently originally the same as that of the king of Mercia, 120 pounds, a sum equal to the *wergeld* of six thegns; cf. *ibid.*, p. 194, n. 1 to Alfred 4 §1. Pollock and Maitland, *History of English Law*, p. 51, n. 2, for Continental Germanic parallels to Alfred 4.

[160] Robertson, p. 87. The oath probably necessitates thirty-six compurgators; *ibid.*, p. 330, n. 2 to law.

[161] Robertson, pp. 103, 205. The triple ordeal is provided for as alternative to the oath in VI Aethelred 37 and as the sole means of clearing the accused in Cnut's law.

society. 'It is the greatest of all treachery in the world that a man betray his lord's soul,' Archbishop Wulfstan proclaims in his *Sermo Lupi ad Anglos*, 'and a full great treachery it is also in the world that a man should betray his lord to death, or drive him in his lifetime from the land; and both have happened in this country: Edward was betrayed and then killed, and afterwards burnt, and Aethelred was driven out of his country.'[162] Alcuin in a letter to Charlemagne in A.D. 801 praises 'Torhtmund, the faithful servant of King Aethelred, a man proven in faithfulness, vigorous in arms, who has bravely avenged the blood of his lord,' after the slaying of that Northumbrian king in A.D. 796.[163] To avenge one's lord in honest feud was not murder and is not condemned as sin by Alcuin. 'A traitor to his lord' is the solitary exception made by one Anglo-Saxon writer when he asserts that Hell need not be feared by any who observes the proper fasts.[164]

These attitudes toward treachery are the ones also reflected in the laws. The provisions against plotting against the king are generalized to plots against any lord, and the stringent penalties are the same. This is found first as early as a subsidiary doom to Alfred 4, with forfeiture of life and all property as penalty.[165] Pollock and Maitland, in their brief discussion of treason in Anglo-Saxon law, make a distinction between the capital crime of plotting against the king, which they maintain probably 'does not represent any original Germanic tradition, but is borrowed from

[162] Whitelock, ed., *Engl. Hist. Doc.*, pp. 856–857; this famous sermon, preached under the alias of *Lupus*, the Wolf, was probably delivered first in A.D. 1014; *ibid.*, p. 854. The references are to King Edward the Martyr, killed at Corfe in A.D. 978, and to Aethelred II, who was forced to flee to Normandy in 1013 during the invasion of Sweyn Fork-beard.

[163] *Mon. Ger. Hist.*, *Epistolae*, IV, Ep. 231. Torhtmund is in the company of Archbishop Aethelheard of Canterbury and is recommended by Alcuin to Charles as they pass through the latter's realm on their way to Rome.

[164] From MS. Tiberius A. iii, ed. by A. Napier, 'Altenglische Kleinigkeiten', *Anglia*, XI (1889), p. 3.

[165] Alfred 4 §2; Attenborough, p. 65. In the same code (1 §1) an oath to betray one's lord is better broken than kept, in spite of the importance of oath-keeping. For a good treatment of the whole subject, cf. Floyd S. Lear, 'Treason and Related Offences in the Anglo-Saxon Dooms', *The Rice Institute Pamphlet*, XXXVII (1950), pp. 1–20.

the Roman law of *maiestas*', and 'the close association of treason against the king with treason against one's personal lord who is not the king, [which]is eminently Germanic'.[166] The evidence cited for the Roman origin of the 'formal enunciation' of the former is its appearance first in the laws of Alfred, 'and when an idea first appears in England in Alfred's time, there is no difficulty whatever in supposing it imported from the continent'.[167] The association of treason against the king and that against a personal lord is, however, also found for the first time in law in Alfred's code, and its 'eminently Germanic' origin is admitted. Traitors in early Germanic tribes were in fact, as Tacitus informs us, executed by hanging.[168] Surely neither notion need rely on Roman legal principles. Both are an attempt to maintain the security of a society and its ruling part, seen in terms of a Germanic societal context of both *comitatus*-relationships and a king the 'peace' of whose person was already embodied in the earliest Anglo-Saxon dooms. What is new in development is the legal extension of jurisdiction and its territorialization beyond the originally sacral presence of the king's person alone.

In the post-Alfredian period, loss of life is inflicted also in II Athelstan 4 against 'one who is accused of plotting against his lord . . . if he cannot deny it, or (if he does deny it and) is afterwards found guilty in the threefold ordeal'; forfeiture of life and property as well as provision for the triple ordeal is found in II Cnut 57, which concerns plots against either the king or the personal lord.[169] Both penalty and triple ordeal parallel the dooms on treason to the king because treachery to one's lord is a general category calling for the severest punishments. Only the king can spare the life of a proved thief or one 'who has been discovered in treason against his lord, whatever refuge he seeks', according to III Edgar 7 §3.[170] When II Cnut 26 repeats this law, it omits

---

[166] Pollock and Maitland, *History of English Law*, pp. 51–52.

[167] Pollock and Maitland, *History of English Law*, p. 51.

[168] Tacitus, *Germania*, c. 12; W. Peterson, ed., *Germania* (Loeb Classical Library; London, 1914), p. 280.

[169] Attenborough, p. 131; Robertson, p. 205.

[170] Robertson, p. 27.

the saving grace of the king,[171] but that the latter is still valid is shown in another law of the same code, that 'if anyone does the deed of an outlaw, the king alone shall have power to grant him security'.[172] The importance of loyalty—especially to the king—is also seen in Aethelred's law that anyone who 'deserts an army in which the king himself is present' risks losing 'his life or his *wergeld*', while 'he who deserts any other army shall forfeit 120 shillings'.[173] Cnut also places treachery toward one's lord (*hlafordswice*) as one of the 'crimes for which no compensation can be paid',[174] an act which placed the malefactor outside the pale of society, so that the societal framework of compensation, by which crimes were recognized and the law-breaker permitted to be re-involved in the folk, no longer applied. It is this principle which is seen earlier when the Laws of Edward and Guthrum rule that 'if he (anyone) so acts as to bring about his own death by setting himself against the laws of God and the king, no compensation shall be paid for him, if this can be proved'.[175]

Resisting the dooms of the heavenly and earthly monarchs thus placed one outside the world of law shored up by those laws, so that the 'out-law's' kin could not claim compensation as though he were still within that world. This involves more than earthly law. Traitors and those who desert their lord when he has need of them are, according to Wulfstan, 'hated by God', if they do not repent through 'ecclesiastical and secular compensation'.[176] Although the king appears in conjunction with other earthly lords, his earlier, pagan, special sacral character is probably

---

[171] Robertson, p. 189.

[172] II Cnut 13; Robertson, p. 181.

[173] V Aethelred 28–28 §1; Robertson, pp. 87, 330, n. 2 to law. It is repeated in VI Aethelred 35 (*ibid.*, p. 103), but only 'at the risk of losing his property', and the clause concerning armies not led by the king is omitted. Cf. Ine 51 on necessity of military service by both noble (including non-landholding nobles) and non-noble; Attenborough, p. 53.

[174] II Cnut 64; Robertson, p. 207. The others are 'assaults upon houses, arson, theft which cannot be disproved, murder which cannot be denied'.

[175] Edward and Guthrum 6 §7; Attenborough, p. 107.

[176] Homily LI; K. Jost, *Wulfstanstudien*, p. 105. Murderers, liars, and oath-breakers are placed in the same category.

reflected in a synodical decree much closer in time to the period of the Conversion. The Synod of A.D. 786 binds 'with the chain of eternal anathema' any who shares in a plot on the king's life *quia christus Domini est*, and any cleric—of episcopal or other rank—who adheres to such a plot is to be deposed *sicut Iudas ab apostolico gradu eiectus est*.[177] The crime of treason against the king is a sin invoking excommunication, and a Judas-like ecclesiastic who betrays the royal *christus* is cast out from the elect of Heaven and earth. 'An attack upon the ruler,' as Heinrich Fichtenau claims for the contemporary Frankish Carolingians, 'was an attack upon a person removed from the sphere of everyday life by a heavenly mandate and invested with a "taboo". The person of the ruler was sacred *ex officio*.'[178] Further, a charter of Aethelred demonstrates that anyone killed resisting the law was denied Christian burial, but that the king—almost as *rex episcopus*—could put aside that ban and permit such a one 'to repose with the Christians'.[179] God's laws had royal sanction, and royal laws had divine sanction, as again the coalescence of religion and law is manifest. Sin and crime tend to be identified, since one 'setting himself against the laws of God and the king' invokes the wrath of both.

We have seen this in the use of secular punishments of fines set in royal laws for ecclesiastical offences. It is also clearly seen in the use of excommunication as punishment for crimes later ages would judge to be secular. Not only is excommunication proclaimed by the royal laws for the sins of illicit

[177] *Mon. Ger. Hist., Epp.*, IV, p. 24; Liebermann, ed., *Gesetze*, II:2, p. 511, *Hochverrat*, sect. 1c. The German synod of Hohenaltheim in A.D. 916 also excommunicated any who committed the sacrilege of rebelling against the *christus Domini*, the king: *Mon. Ger. Hist., Const.*, I, p. 623; E. Eichmann, 'Königs- und Bischofsweihe', *Sitzungsberichte der Bayerischen Akademie der Wissenschaften, Philol.-Philos. und Hist. Klasse* (1928), no. 6, p. 68.

[178] H. Fichtenau, *The Carolingian Empire* (Oxford, 1957), p. 56.

[179] The charter (Kemble, no. 1289), dated A.D. 992–995, is a grant by King Aethelred to Aethelwig, his thegn, of land forfeited by three brothers who had defended a thief. On outlawry, cf. F. Liebermann, 'Die Friedlosigkeit bei den Angelsachsen', *Festschrift Heinrich Brunner zum 70. Geburtstag* (Weimar, 1910), pp. 17–37. On the charter, cf. Whitelock, ed., *Engl. Hist. Doc.*, pp. 525–526.

union,[180] non-payment of Church dues,[181] the committing of perjury and practice of sorcery,[182] apostacy by a priest or monk,[183] marrying a female religious,[184] and slaying a priest,[185] but for the less strictly religious crime of selling anyone out of the country.[186] Alfred invokes it in the case of perjury not for the breaking of one's pledge but only for escape from prison.[187] The Penitential of Pseudo-Egbert calls for excommunication against anyone who has been wronged but will not accept justice when it is offered;[188] the same sentence is elsewhere launched against one who delays appearing before a secular court.[189]

'They broke the King's word, the excellent command of the

[180] Wihtred 3, 4 §1; Attenborough, p. 25.

[181] I Edmund 2; Robertson, p. 7.

[182] I Edmund 6; Robertson, p. 7. II Athelstan 26 refuses burial in consecrated ground to an unrepentant perjurer; Attenborough, pp. 141–143. An earlier law, Alfred 1 §7, however, enjoins excommunication not for breaking a pledge but only for a perjurer's escaping from prison; ibid., p. 65.

[183] VIII Aethelred 41; Robertson, p. 129.

[184] Cnut's Proclamation of 1020, c. 17; Robertson, p. 145.

[185] II Cnut 39; Robertson, p. 197.

[186] VII Aethelred 5; Robertson, p. 113. This may have in mind, however, especially the sale of Christians to the heathen. Cf. V Aethelred 2: 'Christian men who are innocent of crime shall not be sold out of the land, least of all to the heathen, but care shall diligently be taken that the souls which Christ bought with his own life be not destroyed'; ibid., p. 79. This principle is restated in VI Aethelred 9 (p. 95), VII Aethelred 3, and II Cnut 3 (p. 177). In none of these laws, however, is excommunication invoked. Ine 11 exacts wergeld and 'full atonement with God' for selling a fellow-countryman ofer sae but does not mention the special heinousness of selling to the heathen, which may have arisen only after the Viking invasion; Attenborough, p. 41. Cf. D. Bethurum, ed., Homilies, pp. 358–359, n. to ll. 44–45 of Wulfstan's Sermo ad Anglos, on sale of Christians to heathen.   [187] See above, n. 182.

[188] Bk. II, c. 18; T. P. Oakley, English Penitential Discipline and Anglo-Saxon Law in their Joint Influence (Columbia Univ. Studies in History, Economics, and Public Law, CVII:2; New York, 1923), pp. 168–169.

[189] But not in royal laws; cf. Liebermann, ed., Gesetze, II:2, p. 396. 'Exkommunikation', sect. 11p. For ecclesiastical penance required for what Liebermann regards as semi-ecclesiastical offences—breach of pledge, perjury, violation of church-peace, homicide by a cleric, theft and perjury of clerics, the slaying of clerics or of monks, secret murder, etc.—cf. Oakley, English Penitential Discipline, pp. 141–142, 144–146.

Scriptures,' the Anglo-Saxon poem *Christ* says of those in Hell, 'therefore they who here mocked the majesty of the kingdom of Heaven must needs abide in eternal night.'[190] So also those who break the behests of the earthly king and thus mock the majesty of both heavenly and earthly kingdoms are often equally doomed to eternal night. Excommunication for breaking royal law cuts the offender out of earthly society as well as the Kingdom to come. But, as Grace holds open the door of Heaven to the sinner, so for the criminal the king's mercy may bring pardon and 'peace'. The asylum granted by the presence of the sacral monarch is the quasi-divine personal intervention in the punishment due a sinner. It is to this that we now turn.

The question of asylum, as has been observed,[191] is intimately linked with the transition from the old to the new religion in the light of tribal culture. The 'peace' of certain places and the right of asylum, stemming not from constitutional but from sacral realms,[192] are common in Anglo-Saxon law and reflect sacral ruler-cult, although now in Christianized terms. Punishment for offences is more severe if breach of the Church's sanctuary or breach of the king's peace in his own presence is involved. As early as Ine's laws, sanctuary for one fleeing to a church is to be found. The sanctuary provided by the king's person occurs first explicitly in the Laws of Edward and Guthrum, but the special nature of these two powers is seen even in the earliest code, that of Aethelberht, in which premises of Church and king aggravate the offence, and the presence of the king's person doubles the compensatory penalty.[193] The declaration in Edward and Guthrum's decrees that 'sanctuary within the walls of a church and the

---

[190] *Christ*, ll. 1629–1633; G. P. Krapp and E. V. K. Dobbie, eds., p. 48.

[191] See above, pp. 76–77; cf. my 'Paganism to Christianity in Anglo-Saxon England', *Harvard Theological Review*, LIII (1960), pp. 215–217.

[192] Ortwin Henssler, *Formen des Asylrechts und ihre Verbreitung bei den Germanen* (Frankfurt-am-Main, 1954), pp. 54–55. A recent study by Charles H. Riggs, Jr., *Criminal Asylum in Anglo-Saxon Law* (Univ. of Florida Monographs, Social Sciences, No. 18, Spring, 1963; Gainesville, Florida, 1963) analyses the laws of asylum from a constitutional and legal basis.

[193] Ine 5, Edward and Guthrum 1, Aethelberht 1–5; Attenborough, pp. 39, 103, 5. On the laws of Edward and Guthrum, see above, n. 27.

protection granted by the king in person shall remain equally inviolate' is repeated in principle in II Edmund 2 for penalties 'if anyone flees (for sanctuary) to a church or to my premises, and anyone attacks or injures him there'.[194] Equal right of sanctuary is also decreed in VI Aethelred 14 and I Cnut 2 §2.[195] The term used for the king's protection in these dooms of Edward and Guthrum, Aethelred, and Cnut, and also in the eleventh century *Grith*, which repeats Cnut, is of particular interest; it is *cyninges handgrith*, peace from the hand of the king.[196] The *heil*-giving power of the royal sacral hand was associated with fertility, peace, and protection in the Germanic North, as our analysis has already shown.[197]

Royal and ecclesiastical sanctuary are thus both inviolable. The king, an archbishop, or a church can give sanctuary for nine

[194] Edward and Guthrum 1; Attenborough, p. 103. II Edmund 2; Robertson, p. 9. The penalty is outlawry and forfeiture of property; *ibid.*, p. 296, n. 3 to this law.

[195] Robertson, pp. 97, 155. The penalty in Cnut's law for violation of protection of church or king is loss of both land and life, 'unless the king is willing to pardon him'. III Aethelred 15 provides that 'if a man robs another in daylight, and the latter makes the deed known in three villages, he shall not be entitled to protection of any kind', an apparent, but uncertain, denial of the right of sanctuary; *ibid.*, pp. 71, 322, n. 3 to law. Other laws concerning ecclesiastical sanctuary alone are Ine 5–5 §1, Alfred 2–2 §1, 5–5 §4, and 42 §2, and II Edgar 5 §3; Attenborough, pp. 39, 65, 67, 83, and Robertson, p. 23.

[196] It is the term used in Edward and Guthrum 1, VI Aethelred 14, I Cnut 2 §2, and *Grith*. For *Grith*, cf. Liebermann, ed., *Gesetze*, I, p. 470, where the editor translates *Sonderfriede aus der Hand des christlichen Königs*. *Grith* has been attributed to Wulfstan; D. Bethurum, ed., *Homilies*, p. 45. III Aethelred 1 refers to the king's peace *þaet he mid his agenre hand sylð*; Robertson, p. 64. Karl Jost, who regards VI Aethelred as a *Privatarbeit* of Wulfstan and V Aethelred as the laws of the council of *Eanham*, points out that this reference to the king's hand-peace (and to church-peace) does not occur in the latter; Jost, *Wulfstan-studien*, pp. 108, n. 1, 83–85 (where he compares VI Aethelred 14 with I Cnut 2, Polity, and Wulfstan's Homily L). The term is used in Polity (It is right . . . that church-'grith' stand everywhere between walls, and a hallowed king's hand-'grith' equally inviolate); B. Thorpe, ed., *Ancient Laws and Institutes*, II, p. 339. Cf. Wulfstan's Homily LI (the hand-'grith' of the anointed king); Jost, p. 105. The homilist's reference to the anointed ruler is absent in the laws and is perhaps an ecclesiastization of an older belief.

[197] See above, p. 116, n. 130–131.

nights, however, while a bishop or abbot—like a thegn or *ealdor-man*—can give respite for only three nights.[198] This royal right of asylum is recognized also in the eleventh century laws *Be Grithe and be munde*, but in the latter this right, which is granted also to an archbishop or a prince, can be extended beyond the nine nights by the king.[199] Here in these laws we note the 'king's number', the nine of magic and folklore, which is used also to measure the sacral area of the king's peace, in the private treatise *Grith*, extending 'three miles and three furlongs and three lineal acres and nine feet and nine *scaeftamunda* and nine barleycorns'.[200] The significance of the number nine is equivalent in the pagan North to the magic seven of the Christianized Mediterranean and is intimately associated with sacral concepts, such as fertility, protection, and peace, which are intertwined with the cult of rulership.[201] If this indeed, was the original, pre-Christian duration of asylum for one reaching the king's person, it is easy to understand why the three nights sanctuary for a monastery and seven nights for any church consecrated by a bishop, in the earliest laws to mention specific durational periods of ecclesiastical asylum,[202] were changed by Athelstan's reign. The ecclesiastical

[198] IV Athelstan 6 §1–2; Attenborough, p. 149 (where *noctes* is modernized as 'days'). In the Anglo-Saxon fragment of this code the bishop is substituted for archbishop as sharing the privilege of nine nights sanctuary and is omitted from those granting it for three nights; this may be due, as Liebermann suggests, to an attempt by the Rochester scribes to enhance that see; *ibid.*, pp. 151, 210, n. 1 for IV Athelstan 6 §2. The Germanic method of counting by nights instead of days is used; cf. *Germania*, c. 11. Variations, of course, occurred, as in the thirty-seven days and nights sanctuary in the territory given to the dead St. Cuthbert; Whitelock, ed., *Engl. Hist. Doc.*, p. 261 (from anonymous *History of St. Cuthbert*).

[199] Liebermann, ed., *Gesetze*, I, p. 470.

[200] From *Pax*, dating c. A. D. 910–c. 1060, in Liebermann, ed., *Gesetze*, I, p. 390 (with Latin text of Quadripartitus, p. 391). See my 'Paganism to Christianity', pp. 216–217.

[201] A study of this number in relationship to Germanic law is made in my article, 'Aethelberht's Code and the King's Number', *American Journal of Legal History*, VI (1962), pp. 151–177.

[202] Alfred 2 (allowing the three nights for 'any monastery which is entitled to receive the king's food rent, or to any other free community which is

P

and indeed Mediterranean seven, a number perhaps natural to Churchmen in assigning durational asylum, would have been eclipsed by the royal nine if allowed to continue unchanged. Thus, since the protection of king and Church is equally sacred, as is stated even prior to the time of Athelstan, the latter's dooms elevate the ecclesiastical seven of Alfred's code to equality with the 'king's number'. As a result, a church, as well as an archbishop, although not a bishop, shares with the king the right of granting asylum for nine nights.

The sanctity of kingship as seen in the laws goes even further, however, and here again relates to the sacral character of its pagan past. We have seen from Bede's story of the *pontifex sacrorum* Coifi defiling the heathen temple at Goodmanham that priests of the Angli were forbidden to carry arms and that weapons were banned from their temples, as they were in Scandinavia.[203] This priestly peace is continued in Christian times in the same area of the North in the Law of the Northumbrian Priests: 'If a priest comes with weapons into the church, he is to compensate for it.'[204] Icelandic saga parallels this with the forbidding of outlaws by the god Frey from entering even the vicinity of his temple; this and the northern concept that the area surrounding the king was *mikill grithastathr* (a place of great peace)[205] are no doubt based, it has been noted, on the premise that one who enters a holy area becomes himself filled with *heil*.[206] Thus a fugitive from justice partakes by his nearness to the royal presence or to a religious sanctuary of its sacral character and is consequently, as we have seen, granted asylum for the length of time measured by the number sacred to that 'place of peace'—nine nights for the king's presence and seven for a church, until the latter was increased to equate with the royal sanctuary.

---

endowed') and 5 (seven nights sanctuary for a church consecrated by a bishop); Attenborough, pp. 65, 67. The royal guardianship of churches is specifically stated.

[203] See above, pp. 61–62.   [204] Whitelock, ed., *Engl. Hist. Doc.*, p. 437.
[205] H. M. Chadwick, *The Origin of the English Nation* (Cambridge, 1924), pp. 302–303.
[206] O. Henssler, *Formen des Asylrechts*, pp. 71–73.

But the laws carry the notion of the sanctity of the king's person even further. King Edmund decrees in his first code, promulgated in the 940s: 'If anyone sheds the blood of a Christian man, he shall not come anywhere near the king until he proceeds to do penance, as the bishop appoints for him or his confessor directs him.'[207] This is further elaborated by Edmund in his second code: 'Further, I declare that I forbid anyone (who commits homicide) to have right of access to my household, until he has undertaken to make amends as the church requires, and has made—or set about making—reparation to the kin, and has submitted to every legal penalty prescribed by the bishop in whose diocese it is.'[208] Thus a person polluted by the sin of homicide is not allowed to approach the king except by the mediatorship of the bishop. As an outlaw was not permitted in the neighbourhood of Frey's temple, so was he banned from the vicinity of the Woden-sprung Anglo-Saxon monarch. Even though Miss Whitelock is probably correct in maintaining that this law is part of the 'movement to emphasize the sanctity of kingship discernible in other texts in this century',[209] nonetheless the form this emphasis—or rather re-emphasis—takes parallels the ruler-cult of pagan Germanic antiquity. It is not surprising that this would come in terms familiar to the folk. Thus only after a ritual cleansing by penance can the criminal enter the area of peace, the region of the king, and approach the royal person. Indeed the king who issued this law was killed when he tried to rescue his seneschal when the latter attempted to stop a criminal, Leofa, from entering the royal residence of Pucklechurch.[210]

A. J. Robertson, the editor of Edmund's code, suggests that the laws are to prevent suppliants for protection from drawing near the king.[211] However, a doom of Aethelred which forbids any

---

[207] I Edmund 3; Robertson, p. 7.   [208] II Edmund 4; Robertson, p. 11.

[209] Whitelock, ed., *Engl. Hist. Doc.*, p. 332. Its paralleling of pagan sacral kingship and its use to oppose blood-feuds (*ibid.*, p. 58) are not mutually exclusive.

[210] Whitelock, ed., *Engl. Hist. Doc.*, p. 203.

[211] Robertson, p. 296, n. 3 to II Edmund 4. Liebermann's view that the clause 'if he be the king's man' in MS. B of I Edmund 3, although not part of the original law, shows that it was intended primarily to concern nobles of the

excommunicated man to remain near the king before being absolved by the Church adds specifically 'unless it be one who is a suppliant for protection'.[212] The same exception is found in VI Aethelred 36, which rules that 'if those who secretly compass death, or perjurers, or proved homicides presume so far as to remain anywhere near the king, before they have undertaken to make amends both towards church and state, they shall be in danger of losing their [landed] property and all their personal possessions, unless they are suppliants for protection'.[213] The inclusion of *morðwyrhtan*—'those who secretly compass death', i.e. by witchcraft or magic—is interesting further evidence of the ritual pollution of sacral kingship which these dooms oppose.[214] Thus the right of asylum is still upheld, and the royal protector loses none of his prerogatives, but the peculiar character of the Anglo-Saxon king has been reasserted as sacral and not to be defiled by one ritually unclean—unshriven or excommunicated, in the terminology of the new court-religion.[215]

The mediatorship of the bishop, it will be noted in these laws of Edmund and Aethelred, is necessary for the polluted person to approach the king. The image is Biblical to an age which parallels the two worlds, as a God the Fatherlike ruler is approached through the bishop, or 'Christ' as he is often styled in the laws.[216]

---

king's court would not decisively affect the point here. The phrase is, furthermore, not found in the other MSS.; *ibid.*, pp. 295–296, n. 3 to law. Frank Zinkeisen, 'The Anglo-Saxon Courts of Law', *Political Science Quarterly*, X (1895), p. 134, asserts that when in Edgar's laws recourse to the king was made difficult, it was to maintain the jurisdiction of local courts. This is with reference only to the laws directing that cases are not to be brought to the king unless justice has been refused locally, however, and even this local jurisdiction is not a matter of concern in Edmund's laws denying access to the king's person to criminals.

[212] V Aethelred 29; Robertson, p. 87.

[213] Robertson, p. 103. V Aethelred 29, on the other hand, provides for a death penalty: 'It shall be at the risk of (losing) his life or his possessions.'

[214] VI Aethelred 36; Robertson, p. 103.

[215] For the application of these concepts to one of the more complex problems in *Beowulf* (ll. 168–169), see my 'Grendel and the Gifstol: A Legal View of Monsters', *PMLA*, LXXVII (1962), pp. 513–520.

[216] See above, pp. 197–200.

It is the Father who issues His Mosaic dooms, as it is the king who on earth is doom-giver, and it is Christ who is the way to the Throne of Grace, as it is the bishop—or 'Christ'—through whom the sinner is able to come to the throne of God's vicegerent on earth.

A further suggestion of the nature of sanctuary attributed to the monarch is provided in VIII Aethelred 1 §1. 'If ever anyone henceforth violates the protection of the church of God by committing homicide within its walls,' it rules, 'the crime shall not be atoned for by any payment of compensation, and everyone who is the friend of God shall pursue the miscreant, unless it happen that he escapes from there and reaches so inviolable a sanctuary that the king, because of that, grant him his life, upon condition that he makes full amends both towards God and men.'[217] A sanctuary so holy that it would provide protection to such a sacrilegious homicide might be, of course, another church, but the editor of the code is correct in at least raising the question of whether, in view of Aethelred's other laws on royal sanctuary, the residence of the king is meant.[218] Moreover, it is to be noted again that only the king can spare the criminal's life. As Frey frees prisoners in the *Lokasenna*,[219] so the Anglo-Saxon monarch can grant life to the sinner here, as in the laws of Cnut the king alone can grant *frith* to an outlaw.[220] The extension of the king's peace has often been commented on within a constitutional framework, but for a people and monarch living in the point of contact between two worlds, the sacral character of both king and peace is essential to understanding the proper context of royal sanctuary.[221]

Thus, in the tradition of the sacral rulership of Germanic

---

[217] Robertson, p. 117.

[218] Robertson, p. 339, n. 4 to law.

[219] Henssler, *Formen des Asylrechts*, p. 125.

[220] II Cnut 13; Robertson, p. 181. The law says simply that *se ðe utlages weorc gewyrce wealde se cyng ðaes friðes*, but that only the king is meant (and stated explicitly in one MS.), cf. p. 353, n. 2 to law.

[221] Thus it is not surprising that sanctuary was sought at the tomb of King Edward the Confessor even before that sacral king was canonized; F. E. Harmer, ed., *Anglo-Saxon Writs* (Manchester, 1952), p. 13, n. 2. For sacral character of royal burials, see above, pp. 94–105.

paganism, the king in Anglo-Saxon law was enmeshed with both worlds and the natural guardian in law of the relations of his folk with the divine. The heathen king who made *blot* for well-being and who himself had led his people into the new religion was the predecessor of the Christian king who still moved in sacral spheres. Thus, the Anglo-Saxon kingdom under God, of this world and yet tied in goal and law to another world, was to be led in this world through law on its path to salvation by a king working with the Church and the 'deputies of Christ' within it. The worlds were dual and yet the system was one; the leadership was in king and Church, and yet the power was one—and vested primarily in a God-blessed, Woden-sprung, and Church-protecting monarch. His laws reflect this integrated *character mixtus* and show the king embedded in a web which illuminated his cosmic threads as doom-giver and tied him into both worlds. His power was an earthly type of the angelic order of 'thrones, which are filled with such great grace of the Almighty Godhead, that the All-powerful God dwells on them, and through them decides his dooms'.[222]

---

[222] . . . *þaet se Eallwealdenda God on him wunað, and ðurh hi his domas tosceat.* Aelfric's Sermon for the Fourth Sunday after Pentecost; B. Thorpe, ed., *The Homilies of Aelfric* (Aelfric Society Public., I; London, 1844), I, pp. 343–345 (Anglo-Saxon text, p. 344).

CHAPTER VII

The economics of ruler-cult in Anglo-Saxon law

If economists have been accused, like Oscar Wilde's cynic, of knowing the price of everything and the value of nothing, historians, on the other hand, often know the value of everything and the price of nothing. Since value and price are historically related, however, the historian who ignores the economics which both embodies and reflects a value-system and world-view does so at his own cost. Thus, the laws of the early Germanic tribes—and of the Anglo-Saxons in particular, to whom this study is confined—are dominated by virtual tables of prices and compensations for offences and injuries. To the general historian, and even to the medievalist, these are perhaps the least fascinating elements of the laws. Certainly the more cosmic elements of Germanic society almost vanish here beneath the weight of numbers. Nonetheless, even these apparently raw economic sources reveal, upon investigation, not only societal structure and the relationship of church and state but a concept of kingship which is the key to both. As the heathen king, the representative of the gods among the folk, was responsible for the tribe's right relationship with the divine, so his Christian successor continues the same function in later terms.[1] The legal terminology in which this was done, however, was rooted in the Germanic past; it was technical in that it applied to specific Anglo-Saxon practice, and consequently the Romans, not having the practice, did not have

[1] For this assertion of royal duties in the laws, cf. the preamble to II Edmund, V Aethelred 1, VII Aethelred 1, VIII Aethelred 36, preamble to X Aethelred, II Cnut 40 §2; A. J. Robertson, ed., *The Laws of the Kings of England from Edmund to Henry I* (Cambridge, 1925) pp. 9, 79, 109, 127, 131, 197. This work will be referred to hereafter as Robertson. For parallels, cf. p. 341, note 1 to VIII Aethelred 36.

the terms to describe the practice. Crucial to these customs and to the Germanic society they embodied were the concepts of *wer*, *wite*, and *bot*.

Wer, the value of a man's life, varying with his rank in society, *wite*, the fine to be paid to royal authority, and *bot*, the general Anglo-Saxon term for compensation, filled the laws of the Anglo-Saxons. Common sense, Continental parallels, and the dominance of value-systems in the earliest Anglo-Saxon code all indicate that the hierarchy of rank-related compensations was not introduced either with Christianity or 'according to the example of the Romans', and the role of the king in it must always have been prominent. The distinction between *wer* and *wite* was at least as old as the Germanic society described by Tacitus in the first century, when fines, paid in horses and cattle, went in part to the injured man or his relatives (*wer*) and in part to the 'king or state' (*wite*).[2] The king's own value always shows his higher rank. His *mundbyrd*, the *bot* for violating his peace, is fifty shillings in the earliest Kentish laws, while that of the freeman or *ceorl* is six.[3] Further, a double compensation is assessed against an offence committed at a gathering of his lieges summoned by the king or at a feast if the king is present.[4] That this double fine was in virtue of his office—the king's 'body corporate', to use later legal terminology[5]—is suggested by analogy with north English custom. In

[2] Tacitus, *Germania*, ch. xii: *pars multae regi vel civitati, pars ipsi qui vindicavit vel propinquis eius exsolvitur.*

[3] Aethelberht 8, 15; F. L. Attenborough, ed., *The Laws of the Earliest English Kings* (Cambridge, 1922), pp. 5, 7. This work will be referred to hereafter as Attenborough. The code's date probably falls between Aethelberht's conversion and his death in A.D. 616 (or 617). The Kentish silver shilling was four times in value the shilling of later Wessex. *Ibid.*, p. 176, note 1 to Aethelberht 16. For payment of the royal *mundbyrd*, cf. Aethelberht 2, 10, and perhaps 6; *ibid.*, pp. 5, 175, note 1 to c. 6.

[4] Aethelberht 2–3; Attenborough, p. 5. In the former case, fifty shillings, the amount of the king's *mundbyrd* and the compensation to be paid for slaying a man in the king's *tun* (Aethelberht 8, 5), is also to be paid to the king. For double compensation due for breach of the peace of a church or meeting place, cf. Aethelberht 1.

[5] Cf. the seminal study of Ernst H. Kantorowicz, *The King's Two Bodies* (Princeton, 1957), esp. ch. vii, 'The King Never Dies', pp. 314–450.

the *Northleoda Laga* and *Myrcna Laga* a double *wergeld* is assigned
to the king, the Mercians stating that 'on account of the kingship
there belongs a second equal sum as compensation in payment for
a king. The *wergeld* belongs to the kinsmen and the royal-
compensation (*cynebot*) to the people.'[6] In *Northleoda Laga*, on a
similar principle, 'the payment for a king of the North people is
30,000 *thrymsas*, 15,000 *thrymsas* belong to the *wergeld*, 15,000 to
the kingship; the *wergeld* belongs to the kinsmen and the royal-
compensation to the people'. The payment for 'office' doubles
the simple royal *wergeld*, which is also 15,000 for an *aetheling*
(prince) or an archbishop.[7] The king's 'body natural'—again to
use later legal terminology—is thus owed a regular *wergeld*, paid
to relatives, while the 'body corporate' of kingship, the later
'Crown', is compensated by an equal amount.[8]

The amount of *wite* to the king varied in Kentish law with the
crime,[9] as is also true for compensation to the king in the codes
of Wessex.[10] The customary fine in West Saxon law for in-

[6] *Myrcna Laga* 3 §1–4. The king's *wergeld* is that 'of six thegns by the law of
the Mercians, namely 30,000 *sceattas*, which is 120 pounds in all' (c. 2). Liebermann, *Die Gesetze der Angelsachsen* (Halle, 1912), I, p. 462; F. Harmer, ed.,
Select English Historical Documents of the Ninth and Tenth Centuries (Cambridge,
1914), p. 89. H. M. Chadwick, *Studies on Anglo-Saxon Institutions* (Cambridge,
1905), pp. 13, 17–18; Attenborough, p. 194, note 1 to Alfred 4 §1.

[7] *Northleoda Laga* 1–2; the *wergeld* of a bishop or *ealdorman* is 8,000 (c. 3).
Liebermann, *Gesetze*, I, pp. 458–460; Harmer, *Select Documents*, p. 89. Trans-
lations of the *Myrcna Laga* and *Northleoda Laga* are to be found in Whitelock,
English Historical Documents, pp. 432–433.

[8] Chadwick, *Anglo-Saxon Institutions*, p. 133, suggests this distinction as the
basis of the double compensation for *mundbryce* of king and earl. The distinction
between person and office is seen also in the early Welsh law of Hywel Dda:
'The law says that the limbs of all persons are of equal worth; if a limb of the
king be broken that it is of the same worth of the bondman. Yet nevertheless
the worth of *sarhad* to the king or to a *brëyr* is more than the *sarhad* of a bondman if a limb of his be cut'; Melville Richards, ed., *The Laws of Hywel Dda*
(Liverpool, 1954), p. 64.

[9] For example, twelve shillings: Hlothhere and Eadric 9, 11, 12, 13; fifteen
shillings: Aethelberht 84; fifty shillings: Hlothhere and Eadric 14. Attenborough, pp. 21, 15.

[10] For example, thirty shillings: I Edgar 5 §1; sixty shillings: III Edgar 8 §3
(but the two fines on buyer and seller total the customary 120); 200 shillings:

subordination to the king, however, is 120 shillings.[11] Through it and *wergeld* payments to the king can be traced the extension of the king's 'peace' (*frith*)[12] and consequently royal jurisdiction, from the king's own residence[13] and kin[14] to foreigners,[15] illegitimate children and kinless men,[16] and especially the Church, to an increasing state control over individuals and assertion of central authority.[17]

It is only as new Christian kingship is seen against the background of the Church, however, that the *wergeld* and other payments are relevant here. And in this respect too, the hierarchic arrangements of these fines and penalties demonstrate the growth of royal authority. Both the high role of the king and his relationship to the realms of religion will be evident. In the earliest dooms,

---

II Edgar 4 §2. Robertson, pp. 19, 29, 23. On the term *wite* and its amounts in West Saxon law, cf. Chadwick, *Anglo-Saxon Institutions*, pp. 127–134.

[11] For example, Ine 45, Alfred 37 §2, II Aethelstan 1 §5, 3, 6 §1–§3, 20–20 §2, 22 §1, 25–25 §1, IV Aethelstan 4, 7, V Aethelstan 1, 1 §2–§4, VI Aethelstan 1 §5, 8 §4, 11, III Edmund 2, 6 §2, 7 §2, II Edgar 4 §1, III Edgar 3, 7 §2 I Aethelred 4 §3, IV Aethelred 6, 9 §2, V Aethelred 28 §1, VIII Aethelred 5 §1, 10 §1, 11 §1, I Cnut 3a §2, 9, 10, II Cnut 15a §1–§2, 25a §2, 29 §1, 33 §2, 44 §1, 65, 80 §1. Attenborough, pp. 51, 81, 129, 131, 137, 139, 141, 149, 151, 153, 155, 159, 165, 169; Robertson, pp. 13, 15, 23, 25, 27, 55, 77, 79, 87, 119, 121, 159, 165, 181, 183, 189, 193, 199, 207, 215. There are numerous others in which it is less clear that the 120 shillings are paid to the king.

[12] For the identification of royal *frith* with the king's *mundbryce*, for the breaking of which the penalties are the same, cf. Katherine Fischer Drew, *Lombard Laws and Anglo-Saxon Dooms* (Houston, 1956), p. 118.

[13] Ine 45: '120 shillings compensation shall be paid for breaking into the fortified premises of the king'; Attenborough, p. 51.

[14] For example, Ine 76, in which the godson of a king is, when slain, to be compensated for by payment equal to his full *wergeld* to the king, in addition to *wergeld* to the relatives, in contrast to a lower sum for a non-royal godson; the compensation for *wergeld* of a bishop's godson is half that of a king's godson (76 §1). Attenborough, p. 61.

[15] The earliest, other than Wihtred 4 (which does not involve *wite*), is Ine 23–23 §2; Attenborough, p. 43. Cf. II Cnut 40; Robertson, p. 197.

[16] Ine 23 §1, 27, Alfred 1 §3, 31; Attenborough, pp. 43, 45, 63, 77.

[17] Contrast, for example, Ine 39 and Alfred 37–37 §2 on a man moving from one district to another, which Liebermann rightly takes to be a growth of state authority; Attenborough, pp. 49, 81, 198, note 1 to Alfred 37 §1.

those of Aethelberht, a breach of peace in the presence of the king, as previously shown, must be compensated by a twofold payment, the same as an offence in the house of God;[18] theft of the king's property in Kentish law, however, is compensated by ninefold restoration, as is a priest's, compared to twelvefold for the property of the Church and elevenfold for a bishop's property.[19] In the later laws of Wihtred of Kent, however, bishop and king appear on the same level, the *mundbyrd* of each being fifty shillings,[20] and the word of each—the royal and ecclesiasticized *auctoritas suadendi*—is incontrovertible, even though unsupported by an oath.[21] King and bishop sometimes appear as equal in the sharing of *wergeld* when the Church is immediately involved,[22] or in acquiring the 120-shilling compensation for breaking into their fortified premises.[23] In the laws of Ine of Wessex, for example, compensation for fighting in a monastery is 120 shillings, the customary sum for insubordination to the king, as the monastery is placed under the king's peace.[24] In the laws of Wessex, the later development shows the relative position of the king as elevated even more in comparison with the ecclesiastical hierarchy.

[18] Aethelberht 1, 3; Attenborough, p. 5.

[19] Aethelberht 1; Attenborough, p. 5. On the significance of nine for royal compensation, cf. W. A. Chaney, 'Aethelberht's Code and the King's Number', *Amer. Jour. Legal Hist.*, VI (1962), 151–177. Richardson and Sayles reject this clause as an interpolation (see preceding chapter, n. 31), pointing out that if it is excluded, 'the first eleven articles are concerned solely with upholding the king's majesty'; *Law and Legislation from Aethelberht to Magna Carta*, p. 4. Their hypothesis would strengthen my own position on the early role of the king, but it must bear, perhaps appropriately for a work published in Edinburgh, the Scottish judgment of 'unproven'.

[20] Wihtred 2; Attenborough, p. 25.

[21] Wihtred 16; Attenborough, p. 27.

[22] Alfred 8, which concerns a nun taken from a nunnery without royal or episcopal permission; Attenborough, p. 69.

[23] Ine 45; Attenborough, p. 51.

[24] Ine 6 §1; Attenborough, p. 39. This is less than the breach of peace in the royal house, which the same code sets at the forfeiture of all the offender's property and the placing of his life in the king's hands: Ine 6. For the relative value of the Kentish and West Saxon shillings, cf. Chadwick, *Anglo-Saxon Institutions*, pp. 12–20.

However, by the time of Alfred the Great, the king is generally superior in the compensatory hierarchy. 'The fine for breaking into the fortified premises of the king shall be 120 shillings,' he decrees, 'into those of an archbishop, 90 shillings; into those of another bishop or an *ealdorman*, 60 shillings.'[25] The customary 120-shilling fine for insubordination to the king, in the earlier West Saxon laws of Ine invoked against those breaking into the fortified premises of bishop as well as king, is now confined to the king alone, and the archbishop is demoted to ninety-shilling compensation. The relationship of king and archbishop, which stood at a ratio of nine to twelve in Aethelberht's code, if Felix Liebermann is right in holding that Augustine had the Church's twelvefold compensation, has now been reversed to twelve to nine.

This translation of relative status and the inviolability of presence and property into financial terms is seen also in Alfred 3, in which penalties for *borg* (in the sense of *mund*) are set at 'five pounds of pure silver pennies for violation of the king's protection', three pounds for the archbishop's protection or guardianship, and two pounds for that of a bishop or *ealdorman*.[26] This is repeated in II Cnut 58, with the addition of the *borhbryce* of a royal prince at the same compensatory value as an archbishop.[27] The archbishop from a value-rank higher than the king himself has been reduced to the level of a member of the royal family, and other bishops from equality with the monarch to a position inferior to an *aetheling*, or prince, and equality only with an *ealdorman*.

Royal ascendancy is seen further in Alfred's laws in the penalties for fighting or drawing a weapon. To do so in the presence of the

[25] Alfred 40; Attenborough, p. 83.

[26] Attenborough, p. 65.

[27] II Cnut 58–58 §2; Robertson, p. 205. In the *Northleoda Laga* an *aetheling*'s *wergeld* is the same as that of an archbishop. Cf. I Cnut 3a §2, in which *grithbryce* of a principal church is the fine for breach of the king's *mund*, 'five pounds in districts under English law, (and in Kent for breach of the *mund*, five pounds to the king and three pounds to the Archbishop)', the parenthetical clause added by MS. G; Robertson, pp. 157–159, 348, note 2 to law, with reference to equality of king and bishop in *Be Grithe* 6.

archbishop entails the high compensation of 150 shillings, but in the king's hall it costs the offender's life, unless the king spares it. Bishop and *ealdorman* are equated again, with one hundred shillings' compensation.[28]

The relative status thus continues to shift in favour of the king; while in Aethelberht's laws the archbishop and even bishop in some measure outranked the king in compensation, in Ine's code king's and bishop's *mund* was equal, and in Alfred's the bishop's *mund* was one half and two fifths that of the king. By the late tenth century, the ratio is also one half in at least one other respect; 'in the case of an action brought by the king, six half-marks shall be deposited as security, and in the case of one brought by an earl or a bishop, twelve ores'.[29] Finally, in the so-called Laws of William I, perhaps reflecting late Anglo-Saxon custom, the violation of the king's peace in Mercia is five pounds or one hundred shillings, the customary West Saxon and Mercian fine for that offence, but breach of the archbishop's protection is now only forty shillings in Mercia and that of a bishop's or earl's only twenty;[30] thus the ratio in compensation due to archbishop and king is two to five and between bishop and king is one to five, completing the relative elevation of the king in compensatory fines in the Anglo-Saxon period.

As important as this increasing episcopal and archepiscopal 'compensatory inferiority', however, is the bare fact of the embracing of their privileges in royal law. It is not that the bishop loses his essential status; it is that the king gains in authority. Episcopal authority, though, is to be protected by the king. As earlier the king was the vested custodian of the divine protection of his tribe and hence the natural guardian of religious rights, so in the Christian era he is cast in the same vital role. A traditionally powerful priesthood, unknown in Anglo-Saxon paganism, recast

[28] Alfred 7, 15; Attenborough, pp. 69, 73.

[29] III Aethelred 12; Robertson, p. 69. A mark contained eight ores (*aurar*), so the amount deposited against a king's action, three marks, is twice the amount for a bishop's action. *Ibid.*, p. 319, note 2 to III Aethelred 1 §2. For the same ratio in compensation for royal and episcopal godsons, see above, note 14.

[30] (So-called) Laws of William I 2, 16; Robertson, pp. 253, 261.

the problem of royal and divine relationship in the new religion. As a result, the Anglo-Saxon monarch seems at first to have paid a high price by the necessity of integrating the Church's hierarchy into the tribal system. The sharing of sacral character with the new priesthood led to a sharing also of legal status and compensation. By the time of Alfred, however, royal authority in these areas had become increasingly dominant, although such a trend can be seen even earlier; the lost laws of Offa would probably shed crucial light on this transition. At all times, however, royal and ecclesiastical representatives of God were not so much rivals as co-guardians of divine favour. Here too continuity between the old religion and the new is to be noted.

Thus, the bishops, 'whom we ought never to disobey in any of those matters which they, as representatives of God, prescribe for us',[31] are acclaimed as 'God's heralds and teachers, and they shall proclaim and zealously give example of our duty towards God'.[32] In Cnut's Proclamation of A.D. 1020, he not only declares that he 'will not fail to support the rights of the church' and prays his archbishops and diocesans 'to be zealous' with respect to these, but also urges 'my *ealdormen* to support the bishops in furthering the rights of the church and my royal authority and the well-being of the whole nation'.[33] Throughout the history of Anglo-Saxon England, ecclesiastical matters are decided in regular courts, for special courts to decide only Church affairs do not exist. Not only do royal laws decide on the latter, but the Church is called on to assist in what later times would come to regard as lay matters, such as the exacting of the fine for disobedience by a king's reeve.[34] This merging of secular and religious spheres is no more unusual for the early Christian Middle Ages than for Germanic heathenism, but it led to opposition by purists. The papal legates who held councils in England in A.D. 786, for example, reported to Pope Hadrian: 'We saw there also that bishops gave judgment on secular matters in their councils, and we forbade them with the apostolic saying: "No man, being a

[31] IV Edgar I §8; Robertson, p. 33.   [32] I Cnut 26; Robertson, p. 173.
[33] Cnut's Proclamation of 1020 I, 8; Robertson, pp. 141, 143.
[34] II Aethelstan 25 §1; Attenborough, p. 141.

soldier of God, entangleth himself with secular business, that he may serve Him to whom he hath engaged himself".'[35] In England, however, royal authority and ecclesiastical authority, in the tradition of northern politico-religious power, are seen not in conflict but as mutual pillars supporting the realm in its safety and health.

Laws concerning churches and clergy will now be examined to demonstrate this merging of secular and ecclesiastical in royal concern. Legal protection accorded churches and their own right of granting protection, for example, are as old as Anglo-Saxon written law itself. It has already been seen that theft of the Church's property and breach of its peace were topics of the first decree of the first code.[36] Its *mundbyrd* is set at fifty shillings, 'like the king's', by Wihtred.[37] By the time of Alfred the Great, theft from a church is compensated for by only the value of the article stolen and the fine appropriate to the value, in contrast to the twelvefold compensation of Aethelberht's law, but also 'the hand shall be struck off which committed the theft' unless the thief redeems it with a fine in accordance with his *wergeld*.[38] With the increasing extension of the king's peace in the time of Alfred,[39] the compensation due the Church has diminished, but what may be regarded as the civil penalty for the offence—the fine and mutilation—has increased. The element of protection, however, is still present, as it is also in II Athelstan 5, which asserts simply that breaking into a church, after the accused has been found guilty by ordeal, shall be compensated for 'as the written law declares'.[40] Since, the previous extant law on this subject is that of Alfred, presumably the punishment is the same.

[35] C. 10 of councils, quoting II Timothy 2:4; A. W. Haddan and W. Stubbs, eds., *Councils and Ecclesiastical Documents Relating to Great Britain and Ireland* (Oxford, 1871), III, p. 452.

[36] See above, p. 225, and notes 18, 19.

[37] Wihtred 2; Attenborough, p. 25.

[38] Alfred 6–6 §1; Attenborough, pp. 67–69. The value of the object with no increase is suggested by Pope Gregory I to Augustine for theft from a church; Bede, *Hist. Eccl.*, Bk. I, ch. xxvii, *responsum* 3.

[39] F. Stenton, *Anglo-Saxon England* (2nd ed.; Oxford, 1947), p. 273.

[40] Attenborough, p. 131.

With the renewed Danish assaults on England, the need for emphasis on the protection for churches is increased. Probably as the result of their destruction in these wars, the assembly convened by King Edmund at London sometime in the 940s 'ordained that every bishop shall restore the houses of God on his own property, and also exhort the king that all God's churches be well put in order'.[41] In the troublesome times of Aethelred the Redeless, these injunctions appear with increased frequency; as his reign produced more law codes than that of any other Anglo-Saxon monarch, implying the greater need for renewing and repeating legal restraints, so the recurrence in them of the divine and royal protection of churches indicates the greater need for such protection.[42] The decree of V Aethelred 10 §1, 'All churches shall be under the special protection of God and of the king and of all Christian people', is repeated verbatim in VI Aethelred 13, as the latter code also exhorts the king's friends 'that they should diligently maintain the security and sanctity of the churches of God everywhere'.[43] His eighth code, in A.D. 1014, which has already been noted for its explicit description of a Christian king as 'Christ's deputy', not only begins by ruling in the first doom 'that all the churches of God be entitled to exercise their right of protection to the full', but devotes several of its opening laws to protection in that sense, that is, the Church's right of protection, inseparable from protection of the Church.[44] Here violation of the Church's protection is also brought into the realm of economics,

[41] I Edmund 5; Robertson, pp. 7, 296.

[42] This is true in spite of Robertson's comment that the homiletic last codes of Aethelred's reign give 'small sign of any practical policy with regard to the difficulties of the time'; Robertson, p. 49.

[43] Robertson, pp. 83, 97, 105. Jost regards V Aethelred as the authentic laws of *Eanham* and VI Aethelred as Wulfstan's *Privatarbeit* for that council. K. Sisam holds the former to be laws of this council of A.D. 1008 in the form for general circulation and the latter to be a version for parish priests in the province of York; K. Jost, *Wulfstanstudien* [Swiss Studies in English, XXIII] (Bern, 1950), pp. 13–44; K. Sisam, *Studies in the History of Old English Literature* (Oxford, 1952), Note A, pp. 278–287; Dorothy Bethurum, ed., *The Homilies of Wulfstan* (Oxford, 1957), p. 44.

[44] Robertson, pp. 117–119.

to be compensated for by payment to it of 'the full fine for breach of the king's *mund*', five pounds, as the parallel between king and Church is again clearly seen and *bot* is inflicted by the former to protect the latter. By his reign, however, it is necessary to distinguish among churches in what may be called their 'civil status', for while 'from the side of religion they all possess the same sanctity', yet their relative importance changes their 'worldly worth' in law. All are protected by the king's law, however, even as the latter defines the gradations of this *worldlice wirthe*, and for the two most important ranks the parallel with the monarch's values is maintained. The greatest churches are compensated for violation of their protection by the payment of a sum equal to that paid for violation of the king's *mund*, five pounds—ecclesiastical *bot* made equivalent to royal *wite*—while a medium-rank church (*medemram mynstres*) is compensated by the amount of fine for insubordination to the king; smaller churches are paid sixty shillings and country chapels thirty shillings.[45]

When Cnut the Great succeeded to the throne of England, his tendency of maintaining the former customs of his new domain is seen in his repetition of earlier legal injunctions concerning protection of churches. Again the laws portray divine and royal favour to churches, with the king's role next to that of God: 'Every church is rightly in the protection of Christ himself and it is the special duty of every Christian man to show great respect for that protection, for the protection of God is of all kinds of protection most especially to be sought after and most zealously to be upheld, and next to that the protection of the king.'[46] For a usurping king not of the Woden-sprung English line, especially, this implied blessing of royal authority was as important as his own continuation of the tradition of royal protection of churches. As Cnut's marriage with the widow of his predecessor, the renewal of a pagan custom, placed the new king more firmly in the Anglo-Saxon tradition, so this protection of churches by the 'warden of the holy temple', as northern poetry styled the heathen

[45] VIII Aethelred 5–5 §1; Robertson, pp. 119, 339.
[46] I Cnut 2 §1; Robertson, p. 155.

Q

ruler, placed him in parallel with the Christian God.[47] Cnut
repeats Aethelred's provisions for the compensation of churches
and the distinctions in their 'civil' gradations.[48]

Interestingly, it is not until the reign of Alfred the Great,
noteworthy for its concern for monastic foundations,[49] that
protection of nuns is brought under *wite* and *bot*, and not until
Edward the Elder that monks are similarly protected in the laws.
Two dooms of Alfred concern themselves with nuns: Alfred 8
provides that 'if anyone takes a nun from a nunnery without the
permission of the king or bishop, he shall pay 120 shillings, half
to the king, and half to the bishop and the lord of the church,
under whose charge the nun is', with further provision concerning
inheritance by her or by her child. In compensation, therefore,
the abduction of a nun is equated with insubordination to the
king, as she is placed under the monarch's peace, and *wite* is paid
as punishment to royal authority and *bot* to the church. In Alfred
18, his second law on her protection, 'if anyone lustfully seizes a
nun either by her clothes or by her breast, without her permission',
the compensation is set at twice that for a lay-woman.[50] (Presumably if she is seized by her breast with her permission, she is *in jure*
not in need of royal protection.) The sacrilege of an attack on a
nun is also emphasized in a mid-tenth-century law of King
Edmund, decreeing that 'he who has intercourse with a nun,
unless he make amends, shall not be allowed burial in consecrated
ground'.[51] At the end of that century the protection is generalized

---

[47] On Germanic marriage with the widow, cf. H. M. Chadwick, *Origin of
the English Nation* (Cambridge, 1924), pp. 305–320; on the king as 'warden of
the holy temple', cf. Gudbrand Vigfusson and F. York Powell, eds., *Corpus
Poeticum Boreale* (Oxford, 1883), II, p. 478.

[48] I Cnut 2 §5 and 3a §1–2; Robertson, pp. 157–159.

[49] Alfred the Great, for example, gave half his revenues to 'God and the
Church'; of this gift one quarter went to the foundations of Athelney and
Shaftesbury and one quarter to other monasteries in Wessex and abroad;
Asser, *De Rebus Gestis Aelfredi*, c. 102.

[50] Attenborough, pp. 69, 73. The compensation 'if anyone seizes by the
breast a young woman belonging to the commons' is five shillings: Alfred 11;
ibid., p. 71.

[51] I Edmund 4; Robertson, p. 7.

by Aethelred the Redeless, so that 'if anyone injures a nun ... he shall make amends to the utmost of his ability both towards church and state'.[52] Provision against marrying a nun is made in VI Aethelred 12 §1, Cnut's Proclamation of 1020, 16–17, and I Cnut 7 §1, and against fornication with a nun in II Cnut 50 §1.[53] The only one of these providing a specific penalty is the Proclamation of 1020, wherein the offender is ruled excommunicated, with all his possessions forfeit to the king; since the king is the protector of nuns in law, it follows that an offence against them is an offence against the king, and compensation must be paid to him. The royal authority again brings ecclesiastical concerns within its jurisdiction.

Three royal laws concern the protection of priests or others in holy orders, in contrast to the many which exhort to priestly and monastic discipline. The earliest occurs in the laws traditionally assigned to Edward the Elder and the Viking King Guthrum; in it the king (or earl) and the bishop act as 'kinsmen and protectors unless he has some other' for either a man in holy orders or a stranger, if anyone attempts to kill or rob him.[54] VIII Aethelred 33 makes the king alone the 'kinsman and protector' for him for the same crimes 'or if he [that is, the priest or stranger] is bound or beaten or insulted in any way', and II Cnut 39, 40, and 42 also legislate against slaying, robbing and binding, beating, or insulting a man in holy orders.[55] The payment of the penalties displays both

[52] VI Aethelred 39; Robertson, p. 103. Cf. V Aethelred 21 and VI Aethelred 26. *Ibid.*, pp. 85, 99.

[53] Robertson, pp. 95, 145, 163, 201.

[54] Edward and Guthrum 12; Attenborough, p. 109. This code has been attributed, largely on stylistic grounds, to Archbishop Wulfstan; Dorothy Whitelock, 'Wulfstan and the So-Called Laws of Edward and Guthrum', *E. H. R.*, LVI (1941), pp. 1–21. The contents of the laws, however, may come from the period to which they have been traditionally ascribed.

[55] Robertson, pp. 127, 197. Although it is the present fashion to assign as many codes as possible to the authorship of Archbishop Wulfstan, it is difficult to believe that he would make king and bishop the 'kinsmen and protectors' in such cases in one code and the king only in another. This discrepancy is, however, what one would expect if the contents of Edward and Guthrum date from an earlier period—e.g., the reigns of those two rulers—than Aethelred's code.

royal authority and *wite* to it and also the sharing of ecclesiastical protection with the bishop and payment to the latter. The earliest of the three laws provides that compensation shall be paid to 'Christ and the king . . . or the king within whose dominions the deed is done shall avenge it to the uttermost.' The second law, that of King Aethelred, gives the compensation to the injured man and to the king, omitting any reference to the bishop; the last group of laws distinguishes civil and ecclesiastical punishments in decreeing both outlawry and excommunication for murdering a priest, and, restoring the role of the bishop, makes a division between king (or lord) and bishop in accordance with what has been offended against; the offender 'shall pay the fine due to the bishop for sacrilege, in accordance with the rank [of the injured man], and to his lord or to the king the full fine for breach of his *mund*'. It is accordingly recognized that both church and king must be compensated, the former for sacrilege in the failure to respect one in orders, the latter for failure to respect protection assured by the king. The *character mixtus* of both king and law, in their merging of ecclesiastical and secular elements into a unity which denies the possible separation, is here clearly in evidence.[56] The distinction between crime and sin, still not complete in modern jurisprudence, is completely obliterated in Anglo-Saxon law, for which sin is also a crime against the king, God's vice-gerent on earth, with the œconomics of compensatory penalties demonstrating it. The pagan ruler who made sacrifice to undo the wrong relationship of his folk with the gods has his ideological as well as lineal descendant in the Christian Anglo-Saxon monarch whose responsibility it is to punish offences against God and to pronounce dooms compensating for them in *wite* and *bot*.

This royal 'deputy of Christ', sacral in character and in continuity with the sons of Woden who ruled in pre-Christian days, thus by the tenth century holds more firmly than ever the head-ship of the realm of the Anglo-Saxons. This he has gained not by a struggle for power against the ecclesiastical hierarchy of

---

[56] Besides the above, cf. Edward and Guthrum 4, in which, for the punishment of incest, 'the king shall take possession of the male offender, and the bishop the female offender'; Attenborough, p. 105.

Christianity but by the tradition which hallowed his role as vice-gerent of God. He is the leader of a victorious faith and its protector in his dooms. His laws had divine sanction, as, in turn, the Gospels became equivalent of law.[57] Earthly law and divine law—the dooms of the king and the Gospels of Christ—were not in rivalry but were pillars of the same world. Consequently, it cannot be said that the temporal head of state also gained ascendancy over the religion, for the dichotomy is that of a later age. As in northern heathenism, so in Christianity the king mediated between the earthly and divine realms. That this was expressed also in economic terms is to be expected. In such a unity, the king is the counter-image on earth of that heavenly monarch whom he serves, and economics is the reverse side of the coin of sacral values. Like law and religion itself, early English economics is a strand of that ruler-cult which binds the world of *wer*, *wite*, and *bot* to the realm where moth and rust do not corrupt nor thieves break through and steal.

The conflation of the law of 'Christ and the king' into inseparable jurisdictions necessitates also the enjoining of Church law upon civil subjects. One of the earliest problems to appear in the laws of Anglo-Saxon monarchs in this connection is the payment of Church dues. The Church's own immunity from taxation appears as early as the first law of the late seventh century code of Wihtred of Kent: 'The Church shall enjoy immunity from taxation.'[58] The first statement of the other side of this coin of taxation —the right of the Church itself to tax—occurs in the laws of King Ine of Wessex, contemporary with those of Wihtred: 'Church dues [*ciricsceattas*] shall be rendered at Martinmas. If anyone fails to do so, he shall forfeit sixty shillings and render twelve times the

[57] Thus the great Bible manuscripts produced in the monastery of Jarrow were known as Pandects, 'a name transferred from the Justinian Code to the Divine Code'; Bertram Colgrave, *The Venerable Bede and his Times* [Jarrow Lecture, 1958] (Newcastle-Upon-Tyne, 1958), p. 9.

[58] Wihtred 1; Attenborough, p. 25. The subsidiary clause (1[1]) establishes a kind of spiritual taxation on the Church, a Christian equivalent of the pagan necessity of performing *blot* or sacrifice: 'The king shall be prayed for, and they [the clergy] shall honour him freely and without compulsion'; *ibid*.

church dues (in addition).'⁵⁹ Distinct from tithes and probably even older than regular parish organization, *ciricsceat*—'Church-shot' or Church dues—was apparently the offering originally of the first fruits of the seed-harvest.⁶⁰ The payment of the sixty shilling *wite* as a fine to the king and of the twelvefold *bot* as compensation to the Church displays the offence to both civil and ecclesiastical authority.⁶¹

In the late ninth century code of Alfred the Great, Church dues are not mentioned except in the Mosaic law which precedes it.⁶² The laws of Edward and Guthrum state that 'all ecclesiastical dues shall be promptly rendered, on pain of forfeiting God's mercy and incurring the fines which the councillors have imposed' and provide for the payment of tithe, Peter's Pence, 'light-dues', and 'plough-alms'.⁶³ 'Light-dues' provided the church with lights, and 'plough-alms', apparently originally collected for the bishop, were dues from each plough.⁶⁴ The early tenth century code of King Athelstan the Glorious, dealing entirely with ecclesiastical matters, requires payment of Church dues (*ciricsceattas*), payments

---

⁵⁹ Ine 4; Attenborough, p. 37. Cf. Ine 61; *ibid.*, p. 57. It is to be noted that the twelve-fold compensation for failure to pay parallels the twelve-fold compensation for theft from a church in Aethelberht 1. On the date of Ine's code, probably between 688 and 694, cf. Attenborough, p. 34.

⁶⁰ Stenton, *Anglo-Saxon England*, pp. 153–154. Cnut's Proclamation of 1027 sets the feast of St. Martin for the payment of 'first fruits of the crops (*primitiae seminum*), *quae Anglice ciricsceatt nominantur*', undoubtedly a reference to the customary dues, with, as Felix Liebermann has pointed out, *primitiae seminum* merely an incorrect translation of the Anglo-Saxon *ciricsceatt*; Robertson, pp. 152, 347 n. 3 to c. 16. In this present study the term 'Church dues' is used in a general sense; since, however, it is a customary translation for *ciricsceat*, it has been retained for the latter also, but in each case where it has been used in this narrower sense, the word *ciricsceat* has been placed after it in parentheses.

⁶¹ Attenborough, p. 183 n. to Ine 4.

⁶² Stenton, *Anglo-Saxon England*, p. 155.

⁶³ Edward and Guthrum 5 §1, 6–6 §4; Attenborough, p. 105. I discuss the attribution of this code to the homilist Wulfstan above. On the gradual replacement of *ciricsceat* by the tithe as chief dues, cf. Stenton, *Anglo-Saxon England*, pp. 154–156.

⁶⁴ For both of these imposts, cf. Bethurum, ed., *Homilies of Wulfstan*, pp. 342–343.

for the souls of the dead, and 'plough-alms', justifying them by reminding his subjects that 'the divine teaching instructs us that we gain the things of heaven by those of the earth, and the eternal by the temporal'. The king commands that tithes be paid of all his own property, as well as from that of his bishops, *ealdormen*, and reeves. He cites authority for tithes from Jacob and Moses, both quotations inaccurate, as well as from the warning 'in books' (*on bocum*): that God will take away the rest from anyone who withholds the tenth part from Him. Finally, in an implied parallel of dues to the Heavenly King and dues to King Athelstan, he concludes: 'Now ye hear, saith the king, what I grant to God, and what ye must perform on pain of forfeiting the fine for insubordination to me. And ye shall see to it also that ye grant me that which is my own, and which ye may legally acquire for me. . . . And ye must guard against the anger of God and insubordination to me'.[65] The warnings of God's seizing of the nine remaining parts for insubordination to the biblical injunction, and of the king's seizing of the fine for insubordination to him for failure to pay these dues parallel and continue in Christian and legal terms the relationship of divinity and ruler in Anglo-Saxon heathenism. As the pagan Germanic sacrificial king—'the warden of the holy temple'—'made' the year, offering for fertility and plenty, peace, and victory in battle to the gods of the *folc*,[66] so it is still the monarch who presides over the offerings to the Christian God, establishing his people's right relations with the divine.

As might be expected, a theological statement of the importance of prompt payment of Church dues also occurs in the laws of the reformer King Edgar (959-975), and here the heavenly and earthly parallels re-occur, although in reversed order. Although a lord may forgive his tenant, he says, if payments are not made when due, repeated refusals to pay will make the lord so angry that he will take both life and property from the tenant. So will the Heavenly Lord act, since in spite of repeated warnings, laymen

---

[65] I Athelstan, preamble and 1-5; Attenborough, pp. 123-125. Attenborough suggests Genesis 28:22 and Exodus 22:29 as the inaccurate sources.

[66] W. A. Chaney, 'Paganism to Christianity in Anglo-Saxon England', *Harvard Theological Review*, LIII (1960), pp. 209-213.

have refused the Lord His due. Edgar concludes by urging payment gladly, ruling on those who do not pay, making these dues uniform throughout his kingdom, and stipulating the necessity of 'clean life' by those to whom these payments are made.[67] The ecclesiastical punishment of excommunication is invoked by King Edmund for refusal to pay tithes and Church dues (ciricsceat), Peter's Pence, and 'plough-alms'.[68] The payment of Church dues—tithes, 'plough-alms', the hearth-penny, and *sawlsceat* (soulshot, payment for the souls of the dead)—and the observance of festivals, fasts, and the right of sanctuary are the sole topics of Edgar's second code, which he enacts 'for the glory of God, and his own royal dignity, and the good of all his people'.[69]

Felix Liebermann emphasizes that in this code for the first time tithes were made necessary in law for all freemen of various classes, although their payment was the subject of earlier laws under pain of fine or excommunication.[70] Of these I Athelstan is directed primarily to the king's reeves to carry out the provisions for royal property, but the laws of Edward and Guthrum, Edmund, and indeed the early dooms of Ine on Church dues are general in application. There is no change of principle in II Edgar but merely the more detailed spelling-out of old law with

[67] IV Edgar 1 §1–8; Robertson, pp. 29–33.

[68] I Edmund 2; Robertson, p. 7. Peter's Pence occurs only in MS. D and may be an interpolation; cf. Bethurum, Homilies of Wulfstan, pp. 342–343. For a history of this tax in the Anglo-Saxon period, cf. W. E. Lunt, Financial Relations of the Papacy with England to 1327 (Cambridge, Mass., 1939), pp. 3–30. Although it is probable that Peter's Pence originated in England, the problem of which king began it—with Ine, Offa II, and Aethelwulf as the chief probabilities—is apparently insoluble.

[69] Robertson, pp. 21–23. The hearth-penny is apparently Peter's Pence (ibid., p. 303 n. 1 to II Edgar 4), especially as it was due on St. Peter's Day and was paid to Rome. It is also so accepted by Bethurum, Homilies of Wulfstan, pp. 342–343. On sawlsceat, cf. Stenton, Anglo-Saxon England, pp. 152–153, who, noting that it 'may well represent a heathen custom turned to Christian uses', comments on the 'significant resemblance between such gifts made on such occasions and the grave-furniture which had once accompanied heathen burials'.

[70] F. Liebermann, ed., Gesetze, II:2, 749; cf. Robertson, p. 302 n. 1 to 1 §1. It is, of course, the first code binding on all England in which tithes are necessitated in law; cf. Stenton, Anglo-Saxon England, p. 155.

application to various types of churches and social orders. This is typical of the ecclesiastical emphasis of much of Edgar's reform legislation. There is, however, a new element in Edgar's legislation on these payments: he issued his fourth code (A.D. 962–963) as a result of a pestilence which he related in origin to sin and the non-payment of tithes.[71] The lengthy injunctions about tithing are the king's attempt to stop the crisis. Church dues were a subject of royal dooms previously, but never as an equivalent for *blot* or sacrifice to end the anger of the deity. For a people emerged from the Germanic paganism of their tribal past, such sacrifice to end calamity to the folk would blend with societal custom.[72] So as pagan priest-kings stave off tribal calamity by offering *blot*— even themselves—to the gods, so Anglo-Saxon kings of the New Dispensation ordered religious duties to be fulfilled by the folk for the same reason.

Church dues are a recurring subject for legislation in the ecclesiastical codes of King Aethelred II. II Edgar is the basis for the injunctions of V Aethelred 11–12, VI Aethelred 16–21 and 43, VII Aethelred 1 §2–3, 4, and 7, and VIII Aethelred 6–15.[73] King Cnut continues these dooms in his Proclamation of A.D. 1027, following his journey to Rome, to provide *omnia debita quae Deo secundum legem antiquam debemus*—tithes, 'plough-alms', Peter's Pence, and *ciricsceat*—before his return to England. His laws provide for them also in I Cnut 8–14 and II Cnut 48.[74] Of these Aethelred's seventh code is of particular interest as evidence of the rendering in Christian terms of the older notion of sacrifice to the gods for victory and plenty. It was issued at Bath in a year of Danish invasions[75] and the laws answer the crisis by tightening

[71] Robertson, p. 29.

[72] See above, ch. III.

[73] Robertson, pp. 83, 97, 105, 109, 111, 113, 121–123. With VII cf. VII Aethelred (A.S.), 2 §2–3; *ibid.*, p. 115. VII Aethelred 4, 7, are, however, missing in the Anglo-Saxon version.

[74] Robertson, pp. 152, 165–167, 201. In the laws, besides the dues mentioned in the Proclamation, 'light-dues' and *sawlsceat* are also provided for in I Cnut 12–13.

[75] For problems of dating—with 992–995, 998–1000, 1004–1006, 1009–1011, and 1015 as the possibilities—cf. Robertson, pp. 49–50.

the religious discipline of the country. A three day fast, the singing of masses 'against the heathen', prayers and psalms, and the payment of Church dues are the principal measures taken against the Danes.[76] Then, in a direct statement of the relation of Church payments and victory and peace, the old goals of sacrifice, the king concludes: 'And every year in future God's dues shall be rendered in all cases specified above, for love of God and all the saints, so that God omnipotent may show mercy towards us and grant us victory over our foes and peace.' As in Scandinavia the king celebrated the great festival for victory (*til sigrs*) at the beginning of Summer, making sacrifice to Othin to mark the war-year, and the festival for plenty and peace (*til ars ok frithar*) on Winter's Day, as well as for victory and peace on emergency occasions,[77] the Woden-sprung King Aethelred calls for sacrifice of the Mass and other offerings to the divine when he must bring victory and peace to his folk.

Not only in the parallel of Christian dues and ancient *blot* for victory and peace, and in the concept of the ruler as instrumental in enforcing the necessary gifts to ensure divine favour, does one find the elements of continuity with Anglo-Saxon pagan sacral kingship. The dating of these ecclesiastical requirements is also pertinent. When the fourth doom of Ine of Wessex, the earliest law to concern the time of payment, states that 'Church dues [*ciricsceat*] shall be rendered at Martinmas',[78] it should be noted that St. Martin's Day was (and is) November 11th, the Christian feast day closest to the old Winter's Day festival, on which the king sacrificed for a good year, for plenty and peace. The sacrifice at the beginning of that season can be seen in the slaughter of cattle to the pagan gods in November. As the Venerable Bede tells us, this month was the Old English *blodmonath*, the month of *blot* or sacrifice, the *mensis immolationum quod in eo pecora quae*

---

[76] Miss Robertson describes the code as 'notable for its entire lack of reference to practical measures of defence' (*ibid.*, p. 50), a perhaps unnecessarily narrow and certainly unmedieval view of what constitute 'practical measures'.

[77] *Ynglingasaga*, c. 8; also Ari's *Life of Haakon the Good*, c. 16. Cf. my 'Paganism to Christianity . . .', pp. 211–212, 214.

[78] Ine 4; Attenborough, p. 37.

occisuri erant, diis suis voverent.[79] One of the great high festivals of heathenism was thus the November sacrifice, when the cattle which could not be maintained during the long Winter were sacrificed, probably in England as in the Scandinavian North for 'plenty and peace'—the *blodmonath* of England, the *Thortrunk* and offering *til ars ok frithar* of the North. Now given to the God who triumphed over the old deities, offering of the first crops of the harvest is made to the Church and probably replaced the old feasting of the pagan sacrifice.

That these dues are to be paid 'from the estate and the house where a man is residing at midwinter'[80] may reflect no more than that residences tended to be more fixed during the Winter months, but the possibility is that two of the three great pagan festivals—Winter's Day and Mid-Winter's Day—on which the king sacrificed for his people are embedded here in the timing of the sacrificial offerings of the new religion, on which depended the welfare of king and kingdom.

To Martinus maessan as the date for the payment of *ciricsceat* is repeated by King Edgar, Aethelred, and Cnut.[81] Reflecting the mixed character of this dating, tithes in the second code of King Edgar are due at Pentecost, the Equinox, and Martinmas: 'the tithe of all young animals shall be rendered by Pentecost, and that of the fruits of the earth by the Equinox, and every Church due (*ciricsceat*) shall be rendered by Martinmas'.[82] These become the standard divisions of payment in the laws of Aethelred and Cnut,

---

[79] Ven. Bede, *De Temporum Ratione*, c. 15 (*De Mensibus Anglorum*); C. W. Jones, ed., *Bedae Opera De Temporibus* (Cambridge, Mass., 1943), p. 213. On the use of *blotan, blot,* and related words for 'sacrifice', cf. Richard Jente, *Die Mythologische Ausdrücke im Altenglischen Wortschatz* (*Anglistische Forschungen*, LVI; Heidelberg, 1921), pp. 38–41. See above, p. 57.

[80] Ine 61; Attenborough, p. 57.

[81] II Edgar 3, VI Aethelred 18 §1, VIII Aethelred 11, I Cnut 10; Robertson, pp. 21, 97, 121, 165. Ine's original law (4) that failure to render God these dues brought a penalty of sixty shillings and twelve times the *ciricsceat* is probably reflected in the provisions of the last two laws for the payment of 120 shillings to the king and twelve-fold, with the amount due the king increased to the customary fine for insubordination.

[82] II Edgar 3; Robertson, p. 21.

with the non-liturgical Equinox, with its pagan overtones, giving way to the Christian feast of All Saints, later in the calendar as the latter is.[83] Aethelred's eighth code, although as late as A.D. 1014, may show what the transition had been in ruling that the tithe of the fruits of the earth shall be rendered 'by the Equinox, or at least by the feast of All Saints'.[84] Cnut in his Proclamation of 1027, however, refers the payment of the tithe of fruits to *mediante Augusto*,[85] perhaps harking back to the first code of King Athelstan a hundred years earlier, in which all tithes—of livestock as well as the fruits of the earth—were to be paid on 'the day on which Saint John the Baptist was beheaded', i.e., August 29th.[86]

The September Equinox, when, as we have seen, the fruits of the earth were to be paid, also marked a heathen high-feast. The Germanic Autumn festival of the harvest occurred then or in mid-September,[87] and the Fall procession of Frey for the plenty of the earth has been associated with this season. That this Autumn festival was known in pagan England is confirmed by the Venerable Bede's appellation of *halegmonath* ('holy month'), the *mensis sacrorum*, to September.[88] These are perhaps related to the appearance of Michaelmas (September 29th) in the dating of dues in Christian times. Sir Frank Stenton, noting that the eleventh century burgesses of Derby paid twelve thraves of grain annually to the king at Michaelmas, maintains that this, 'which obviously represented their church-scot', shows that 'like other ecclesiastical

---

[83] For Pentecost payment of tithes of young livestock and All Saints Day for tithes of fruits of the earth, cf. V Aethelred 11 §1, VI Aethelred 17, VIII Aethelred 9, I Cnut 8 §1; Robertson, pp. 83, 97, 121, 165.

[84] VIII Aethelred 9; Robertson, p. 121.

[85] Cnut's Proclamation of 1027, c. 16; Robertson, p. 152.

[86] I Athelstan 1; Attenborough, p. 123. The requirement in VII Aethelred 7 that all alms in arrears be paid 'between now and Michaelmas', i.e., September 29th, is related to the three day fast preceding Michaelmas 'as a national penalty' in the emergency of invasion and is dated undoubtedly for the occasion; Robertson, pp. 109 (c. 2), (2 [3a]), 113 (7), 115 (1). However, note the Michaelmas payment of grain to the king in eleventh century Derby; see below.

[87] See above, p. 60.

[88] *De Temporum Ratione*, c. 15; C. W. Jones, ed., pp. 211, 212.

revenues of high antiquity, church-scot [i.e., "church-shot" or *ciricsceat*] was occasionally secularized'.[89] The reverse, of course, is also originally a possibility. A payment to the king, made in grain perhaps partly for the practical purpose of providing the royal *feorm* and partly in sacrificial recognition of the king in whose weal is good crops and who sacrificed for the latter,[90] may, because of its primarily religious connotations, have been ecclesiasticized in the new religion. That the first appearance of *ciricsceat* calls for payment at the time when the pagan Germanic king sacrificed for a good year, as we have seen, points in the same direction. So here, in eleventh-century Derby, offerings are still made, related in mode to the harvested crops, in time to the old Autumn harvest festival of the Equinox, and to the king both in his earlier, related laws directing their payment and in their payment by the burgesses to the king himself.

The Christian feast of Easter is, from the reign of Edgar, the customary term of reference for 'plough-alms'. 'Fifteen days after Easter' for their payment is found first in II Edgar 2 §3 and recurs in V Aethelred 11 §1, VI Aethelred 16, VIII Aethelred 12, and I Cnut 8 §1.[91] Here too, however, the origin of a payment from each plough lies almost undoubtedly in pagan custom, in the plough ceremonies originally practiced to guarantee the fertility of the soil. In the survival as Plough Monday in later England, contributions—paralleling 'plough-alms'—were collected as a plough was pulled from one dwelling to another. In Christian England Plough Monday was the first Monday after Epiphany, but in Germany these ceremonies occurred in the Spring, 'sometimes about the beginning of Lent or at Easter'.[92] There is no evidence for them in pagan Anglo-Saxon England, of course, considering the scanty sources for paganism, but as these later

[89] Stenton, *Anglo-Saxon England*, p. 154.

[90] The *feorm* was the provision necessary to feed the king and his followers for a certain period of time.

[91] Robertson, pp. 21, 83, 97, 123, 165. The early references to payment of 'plough-alms' in Edward and Guthrum 6 §3, I Athelstan 4, and I Edmund 2 set no time for their payment; Attenborough, pp. 105, 125; Robertson, p. 7.

[92] H. M. Chadwick, *Origin*, p. 223.

survivals in Germanic lands show plough ceremonies near Easter and in England a secularized plough-alms, the possibility is surely present that 'plough-alms' near Easter in Anglo-Saxon law are a Christianized form of a pagan custom. The purpose of the latter was to assure the land's fertility, which was part of the king's function in Germanic tribal society. Indeed, 'mildness of the seasons' and 'abundance of crops' are still among the blessings which rest 'in the king's righteousness' that the Christian Alcuin described to King Aethelred in A.D. 793.[93] Thus, continuing the royal role as guarantor of his land's well-being and as mediator with the divine for its fertility, it is not inappropriate that the Christian Anglo-Saxon monarch issued his dooms for an Easter-related 'plough-alms' in support of the religion of the new God.[94]

'Light-dues'—for candles for the churches—also a subject of the laws, are determined, when time is mentioned, in accordance with liturgical feasts. The first reference to them provides merely for a fine for their neglect.[95] Aethelred's fifth and sixth codes call for their payment 'three times in the year' but do not specify which three times these are to be.[96] Christmas, Candlemas appropriately (February 2nd, the feast of the Purification of the Virgin Mary), and Easter are, however, the three times assigned by the homilies of Wulfstan,[97] although the early eleventh century laws of Cnut, substituting All Saints for Christmas, provide that they shall be paid 'first a half-pennyworth of wax from every hide on Easter Eve, and as much afterwards at the feast of All Saints, and as much afterwards at the feast of the Purification of St. Mary', that is, Candlemas.[98] Candlemas is the only feast required for their rendering in Aethelred's eighth code, but 'he who so desires may give them more frequently'.[99]

Appropriate as the recurrence of Candlemas is in Christian

---

[93] See above, p. 89.

[94] In England as late as A.D. 1493 the purpose of plough-ceremonies is to help 'make the year': 'the ledingh of the ploughe aboute the fire as for gode beginning of the yere that they schulde fare the better all the yere follouwying'; Chadwick, *Origin*, p. 224.

[95] Edward and Guthrum, 6 §2; Attenborough, p. 105.

[96] Robertson, pp. 83, 97. [97] Robertson, p. 328 n. 3 to 11 §1.

[98] Robertson, p. 165. [99] Robertson, p. 123.

liturgical terms, a February association with a feast of lights would make the transition easier from the old to the new religion, since Germanic paganism observed a February festival of the advancing sun. An eighth century list of pagan practices, often attributed to Boniface, includes 'the swinish feasts of February', the sacrifice of swine accompanying the festival.[100] If the payment of 'light-dues' was first instigated by Archbishop Wulfstan,[101] they may well have been introduced to offset an invigorated observance of the pagan feast in the Danish-occupied regions, but that the use of 'light-dues' is, like the pagan feast of light, much older is shown by the existence of this tax on the Continent as early as A.D. 779.[102] The claim for Wulfstan as its originator is further brought into question by King Offa of Mercia's gift of three hundred and sixty-five mancuses annually to Rome for the support of the poor and for lights, apparently as a thank-offering to St. Peter.[103] Moreover, the will of King Aethelwulf, Alfred the Great's father, provides for one hundred mancuses to buy oil for the lamps of St. Peter's in Rome on Easter Eve and at cock-crow and one hundred mancuses for lights for St. Paul's, Rome, on the same occasions.[104] These gifts are, of course, not taxes for 'light-dues', but their purpose may shed light on the antiquity of the concept.

Thus Church dues in Anglo-Saxon England continued concepts of both the earlier Germanic heathenism and the sacral kingship which was central to it. Altered to the teachings and needs of the new religion, these dues nonetheless still united the tribal obligations and notion of well-being to the cosmic structure into which the folk was integrated, with the monarch, through whose laws these obligations were directed, serving as the central link be-

---

[100] J. T. McNeill and H. M. Gamer, eds., *Medieval Handbooks of Penance* (Records of Civilization, XXIX; New York, 1938), p. 419.

[101] Bethurum, *Homilies of Wulfstan*, p. 343.

[102] Bethurum, *Homilies of Wulfstan*, p. 343.

[103] Stenton, *Anglo-Saxon England*, p. 215, n. 1, discusses this grant and argues against it as the origin of Peter's Pence. The latter, appropriately, is always to be paid by St. Peter's Day, according to the laws; II Edgar 4 (hearth-penny), V Aethelred 11 §1, VI Aethelred 18, VIII Aethelred 10, I Cnut 9; Robertson, pp. 23, 83, 97, 121, 165.

[104] Asser, *De Rebus Gestis Aelfredi*, c. 16.

tween the two worlds, as he had under heathenism. In the payments themselves, in the deity-related areas of tribal life and the seasons associated with these payments, and in the role of the ruler who issued his dooms concerning them, Anglo-Saxon Church dues, rooted in the pagan past, lived on, to demonstrate the power of historical continuity, in Christian England.

Christian kingship and Christian Church

The problem of rendering to God what is God's is no less complex when Caesar is himself a Christian. In the full flood of Christian monarchy in England, the ruler still participates in cosmic and earthly realms, a position presaged by that of his heathen ancestors but involving, inevitably, changing forms and problems. Our concern, however, has been with the sacral role of the Anglo-Saxon king in the transition from paganism to Christianity and with the influence of heathen rulership upon Old English political and religious life. The royal role in monastic reform and other features of developed Christian kingship are beyond the scope of this study.

'For a Christian king is Christ's deputy among Christian people.'[1] So, it has been seen, did the laws of Aethelred II epitomize the role of the Christian monarch, and it is this basic concept that permeates the Old English view of Christian kingship. The king was still the head of the folk under divine auspices, and a separation of religion and royal function was as unthinkable as under paganism. In common also with Christian kingship on the Continent, the English ruler stood in a special relationship to the Divine King. The doctrine of separation of powers between ruler and Church was as abhorrent to the latter, which had inundated the kingdoms on the tide of royal favour, as it was impracticable to the monarch. The ruler was expected to play a theological and eschatological role for his folk. The view of the king as *doctor* of his people—the *tuba praedicationis*, as Alcuin hailed

---

[1] VIII Aethelred 2 §1; A. J. Robertson, ed., *The Laws of the Kings of England from Edmund To Henry I* (Cambridge, 1925), p. 118. On general concept of king as Vicar of God, cf. F. Kern, *Kingship and Law in the Middle Ages* (S. B. Chrimes, tr.; Oxford, 1939), pp. 8, 11, 50; A. Harnack, 'Christus praesens-Vicarius Christi', *Sitzungsberichte der Preussischen Akademie der Wissenschaften, Phil.-hist. Klasse* (1927), pp. 415-446.

R

Offa of Mercia[2]—leading them to judgement, cast a religious aura about him which was to continue a ruler-cult in Christian terms.

One reflection of this is the parallelism of the king and the divine in the framework of the new religion. Thus Bede reports that Paulinus accompanied Ethelburga of Kent north to her marriage with King Edwin, so that, Northumbria being converted, 'he might present her as a chaste virgin to Christ the one true husband'.[3] The parallel of the country led as a bride to Christ and the princess as a bride to Edwin was not unsuitable to an author and a people to whom the ruler was Christ's earthly *gespelia*. The king as the Good Shepherd and *pastor* of his flock also appears. *Te magis agnosce pastorem et dispensatorem donorum Dei quam dominum vel exactorem*,[4] King Cenwulf of Mercia is exhorted by Alcuin, the same author who greets Charlemagne with the words, *Grex est quippe tuus, tu pastor amabilis illi*.[5] *Estote rectores populi, non raptores; pastores, non predatores*, he writes to King Aethelred of Northumbria.[6] An Anglo-Saxon commenting on the duties of a Christian king projects the same image: 'Thou wilt have at God's judgement to produce and lead forth the flock of which thou hast been made the shepherd in this life, and then give account how thou heldest that which Christ afore purchased with his own blood.'[7] The eschatological royal mission is that of *pastor*, leading his flock to the Divine Shepherd.

In the Christian concept of monarchy, as in its northern

---

[2] *Vos estis decus Britanniae, tuba praedicationis, gladius contra hostes, scutum contra inimicos*: Alcuin to Offa of Mercia, A.D. 790; *Mon. Ger. Hist., Epp.*, IV, p. 107.

[3] Bede, *Hist. Eccl.*, Bk. II, c. 9; J. E. King, ed., *Baedae Opera Historica* (London, 1954), I, p. 249 (Latin, p. 248). The reference is II Corinthians 11:2.

[4] Alcuin to King Cenwulf, A.D. 797; *Mon. Ger. Hist., Epistolae*, IV, Ep. 123, p. 181.

[5] *Mon. Ger. Hist., Poet. Lat.*, I, p. 247. Franz Kampers, 'Rex et Sacerdos', *Historisches Jahrbuch*, XLV (1925), pp. 504 ff., traces the concept of the Good Shepherd primarily from Greece and Byzantium, rather than from the Old Testament, to the West. Cf. I Cnut 26 §1, 3, with metaphor of shepherd but with reference to bishops; Robertson, ed., *Laws*, p. 173. Cf. II Cnut 84 §2–2a; *ibid.*, p. 216.

[6] A.D. 793; *Mon. Ger. Hist., Epistolae*, IV, Ep. 16, p. 44.

[7] W. Stubbs, ed., *Memorials of St. Dunstan* (Rolls Series, vol. LXIII; London, 1874), p. 356; for commentary on this work, see below, pp. 257–259.

heathen background, it must be noted again that kings gain their
realms by God's favour and lose them by His disfavour. It is
'Jesus Christ, the Saviour of the World, ... through Whom
kings rule and divide the kingdoms of the earth'.[8] So, for example, 'He has given and granted to King Edward the fair island
of Britain, as he did of yore to his kinsmen.'[9] But it is not only
their ancestral realms which God gives to monarchs. He increases
the earthly power of his faithful vicegerents. Thus, King Oswald,
after his instruction by Aidan, 'did not only learn to hope for the
heavenly kingdoms unknown to his forefathers, but also won
earthly kingdoms more than any of his ancestors did, by the
power of the same one God who made Heaven and earth'.[10] As it
is expressed in the later Peterborough Chronicle of Hugh Candidus concerning Penda's son, Wulfhere of Mercia, 'because he
was faithfully subject unto Christ everywhere, the neighbouring
kings were subject to him'.[11]

As with earlier pagan rulers, so with Christian kings unfaith-
fulness and the consequent loss of God's favour, however, can
bring the collapse of royal power. It is not surprising that the new
religion regards this as the fate of heathen monarchs, as when at
the Battle of Wednesfield or Tettenhall in A.D. 910 'Ivar lost his

[8] Grant by King Ceolwulf I of Mercia to Archbishop Wulfred at witen-
agemot on occasion of the royal consecration, September 17, A.D. 822 (Birch
No. 370); A. W. Haddan and W. Stubbs, eds., *Councils and Ecclesiastical
Documents relating to Great Britain and Ireland* (Oxford, 1871), III, p. 589.

[9] A. J. Robertson, ed., *Anglo-Saxon Charters* (Cambridge, 1956), no. 104,
p. 195 (Anglo-Saxon, p. 194). Among many, cf. grant by King Athelstan of
Amounderness, June 7, A.D. 934 (Birch 1344), transl. in D. Whitelock, ed.,
Engl. Hist. Doc., p. 506: 'I Athelstan, king of the English, elevated by the right
hand of the Almighty, which is Christ, to the throne of the whole kingdom
of Britain ...' Birch, 667 (A.D. 930) states that Providence has honoured
Athelstan with his father's throne and fame. 'He [God] has endowed with a
kingdom Edred, King of the Anglo-Saxons and Emperor of the whole of
Britain'; grant by King Edred to Aelfsige Hunlafing, A.D. 955; A. J. Robertson,
ed., *Anglo-Saxon Charters*, no. 30, p. 57 (Anglo-Saxon, p. 56).

[10] Bede, *Hist. Eccl.*, Bk. III, c. 6; King, ed., I, p. 351.

[11] C. Mellows and W. T. Mellows, eds., *The Peterborough Chronicle of Hugh
Candidus* (Peterborough Museum Publications, New Series, vol. I:1; Peterborough, 1941), p. 7.

sovereignty and hastened to the court of Hell', overthrown and slain by the Christian armies of Mercia and Wessex.[12] But opposition to the Church can bring God to abandon Christian kings also. Thus Alcuin encourages Archbishop Eanbald in A.D. 801, in the midst of the latter's adversity, by reminding him: 'You yourself have seen how kings perished, princes who were opposed to your predecessors and the Church of Christ. Does God sleep in their crimes, because they think they can rage with impunity, and think not that the eye of God watches over their madness?'[13] Similarly, the ancient estate-roll known as the *Historia de Sancto Cuthberto* tells how the Northumbrian kings Osbert and Aella took away part of the property of the monks of St. Cuthbert, whereupon the *ira Dei et sancti confessoris* caused them to lose both life and kingdom.[14] St. Boniface, in his famous letter of A.D. 746–747 to King Aethelbald of Mercia, reproaching him for violating the privileges of the churches, recalls the fates of Ceolred of Mercia and Osred of Northumbria: 'Condemned by the just judgement of God, thrown down from the regal summit of this life and overtaken by an early and terrible death, they were deprived of the light eternal and plunged into the depths of hell and the abyss of Tartarus.' Ceolred, a violator of nuns and ecclesiastical privileges, went mad while 'feasting in splendour amid his companions', and Osred, 'driven by the spirit of wantonness, . . . lost his glorious kingdom, his young life, and his lascivious soul'.[15] This necessity for obedience to the precepts of the Church in order for the realm to be held in safety parallels the pagan necessity for *blot* to preserve the *heil* of the folk and is found commonly in the medieval West.

[12] Aethelweard's Chronicle, Bk. IV, c. 4, *sub anno* 909 (but 910 in Anglo-Saxon Chronicle, MSS. A, B, D, E, and Mercian Register); J. Stevenson, ed., *The Church Historians of England* (London, 1854), II:2, p. 438.

[13] *Mon. Ger. Hist., Epistolae*, IV, Ep. 232, p. 377; Whitelock, ed., *Engl. Hist. Doc.*, p. 796.

[14] Anonymous *History of St. Cuthbert*, c. 10; T. Arnold, ed., *Symeonis Monachi Opera Omnia* (Rolls Series, vol. LXXV:1; London, 1882), I, pp. 201–202; for date of ms., cf. pp. xxv–xxvi.

[15] Haddan and Stubbs, eds., *Councils and Eccl. Doc.*, III, p. 355; Whitelock, ed., *Engl. Hist. Doc..* p. 755.

What was taken with one hand, however, was given with the other. The Church demanded obedience to God and to the new institution which interposed itself between the divine and human, but it also consecrated the royal authority and gave new sanctions to it to replace the old. Paganism, as we have seen, bestowed a priestly character upon the heathen sacrificial king. The Church destroyed the sacrificial king in a sacramental sense—no king, for example, celebrates Mass—but it substituted the widespread Christian concept of the king as the *christus Domini*, 'the Anointed of the Lord'.[16] Both royal and sacerdotal heads are anointed and thus are *christi*; both are worthy to be made great, the priest because of the saving power of his office, the king, in Bede's words, *ut devictis omnibus adversarius nostris ad regnum nos immortale perducat*.[17] This eschatological task is thus bestowed on the monarch in his capacity as the Lord's Anointed, and its effect was to give him a special mission in the Christian cosmic scheme.

[16] The application of this Old Testament title to monarchs is found in Anglo-Saxon England as early as the Ven. Bede, who, as George H. Williams has pointed out, 'may very well be one of the sources of the theory of the royal and sacerdotal *christi*'; G. H. Williams, *The Norman Anonymous of A.D. 1100* (Harvard Theological Studies, vol. XVIII; Cambridge, Mass., 1951), p. 162, n. 548. In England the first definite evidence for the anointing of kings is the sacring of the aetheling Ecgferth, the only son of Offa of Mercia, in his father's own lifetime in A.D. 787; Anglo-Saxon Chronicle, *sub anno* 785 (787). The anointment of Charlemagne's sons, Pepin and Louis, as kings by Pope Hadrian I only six years prior to this has often been cited as the model which inspired a Mercian *imitatio*, especially since contact between Offa and the Frankish monarch is certain; Frank Stenton, *Anglo-Saxon England* (2nd ed.; Oxford, 1947), p. 217. On letters of Charles and Offa, cf. Haddan and Stubbs, eds., *Councils and Eccl. Doc.*, III, pp. 486–487, 496–498. However, it is possible that the influence was also in the reverse direction, for the earlier anointment of King Pepin I, Charlemagne's grandfather, was performed by the Anglo-Saxon missionary Boniface. If the latter were aware of earlier Celtic royal sacring in his own homeland and was not basing this legitimization of the Arnulfings simply on Biblical antecedents of anointment, Offa's ultimate precedent would be in his own island. On the whole problem of anointment, cf. E. Eichmann, 'Königs- und Bischofsweihe', *Sitzungsberichte der Bayerischen Akademie der Wissenschaften, Philol.-philos. und hist. Klasse* (1928), no. 6.

[17] M. L. W. Laistner, ed., *Expositio Actuum Apostolorum et Retractatio* (Cambridge, Mass., 1939), p. 405.

Anyone who thwarted the royal *christus*, therefore, gained the enmity of the Heavenly *Christus*. This divine protection which enveloped the king in a sacral character was presented clearly and in strong terms by the papal legates who visited the kingdoms of England and reported to Pope Hadrian in A.D. 786. In the decrees read at the councils of King Aelfwold of Northumbria and King Offa of Mercia at the instigation of this well-known legatine mission was the injunction: 'Let no one dare to conspire to kill a king, for he is the *christus Domini*, and if anyone take part in such a crime, if he be a bishop or anyone of the priestly order, let him be expelled from it and cast out from the holy heritage, just as Judas was ejected from the apostolic order; and everyone who has consented to such sacrilege shall perish in the eternal fetters of anathema, and associated with Judas the betrayer, be burnt in the eternal fires.'[18] The parallel of Judas Iscariot with the murderers of a king, and indeed with those who even consented to the crime, casts the Anglo-Saxon king into sharp relief as the earthly counterpart of Christ. Even the sacerdotal *christi* are subordinated here to the royal, for they too, like Judas, are to be cast out *a sancta haereditate* if they plot against the king.[19] The sacred character of the Christian ruler, unlike that of the pagan sacrificial king, makes him, in theory, inviolable.

[18] Report of the legates Bishops George of Ostia and Theophylact of Todi to Pope Hadrian, A.D. 786, c. 12 (*De ordinatione et honore regum*) of canons of the two councils held by them. Haddan and Stubbs, eds., *Councils and Eccl. Doc.*, III, p. 454; Whitelock, ed., *Engl. Hist. Doc.*, p. 771. On this mission, cf. Helene Tillmann, *Die Päpstlichen Legaten in England bis zur Beendigung der Legation Gualas (1218)* (Bonn, 1918), pp. 5–7, 156–158. That this twelfth canon may have been influenced by the murder of King Cynewulf of the West Saxons in A.D. 786 (Anglo-Saxon Chronicle, *sub annis* 757 [755], 786 [784, 783] has been suggested by Haddan and Stubbs, eds., III, p. 447.

[19] This emphasis on the royal *christus* over the sacerdotal is found in extreme form in the later royalist tractates of the Norman Anonymous (A.D. 1100), which, even though most probably authored by William Bona Anima, Archbishop of Rouen, may well have been influenced by earlier English development. Cf. G. H. Williams, *The Norman Anonymous, passim*. On the comparison with Judas, cf. Anglo-Saxon Chronicle, *sub anno* 1087 (1088), in which, in a plot against Rufus, Bishop William of Durham 'thought to do to him as Judas Iscariot did to our Lord'.

This Anglo-Saxon canon appears early in the history of Christian ruler-cult among the Germanic peoples. One hundred and thirty years later this royal immunity against murder occurs on the Continent at the Synod of Hohenaltheim (A.D. 916) by the branding of revolt against the king, 'the Anointed of the Lord', as sacrilege, with excommunication for its perpetrators.[20] That this may have been influenced by Anglo-Saxon precedent, undoubtedly known to the English missionaries who preached the Gospel to the Continental tribes and occupied Germanic bishoprics and abbacies, can only be suggested. Certainly the strong ecclesiastical prejudice against slaying the Lord's Anointed continued in England, and an emphasis on a more complete submission to the ruler, never a part of Germanic tradition, was strengthened. A plot to dethrone King Aethelwulf is described, for example, by his son's biographer Asser as 'contrary to the practice of all Christians . . . unheard of in all previous ages'.[21] It cannot be assumed that Asser knew nothing of the history of seventh and eighth century Northumbria, to cite an extreme case, or even of his own Wessex; rather the ecclesiastical theory of the sinfulness of destroying the royal *christus* overwhelmed both the facts of the historical Anglo-Saxon past and the Germanic tradition of sacrificing the ruler. Sacral Germanic kingship called for the ritual deposition of the ruler; it was replaced by a Christian sacral kingship which forbade deposing the Lord's Anointed. So Alcuin writes of 'the earth polluted by the blood of lords and princes' as a sacrilege ranking with 'the most holy places devastated by the pagans, altars defiled by perjuries, [and] monasteries violated by adulteries'.[22]

[20] *Mon. Ger. Hist., Const.*, I, p. 623. Cf. E. Eichmann, 'Königs- und Bischofsweihe', p. 68. On treason in Anglo-Saxon law, see above, pp. 207–211.

[21] Asser, *De Rebus Gestis Aelfredi*, c. 12; W. Stevenson, ed., *Asser's Life of King Alfred* (Oxford, 1904), pp. 9–10. Cf. the later account by Henry of Huntingdon of the rebellion against King Moll of Northumbria by his thegn Oswin, who, *committens proelium erga dominum suum . . ., jure gentium spreto, jure Dei occisus est*; T. Arnold, ed., *History of the English, by Henry, Archdeacon of Huntingdon* (Rolls Series, vol. LXXIV; London, 1879), Bk. IV, c. 22 (*sub anno* 761), p. 125.

[22] Alcuin to King Offa of Mercia, A.D. 796; *Mon. Ger. Hist., Epistolae*, IV, Ep. 101, p. 147.

Even more specifically, the anonymous *Vita* of St. Oswald the Archbishop, written between A.D. 995 and 1005, says of the nobles who plotted the murder of King Edward the Martyr at Corfe that 'they possessed minds so accursed and such dark diabolical blindness that they did not fear to lay hands on the Lord's Anointed'.[23] In a grant to his mother in A.D. 996, King Aethelred II launches the usual comminations against anyone who refuses to consent to it 'unless he make amends ... for what he has done with spiteful machination against our decree'; then he adds, 'because it is said by the psalmist: "Touch ye not my anointed".'[24] That this necessity of submitting to the king is dependent on his hallowing as the *christus Domini* and not on any *mana* indwelling the *stirps regia* is demonstrated by the homilist Aelfric. 'No man', he states in a Palm Sunday sermon, 'may make himself a king, for the people have the option to choose him for king who is agreeable to them; but after that he has been hallowed as king (*to cyninge gehalgod*), he has power over the people, and they may not shake his yoke from their necks.'[25] Thus a people may choose a monarch but may not depose him once he is anointed. *Mana*, in the Church's view, no longer abides in the divine descent of the king from Woden but in its sacring of his power as

[23] Anonymous Life of St. Oswald, Archbishop of York, by a monk of Ramsey Abbey; J. Raine, ed., *The Historians of the Church of York and Its Archbishops* (London, 1879), I, p. 448. Transl. in Whitelock, ed., *Engl. Hist. Doc.*, pp. 841–842.

[24] Grant of King Aethelred to Aelfthryth of Brabourne, etc. in Kent; Whitelock, ed., *Engl. Hist. Doc.*, p. 532.

[25] B. Thorpe, ed., *The Homilies of Aelfric* (E.E.T.S.; London, 1843), p. 212 (transl., p. 213). Karl Jost, 'The Legal Maxims in Aelfric's Homilies', *English Studies*, XXXVI (1955), pp. 204–205, shows that Latin versions in a forged decretal of Pope Leo VIII and in a pamphlet of an anonymous cardinal, c. 1098, cannot be Aelfric's source; however, he points out a third version in the *epistolae* of Bishop Atto of Vercelli (d. A.D. 961), in which it is quoted from an unlocated passage of St. John Chrysostom; this may have been the origin, since Atto's works were known in England a generation after his death. Of these versions only in Aelfric does it occur in a theological and not a political context and no source for his following passage, paralleling a tyrant-king and the Devil, has been located.

a quasi-priestly *christus*.[26] The king is now *heilerfüllt* through his hallowing, but this new form of sacral kingship is hedged about not only with divinity but with responsibilities to the Church which bestowed it.

A Christian ruler, like his pagan predecessor, is thus given a sacral quality, but, also as in earlier times, this is balanced by the duties which it entails. Besides the dooms, which have already been discussed, several specific documents supply us with information on what the duties of a Christian king were in Anglo-Saxon England. The necessity of royal obedience to bishops is stressed in the earliest work of length devoted to this topic, the report, previously mentioned, of the papal legates George and Theophylact to Pope Hadrian I, dating from A.D. 786. The eleventh canon of the conciliar decrees accepted during this legatine mission by King Aelfwold of Northumbria and Offa of Mercia taught *de officio regum et excellentia sacerdotum* that kings should govern *cum magna cautela et disciplina* and judge *cum justitia*. The pre-eminence of the priesthood is supported by Biblical texts; kings and princes are admonished 'to obey their bishops heartily with great humility, because to these are given the keys of heaven, and they have the power of binding and loosing'. The importance of 'prudent counsellors, fearing the Lord, honest in habits' is also urged on the kings, so that their subjects might profit from the good examples of their rulers.[27]

Further, the coronation oath of the Anglo-Saxon king expresses the duty of a Christian monarch in three promises. These survive not only in Latin in the Pontifical of Egbert and in the coronation *ordo* for King Aethelred's coronation but in Anglo-Saxon, which 'is written, letter by letter, after the writing that Archbishop

[26] An ecclesiastical corollary of this priestly character of the king as *christus Domini* is the necessity of his legitimate birth; here the qualifications for the priesthood of the altar are applied to the royal priesthood of the throne. Cf. Haddan and Stubbs, eds., *Councils and Eccl. Doc.*, III, p. 453 (canon 12 of legatine report to Pope Hadrian, A.D. 786); F. Kern, *Kingship and Law in the Middle Ages* (Oxford, 1939), p. 29, who emphasizes that this upheld the sanctity of marriage.

[27] Canon 11; Haddan and Stubbs, eds., *Councils and Eccl. Doc.*, III, pp.452-453.

Dunstan delivered to our lord (King Edgar) at Kingston on the day that they hallowed him king (May 11th, A.D. 973)'.[28] This brief *promissio regis*, which the king 'laid up on Christ's altar, as the bishop directed him', pledges three things: 'true peace' to the Church and people, the prohibition of 'robbery and all un-righteous things to all orders', and 'in all dooms justice and mercy, that the gracious and merciful God of his everlasting mercy may forgive us all'. The first promise, therefore, of this solemn oath is directed to that peace which was essential for the flourishing of the Church but which also was a cult-relation of pagan rulership. The entire pledge, however, displays a Christianization of the royal duty and is to be viewed in the line of the Christian ecclesi-astical tradition of peace, justice, and mercy.

This *promissio* is elaborated in the Anglo-Saxon statement on the duties of a Christian king which immediately follows the coronation oath in two manuscripts.[29] In this, possibly a work of Dunstan himself, worldly honour and the mercy of God are promised to the monarch who keeps the oath, but 'if he violate that which was promised to God, then shall it forthwith right soon grow worse among his people, and in the end it all turns to the worst, unless he in his life first amend it'. Here the ancient relation of the king's *blot* and the well-being of the folk is con-jured up, but this need not militate against Dunstan's authorship of it, since the equally devout Alcuin re-states the *heil* residing in the king's person even more explicitly.[30] After imaging the king as the shepherd leading his flock to judgement, the author then specifies the royal obligations. 'The duty of a hallowed king [*gehalgodes cynges riht*] is that he judge no man unrighteously, and that he defend and protect widows and orphans and strangers, that he forbid thefts, and correct unrighteous intercourse, and annul and altogether forbid incestuous alliances, extirpate witches

[28]Cotton MS., Cleopatra B. 13, fol. 56; the following *Promissio Regis* is also in Vitellius A.7. Printed in W. Stubbs, ed., *Memorials of St. Dunstan*, p. 355; A. J. Robertson, ed., *Laws*, p. 42.

[29] MSS. cited in previous note. For text, cf. W. Stubbs, ed., *Memorials of St. Dunstan*, p. 356, and for comment, A. J. Robertson, ed., *Laws*, p. 41.

[30] See above, pp. 64–65.

and enchanters, drive out of the land kin-slayers and perjurers, feed the needy with alms, and have old and wise and sober men for counsellors, and set righteous men for stewards, for whatsoever they do unrighteously by his fault, he must render account of it all in the judgement day.'[31] As we have noted, these have parallels in the law codes, particularly those of Aethelred, but the principal comparison is with one of the major sources on the structure of Anglo-Saxon society, the so-called *Institutes of Christian Polity*.

Almost the only work in Old English and one of the earliest anywhere to define the duties of the various classes of society, the *Institutes* may well fulfil the claim made for it that 'when it is better known, perhaps it will usurp the place of [the Norman Anonymous] . . . as one of the earliest documents on a subject of supreme importance in medieval history'.[32] It enters our province, however, only for its discussion of royal power and obligations. Generally attributed to the authorship of Archbishop Wulfstan (d. A.D. 1023),[33] it is of great importance as a statement by a leading royal counsellor and ecclesiastic of the duties of a Christian

---

[31] W. Stubbs, ed., *Memorials of St. Dunstan*, p. 356.

[32] Dorothy Bethurum, ed., *The Homilies of Wulfstan* (Oxford, 1957), p. 46. She also asserts (p. 76) that 'it is the only work in Old English' which 'defines the duties of all classes of men, and in the process defines also the limits of power and therefore the interrelation of the church and the secular arm'. However, no. 50 in A. S. Napier, *Wulfstan: Sammlungen der ihm zugeschriebenen Homilien nebst Untersuchungen über ihre Echtheit* (Berlin, 1883), which, as Miss Bethurum herself points out (p. 39), 'comes near being a condensation of Polity', also discusses the duties of the estates from the ruler on down as well as their relationships to the Church. Plummer and Jost both suggest that this may have been the coronation sermon preached before Edward the Confessor; Miss Bethurum considers it not a homily but possibly the notes for an address by Wulfstan, whose writings make up its principal contents, to a witan. For these views and the evidence of Wulfstan's authorship, cf. Bethurum, *Homilies*, pp. 39–41. Since its material on the duties of the king repeats the *Institutes of Christian Polity*, I have here used only the latter, which is fuller in its treatment.

[33] Bethurum, *Homilies*, p. 46, an attribution with which Jost agrees; K. Jost, ed., *Die 'Institutes of Polity, Civil and Ecclesiastical'. Ein Werk Erzbischof Wulfstans von York* (Swiss Studies in English, XLVII; Bern, 1959).On the life of Wulfstan, see Bethurum, pp. 54–68.

king after the full effect of the monastic revival had been felt. The work opens with a discussion of rulership in which is re-asserted the concept underlying VIII Aethelred 2 §1, that 'a Christian king is Christ's deputy among Christian people'. 'It is very right,' *Polity* states, 'that a Christian king be in the position of a father to a Christian people, and in watch and ward Christ's deputy, as he is so considered.'[34] A brief consideration of the king-ship of God, 'the Glory of kings', is followed immediately by that of earthly kingship. It is the monarch's duty to raise up Christ-ianity, to establish peace, to love righteousness, and to support the just and punish evil-doers. 'Lo! through what shall peace and support come to God's servants and to God's poor, save through Christ, and through a Christian king.' Not only is the parallel with the divine again made clear, but immediately it is succeeded by a Christianization of the ancient pagan belief that the well-being of the folk rests in the king. 'Through the king's wisdom, the people become happy [*gesaelig*], well-conditioned, and victorious, and therefore shall a wise king magnify and honour Christianity and kingship, and he shall ever hinder and abhor heathenism.' Thus the right relationship with God, bringing victory and health, now requires diligence against the old faith which had ascribed the same gifts to sacral kingship. As the king offered heathen *blot* to purify the folk, so now, 'let him purify his people before God and before the world, if he will merit God's mercy'. However, the Christian aspect of royal duty is continually em-phasized in the *Institutes*. The 'seven things befitting a righteous king', for example, are 'first, that he have very great awe of God, and secondly, that he ever love righteousness, and thirdly, that he be humble before God, and fourthly, that he be rigid towards evil, and fifthly, that he comfort and feed God's poor, and sixthly, that he further and protect God's church, and seventhly, that, towards friends and towards strangers, he be guided alike to just

[34] The document, from CCCC MS. 201 and Nero A 1, is printed in B. Thorpe, ed., *Ancient Laws and Institutes of England* (London, 1840), pp. 422-440, and in K. Jost, *Institutes*, pp. 39-165. In Thorpe (whose translation is used here), the sections on kingship are c. 1-4; in Jost's edition, pp. 39-58. Bethurum, *Homilies*, p. 77, n. 1, suggests a parallel with Sedulius Scotus.

judgement'. The dominantly ecclesiastical tone, certainly to be expected of Archbishop Wulfstan, runs through the concept of duties of all levels of society, nor is it at variance with the view of the kingly office seen in the homiletic laws of King Aethelred, which were a product of the same hand.

Thus Christian kingship in Anglo-Saxon England both continued the earlier Germanic sacral kingship and altered it to the teachings and needs of the new religion. The Church had not been there before; now there was a new mediatorship, an institutionalizing of the way to God outside the regular and earlier politico-social structure. The need to take it into account is seen as early as the codification of the first English law code. In the long run, it resulted in a separation of royal functions, the sacrificial-priestly role of the Germanic tribal monarch going to the Church hierarchy and that of sacral protector remaining with the king. This separation of powers manifested itself not in the obliteration of the religious nature of kingship but in the establishment of a sphere of action by and for the *ecclesia* apart, to a greater degree, from that of the *regnum*.[35] However, the Church-blessed Christian monarch remained in direct descent from the sacral ruler of Germanic heathenism. Because the king had been absorbed into the new system of salvation, there had been no major opposition to it in England. The key to pagan tribal religion had been the king and clan. With the conversion of the former and the blessing of his power, the folk was led by its royal *pastor* into the new religion, and his sacral role flourished in it as it had in the old.

---

[35] William I's ordinance issued between 1072 and 1076 can no longer be seen as a separation of new spiritual courts from temporal ones, but in the view of its advocates as 'restoring to the bishop jurisdiction which properly belonged to him, and as purifying the way in which it was exercised'; Colin Morris, 'William I and the Church Courts', *English Historical Review*, LXXXII (1967), pp. 449–463 (quotation on p. 450). One must wait until the twelfth century for Church courts whose jurisdictions and procedures are clearly separated from temporal ones; *ibid.*, pp. 462–463.

Index

Hundred: as governing unit, 7
Husdrapa: of Ulf Uggason, 125
Hyndluljoð, 20, 125
Hywel the Good, king: pedigree of,
    42; laws of, 66–67

Ida, king of Bernicia: descent of, 31,
    32; mentioned, 30
Indictions: adopted in Kent, 8n
Illegitimacy: and succession to throne,
    24
Ine, king of Wessex: laws of, 43, 106,
    178–79, 182, 184, 187, 189, 203,
    206, 213, 225, 226, 227, 235, 238,
    240; and agricultural cult, 90; gives
    land to St. Cyngar, 152; mentioned,
    82
Ing: and Frey, 51; cult of, 131
Inglingehögen, 104
Ingvaeones, 131
Institutes of Christian Polity: on duties
    of king, 186–87, 257–59
Istvaeones: and Woden-cult, 33
Italicus, king of the Cherusci, 10n
Ivar, 249–50

Jacob, patriarch, 201, 237
Jaellinge Heath, 91
Jaruman, bishop: mission to Essex,
    160
John the Baptist, St., 60, 242
Jolliffe, J. E. A.: on sacrificial king,
    85
Jomsvikings, 115
Jordanes, 5
Judas Iscariot: as parallel of king's
    murderers, 252
Judith: and Balder, 52; on raven, 133
Judith, queen of Wessex: marries
    stepson, 27
Julian the Apostate, 83
Justin, bishop, 159
Justinian, emperor: gives ruler to
    Heruli, 20–21; mentioned, 141

Kemble, J. M., 97
Kenelm, king of Mercia: as saint, 78,
    79

Kenneth, king of Scots: visit to
    Edgar, 66
Kennings: for God, 46–48; and
    helmet, 139; for king, 177
Kent: multiple-rulership in, 9; divine
    descent in, 30; paganism banned in,
    43; ecclesiastical foundations of, 49;
    conversion of, 157–59; apostacy in,
    167; mentioned, 164
Kenwulf, king of Mercia: letter to,
    83
Kern, F.: on *stirps regia*, 16
Kerunnos: and stag-sacrifice, 130
Ketils Saga Haengs, 96–97
King: terminology for, 7–8, 21; as
    sacrificer, 14 *and passim*; as war-
    leader, 14 *and passim*; as priest,
    63–65 *and passim*; as homilist, 64,
    200–03; as purifier of his people,
    71–73, 258; and peace, 183, 184,
    205–07, 213, 215, 216–19, 222, 224,
    229; as Christ's deputy, 185, 192,
    193, 200, 204, 230, 234, 247, 248,
    258; obedience to, 193–95; plotting
    against, 207–11; compensation for,
    222–28; paralleled to Christ, 248;
    as pastor, 248, 259; and eschatology,
    251–52; as Lord's Anointed, 251–
    255; duties of, 255–59. *Also passim*
Kings, as saints. *See* saints, royal
'King's evil', 73, 83
King's person, sanctity of, 216–19
King's residence: as sanctuary, 219.
    See also palace
King-slaying, 78–79, 86, 113–20, 151
Kingston: Edgar's coronation at, 256
Kinship: and king, 21
Knee: as sacral object, 5, 116

Lance. *See* spear
Langobardi: kingship among, 9
Laurentius, archbishop, 159
Law, Anglo-Saxon: influences on,
    174–76; alliteration in, 175; nature
    of, 176; codes of, 177–81; and unity,
    193–94. *See also* chs. VI–VII, *passim*;
    names of rulers
Law, Mosaic, 43–44n, 236